Bobby Joe: In The Mind of a Monster

Bobby Joe:
In The Mind Of
A Monster

The Chilling

Facts Behind

The Story Of

A Brutal

Serial Killer

COOL HAND COMMUNICATIONS, INC.
BOCA RATON, FLORIDA

ISBN: 1-56790-093-3

First Printing

COOL HAND COMMUNICATIONS, INC.
1098 N.W. Boca Raton Boulevard, Suite 1
Boca Raton, FL 33432

Printed in the United States of America

Cover and book design by Cheryl Nathan

Cover photo courtesy of The Tampa Tribune

Unless otherwise indicated, all interior photos courtesy of The Tampa Tribune

Ward, Bernie, 1935-
    In the mind of a monster / Ward Bernie.
        p.   cm.
    ISBN 1-56790-093-3 : $12.95
    1. Long, Bobbie Joe, 1953-   . 2. Murderers--Florida--Biography.
  3. Serial murders--Florida.-- 4. Rapists--Florida--Biography.
  5. Rape--Florida. I. Title.
  HV6248.L78W37   1994
  364.1'523'0975965--dc20   94-42954
                                                                  CIP

TO THE VICTIMS,
LEST WE FORGET

Contents

A LETTER FROM BOBBY

    They were all slutes. Really! I've
raped probably 50 women, from 12 yr old
virgins to 40 yr old housewives. But
they were regular people, and I never
caused them any physical pain or terrified them. No shit, half or more of em
loved it and got off themselves. If you
want, I'll tell you about a couple.
They're good stories, and true.

Introduction

In the decade that has passed since a cunning serial killer stalked the Tampa nights, the State of Florida has tried five times to execute the confessed slayer, and failed.

As recently as January, 1994, Bobby Joe Long was convicted of one of those ten murders—for the third time.

In February, 1994, the jury recommended that Bobby Joe Long die in the electric chair—for the third time.

In March, 1994, the judge ordered Bobby Joe Long be put to death by electrocution—for the third time.

Add to that the two other times Bobby Joe Long has been sentenced to die for killing.

Should he beat the chair, looming before Bobby Joe Long are the twenty-eight life sentences on multiple charges of kidnaping, sexual battery and murder he received in connection with the string of heinous killings in Hillsborough County, the six life sentences handed down for a vicious home invasion rape-robbery in Pinellas County, and the 693 years he was sentenced to serve for terrorizing, raping, and robbing a Pasco County, woman—one of 100 young girls and women Bobby Joe Long attacked in his persona as "The Ad Man Rapist."

All of which beg the questions: Why, after all these years, is serial killer/serial rapist Bobby Joe Long alive and well and still beating the Florida justice system like a little toy drum? And why, why did he do it?

Bobby Joe: In the Mind of a Monster may or may not answer those questions, but it does tell the story. All the gore one might expect from a sex/murder spree is here. So too, are the experts'

contradictory analyses of Bobby Joe's grotesque psyche, along with the shocking words of the killer himself—a rare and perhaps unprecedented peek inside the mind of a serial killer.

The Bobby Joe Long story is a combination detective story and psychological thriller...an unprecedented descent into the malevolent mind of a serial killer as seen through the eyes of potential victims who survived, the man hunters who ran the killer to ground, and the words of Bobby Joe Long himself, as delivered in scores of letters written while he was behind bars.

Long's own words are taken from a series of 100 or more of these letters he wrote while being held in the Hillsborough County Jail. They were smuggled to inmate Jay Scheidler, another convicted murderer, who used his proximity to Long to try and con his way into a lighter sentence.

Some of these "Letters from Bobby" read like a pornographer's fantasy run wild and the first inclination is to dismiss them. But that's the easy way out! Ironically, it is the words of the rapist himself, more than anything the victims might say, which betray his actions as ruthless, dehumanizing expressions of power and force. Even though Bobby Joe Long lingers obscenely over explicit sexual details, sex was secondary. Pain, revenge, and humiliation were foremost. A selection of these letters are printed here, unedited.

The names of some of Bobby Joe Long's victims have been changed. These were women who were raped and brutalized by Bobby Joe Long and lived to tell about it. They and their families have suffered enough without being subjected to more public attention after so many years of struggling to put the terrifying experience behind them. Names which have been altered are marked with an asterisk on first reference.

Over the past decade, during the many appeals and retrials in Bobby Joe Long's desperate attempt to escape the electric chair, Lisa McVey has been there to take the witness stand and tell her story again in all its graphic and embarrassing details if it meant ensuring Bobby Joe Long would never leave Death Row—alive. By taking such an aggressive public stand, Lisa has refused consistently to spend the rest of her life as one more casualty in Bobby Joe

Long's one-man mission to destroy. She has fought back, and with remarkable élan has emerged from the dreadful experience as a strong and vibrant young woman. Others touched by Bobby Joe Long have not been so resilient or so fortunate.

Bobby Joe is a disturbing horror story....

LISA

A LETTER FROM BOBBY JOE

They loved it. They're all whores, long as they know your not gonna beat em or kill them, or fuck em with a broom or something. Just like guys really, once they see they don't have to play the role any more and can let go, they love to fuck as much as we do.

▲   ▲   ▲

The first hint that a sadistic sexual predator was loose in their midst didn't raise much interest among the crime-jaded folks of Tampa, Florida.

Buried on page 9B of the May 14, 1984 edition of the Tampa Tribune was a brief, three-paragraph item that most bleary-eyed Monday morning readers probably missed. It read:

"A young boy taking a walk discovered the nude decomposed body of an unidentified woman, Hillsborough County officials reported Sunday.

"The body was found at the dead end of East Bay Road near Simms Road at 6:30 p.m. Sunday. It appeared to have been there at least three days.

"There was no identification and because of decomposition, officials couldn't provide an accurate description of the victim."

That was all. On the surface, it was one more weekend killing

in a city that was rapidly evolving into the sort of urban Everywhere in which butchery, such as that found on East Bay Road, was becoming too routine to notice. The bodies of several other young women had been dumped throughout the Tampa Bay area and, while their murders appeared unrelated, the effect of all the killings was to blunt the edge of concern for an ominously accelerating murder rate throughout the historic Bay Area (which included Hillsborough and Pinellas Counties, plus the cities of Tampa, St. Petersburg and Clearwater, along with their burgeoning Sunbelt suburbs.)

Sprawling Hillsborough County, which includes everything from citrus to shipping and from football to phosphate (not to mention a thriving underground sex industry), wraps itself around the eastern shores of Tampa Bay, one of the best natural ports in the Hemisphere. It includes the city of Tampa, with its major suburban growth spreading north into Florida's hilly horse country.

Until 1984, the Hillsborough County Sheriff's Office could expect thirty to forty homicides a year. But beginning that year, the bodies began piling up at an alarming rate. Several were those of young women, slain and dumped on side streets or along lonely country roads. Some were drug killings. Some were the results of violent lovers' spats. And it was that obviously related handful of raped and strangled young women that captured the attention of law enforcement, from the cop patrolling North Tampa's raunchy "Hooker's Alley" to the FBI's elite new psyche squad based in Quantico, Virginia.

So the report of the remains of a young woman found face down in the weeds at the end of East Bay Road elicited a sort of "So what" response. The exception in this case was the nudity, a detail reporters loved to linger over. The fact that the victim was unclothed suggested she might have been doing something she shouldn't have been doing. Prostitute, maybe, who ended up just where decent folk expected to find her, splayed and strangled and left to parboil in the relentless Florida sun.

That day that some mother's daughter was found rotting in the weeds was a Sunday.

Mother's Day.

Otherwise, just another dead unmourned hooker.

The public's general apathy over the rape-murders of young women from the Tampa streets continued even after the second body was discovered a few weeks later. This time, a composite drawing of the Jane Doe victim accompanied the Tribune item, dated May 30:

"The Hillsborough County sheriff's officials Tuesday released a composite of a young woman found Sunday in woods near Plant City. They describe her as in her late teens or early twenties, approximately five feet five inches tall, weighing 119 pounds, with dark brown shoulder length hair and brown eyes. The Sheriff's Office said she was wearing a size eight white polyester-type jumpsuit and white pantyhose. Anyone with information is asked to contact the Sheriff's Office Major Crimes Bureau..."

The idea that the dead woman was merely one more lowlife was reinforced when the newspaper later reported: "Investigators have shown pictures of the unidentified victim and interviewed people in more than two hundred businesses, mostly night spots and bars in Hillsborough, Pasco and Polk Counties."

The first two bodies were found in late spring and early summer of 1984. Six months later, by the time the "unknown" victims had each acquired a name, a face, and a morgue number, that "so what" attitude had changed dramatically. By then, eight more bodies had been found, and the entire Bay Area was in a near panic, aware that a serial killer was prowling the streets.

Every cop's nightmare—a serial killer who had committed at least eight murders and almost certainly more. Tampa Bay area authorities were at last reluctantly admitting to the public that the gruesome, sexually motivated murders were indeed the work of one man. Already, the man was killing at the rate of one every two

or three weeks and everyone, from the hotshot FBI agents called into consult to the newest rookie on the street, knew that the son of a bitch wouldn't quit killing until they stopped him themselves. By now, the guy had acquired a vampire-like thirst for brutal rape and the act of murder.

In an all too familiar orgy of brutal sex, torture and murder, the killer's M.O. was to pick up women on the street, somehow subdue them and drive them to isolated areas, mostly outside the city of Tampa in rural Hillsborough County. There, the women were raped and murdered, and their bodies unceremoniously dumped in the weeds. The victims were between eighteen and twenty-eight; most were hookers, a few were not. All the women were strangled, although one was also shot while another was beaten and had her throat cut for good measure. Some were still bound when their remains were discovered, and the similarities in the ligatures told the cops that most likely the same man was responsible. So did some peculiar red fibers that were found with each victim, but at that point in the investigation the existence of the fibers was a closely guarded secret. If word leaked out about the existence of evidence linking the murders, police feared the killer would clean up his act, ending whatever chance they had of hanging the guy with the almost invisible little red fibers he unwittingly left behind.

Since nearly all the killings apparently occurred in county juris-diction, the burden for investigation fell on the shoulders of Lt. Gary Terry who headed Sheriff Walter Heinrich's Major Crimes Squad.

Lt. Terry hoped to keep the investigation low key as his detec-tives went about routine chores that normally make up a murder investigation: Check the victims' backgrounds. Look for violent boyfriends, pimps who felt cheated, drug ripoffs. Anything, at first, but a serial killer.

That was Lt. Terry's intention. Events soon ripped those good intentions right out of his hands and splashed them all over the front pages of the Tampa Tribune, the St. Petersburg Times, the other area newspapers, and guaranteed a lead spot on every area newscast.

It started slowly, but the fear that spread through the community as each new body turned up was in direct proportion to the blaring headlines that chronicled the killings. Neither the public who followed them nor the news media who supplied them would ever admit to it, but the stories held a morbid fascination for both. The headlines through the summer and fall of 1984 were barometers of that escalating, gut-deep terror that news of a serial killer on the prowl is certain to arouse:

YOUNG WOMAN FOUND DEAD IN
EASTERN HILLSBOROUGH GROVE

LINKS DISCOVERED IN 'BRUTAL'
SLAYINGS OF 2 LOCAL WOMEN

UNIDENTIFIED BODY FOUND
IN ROADSIDE DITCH

FEAR OF KILLER SPREADS AMONG
CLUBS IN TAMPA'S NIGHT LIFE

WOMAN'S SLAYING MAY BE
CONNECTED TO OTHER MURDERS

19 YEAR OLD DANCER IDENTIFIED
AS WOMAN FOUND DEAD IN DITCH

AGENCIES FORM TASK FORCE
TO INVESTIGATE SERIAL KILLINGS

And, finally, the headline everyone had been praying for:

SUSPECT CHARGED IN 9
HILLSBOROUGH RAPE-MURDERS

The hunt for the serial killer who stalked the night took on a sensational aspect early in the investigation, when Sheriff Heinrich threw out the term "sexual overtones" to describe similar circumstances in the murders. Reporters instantly snatched up the quote and repeated it in every news item until the killer was caught.

Five months after the first victim was found, authorities formed a Task Force and went hunting. About thirty seasoned investigators made up the task force, which included homicide and forensic specialists from the Hillsborough County Sheriff's Office, the Tampa Police Department, the Florida Department of Law Enforcement, the Pasco County Sheriff's Office, and the FBI's recently formed Behavioral Science Unit.

Yet for all their crime-fighting expertise and high-tech detecting, when it finally came down to the nut cuttin', the job of catching the killer fell on the unlikely shoulders of a sweet-natured, lonely, sexually abused seventeen year old girl-child who had dropped out of school to care for an ailing, double amputee who claimed to be her father.

The beginning of the end for the serial killer who had terrorized Tampa's women of the night, started early on that November, 1984, morning while the sun was still crawling up out of the Atlantic preparing to march across Florida's grove and cattle countries to spread the day across the broad blue-green bowl of the Bay.

Lisa McVey was just getting off work at the Krispy Kreme Donut Shop just north of the Florida and Waters Street intersection on Tampa's North Side. Her time card showed she clocked out at 2:25 a.m. About the same time, she telephoned Marce Rhodes, the double amputee who had taken Lisa in two years earlier in the midst of a family dispute and now held her virtual hostage through threats and sexual intimidation. The two of them shared the house on River Shore Way, a short street running west from the Hillsborough River to Rome Avenue and just a block over from the

large Tampa Catholic High School campus. As far as the neighbors knew, Marce was Lisa's loving stepfather and she the devoted daughter who had dropped out of school to care for the ailing old man. "Her daddy, that's all she has," clucked a neighbor. "They used to yell good-bye to each other as long as they could until she pedaled out of sight."

The old frame house with the faded siding was four miles from the Krispy Kreme Donut Shop. Every day and every night, rain or shine, Lisa had to make the eight-mile round trip on her bike. Marce Rhodes could no longer drive, and there was no other means of transportation. She'd been working at the Florida Avenue Krispy Kreme for about three months, after transferring from one of the company's shops down on Kennedy Boulevard. The Kennedy Krispy Kreme was a lot closer to home, but going up to Florida Avenue meant overtime pay and Marce Rhodes made her change.

As Lisa later told investigators, "Rhodes made me ride a bike to work every day. So, that night I was at Krispy Kreme on Florida Avenue. I worked overtime, like two-thirty in the morning. Usually I'd work like two o'clock in the afternoon 'till about eleven o'clock at night. But on Friday nights, it was overtime all the time."

Lisa was still trapped in that abusive father-daughter charade that November morning when she picked up the phone at Krispy Kreme and dialed Rhodes' number. "I'm all through here. I'm coming straight home," she told him.

Minutes later, clutching a plastic bag containing her few precious makeup items and a second bag holding Marce's favorite cinnamon donuts, Lisa climbed on her beige, three-speed Huffy bike and began the long, lonely ride home through the dark and seemingly deserted Tampa streets.

But the streets weren't entirely empty. And Lisa McVey wouldn't make it home for another twenty-six terror-filled hours.

Leaving the donut shop, Lisa pedaled to the corner of Florida and Waters, turned right and rode past a string of used car lots, radiator shops and late night beer-and-a-shot joints. In fact, about the only sign of life aside from a few passing cars and trucks was the flickering neon signs from all those blue collar-bars.

11

It scared her sometimes, riding alone in the dark. And some- times there was good reason to be afraid of the shadows. It was only four or five months before, when she was coming home from the Kennedy Boulevard shop at night, that one of those shadows sprang suddenly to life, knocked her off her bike, snatched her purse, and disappeared back into the night. Bruised, shaken, and in tears, Lisa continued on home, where she knew old Marce waited to pounce on her and rail at her for being so dumb that she let some- body steal her purse.

A mile down Waters, Lisa crossed over and turned left onto Rome. It was like entering a long, dark, spooky tunnel formed by huge, old, live oak trees overhanging the street. The street lights were few and far between, the houses set far back on large lots that only enhanced the sense of isolation. At least on Waters there was some traffic and lights. Here it was all dark and silent except for the shush-shush of the bike tires on the asphalt and the distant barking of a backyard dog.

Lisa pedaled fast for the next mile or so, trying not to think about what might be hiding in the darkness. Or about the big car that passed her a couple of times. At least it looked like the same car.

"So, I was riding my bike home in the morning," Lisa later recalled. "I crossed Rome and Sligh, and I saw this van sitting beside the baseball park, and I saw a car sitting in the church parking lot. And it was kind of strange, because I had never seen a car that late at night sitting in the parking lot.

"The van neither, and I always took that route. And so, I was looking at the car and turned my head and this—I saw a black shad- ow that just yanked me off my bike. And I started screaming, saying 'Oh, my God!'

"And he said, 'Stop screaming or I'll blow your brains out.' And he put a gun to my left temple. And then he drug me off across the street into the car, and kept telling me to keep my eyes closed. And told me to strip."

The man who grabbed Lisa McVey had been lying in wait for the girl, watching from his vantage point behind the van parked parallel on Rome just a hundred feet or so south of the Sligh

Avenue intersection. It was the perfect trap. No traffic on either street. A vacant parking lot for the North Rome Baptist Church on the opposite side of the street where the man had parked his car. No stores open. No houses close by whose occupants might be aroused by a screaming girl. Perfect! thought the hulking figure, seconds before he leaped from behind the van, body-blocked the bicycle, and grabbed the startled girl before she hit the ground.

Despite the warning, Lisa started to scream, but the powerful arm around her throat choked off any sounds. Suddenly, all those images of dead girls she'd been hearing about on the television news flashed through her mind as the man quickly dragged her backwards across the street to his car, which was parked in the church parking lot.

"I watched the news all the time, and all the missing bodies and stuff. That was going through my mind, that bodies were being found and stuff. And what I was thinking about was I was going to be dead, just like them. And I would be found somewhere, you know. I was saying, 'God, just let it be over,' you know. So, he dragged me over to the car and told me to strip."

Red car. White seats. Those were the first things she remembered noticing about the car. That and the fact that the lights didn't come on when he opened the door like they usually do. And the man did something to make the back of the passenger's seat go all the way down so it was kind of like a bed.

"He like threw me into the passenger side from the driver's side," she continued. "And, you know, he told me to strip and I said, 'What?' and he goes, 'Strip!' real loud. So, I stripped— because he had that gun to my side.

"He told me to keep my eyes closed and they were shut. Before we got even into the car, he said, 'Just keep your eyes shut; keep them closed.' And I said, 'All right. They're closed,' you know.

"I yelled something about just don't hurt me. And he said, 'Shut up!' and I said, 'Okay.' So, we were driving off and he was touching me. And he made me go down on him in the car while he was driving.

"And after that, we was driving around along the interstate, you

know, because the window was open and I could hear the different air pressure. When you go on the interstate, it sounds like you're going faster. And so, then the next thing I knew, we were in this parking lot."

About three hours later, Tampa police officer J.J. Thiel checked out what his dispatcher told him was the scene of some kind of accident just south of Sligh on Rome.

An agitated, gray-haired woman and her male companion were waiting for him. She identified herself as Elizabeth Kessler, fifty-six, from the little retirement town of Land O'Lakes, just north of Tampa. The man with her, Jerry Maddox, was her roommate.

Mrs. Kessler pointed to a bicycle abandoned at the side of the road and identified it as belonging to her seventeen-year-old grand-daughter, Lisa Rhodes (the name she was being forced to use at the time).

According to Thiel's report: "...w/f Keeler advised that her granddaughter was missing. I observed w/f Rhodes bicycle on the west side of the road, and her personal belongings strewn about the area. I contacted Cpl. Olinski and we checked the surrounding area for w/f Rhodes. We had the office man contact the area hospitals with negative results. Cpl. Olinski checked the van that was at the scene, and the owner w/m Benton advised he ran out of gas at 2400 hrs. and left his van there and the bicycle was not at the scene. The scene was protected and the immediate area was searched with negative results."

About the same time, another Tampa patrolman, George Clark, was sitting down at 1531 River Shore Way to take a missing persons report from a gruff, ill-tempered old guy in a wheelchair who gave his name as Marce C. Rhodes.

Rhodes told the officer that he'd last heard from his daughter at approximately 2:25 a.m., when she had called from work to tell him she was coming straight home. Lisa usually made it home by 3 a.m., Rhodes said, and he figured something must have happened to her because she'd never gone out after work before. She didn't have any boyfriends, she didn't date anybody, didn't even have any

14

close girlfriends her own age so far as Rhodes knew, just went to work and came home to take care of him.

Clark took the picture Rhodes handed him of a pretty, smiling, laughing-eyed girl. What's going on here? he thought to himself. What's a pretty kid like this doing out at three in the morning riding a bike home from work? And why's she stuck here taking care of this old goat instead of in school and out having fun with her friends?

But those suspicions never showed up in the police files. Clark stuck strictly to the facts, at least as they appeared to be, stating in his report:

"When she did not return home by 0315 hrs. he began to become disturbed. He then received a phone call from his daughter's grandmother, w/f Kessler, at which time he advised her that Lisa had not returned home. He advised that since he is an invalid (had both of his legs amputated in Dec. 83), he asked Kessler to begin looking for Lisa...Approx. one and a half hours later he was advised by Kessler that she had found his daughter's bike.

"His daughter has been living with him for approx. two years and he had adopted her. Mother is currently living in Pennsylvania and she and her mother do not get along. Advises his daughter has no other relatives in Tampa except her grandmother, Kessler."

In the statement she gave police, Elizabeth Kessler confirmed she was Lisa's grandmother and didn't dispute Rhodes' claim that he had adopted the girl. She told police that she and Jerry Maddox had been out at Seminole Bingo and didn't get home until after 3 a.m. She decided to call Rhodes, an old boyfriend, to see how he was doing and learned that Lisa had not returned home.

Concerned, she and Maddox drove into Tampa and started backtracking along the route Lisa normally took home from the donut shop. It was about a few minutes after 5 a.m., when they came upon her bicycle in the grassy swale alongside Rome Avenue and notified police.

Other than Lisa's cosmetics that had spilled out when the bike upset, and the bag of Marce's cinnamon donuts, Clark observed in

15

his report that "Although it appeared that the items had been spilled to the ground, it did not appear as if a violent struggle had occurred. No signs bike had taken any type of forceful impact although it appeared it may have been thrown."

It was as if a giant hand had reached down and plucked Lisa McVey off her bike. Just disappeared into thin air leaving the cops, Grandma Kessler and old Marce Rhodes scratching their heads.

And then, just as suddenly, she reappeared—exhausted, in pain from being raped and sodomized a half dozen times or more, her jaws aching from the long hours she'd been force to suck the man's penis. Exactly twenty-six hours after she had been reported missing, Lisa McVey, wearing a man's black pullover shirt, stumbled up the walk to 1531 River Shore Way, sobbing for help as she pounded on the door.

At 7:40 a.m., Marce Rhodes notified Tampa police that his "daughter" had returned, telling a wild story of being kidnaped and sexually assaulted numerous times. Detective B.D. Black was among the first officers to arrive at the Rhodes home. Lisa was obviously shaken and on the verge of slipping over the edge into hysteria, now that she realized she was actually free and would not be killed. This girl needed medical attention, Black told the man in the wheelchair. He gathered up the clothing Lisa had been wearing as evidence—a pair of tan ladies' panties, white bra, a white blouse and a flowered piece of cloth that had been used to as a blindfold—wrapped the trembling girl in a blanket, and set out for the emergency room at Tampa General. Enroute, he radioed headquarters requesting that the on-call rape investigator meet him at the hospital.

Detective Polly Goethe was the officer on duty. She arrived at the emergency room and took over the investigation of the abduction and rape of Lisa McVey. That morning, and again two days later after Lisa had regained her composure, Detective Goethe interviewed her, gently urging the girl to remember as much as she could about her attacker and the place she was held prisoner. During those interviews, Lisa astonished police with almost total recall and her ability to remain so cool-headed throughout the ter-

rifying ordeal. Incredible! Goethe marveled to herself. Anybody else would have been a blubbering idiot by now. She was also stunned by Lisa's fierce resolve, after the initial shock wore off, to get the guy who had done such terrible things to her.

Lisa told Detective Goethe that while she was being held in the guy's apartment, she promised herself that if she got out alive she would tell the police everything she could remember to catch him, and wouldn't hesitate about calling the police even if he threatened to kill her and her family if she did.

"He's a sick person, you know, just creepy and disgusting," Lisa said heatedly. "I just hated him. Just didn't even want him touching me or anything. I just couldn't believe it was happening to me...

"Right now, my feelings, I think he should go to the electric chair...I'm lucky. I mean I could be dead, you know. Right now. I can't stand him. I wish he was dead, I really do. Because you know, he hurt me, you know. Not physically, but he hurt me...I think he should be punished for his crime, he deserves it. And I think he should take his punishment, what he has coming to him, the electric chair.

"There was never a doubt in my mind," Lisa continued. "I just knew he was going to kill me any time. I mean, 'He's gonna kill me now, he's gonna kill me now.' That's all I said.

"I don't know what I did right. Just—I was real calm. I told myself to be calm and everything and the whole thing would be over. Just don't say anything bad to him or nothing like that, just do whatever he wants and you're free; you're gone. And he just let me go."

Lisa told Detective Goethe that as soon as the man got her in the car and forced her to disrobe, he drove away fast, turning, she thought on Sligh headed east. She estimated they drove for almost thirty minutes, with the man forcing Lisa to perform oral sex, grunting and roughly thrusting his penis deep into her mouth. She sensed the man was about to ejaculate, but before he did, he made Lisa stop and lie back in the passenger seat with her eyes closed.

According to Goethe's report:

When they stopped, he told her that they were at an office building and he was going to take her to the top floor. Still having her keep her eyes shut, he put her white work shirt and white pants on but left her underwear and shoes and socks in the car. He then put a blindfold on her, before they got out of the car. To the best of her knowledge, this was the same blindfold that she had with her when she returned home and was later recovered by the police. The blindfold was on somewhat loosely and she was able to peek out the bottom of it. She again saw that he had a gun. She estimated they had traveled about twenty-five or thirty minutes before arriving to their destination. He got her out of the car and walked her up to the building. He opened some kind of gate which they passed through. They then walked up two flights of red carpeted stairs with a railing on each side. He opened he door with a key. He had the key and the gun in the same hand. They then went inside.

"I peeked under the blindfold, he didn't tie it tight, and I saw all these trees," Lisa said. "And it just seemed like a small parking lot to me. All I could see was like a white wall in front of me. And as we were walking, I could see the color of the stairs. I thought that they were red. And we walked up there, two stories. There was a handrail, I think it was brown, but I couldn't tell what it was made of. I remember seeing the door. Under the blindfold, I saw a white door. And his left hand—he opened the door with his left hand and the gun was in his left hand.

"I remember a gate, I believe—I thought it was like a rod gate, a metal gate.

"Let's see. Okay. We entered the apartment and he took my blindfold off and told me to keep my eyes shut. Then we went straight to the bathroom and took my clothes off."

As soon as she had disrobed the second time, the man also took his clothes off and made Lisa bend over with her hands on the toilet seat. She said she felt the man press his bare body against her

18

buttocks. He grabbed her tightly by the shoulders and she suddenly felt a searing pain as he jammed his penis into her rectum.

"Don't!" she cried, trying to wrench away from the man's grasp. "Don't! Oh, it hurts! It hurts."

"Okay, okay," the man ordered. "Stop your goddamn crying!"

The man pulled her out of the bathroom into the adjoining bedroom, threw her on the floor on her back and fell on her. "He raped me," she said. "Right there, on the floor between the bathroom and the bedroom."

After the man climaxed, he pulled Lisa to her feet, took her back to the bathroom and turned on the shower.

"We're going to take a shower," he told her, "but you keep your eyes shut or I'll kill you."

Lisa nodded. Anything, she told herself silently. Just go along with the guy.

Afterward, the man put a hairbrush and dryer in her hands and told her to dry her hair while he sat on the toilet watching. But not close enough. Carefully and surreptitiously, Lisa was checking out her surroundings. Observing details. Remembering what she saw.

"I was peeking out from under my eyes. And I remember seeing the bathroom and the shower from underneath my eyes. It's like, I guess it was pink walls. I believe it was pink, but I'm not sure. And I remember seeing a picture in the bathroom of an owl. And I remember seeing a counter, a sink and counter, and I remember seeing a pair of sneakers with—it sounds funny, an engraved chicken on it. They were like blue striped in the middle with an engraved chicken on it, on both sides of the shoes. And they were just regular sneakers.

"And so he told me to go into the bedroom. He had his hands around my waist...All I was thinking about was he was going to shoot me with the gun. I opened my eyes just a little and I saw another picture on the wall, but I didn't make out what it was... the wall was white, the room was small, and he had a water bed.

"He put me on the bed and then he rolled over me when he got in bed, and the gun like, went over my stomach or hit my arm,

and he said, 'That's just to let you know I still have it.'

Usually, Lisa wore her hair in a ponytail and pinned up, the way they wanted her to wear it at the donut shop. But just before leaving Krispy Kreme, she loosened the ponytail and shook out her long, soft, brown hair, leaving only two barrettes to hold it. Just before she got in the shower, the man removed one of the barrettes. Later, Lisa took the other one out and dropped it beside the bed. "I just pulled it out of my hair and dropped it beside the bed," she later explained. "He didn't know I put it there."

Although the lights were turned off, there was a digital clock radio on the headboard above the bed, with red numerals that cast a faint ruby glow over the room.

For a few minutes, they lay side by side in the darkness.

Then the man rolled over on top of her. Over the next several hours, Lisa told police the man repeatedly raped her and, in between, forced her to perform fellatio.

"He raped me like four or five times in the bed," she recalled. "And he ejaculated every time. He made me—he would also make me say things to him about what I wanted him to do to me. He would make me say, 'Lick my body, lick my tits, fuck me and fuck my pussy.' He would also say 'right' a lot. And then he kept asking me about what kind of girlfriends I had, describe them, their breasts, everything to describe them, you know."

At one point, Lisa screwed up her courage to ask the man, "Why are you doing it to me? What did I do to you? I didn't hurt you."

"Do you want me to slap you?" the man replied.

"And I said, 'No,' and just shut up and didn't say anything else.

"But he had mentioned in the car that he did this to other girls. And that he hated women in general. Then on the bed when we were talking there, he said he had just broke up with his girlfriend and he was real mad at her. And he said this is the way he could get even with other girls, because of this one girl."

In time, the man, wearied of the marathon sex, dozed off, but Lisa remained awake. Her arms and feet were loosely tied with strips of bed sheeting. Sometime early in the morning, the man

awoke and untied the sheets. "I guess I trust you now," he told her.

Months later, during one of the many pre-trial depositions in which Lisa McVey told and retold her story, this exchange between the girl and one of the attorneys took place:

Q. *Let me stop you for a minute, Lisa. When you first were grabbed off the street, you said you figured you were going to end up dead.*

A. *Uh-huh.*

Q. *When, if ever, did that change? Did you think you might be released?*

A. *When I started talking to him.*

Q. *When was that?*

A. *When we were on the bed like for a good eight hours, we were on the bed and he just started talking to me. And I was just laying there listening to him. And he wanted me to answer back, so I answered back.*

So, then it's like he's started to trust me. I felt he was starting to trust me. But, he didn't say anything like that. And he got up one time out of the bed and I heard the gun. It's like this is when the room was dark, you know. And I heard like something hit the drawer or something. Like bullets falling out of the gun or something and then--but then he came back to bed and I heard the gun hit the headboard, again. I don't know what he was doing; I don't know if he emptied the gun or what.

Q. *He never said anything about taking the bullets out?*

A. *No, he did not. Only in the car, he said he had a knife, too.*

Q. *On the way to the apartment?*

A. *Uh-huh.*

Daylight seeped through the heavy curtains covering the bedroom window, but the man gave no sign that he was ready to end the ordeal. They remained on the waterbed most of the day. When he wasn't forcing another round of intercourse on Lisa, or making her suck his penis, the man simply lay beside her stroking her body, kissing and sucking on her breasts.

He was intensely curious about Lisa's prior sex life. Had she

had sex before? Who with? How many times? What was it like?

"At first," she said, "I told him I hadn't had sex before, but he got mad and said real mean like, 'Don't bullshit me!' So I said yeah I had, with a guy in high school. That wasn't the truth at all. I didn't tell him about Rhodes. I just said it so he wouldn't keep nagging me."

One minute the guy would be nice and gentle with her, but would turn mean and nasty the next, handle her roughly or yell at her in a gruff, harsh voice. Gradually, Lisa was learning to recognize the signs that set him off, so when she talked at all it was quiet and obedient. Don't make him mad. The next time he got pissed off he might just say Fuck it! and kill her on the spot.

Once, after she had sucked him to yet another erection, the man made her get on her knees and again attempted anal intercourse. This time, even without lubrication, he was successful, and although the pain was excruciating, Lisa bit down on the bed sheet and willed herself not to scream. Anything, she reminded herself for the hundredth time. Just anything not to make him mad.

Afterward, to her surprise, the man rolled off her, said "Thank you" softly and drifted off to sleep. The man napped often, but for short spells, so Lisa was fearful that if she attempted to untie her bonds and flee, he would awaken and then probably kill her. Sometimes, when he was finished having sex, he put the blindfold back on her; other times he left it off, but ordered her to keep her eyes closed. Besides, the windows were covered with such heavy, dark curtains that very little light filtered in. Even without the blindfold, she still couldn't make out much in the room other than the red glow from the clock radio on the headboard.

When he wasn't touching her, he made Lisa fondle his penis or rub his back and right arm that he said were sore from lifting something heavy at work. He also urged her to touch his head softly and sort of crooned to himself when she did it just right.

He started calling her "babe" instead of "bitch" or "slut." When he asked her name, she lied and said it was Carol. Once, before falling asleep again, he told Lisa, "I'm sorry, but I gotta do this; I gotta put the blindfold back on you. You know why."

"Yeah," she sighed. "I know why."

Only twice did he allow her to use the bathroom. The first time was after she'd been held prisoner for what Lisa guessed must have been eight or nine hours, and he only did then because she warned that she'd pee in the bed if he didn't let her. Each time, he urinated after she did, and although the lights in the bathroom were turned on at the time, he made her keep her eyes shut.

As the hours dragged on, the man seemed to relax more and become less rough and demanding of her sexually. He became almost apologetic. Several times he told Lisa, "I don't want to hurt you, babe. I don't know why I did this, you're such a nice girl. I don't know why I did this, revenge, I guess. I just broke up with my girl and got tired of women, in general, walking all over me."

And during the time they spent talking in the darkness, Lisa became aware of the man's peculiar voice, something she hadn't noticed back in the car or when they first arrived at the apartment, so terrified was she that the next second might be her last. But now she had time to listen. And Lisa swore that, if she lived through this, it would be a voice she'd remember for the rest of her life—thin, high-pitched, nasal; sort of whispery at times, its edges burred off by the subtle slide of a gentle Southern accent. She couldn't see the guy, but Lisa could tell by feel that he was big and burly, that he had thick hair and a bristly mustache, the kind of body that you'd expect to house a deep, rumbling growly kind of voice. But this guy sounded, well, almost girlish. Real effeminate. Not what you'd expect in a guy who kept going like a runaway sex machine.

Under the man's prodding, Lisa told him a little about her home life, leaving out the history of sexual abuse or that Rhodes was a double amputee. "I was afraid that if he let me go and he knew that about Rhodes, he'd come to the house and make trouble," Lisa explained. She did tell him that her "father" was seriously ill, that he'd already suffered two heart attacks, and that she had quit school to take care of him. Her job at Arby's (another lie so he couldn't track her down later) was all the income the pair had to live on.

The hours dragged by and the dim light filtering through the

curtains faded. Lisa sighed. Another night was coming. How long was he going to keep her? And what was he going to do when he was finished with her?

"So, I'm laying there," she recalled, "and all of a sudden he says, 'Do you want something to eat?' And I said, 'No.' And he said, 'You've got to have something to eat.' And I said, 'Alright.'

The man got up, rummaged through his closet, and tossed her a pair of his own shorts that fit her almost perfectly and a black pullover top. After Lisa was dressed, he tied her hands and feet with strips torn from a sheet, but loose enough that she could still hobble about the apartment and use her hands. He also tied her hands and gagged her with more of the same material.

"I'm sorry I have to do this again," he told her, "but I have to gag you so I know you won't scream. And I have to blindfold you."

Taking her by the arm, the man guided her into the living room, sat her down on the couch and switched on the television. Lisa instantly recognized the theme song from the program playing; it was "Airwolf." That means it's 8 p.m. Saturday. Seemed like she'd been here for ages but it was really only, she figured in her head, like about fifteen, sixteen, or seventeen hours.

Off to the side, in what she assumed was the kitchen, she could hear the man opening the refrigerator and the cupboards, setting things out on the counter.

"You hungry?" he called.

Gagged as she was, Lisa could only shake her head from side to side.

Apparently, the man had been watching her because he answered, "Well, you gotta eat something. I'm making sandwiches." While the man worked, Lisa leaned back on the couch and found she wasn't totally blind.

"The blindfold is like thin almost, and I could see around the room." she said. "I could see the picture of the T.V., the color, and I could see where the chair was sitting. I was on the couch. And there was a coffee table in front of me.

"And I believe there was a chair right across from me...And what's like, I guess—I don't know, sliding glass doors or some-

thing...I saw the kitchen. I saw the light in there. I believe I seen a white table that I seen when I first came into the apartment. I looked to my left and saw a white table. I guess it was. And so, he goes back to the couch and has his sandwich and a soda. He took the gag out and asked if I was thirsty and I said, 'Yeah. I'll take a sip of Coke.'"

The sandwiches were made of ham. There were sesame seeds on the bread. For a few minutes, Lisa nibbled at the sandwich and sipped the soda, but she remained blindfolded with her hands and feet bound. Suddenly, the exhaustion of the sleepless night and day, compounded by the still awful fear that she might die at any moment, overwhelmed Lisa and she began to cry.

"What's the matter?" the man demanded.

Lisa shook her head. "Nothing," she sobbed.

"Bullshit! Tell me what's wrong."

"I'm just tired of being tied up all the time," she answered.

"Well, stop it," the man said. "Don't cry. I don't like to see you cry, but I don't want to hurt you. Maybe I'll just keep you. What would you think of that?" he asked, pulling her to her feet and maneuvering her back to the bedroom.

Oh God, she thought. I don't know what's worse. Killing me or making me stay with him. And now he's going to rape me again.

But she pulled herself together: "I just agreed, I said, 'Sure, keep me, just keep me.' You know. And he goes, 'No, I can't do that. But I wish we had met some other way.'"

Back in the bedroom, Lisa steeled herself for another inter-minable round of sex. The man untied her, much to her surprise, and told her to lay down on the water bed. She was still clothed, but the man stripped down to his bikini underwear. He turned off the light and then removed her blindfold.

The man lay down beside her and for a while did nothing but lick her ear, and kiss and nibble her neck. He then took her shirt off and sucked on her nipples for several minutes. Then, like an infant who had nursed his fill, the man put his head on the girl's breasts and told her, "Just rest now," and quickly fell asleep. Lisa waited, with the weight of the man's head pressing down on her,

unable to sleep; afraid, almost, to breath least he come awake in a rage. So close. The worst, she scarcely dared dream, was over.

Lisa eventually dozed off herself and was jolted awake when the radio alarm went off about 2:30 a.m. The man stirred and slid off the bed, stretched and yawned. "It's getting late," he said. "I've got to get you home. Where do you live?"

"Just off of Hillsborough and Rome," she answered.

"Okay. Come on and get dressed but keep your eyes closed and don't look at me."

Following his instructions to the letter, still afraid she might upset him and make him change his mind, Lisa donned the clothing she was wearing when the man snatched her off her bike twenty-four hours ago, except for the white shirt she'd been wearing. It's too dirty, he said. Wear this, handing her the same black pullover she'd worn earlier. When she was dressed, the man again blindfolded her with the strip of flowered shirt, steered her back downstairs, and helped her into the car.

As she was getting in on the passenger side, she bumped her head on the car roof, prompting an apology. "Oh, I'm sorry, babe, I should have guided you in." The seat back was reclined like it was when he first grabbed her. While she was lying there, the man put Lisa's shoes and socks back on her feet. "Now, isn't that service?" he asked. He started the car, leaned over and kissed her on the mouth, and then drove out of the parking lot.

Once underway, the man told her, "Look. I gotta stop and get some money and get some gas. Can I trust you not to get out and run?"

Lisa nodded, assuming the man still had the gun with him and would use it if she tried to get away. They drove for what she guessed was five or ten minutes and stopped at a bank. The man got out, and Lisa could hear the noises the automatic teller machine made as he withdrew money.

"The seat was sitting up then and I could see under my blindfold a little bit," Lisa recalled. "I couldn't tell what kind of bank it was. All I saw were windows with lights hanging from the ceiling. Then he got back in the car and drove a few more minutes to this

26

gas station. I couldn't make out what kind it was. I just know it was a gas station. And all this time, I'm sitting upright in the passenger seat with the blindfold on. And I'm shocked because no one saw us. And I don't know how. He said something about slide down or something, but I guess no one seen me, because he said, 'Make sure you stay in the car.' So, I stayed in the car.

"After the gas station, he pulled me over, made me snuggle next to him and we were driving along and I could see out the window. And I'm trying to tell myself, try to identify something, you know.

"And I saw a Quality Inn and a Howard Johnson—first, I saw the Howard Johnson then we went under the interstate and I saw a Quality Inn and we took the interstate. It wasn't not even five minutes apart seeing Quality Inn and Howard Johnson's. It's like from the gas station to the Howard Johnson's is about eight, ten minutes. Then I saw Howard Johnson and Quality Inn within a few minutes of each other."

As they sped along the crosstown highway, the man told Lisa he would let her go but worried over what she might tell the police after she was freed.

"Are you going to tell the police on me?" he asked.

"No, I promise I won't tell the police on you," she insisted.

"Yes, you will. Do me a favor. Don't describe me. Or describe me as somebody else. Tell 'em I'm I have long hair, a big beard and that I'm short."

Lisa promised she would.

Then he asked, "Are you going to tell your father or, you know, Rhodes? Those people deserve it, letting a seventeen-year-old out this late at night on a bicycle. They deserve all this. Just tell 'em some guy abducted you at gunpoint and borrowed you for a few hours."

Following Lisa's directions, the man exited the Interstate and drove to central Tampa and the Wellswood area of the city bordering the west bank of the Hillsborough River. At the intersection of Rome and Hillsborough Boulevard, the man pulled into the deserted parking lot and parked behind a vacant building.

The man put his arms around the girl, hugged and kissed her and told her he didn't want to let her go. He reached across, opened the passenger door and told Lisa to get out. He pushed a bundle of clothing into her hands that turned out to be the girl's work shirt and her underpants.

"Here's your stuff," he said. "When you get out of the car, just stand there and for about five minutes till I take off. Then you can take the blindfold off.

"Take care."

Seconds later, when she heard the car speed away and was sure the man was safely out of sight, Lisa pulled the blindfold down around her neck and found herself standing alone in the dark, foreboding parking lot, still more than half a mile from home.

"At first, I just sat down and start crying, just sat there and cried my eyeballs out," she said. "Then I got scared he'd come back so I started walking home. Every time I heard a car, I hid, like maybe he was coming back to get me again. I never thought I'd be home again."

Since his arrest, Bobby Joe Long has never explained satisfactorily why he didn't kill Lisa McVey, knowing full well that she could lead the police right to his doorstep. He once told CBS News reporter Victoria Corderi: "It's like it was pretty easy to tell from the very minute I grabbed McVey that she wasn't like the others. And that's probably why she is still alive walking and talking today. I understand that she would love to see me in the electric chair. And I can't blame her, you know, I really can't blame her. I might feel the same way, but I didn't hurt the girl, you know."

After studying the case and visiting Long on Florida's death row, author/psychologist Dr. Joel Norris offered this explanation for why Lisa McVey was allowed to live:

Bobby Joe Long's description of the final days before his arrest exemplify the serial killer's well-tuned sense of survival. Long knew that because of the growing public clamor over the North Tampa murders the police were patrolling the area in

greater numbers. He also knew that his own pattern
of crimes, the places where he found his victims,
and the types of victims he chose were a matter of
public record. He had read about them in the newspaper. He also heard on the news that local and state
authorities had formed a task force to catch him.
"At that point, I could have gone to Miami or even
back to California," he later explained from his
cell on death row. "I could have gone back to West
Virginia for a visit. I could simply have walked
away from Tampa and stopped picking up girls there,
and I'd still be a free man today because the police
had no idea who or where I was until I let McVey go
and she went to the police." Even then, he explains,
he could have fled the area, but he didn't. He was
steps ahead of the police. He was caught because he
wanted to get caught. He wanted the murder spree
that was killing him as well as his victims to stop,
but he couldn't stop it himself. What is most important, however, is that the police couldn't stop him
until he revealed his whereabouts to the task force
by releasing his next to last victim. Then and only
then did the police have the clues to establish his
identity.

Cops scoff at Long's claim that by freeing Lisa McVey, he was
asking to be caught because he couldn't stop the killing himself.
They point to the fact that only days after he let Lisa go, he went
out trolling again and found Kim Swann, his final victim.

"Bobby Joe wasn't ready to stop killing and let the McVey girl
go so we'd catch him," insisted Lt. Gary Terry. "He still thought he
was smarter than we were. Maybe he thought he'd be caught sooner or later, but I know for damn sure he was real surprised that we
were that close to him.

"He still thought he was smarter than we were. We would have
gotten him eventually, but I don't know how many more victims
there would have been without Lisa.

"And I have no idea why he didn't kill her. We asked him that

and Bobby couldn't even give us an answer. I think that during that time they were together, he formed an attachment for her and decided not to kill her. It was just her personality. Lisa's like everybody's kid sister. As far as we can determine, she was the only victim he took to his residence. I'm sure of that.

"And I know this: If Bobby Joe Long were by some miracle set free today, you could find him again just by following the trail of bodies. Because Bobby Joe Long, given the opportunity, will kill and kill and kill again because he enjoys it."

Sgt. Bob Price, one of the Tampa police detectives on the Task Force and one of the two seasoned investigators Terry chose to pry a confession loose from Long, once offered his own solution to the puzzle of why Lisa McVey survived when so many others died:

"Well, sir, it's the wildest thing you'll ever read in your life (the McVey case), I assure you, because we're talking about a man who abducted a young girl, took her to his home, gave her a bath, washed her hair, combed it out for her, fed her. We're talking pampered, pampered. In fact, at one point, and I believe Mr. Long when he says in all honesty that she just broke down and says, 'Look, can I take this thing off? (blindfold). I'd like to stay,' you know.

"And Lisa McVey, her home environment was not the best. We ended up arresting her guardian for involuntary sexual battery, who was a double amputee. The only thing that kept Lisa McVey alive, in my opinion, was her home environment. Being abducted and forced into sexual acts was nothing new to this girl, and that's exactly the way she responded, just it's no big deal, you know. I get the same thing at home."

Several days later, after finishing her interviews with Lisa McVey and reviewing the scanty evidence at hand, Detective Polly Goethe sat down to write her report of the bizarre affair. She concluded:

McVey said she got home sometime around 4:30 a.m. She had to knock on her father's bedroom window to waken him and by the time she finally got inside she was hysterical and crying. She said she even passed

out at one point. She said it took her about two hours to calm down.

McVey described the suspect as a W/M, possibly in his mid 30s or older, because he told her he was old enough to be her father. While they were in bed, he allowed her to touch his face. She remembered from the glimpse she had of him that his hair was brown and it felt that it was about an inch long in a layered cut. He had skinny eyebrows and a short mustache. His face felt rough as if he hadn't shaved in a couple of days. It seemed like he had a big nose and small ears. His teeth seemed good. His lips seemed skinny and his eyes seemed small. She estimated that he was around five feet, seven inches and weighed approx. 150 lbs. with a slightly overweight build. He was not muscular although he seemed strong at first when he grabbed her. His legs and lower back were hairy but he did not have hair on his chest. He did not wear glasses, he did not smoke, and did not drink or use drugs while she was with him. He did not have on any jewelry. He was possibly wearing jeans, possibly a white shirt with red trim on the shoulders, and possibly sneakers. When he dropped her off, he was wearing some kind of baseball type cap, because when she hugged him, she felt the back of the cap. He did not have any noticeable foreign accent. She described the gun as a revolver, silver or chrome colored with a brown grip, possibly four inch.

She described the car as dark red or maroon in color, solid red, two door full size vehicle. The dashboard and steering wheel were red. The seats and interior walls were white. On the dashboard was a brown strip with the word "Magnum" in silver letters. There also a digital clock on the dashboard with green numerals. The seats were white and were divided with an arm rest in between. She did not remember the carpet but thought they were floor mats, maybe black. She caught a glimpse of the back seat when she first got into the car and it seemed

empty. She did not recall anything on the dashboard.
The vehicle had an automatic transmission, a radio
tuned to Q105, and electric door locks that did not
have a knob at the top. The car also was noisy,
either a mechanical engine noise or a noisy muffler
and seemed to vibrate a lot.

She described his apartment building as being
light colored stucco on the outside. Suspect had to
open some kind of gate before they got to the
stairs which were carpeted with red carpet and had
stair rails on both sides. The door and the interi-
or walls were white. The apartment carpeting was red
also. After they entered, she thought there was a
bedroom to the left and a bathroom to the right,
then the living room, then the kitchen. The bathroom
was pink. One bathroom wall had a picture of an owl
on it. There was a blue rug around the toilet
although she could not remember the toilet color.
There were a pair of jogging type shoes or sneakers
on the bathroom floor. They were a little dirty.
They were white with a medium blue stripe on both
sides, lace up, with a little chicken or a rooster
on the sides. The bedroom also had red carpet with a
waterbed and flowered sheets. There was also a light
weight bedspread on the bed. There were weights on
the bedroom floor, a silver bar with gray weights.
There was also a fan on the bedroom floor. In the
living room there was a couch and a coffee table and
possibly a chair nearer to the kitchen. The television was to the left of the couch and the kitchen
was to the right of the couch. She was able to see
the light of the TV. The couch was finished with a
flat velvet like fabric and she could not recall the
color. She did not actually see the coffee table but
heard him set things on it. She recalled that as
they were leaving the apartment, she had to step
down, walk to a room, and then step up again to go
out the door. She did not remember this step when
entering the apartment. While she was in the apartment, she could hear noises from the outside, cars,
television, and voices.

When she finished typing up the report, Detective Goethe sat back, reread what she had written and shook her head in disbelief. Incredible! she thought. How did the kid remember so much with all that happened to her? Goethe knew from experience that cops rarely were handed so much specific evidence to go on in any crime, but especially not in a rape case, which usually left the victim in a state of shock and too highly traumatized to remember much of anything except the pain and the nightmarish terror.

But there was more. Unaware, Lisa McVey had carried crucial pieces of evidence home with her; specks of almost microscopic red fiber that, when woven together, were large enough to snare a brutal serial killer/serial rapist.

Meanwhile, across town at the Hillsborough County Sheriff's compound, a group of harried homicide detectives sweated away behind closed and guarded doors in a top-secret investigation, growing more desperate with each passing day. Serial murder, in 1984, was a brand-new ball game for most cops. There were no rules to go by, no textbook guides to follow in bringing to bay a modern-day Jack the Ripper who was busy strangling streetwalkers and scattering their remains almost as fast as the coroner could clean up after him. With no precedent to follow, Lt. Terry almost daily found himself either breaking some old, how-to rules of homicide investigation or making up new ones as he went along to fit the circumstances. One of those new "rules," Terry decreed, was that every piece of forensic evidence collected from violent crime scenes anywhere in Hillsborough County (which included Tampa police jurisdiction) be hand-delivered by special courier to the FBI Lab in Quantico and placed in the hands of Special Agent Mike Malone, one of the top experts in the Bureau's Hairs and Fibers Unit. It was a long shot, but maybe the FBI experts would find the missing link that ultimately would put a face on the strangling killer. It was a radical departure from the routine, but this murder case was anything but routine.

Supplemental reports filed by Detective Polly Goethe noted that:

On 5 Nov 84, I was directed by Capt. Martinez to send the clothing and the Sexual Battery kit evidence in this case to the FBI lab. I viewed the clothing evidence, which include a pair of white knit pants, a black knit pullover shirt,(which contained no labels), a white knit shirt, a white bra , a pair of socks, one pair of underpants, and a sexual exam kit, which remained sealed. I also viewed and took a Polaroid shot of a strip of cloth which had been used as a blindfold on the victim. This cloth was white in color with brown and blue print flower design. These items were sealed and were taken to the FBI lab in Washington by Det. Grossi on 6 Nov 84.

On 6 Nov 84, a memo was sent to both Uniform Districts describing the information obtained to this date on the suspect and the vehicle.

But not everyone took Lisa's story at face value. According to one old police hand who took everything he heard with several grains of salt, "... personally it sounded like a fairy tale. You got a young lady who is riding home from work, 2:30-3 o'clock in the morning, she's pulled off of a bicycle, taken to an apartment, stays there for some twenty-six to twenty-eight hours and is released and returns home.

"In all honesty, the first thing you think is, did this young lady and her boyfriend went someplace and stayed too long and that was an excuse to get back in the house type situation?

"Her story consisted of this man who abducted her. Once he got her to the apartment, he gave her a bath, she gave him a bath, he washed her hair, combed her hair, told her how pretty she was, went out of his way to make her comfortable at all times, continually apologized to her about, you know, you're a really nice girl and this shouldn't happen to you and I'm really sorry that this happened. And then he'd have intercourse with her and tell her he was sorry again. He tied her up on several occasions, they slept in the same bed, just kind of hard to swallow, you know.

"In fact, the only reason we sent her stuff to the FBI was because we had nothing to lose. At the time I was up to my ears in

alligators when the Captain told me to put her stuff together and send it. I said, 'No, I ain't got the time to mess with it.'

"He said: 'Send it!'

"We sent it."

And there the investigation rested for almost two more weeks, during which time the mysterious serial killer seized yet another victim off the Tampa streets and left her nude and strangled body sprawled spread-eagled on the slope of an east side highway overpass.

On November 13, 1984, Lt. Terry and one of his lead investigators, Lee "Pops" Baker, were sitting in the office of the Georgia Bureau of Investigation (GBI) in Atlanta, conferring with a specialist whose serial killing baptism of fire came with the Atlanta Child Murders, in which some thirty boys and young men were believed slain by a single predator. Wayne Williams was eventually tried and convicted on only two of the murders. However, based on that conviction, Atlanta police say they cleared twenty-three of the killings. The case against Williams rested primarily on fiber evidence that police said conclusively linked Williams to the victims.

"We were up there to talk about the fiber evidence," Terry recalled. "But there was something else bothering us. At that point, we had eight victims that we knew of. What happened when we got to fifteen, twenty, twenty-five bodies? How would we handle that? We didn't know, didn't have a clue about how to manage an investigation of that magnitude, so we were looking for help. The Atlanta people had been through something similar with the Child Murders and we were hoping they could give us some guidance.

"The Tampa kidnap-sexual battery case involving Lisa McVey was being worked independently of the Sheriff's homicides cases. We were meeting and communicating between the agencies, but we were hitting a stone wall. Bodies kept coming. Every time we had a body we felt we were getting closer with more information, but we still didn't have a name to go with all the evidence we were collecting. At that point, we were starting to send evidence from any violent crime to the Lab, inundating them with other cases."

In the middle of the conference with the Atlanta detectives,

35

Terry received a call from his office informing him that Agent Malone was trying to reach him. Terry called Quantico.

"I hope you're sitting down," an excited Malone began. "If you're not, you'd better, because I just made a fiber match on one of your cases."

"That's great! Which homicide?"

"No, no," Malone replied. "Not one of the murders. This is on a rape case out of the city of Tampa. And the victim survived!"

The stunning news that there was a live victim solidly linked to the killer by the fiber evidence, a victim who could possibly identify him, rocketed Terry out of his chair.

"What?" he exclaimed. "You gotta be kidding!"

Within the hour, Terry was on a plane back to Tampa. While he was airborne, orders went out from Sheriff Walter Heinrich's office to gather the troops. The formation of a special Task Force was authorized. By the time Terry's plane touched down at Tampa International, where an emergency escort with lights and sirens blazing awaited him, officers from several jurisdictions were already gathering at the sheriff's compound in historic Ybor City to coordinate their assignments. Those agencies included in the Task Force were the Hillsborough and Pasco County Sheriff's Office (since one body was dumped a few hundred feet across the line in Pasco County), the Tampa Police Department, the Florida Department of Law Enforcement (FDLE), and the FBI. The officers selected for the Task Force were all homicide and or sex-crime detectives with years of experience dealing with the brutality of murder and rape. All in all, nearly fifty agents and detectives gathered to focus their considerable array of cop skills on a single goal:

Find the guy who raped Lisa McVey and you find the killer.

"And that," said Lt. Terry simply, "is how it broke."

While Terry divided the Task Force into teams and sent them off, Sheriff Heinrich fended off the news media in a hastily called press conference to announce the formation of the Task Force.

"We feel pretty strongly that there is a connection between several of the eight murders that have occurred here in the last six months," Heinrich explained. Asked if a serial killer was active in

the Tampa area, Heinrich conceded, "I think in those cases we have linked I would probably have to say yes. We are working on the theory that others may be connected."

With the stunning news that tiny red fibers had been found clinging to the clothing worn by Lisa McVey when she was abducted, the seventeen year old girl was suddenly a very important person. Detective Polly Goethe was recruited into the Task Force, thanks to the rapport she'd already established with the young victim who now, more then ever, realized just how lucky she was to be alive.

She'd actually spent the night alongside a monstrous serial killer—and had lived to talk about it! Even the violence-toughened street cops who had little reason to believe in miracles were muttering to themselves about this one and asking why. If this really is our guy, why didn't he kill her? But there wasn't much time for pondering the enigma of why one lived when so many others died. This was a time for action.

Goethe was teamed with Tampa homicide detective Sgt. Bob Price and Hillsborough County's Sgt. Randy Latimer. The trio rushed off to pick up Lisa at Beach Place, the state-run shelter where she had been moved after the abuse by Rhodes became known. She was interviewed again and debriefed as the investigators plumbed the recesses of her very sharp memory for the tiniest details that might narrow an already tightening dragnet even more. With Lisa McVey at her side, Detective Goethe began cruising North Tampa, picking out the landmarks that Lisa remembered or searching for new ones that might jog her memory.

They started with her recollections of the motel signs, a Howard Johnsons and a Quality Inn, close to where the kidnaper drove onto the Interstate. Price instantly recognized the description. "I've got eleven years experience on that side of town and what she saw could be only one place—Nebraska and Fowler, block east of the Interstate," Price reported. Lt. Terry pursed his lips and nodded. Nebraska Avenue. It fits, he thought. Most of the murder victims had been picked up along the Nebraska meat market, and scores of detectives had been targeting the Strip for weeks

37

with stakeouts and decoys in hopes of catching the killer as he shopped for his next victim. North Tampa was still a vast area to cover, but at least now they were in the right ball park.

Lisa's estimate of the time it took to drive from the kidnaper's apartment to the automatic teller machine stop narrowed it down even further. In 1984, there was only a handful of ATMs in the entire city, few of them on the north side. A squad of detectives was sent off to subpoena bank records that showed any ATM transaction in North Tampa between the hours of 2:30 and 4:30 a.m. on November fourth. It was an almost impossible long shot, but squads also began backtracking from the point where Lisa was released, checking service stations and convenience stores that were open during those hours, searching for an attendant who might remember the man who stopped for gas.

Lisa's recollection of the word "Magnum" on the dashboard of the kidnaper's car was also highly significant. A check with auto experts revealed that only the 1978 and 1979 model Dodges carried this distinctive mark. A Task Force member flew off to the state capital in Tallahassee and returned with a computer printout of all Dodge Magnums registered in Hillsborough County. The printout ran to fifteen pages and included 278 registrations.

Buried on page fourteen was the name of Robert Joe Long.

While detectives were still running down names on the vehicle registration list, the subpoenaed records from the First National Bank, Barnett Bank, and Southeast Bank were delivered to the Task Force's headquarters. Thankfully, the list was considerably shorter than the list of auto registrations. Southeast Bank had recorded no transactions on its automatic teller machines during the specified hours. However, a Barnett Bank Honor Card had been used at a Florida National Bank ATM located at 58th Street and Fowler Avenue at 3:49 a.m. on November fourth. The time fit. The location fit. And the name that jumped out at investigators just happened to matched one on the list of Dodge Magnum owners: Robert J. Long, W/M, DOB: 10/14/53, of 5802 East Fowler Avenue.

However, even before those two vital clues came to light, Task Force man hunters ran into a Bobby Joe Long, questioned him,

took his picture, and let him go when he refused permission to search his car.

"At this point," Lt. Terry recalled, "the case was going about ninety miles an hour. We had about forty-five or fifty cops on the streets. We knew we were finally closing in on our guy.

"When Lisa was debriefed and explained where she was released, that gave us a focal point, so we flooded north and northeast Tampa with two-man search teams and began scouring the area for a red or maroon car with white interior, based on Lisa's description. Their orders were to stop any red Dodge Magnums and do a 10-80, a field interrogation report. Two city officers going down Nebraska saw the car."

About 11:30 a.m. on November 15, Detectives C.L. Helms and Charles Wolf were driving southbound on Nebraska. They had just crossed Sligh when a red car zipped by them, headed north.

Helms, at the wheel, reached over and slapped his partner's arm. "Hey!" he exclaimed. "That looks like our guy. Let's get him." Helms swung the unmarked cruiser around in a U-turn and flipped on the blue lights. The driver of the red Dodge pulled off into a parking lot at Nebraska and Hamilton, five blocks north of Sligh.

According to Wolf's field interrogation report on the routine street stop:

```
Det. Helms approached the w/m driving this vehi-
cle first and asked the subject for his driver's
license. The w/m gave Det. Helms his driver's
license, at which time I told the w/m subject that
he was stopped because his vehicle fit the descrip-
tion of a vehicle which had been used in a hit and
run traffic accident. After I retrieved the sub-
ject's driver's license, I viewed  same and ascer-
tained that the w/m subject's name was LONG, BOBBY
JOE; DOB: 14 October 53, 5802 E. Fowler Avenue, #6.
His Florida Driver's License Number is L520 070 53
374. W/M LONG was six feet tall, 180 lbs., had hazel
eyes, brown slightly wavy short hair. I observed
that w/m Long's Florida driver's license had expired
and at that time he told me that he had a valid West
```

39

Virginia driver's license. His West Virginia driver's license # was E317181. The address on his West Virginia driver's license was 826 13th Street, Kenova, West Virginia.

I asked w/m Long if he worked; at which time he told me that he was unemployed and that his last job was at Brandon Community Hospital and that he had quit his job in March 1984 because the work was beginning to be too much. He advised that he had worked at Brandon Community Hospital for approximately nine months. I asked w/m Long where he was coming from, at which time he told me that he was coming from the Employment Office downtown. He advised that he was going to eat lunch at this time.

At approximately this time, Det. Wolf came up to w/m Long and he told w/m Long that the reason we had stopped him was that we were investigating a minor hit and run traffic accident in which the suspect had pulled a run on the driver of the second vehicle and that w/m Long's vehicle fit the description of the suspect vehicle and that was why he was being stopped and questioned. Mr. Long was very cooperative as far as answering questions, however, when Detective Wolf asked w/m Long if he could search his vehicle for a firearm, w/m Long refused to let Det. Wolf search the car.

I observed that w/m Long's vehicle was a 1979 two-door Dodge Magnum, burgundy in color, semi-faded, bearing Florida Tag Number 759 AGL. It had an '85 October decal on same. The interior of the vehicle was white leather. The front seat in the car was a bench type seat which had an arm rest which folded down in the middle, the dashboard of the vehicle was red in color, the steering wheel was red in color. The vehicle also had the word "Magnum" written in silver letters on the glove box of the car. Also the word "Magnum" was on a brown wood grain type strip and next to the word "Magnum" was a digital clock. There were no floor mats in this vehicle at this

time. I did observe that the vehicle was very clean on the interior in appearance. I observed that there were some tools and what appeared to be a tool pouch in the back seat of the car and that there was a rod and reel also in the backseat of the car.

The u/signed and Det. Wolf asked w/m Long if he would mind if we took some Polaroid photographs of him at which time he advised that we could. We also asked if we could take photographs of his vehicle and he also stated that we could. At that point, Det. R. Jordan with Auto Theft arrived at the scene and he took several pictures of w/m Long and of w/m Long's vehicle.

The Polaroid photo showed a ruggedly handsome, square-jawed young man staring directly into the camera. His thick, dark-brown hair, slightly parted on the right, swooped down across over his forehead. With the noonday sun directly overhead, the man's already deep-set eyes were cast in dark shadows and the same light angle made him appear to have high, Indian-like cheekbones. No movie star, maybe, but good-looking enough in an open, boyish sort of way. Easy to see why a girl might jump in the car with the guy without thinking twice about what might be lurking behind those flat brown eyes.

While Helms chatted with the man, Detective Wolf got on the radio to Sgt. Price and informed him of they had a guy and a car stopped, and both of them were dead ringers for the description Lisa McVey had provided. Unfortunately, Price was skeptical, and told the excited detective there wasn't much they could do at that point with no warrant and no charges.

"In all honesty," Price later recalled, "the odds of the first car that you stop being the suspect is one in God knows how many billions. But Wolf was emphatic. He felt very strongly that they had stopped the right subject. He said it all fits. He (the suspect) was very nervous. He was fidgety. He didn't respond well to us stopping him, but he didn't object to having his photograph taken...Our guys told him that his vehicle possibly had been involved in some type of hit and run which was why they'd stopped him and they

were sorry for the inconvenience, et cetera, et cetera.

"I told Wolf they should stall him as long as they possibly could while I contacted the sheriff's office. At that point, we picked up surveillance on Mr. Long and continued to keep him under surveillance until he was arrested.

"Also, approximately two hours after Mr. Long had been stopped he called the Department and asked to speak to Detective Helms. He wanted to know if they had in fact found the vehicle they were looking for because he didn't want to be stopped again by other policemen who were also looking for this hit and run car. He asked to be advised when the car was located, which, in my personal opinion, was a strong indicator that we were in the right direction," Price said.

As soon as the man, still grumbling about being stopped, was released and told he could be on his way, the two detectives leaped in their car and raced to the Temple Terrace section of northeast Tampa. Fowler Avenue skirts the southern boundary of the sprawling University of South Florida campus. A few blocks east of the campus, the officers turned left off Fowler at 58th Street and made a quick right turn into the parking lot of a row of two-story buildings at 5802 East Fowler that housed small businesses on the ground floor and apartments on the second floor.

"We went to eyeball the place right away because the guy looked so right to us and we wanted to see if his place matched what the victim in the kidnap and rape case had described," explained Helms. "It was perfect."

"As you turned off of 58th Street into the apartment parking lot, you drove underneath several large oak trees which had a lot of moss hanging from them just the way she [Lisa McVey] described. The parking lot to the complex was very small, so the guy could park very close to the door and when you got out of the the car you had to step up onto a concrete sidewalk to enter building. We didn't go in, but from the outside we could see a stairway that the girl said was there. She talked about going through a squeaky gate before entering the building. There wasn't any gate but the outside door was a storm door type with small windows and grates that someone

wearing a blindfold might mistake for a gate. And it squeaked just like she described."

After checking the apartment, Helms and Wolf returned to police headquarters, met with Sgt. Price and briefed him on what they'd found. They also turned over the Polaroid photos taken of the suspect and his vehicle.

Within the hour, Lisa McVey had tentatively identified that man as the same one who kidnaped and sexually attacked her. With that identification in hand, Lt. Terry reconvened Task Force personnel and began parceling out new assignments.

"About the same time all that was happening," said Terry, "the guys who had been working the vehicle registrations and the ATM records came back with the match. A red Dodge Magnum was registered to Bobby Joe Long. Bobby Joe Long had made a withdrawal from the ATM at 58th and Fowler early on the morning of November fourth. And now Lisa McVey had picked Bobby Joe Long out of a photo lineup. We had everything we needed to take him down, at least for the McVey kidnaping. And by now we were all pretty sure this was the same guy who was responsible for the homicides.

"We began surveillance of Long within about three hours after he was stopped and questioned. When we got in place out on Fowler, he had backed his car into his parking space and we watched him make several trips back and forth to a dumpster and to the woods behind his apartment getting rid of stuff."

Based on the information obtained so far, one squad rushed off to obtain an arrest warrant and a search warrant approved by a circuit court judge; other Task Force members broke up into two-man units and began coordinating a twenty-four-hour surveillance that would stick to Bobby Joe Long like Superglue until he was arrested. Less than three hours after Helms and Wolf spotted the red Magnum on Nebraska Avenue, an invisible surveillance net silently was thrown around 5802 East Fowler Avenue. Other units, including an airborne patrol to minimize the chances Long might spot a tail, were standing by as backup.

While they waited, Lt. Terry called Mike Malone at the FBI

and invited the agent to join the bust. You were as much a part of making this case as anybody, Terry told him. We'd like to have you here when we take him down, and there'll be more fiber evidence to check out once we get into his car and apartment. Malone grabbed the first plane out of Quantico headed for Florida.

In addition, Terry, looking for any edge he could get, sat down with specialists from the FBI's Behavioral Science Unit to talk about guidelines to follow in arresting and interviewing the suspect. How should they approach the guy? How might he react? What interviewing techniques worked best with someone suspected of multiple homicides? In short, what made a serial killer different from your garden-variety murderer, and how should they handle him? With those questions answered, Terry set about assigning Task Force members to different teams that were ready to pounce at the right moment.

One team was selected to physically arrest Long. Another was told to do nothing but watch and listen to the suspect after he was picked up. Terry chose two detectives with exceptional interrogation skills to interview Long after he was in custody. "Their technique," Terry explained, "was to start talking and keep on talking, keep engaging the suspect in conversation so he wouldn't have time to think. In fact, they both talk so much that most people would probably confess just to shut them up," he laughed.

A search-and-seizure team was appointed to handle Long's vehicle, another search team for the residence, and a neighborhood survey team to interview Long's neighbors in his apartment complex before word of the arrest leaked to the media. That's important, Terry emphasized. You have gotta get to those neighbors before the media does. As soon as they hear we have somebody in custody suspected of doing the killings, they'll be all over the place like a swarm of locusts. Anything we get after that will be contaminated.

Finally, with everyone in place, there was nothing to do but watch. And wait. The watchers' minute by minute surveillance logs tell the tale of the next 24 hours, culminating with the final entry:

> 1600 hours the subject left the cinema and Det.
> Radford and Det. Davis arrested the subject in the
> parking lot without incident.

Actually, the arrest of Bobby Joe Long was a bit more melodramatic than the laconic surveillance logs indicate. In fact, for thrills it rivaled the action-adventure flick that Long and, unbeknownst to him, four or five wrapped-tight cops had just sat through--Chuck Norris in a matinee showing of Missing in Action.

Lt. Terry described the scene: "At the movie theater, Long didn't know it at the time but at least four cops went in with him—one on his left, one on his right, one in front of him and one behind.

"The rest of us waited outside. I still had a nagging doubt in my gut that, even though we'd been chasing this guy for eight months, there was still that very slight possibility that he might not be the right one. I sent a detective on his hands and knees crawling up to Long's car to check the tires. He reported back that they were mounted backwards, just as we speculated they might be back with our second victim. There was no doubt then that we had the right guy.

"When he emerged from the movie, we used that special tactical police command that we all learn in the academy:

(Hands up, you son of a bitch, or I'll blow you away!)

"If he had moved, there were so many guns pointing at him that three or four of our own people probably would have been hit in the crossfire!"

When he walked out of the theater, Bobby Joe Long had no hint that he was such a center of attention for so many jittery cops.

Suddenly, the air around him exploded in noise and the shrill screech of tires as a dozen unmarked and marked police cars roared across the parking lot, straight at him. Heavily armed policemen rushed at him all from all sides, seeming to shout all at once,"Don't move, you son of a bitch!" "Hands up, motherfucker!" "On the ground, cocksucker!" Stunned, Long barely moved before several hands grabbed him from behind and threw him face down on the rough pavement. Someone jerked his arms behind his back, and the cold steel of handcuffs bit harshly into his wrists. As he

turned his head slightly to spit out the gravel from the parking lot, one cop planted his knee in the middle of Long's back and jammed the barrel of a .357 Magnum against the side of his head. "One more move, asshole," the man snarled, "and I'll blow your fucking head off!"

▲   ▲   ▲

A LETTER FROM BOBBY

I don't know if you know how they caught me—I think I told you, it was because I let that one girl go. I just couldn't kill her. She was something special. Now, I think hey, you knew she'd get you nailed, what if you had it to do all over again? I think I'd let her go again, should never have fuckin messed with her in the first place. It all just makes me crazy. I've never had troubles picking up pussy, in bars, on raquetball courts, doin my fuckin laundry.

I don't fuck around, I don't bullshit, and I've sure as fuck learned my lesson about "talking". So "you'll" know, those fuckers had all the evidence they needed when they grabbed me. Did you hear how that came down?

I went to the fucking movies over on Dale Mabry and when I walked out the exit theres two grody looking fucks behind me talking about what a good fuckin movie it was next thing I know I'm on the ground with a fucking cannon up against my ear, and I swear at least 100 fucking FBI, Fla Law Enf, Tampa police, Hills Sheriff, all popped up from everywhere and that was it. They nailed me.

I knew it was gonna happen, they pulled me over the day before and had me under constant surveylance since. I thought about splitting, never would have made it even if I tried. So really I just let it happen. Fucked up real good! eh?

I mean they had me so I "thought" if I cooperated

it would go better on me. I was wrong! But I
learned! If I ever get out, shoot first, ask questions later, and don't say shit to the POLICE!
except I want a lawyer! Live and learn. But I don't
forget.

▲   ▲   ▲

Sgt. Bob Price watched the takedown unfold from an adjoining
parking lot along with Latimer, Terry, Agent Malone, and several
other command officers. When Price and the others reached the
scene, Long was already handcuffed and sitting in the back seat of
an unmarked police car while another member of the Task Force
read him the search warrant authorizing authorities to seize Long's
car. Long was told only that he was under arrest for the kidnaping
and sexual battery of Lisa McVey. No mention was made of any
murders, or of his suspected role in the multiple slayings.

Once the reading of the search warrant was complete, evidence
technicians swarmed over Long's Dodge Magnum. The first thing
Detective Steve Cribb did when he opened the car door was to clip
a sample of the carpeting from the right front floorboard and bag
it. Cribb carried the bag to a group of officers standing nearby and
handed it to Special Agent Mike Malone. It would take highly specialized lab equipment and powerful microscopes to tell for sure,
but already in his mind's eye Malone could see these carpet samples matching perfectly with the infinitesimal traces of red fiber
that had been meticulously collected from the multiple homicide
scenes throughout Hillsborough County. Over the past eight
months, Agent Malone had become as familiar with the peculiar
characteristics of those little red fibers as he was with his own best
tie. For months, he'd wrestled with the mystery of where they'd
come from, and how they linked one killer with the deaths of so
many young women. Now, at last, Malone was looking at the source
of those fibers

▲   ▲   ▲

A LETTER FROM BOBBY

They want to fry me REAL bad. I'm the biggest fiend to ever hit Hillsborough County, and they want me barbecued and well done. Never gonna happen. I'll do it myself before those fucks get the pleasure.

▲   ▲   ▲

Sgt. Bob Price walked up to the car, introduced himself to Long and studied the silent suspect, still trembling slightly over the suddenness of the arrest. For the next several hours, Price and Randy Latimer would be as close as skin to Bobby Joe Long, as they took on the mind-numbing task of interrogating a man they were now convinced had murdered many times, cruelly, cunningly, and without conscience. They were going to try to get inside the monster's head, lead him, push him, prod him until they knew far more than they ever hoped to know about what made Bobby Joe Long tick. About what set him off. About why he raped. Why he killed.

As Price approached the car, Detective Cribb was sitting in the back seat with the suspect, reading him the warrant. A dozen or more officers milled about the car.

When Cribb was done, Price opened the car door and introduced himself. Like so many others, Sgt. Price was struck by the soft, oddly high-pitched, almost effeminate voice that came out of the husky looking guy scrunched up in the back seat, hands cuffed behind his back. A Tampa cop for fifteen years, Price at the time was a supervisor in the department's homicide bureau who had interviewed countless murder suspects. He'd developed an intuitive sense, an overactive hunch muscle, some called it, about these guys—when they were telling the truth; when they were lying; when they were about ready to break and what little push might send them over the edge into a no-way-out confession. Price was a master at his craft. He'd played the game with some of the best

48

mind-fuckers in the business, and there was nothing they could slip by him anymore.

Much of Price's success as an interrogator came from knowing his prey. So now he closely studied Bobby Joe Long from behind hooded eyes, sidling up to him "good ole boy" style.

We're going out to your place, Price told the suspect. We want you there when we execute a search warrant. Price climbed into the back seat beside Long. Two other detectives were in the front, and a small caravan of cop cars pulled out of the parking lot and headed east on Busch Boulevard.

Long's demeanor puzzled Price. Not what you'd expect from a guy who suddenly found himself in some deep and serious shit. Not nervous or fidgety. Wasn't all sweaty. Long acted like he was more embarrassed than anything else.

"He didn't like the handcuffs at all," Price recalled. "Obviously when you make an arrest in the way we did, took him down right in front of a crowd coming out of a theater, it was embarrassing to him. And going out Busch Boulevard with traffic bumper to bumper, Bobby kept trying to slide down into the seat so he wouldn't be seen."

No one mentioned kidnaping or murder or rape during the long ride. It was mainly just idle chit-chat.

Recounted Price: "I guess he heard one of the other guys call me Bobby, because he asked me if I liked the name Bobby. Then he said, 'Bobby, these handcuffs are a little too tight.' That's all he complained about.

When they reached the apartment building on Fowler, about thirty other officers had already arrived and the parking lot was filled with cop cars. The high-profile police activity had attracted attention, and crowds of curious onlookers were gathering. The audience of his former neighbors mortified Long. He ducked his head and refused to leave the car while the search warrant authorizing entry to his apartment was read and executed. One former neighbor, straining to get a peek at the figure cowering in the back seat of the police car, expressed shock when told it was the man from Apartment six, and that he'd been arrested for rape. "Oh,

no!" she exclaimed. "Not him. He seemed so shy, so quiet."

"Long became very uneasy," Price remembered. "He made a remark like, 'Oh, my God, the press is here.' I told him, "No, the press is not here. We went through a lot trouble to make sure that the press wasn't here." I said, "Bobby, I don't want to turn this thing into a circus." He seemed to appreciate that.

"I sort of signaled the other two officers in the front seat to get out and leave us alone. I wanted to establish a rapport with Bobby. What little I knew about him, I knew that he had a tremendous ego, still does, and I fed it. We sat there four or five minutes when some young ladies in halter tops and very short shorts and with some little kids walked by the car.

"He said, 'Well, I guess it will be quite some time before I see them again.' And I personally thought he was referring to the young ladies, but he said, 'No, I'm talking about the kids. I've got two kids of my own, but I don't get to see them very often. They live in Hollywood, Florida.'

"About that time I saw Randy Latimer arrive. I went to get out of the car, and I made a remark to Bobby. I said, 'Look, I'm not going to talk about any of this case until we get downtown and you've been properly advised of your rights and signed the forms. But I do want to say one thing'—and I wasn't looking at him when I said it—but I said, 'I want to thank you for not hurting that little girl [Lisa McVey].' And I got out of the car. I did it intentionally. I got out, stayed outside of the car maybe two or three minutes, talked to Randy. I just wanted Bobby to sit for awhile.

"When I got back in the car he said, 'You're welcome.'

"Then he got into, 'Are you the man in charge?' I wasn't. I had nothing to do with the press not being there, but I'm telling Bobby what I want Bobby to know. I wanted Bobby to think that I was absolutely and totally in charge of the situation and whatever I said went. He thought that I'd personally kept the press away, and he was impressed with that.

"So he said, 'Well, then, if you're in charge, is there any reason I have to stay here? Is this necessary? Do I have to be here?' I told him that he could waive the right to be present if that's what he

wanted, so he said, 'Well, then let's get out of here.'

"I got out of the car again, and told Sgt. Latimer and Lt. Terry that Bobby didn't want to stay there. Lt. Terry said, 'Okay Get him out of here.' And we went straight to Hillsborough County Sheriff's Office."

While Sgt. Price sat in the parking lot playing with Bobby Joe Long, the search team went about gathering up and cataloging just about everything in sight in apartment six. Many of the items noted in the search affidavits—crystal salt and pepper shakers, figurines, wall painting—would only become meaningful as the investigation continued to unfold. Others, however, immediately grabbed the searchers' attention.

"When we searched his place, you never would have believed this was the same person who had raped and murdered those victims," Lt. Terry recalled. "The place was spotless. His closet was what I'd called obsessively neat, with all his shoes carefully lined up on shelves and all his clothing hung exactly the same way.

"On the shelf of the closet we also found a box that was filled with different-colored shoelaces—the perfect, untraceable ligatures."

Recalling what Lisa had told her, Detective Goethe walked into Long's bedroom, stooped down by the side of the waterbed and, using a pair of tweezers to avoid contamination, picked up a girl's hair barrette just were Lisa said she'd dropped it. A hair caught in the barrette would later be matched to Lisa, proof that she had, indeed, been held prisoner in this very room—one more solid piece in the mounting pile of evidence that was rapidly burying Bobby Joe Long. "While in the apartment," Goethe later reported, "I noticed many things that confirmed Lisa's description. I noted the carpeted stairway with railings on both sides. The apartment had a waterbed with a bookcase type headboard with a digital clock on the headboard. There was a set of weights in the apartment. I noted bread with sesame seeds on it. I noted the picture of the owl, and a pair of jogging shoes as described by Lisa. I also noted a large square floor fan. The couch in the living room was finished in a velvet-velour type fabric as described by Lisa. There was also a bathrobe which Long had covered Lisa with."

Meanwhile, Deputies Greg Brown and Jon Tillis strung a yellow, "Do-Not-Cross" crime-scene ribbon around the dumpster behind the apartment where Long had been spotted discarding items. Not all of what they found was the kind of trash they expected to find. One envelope contained shockingly explicit photos of a nude woman on her knees in the front seat of a car, reaching back to expose her genitals. Others in the collection showed the same woman in the act of intercourse with a man—once in the missionary position, once from behind. The man's face didn't show, but his erect penis was clearly penetrating the woman. At the time, the detectives who found the prints didn't realize the significance of their discovery. They soon would for, incredibly, they were looking at a rape in progress as recorded by the rapist himself. The ultimate trophy.

"We recovered many other photos of nude women from the dumpster or found them in his apartment," said Terry. "Some turned out to be photos of the victims of his Ad Man home invasion rapes that he'd found and took with him when he left. Some we never identified. He was doing a lot of housecleaning when our surveillance got on him, but he had about a three-hour head start. No telling what he might have disposed of that we never found. Especially pictures. We have reason to believe that there were photos of other victims he'd taken that he may have gotten rid of or that are now in the hands of others."

While Brown and Tillis continued sifting through the dumpster, Detective Pops Baker, following the directions of the surveillance team, began scouring the wooded lot east of the apartment building where the watchers had seen Long apparently throw something away. About sixty feet away, Baker came across a large hunting knife lying in deep grass. The blade was shiny and clean. In fact, Baker noted, the weapon was so spotless that not even a fingerprint smudged its surface. Whoever threw the knife away had made sure it was scrubbed clean before he did it. Baker was particularly interested in any knife that might have belonged to Bobby Joe Long.One victim's throat had been cut—with a knife just like the heavy-bladed hunting knife that now lay at Baker's feet.

Before the search party concluded its work, several pieces of women's clothing, including a pair of zip-up boots, were found in the vacant field where Long had discarded them. All were bagged and placed into evidence.

Leaving Long's Fowler Avenue apartment to the search party, Sergeants Price and Latimer drove Long to the Sheriff's office. They sat him in a small, windowless interview room that held only three folding chairs. Before starting the interview, the two inter-rogators conferred with Sheriff Heinrich and Lt. Terry on what approach to take with the suspect. Remember what the FBI advised, Terry cautioned, with a guy like this don't try bullshitting him. Tell him up front what you've got on him and that you've got him. Price and Latimer entered the room and took chairs on either side of the suspect, deliberately close, crowding his personal space. Latimer carried a yellow legal pad to take notes. Price read the Miranda warning and asked Long to read it again for himself. At 5:52 p.m., Bobby Joe Long, asked for a cup of coffee, signed a Consent to Interview form and the grilling began.

For the first hour and a half the detectives focused solely on the Lisa McVey case—the kidnaping and repeated sexually assaults the young girl suffered during the hours she was held prisoner in the Fowler Avenue apartment. Long seemed relieved it was over. But he was too eager to cooperate, Price and Latimer thought. Too quick to cop to the charges, as though if he admitted this one thing they wouldn't bring up the other stuff. "Yeah, yeah. I did it," Long responded almost as soon as Lisa's name was mentioned.

He insisted he didn't know what drove him to snatch the girl off her bike in the middle of the night and spirit her off to his apartment. Long said that he'd been out driving around earlier in the evening, just cruising, and had stopped for one drink at a bar on Dale Mabry Highway over on Tampa's west side. He was on his way home when the girl passed him on her bike going in the oppo-site direction. Long turned around and followed her, passing her and backtracking a few times to make sure she hadn't turned off or stopped somewhere along the way.

The traffic was light. And due to the lateness of the hour there

53

were no passersby to see what was going on, so Long said he just decided on the spur of the moment to grab the girl. He parked just south of Sligh, took a ready-made blindfold out of the glove compartment, and crossed the street to hide behind a van. (Long admitted that he had made the blindfold a couple of days earlier, knowing he was going to use it but not when or on whom.)

Long described how he grabbed Lisa as she rode past the van, told her he had a gun, and dragged her across the street to his car. He ordered the girl to disrobe and admitted "having sex" with her, but adamantly refused to discuss any specific details about the sex.

For the first time, the cops ran into a curious contradiction that was to puzzle them for the duration of the case. Bobby Joe Long, they discovered, could talk about strangling other human beings, he could describe, without emotion, watching the life fade from their eyes as they slowly died. He could, without remorse, discuss the finer details of murder and body disposal. But when it came to sex, Bobby Joe Long refused to say a word. "Bobby Joe Long never would talk to us about what he did sexually to his victims, the ones who lived or the ones who died," recalled Gary Terry. "Whenever the subject came up, he clammed up. Acted too embarrassed to talk about anything sexual. All he'd say was 'I had sex,' which became a euphemism for yeah, I raped her and sodomized her and forced her into fellatio and performed cunnilingus on her and bit her and stuck my fingers in her vagina and anus.' It got so that when Long said 'had sex,' we pretty much knew what he really meant. But I never figured out why he was that way. Maybe he was just too ashamed of sex to talk about it with other men."

Long tried to convince the two detectives that, after grabbing Lisa, he got scared because he'd never done anything like that before and drove recklessly and aimlessly away from the scene, getting lost in the maze of residential streets before finally finding his way back to Fowler Avenue. Price and Latimer knew it was all crap. A guy who'd kidnaped six or eight or more women off the streets in the past eight months wasn't about to panic now, especially when there were no witnesses. But they let him talk.

At his apartment building, Long continued, he told Lisa to get

dressed, blindfolded her, and walked her up the stairs. And then, according to Latimer's report: "Long stated he had sex with the victim numerous times for the next twenty-four hours."

As he talked, Price and Latimer got the impression that Long was trying to put the best face possible on the abduction and sexual assault on the young victim, portraying himself as a kindly old uncle who, in between rapes, was sensitive and solicitous of the girl's needs. On Saturday, the full day they spent together in the apartment, Long said he fixed a ham sandwich for the girl—after first binding her hands and feet and blindfolding her so she couldn't escape. When she complained of being cold, he tucked his own terry-cloth bathrobe around her. At one point, he insisted, Lisa even told him she didn't want to leave, didn't want to go back to her "father" who had suffered numerous heart attacks and whom she had to care for. Long said he thought she seemed awfully nonchalant about her family and how they'd be worried when she didn't come home. He wasn't sure if this attitude was just to pacify him and keep him from getting upset, or if she really meant what she said.

While still in the apartment, Long continued, he unloaded the .38 revolver he'd used in the abduction and threw the cartridges away. In case something went wrong, he didn't want to be tempted to shoot the girl. And, by the way, he added, two days after freeing Lisa, he threw the gun off the Courtney Campbell Causeway into Tampa Bay, hoping that if the gun was gone, the urge to kidnap again would vanish with it. *Uh-huh, Latimer thought. Has nothing to do with the fact that one of the murder victims was shot in the back of the neck with a gun just like that one, does it, Bobby? No gun, no ballistic evidence, right, Bobby?*

As he talked, Long constantly expressed his concern for the girl's welfare. "Is she all right? Is she doing okay?" he asked. "She's really a nice girl. Do me a favor. Don't bullshit me. Promise me that you'll tell her that I'm really sorry that I had to put her through that."

After releasing Lisa early that Sunday morning, Long continued, he went home and slept until late that night. When he awoke,

Long was dismayed to find that the urge to kidnap and rape was still with him, an almost uncontrollable obsession that had driven him for years, beginning back in the seventies when he was still married. It seemed that the urge became stronger after he lost a job or some other setback plunged him into a deep depression. That's when he'd get in his car and start driving for hours on end, searching for someone like Lisa. He told the detectives that, in the past two years, he had racked up more than 50,000 miles on his Dodge cruising the streets, and had put on ten or twelve used tires during that period. But, he added quickly, he hadn't done anything like that since the incident involving Lisa McVey.

Price caught Latimer's eye and nodded slightly as if to say: Yeah, well we'll see about that.

Latimer picked up a folder and flipped it open. "Speaking of tires, Bobby," he asked, the tone of his voice taking on a harder edge, "are you familiar with forensic evidence—tire impressions, fingerprints, fibers, stuff like that? You know about the FBI and their reputation with that kind of evidence?"

Long nodded, suddenly wary.

"Well, in all those tires you bought, did you ever buy a Vogue tire?" Latimer pressed, pulling his chair closer to the suspect.

Long shifted slightly in his chair and shrugged off the question.

At that point, Bob Price excused himself and stepped into the hallway. He thumbed through a thick case file, pulled out a set of five photographs, and returned to the interrogation room.

Long glanced away from Latimer, who was now only inches from his face. When he spotted the photos Price handed to Latimer, a thin sheen of sweat broke out on his forehead. He straightened up, crossed his arms, and leaned far back in his chair, all the subtle signs that Price had been watching for. Price smiled to himself. Got ya, you son of a bitch!

"Tell me, Bobby, did you ever pick up any prostitutes?"

Long nodded again, his voice even softer and now nearly inaudible. "Yeah. Down in Miami."

"What about here in Tampa?" Latimer bore in. "Ever pick up hookers around here?"

"I— I don't think I want to answer that."

Latimer shoved the top photo into Long's hands. It was a picture of Kim Swann, whose body had been discovered on a highway overpass on November twelve, only four days earlier. "Ever see her?" Latimer demanded.

Long glanced at the photo and shook his head.

Latimer repeated the process with the next four photos:

Karen Dinsfriend.

Chanel Williams.

Michelle Simms.

Lana Long.

Each time, Long shook his head. Pale and shaky, he asked to use the rest room. When he returned to the interview room, Latimer resumed his relentless questioning. Did you know this girl? Have you ever seen this one? After again studying the photo of Kim Swann, Long conceded, "I might have seen her around someplace, but I don't know for sure."

Up to that point, Price recalled, the atmosphere in the cramped room was "almost friendly." But now, perhaps sensing he was cornered and the rat catchers were closing in, Long suddenly became belligerent.

"Look," he complained, pointing at Price, "I don't like— don't like the atmosphere since you came back in. The complexion of things have changed since Price came back. I think I might need an attorney."

"Why would you need an attorney?" Price said, "Nothing's changed. Bobby, listen, you know, we've been honest. We're going to continue to be honest. And there is no way that you can tell me— when we arrested you this afternoon you knew that this investigation would end up talking about these young ladies.

"We're not here to ask you if you did this. We know that you did this, and we want to know why."

Latimer interrupted. "We've got impressions of that Vogue tire with the whitewall turned inside out, just like it is on your car. We have fibers that came out of your car, and we had FBI experts fly in here from Washington to examine your car. We have connected

those fibers to four or five homicides. We've connected them. We've got you. There's no doubt."

"Look," Price added, "it's not a matter of did you do this. We know you did this. We can prove you did this. This is not to make our case; our case is made or you wouldn't be here. It's that simple."

Bobby Joe Long listened and took a deep breath. He looked up, he looked down. He looked longingly at the closed door, realizing now that he would never leave this room a free man, and quietly remarked:

"Well, I guess you got me. Yeah, I killed them. All the ones in the paper. I did them all."

He picked up the five photographs and shuffled through them. Without looking at the detectives, he said softly:

"There's three missing."

▲   ▲   ▲

A LETTER FROM BOBBY

Not surprised Latimer has a lot of enemies as well as Price. I was laying the groundwork for this shit when they caught me, they trust & believe me. I talked, but never mentioned my kinky friends. They're all gone, her back to California him back to Miami. I thought it may help if I talked, they had me anyway man, they were on me for like three hours before I said shit, then they had told me some things that proved they did have me, or I wouldn't have talked at all. So by talking I get maybe three more murder charges, so what! six-to-nine, whats the difference. I figured on the hunt a long time ago. I figured if I ever got caught that would be a good way out, even thought about planting a real well greased piece somewhere. I had about eight-to-ten laying around from the rape robberies. Just never went thru on it wish I had.

▲   ▲   ▲

Part Two

BOBBY
JOE

A LETTER FROM BOBBY JOE

I look at my folks, they're pitiful. They're hypocrits, their [sic] both now good "Christians." Fuck em both. If I ever lay eyes on either one of em again its too fuckin soon. I've tried to shield my Bitch Mother, now no more kid gloves. Its all coming out, I don't care anymore. They lie, they pass the buck, they're shit.

I don't have parents as of now. My mothers the biggest bitch, hypocrite, slut that ever lived...Thats it, I've had it, no more kid gloves.

My father has the backbone of a worm, he's so pussy whipped by my mother, it makes me wanna puke.

Its been coming to this, they're both so full of shit its pitiful. Man I thought serious about killing my mother before Cindy ever came along. Probably should have, maybe I wouldn't have hurt all the innocent people I did, and cause the pain & suffering I have. Fuck em, I've had it.

No more letters, no more nothin, I'm done with em.

▲   ▲   ▲

Kenova, West Virginia boasts that it's the "Town of Nice People."

Kenova is perched on a promontory just below Huntington, where West Virginia juts out to wedge itself between Ohio and

59

Kentucky. Here the Ohio River splits, the main branch heading west to form the border between Ohio and Kentucky, while the smaller branch, now known as the Big Sandy, rolling south to form the division line between Kentucky and West Virginia. Someone looked at the map back in 1889 when they were first plotting out a town on the site, noticed how the three states merged and used the abbreviations of Kentucky, Ohio, and Virginia to reflect that geographical quirk.

Like most other West Virginia villages and cities, the rail-junction town of Kenova is hill country. The main spine of the Appalachian range cuts through the heart of the state to the east, with the foothills sloping off toward Ohio and Kentucky. As much as they'd like to escape the stereotype, Kenova residents and other West Virginians who share their roots are stuck with the hillbilly image of the Hatfields and McCoys fussin' and fuedin' back in the hills, or the Deliverance types busy inbreeding down in the hollows. Just enough of it's true to keep the stereotype alive and kicking.

In the case of Bobby Joe Long's roots, the stereotype is not too far off the mark.

Joe Long was born in 1929, Louella Lucas six years later in 1935. The union of the two households, both predisposed to alcoholism and mental illness, laid the foundation for yet another generation doomed to carry on the seeds of disorder. In the words of one of the many psychiatrists who later studied him, "Bobby Joe Long's problems began in the womb. There is a history of mental illness on both sides of Mr. Long's family, that is, his mother's side and his father's side. Specifically, on the father's side there's a history of alcoholism. On the mother's side there's a history of emotional disease and emotional instability. Both of these are important to this particular mental defect because they are connected to and related to a higher level of impulsivity, of irritability, of short-temperedness in a human being right from the time of their birth."

Bobby Joe Long was born on October 14, 1953, at the old Rife-Ferguson Hospital in Kenova. According to the wishes of his parents, the birth certificate officially proclaimed his name as Bobby

Joe. Only later, as an adult, did he present himself as Robert J. Long, which made him sound more sophisticated and less of a hillbilly.

TESTIMONY OF LOUELLA LONG

A. I got married to Joe Long when I was seventeen years old. He was twenty-three. We went over to Indiana to get married but we was living in West Virginia, in Kenova. Back then, in 1952, it was a lot smaller than it is now, three thousand people, maybe. I worked at a little drive-in restaurant, and I met Joe there. His father had a restaurant in town.

I knew Joe's family. In a small town you know everybody pretty well. They all drank. I don't know if it was really alcoholism but they all drank. Joe used to, but he doesn't anymore. He hasn't drank in years. But back when Bobby was a child he drank quite a bit. And there were mental problems on his side of the family. His mother's sister—he had one die in a mental institute, and she was just twenty-some, and then another one died of a brain tumor. She was in the thirties, early thirties. And my mother-in-law just had a tumor operation. She had one the size of a grapefruit removed about five years ago. It had been there for about twenty-some years the neurosurgeon said.

Q. I'd like to ask you a little bit about your family background at this point. Why don't you describe your home life as you grew up.

A. Well, I don't remember much of it. I don't remember my mother, even. My daddy died when I was two, and my mom had three little girls. My dad was about twenty. They both were—mom got married when she was thirteen; so, she had three babies, and she had a third grade education. She worked in the field and everything, tobacco field; and, so, um, I don't

remember my mother when I was little at all. I don't remember her ever holding or kissing me or ever nothing. Um, I know she was there, but that's about it and I kind of raised myself. My mom never taught me anything, truthfully. I never knew love in my life to tell you the truth.

My sisters are Idella and Luwana and there's been a lot of emotional problems in all of us. I have another sister, a half-sister, and all of us have a very bad emotional problem. We've kind of straightened them out now that we've gotten older, but just recently I would say that we have.

I was eighteen the year when Bobby was born, the year after we got married. He was a month overdue and I put on a lot of weight. I gained sixty-seven pounds. I had been working as a car hop and I went back to work when he was a few weeks old, three or four weeks old. Joe wasn't working then. He couldn't find a job. He had been injured on his hand. He had a whole hand cut out and it was very difficult for him to find a job,

And then, well, we separated when Bob was eight months old. I went and lived with my mom sometimes and then I lived in Huntington with an aunt by marriage, an older aunt, at the time she was around sixty-five or seventy when she was taking care of Bobby. I moved around quite a bit after the separation.

Then when Bobby was two and a half years old we moved down here. We moved to Miami. Well, we lived in so many homes—I can't remember. We lived with one lady on the lake for, um, I worked at a drive-in there, and we lived with her for about a year, year and a half, and, um, after that, we lived with--and I think when we first came down we had a hard time finding somebody that would be good to him and treat him like their own child. And I worked at night as a car hop and I only went to the ninth grade, and I didn't have that much education; so, it's kind of hard to get a job, too, and, um, so we lived in a

lot of different homes even then when we first came down, because I didn't know my way around. I was very ignorant of everything. I didn't know how to do anything, really.

▲   ▲   ▲

At twenty-three, Joe Long was a bridegroom who was still busy sowing his wild oats. Louella Lucas at seventeen was a giddy, love-starved, not- too-bright kid who was smart enough to know she did-n't want to be stuck in this cold, grim, backwater mountain town, being ground down by poverty and hard work into a woman, wrinkled and old before her time, like her mama. The instant Joe and Louella met, it was flint on flint and sparks flew. They rushed off to get married in '52; had a baby boy named Bobby Joe in '53; split up in '54; divorced in '55 and, during the short spaces in between, battled each other like one was a Hatfield and the other a McCoy. Once, Joe and Louella remarried, but they continued to live apart—far apart. Before long, they were divorced again. They finally remarried for good when Bobby Joe was grown.

"We were pretty young," Joe Long admitted. "She didn't want to live up here, and I didn't want to live down there."

"Down there" was South Florida, where Louella Long rode on a Greyhound bus with her two year old Bobby Joe squirming on her lap, just to escape the cold and ugly winters and Joe Long's liquored-up ways that often turned mean.

One snapshot in the Long family album from that period shows a tousle-haired Bobby Joe, about three years old, standing in a sun-dappled yard with swaying palms portraying a balmy background. Next to him is his mother. Still in her early twenties, the photo is of an attractive woman with short dark hair, a tight, white, one-piece swimsuit accentuating her tanned legs and shapely figure. Easy to see why, in the skimpy tights and the spray-on tops she wore to work, why she was so popular with the regulars at Big Daddy's and the other redneck lounges where she hustled drinks. Miami of the mid-1950s was still a relatively small town, serving mainly the good

ol' Southern boy trade, while glitzy Miami Beach, across the bay, took care of the rich snowbirds from the North.

Even though both are smiling at the camera in that old photo, Louella Long is clutching Bobby Joe by the wrist, not holding his hand in a protective, mothering way, leaving the impressing that she is reluctantly dragging the boy around behind her like excess baggage.

"He was such a sad, lonely little boy back then," his mother sighed.

TESTIMONY OF DR. HELEN MORRISON*

There's an indication that, even at the time of birth, there were problems with Mr. Long. His mother reported to me that she had gained sixty-seven pounds during her pregnancy, that he arrived one month late and caused her a great deal of difficulty during labor, because his birth weight was about nine pounds, one ounce. By the time Mr. Long was one year of age, there were indications that he was failing to thrive. He was an infant who was losing a good deal of weight. There seems to be no physical cause for this, and it appeared to be related to the lack of contact that both parents had with him during his infancy, which was later continued through his childhood and adolescence. His family situation was extremely chaotic. There was indication that mother was absent physically as well as emotionally in regards to consistent working and being out of the home, indicating that father had trouble with various substance abuse and a subsequent divorce and separation between the parent when Mr. Long was two and a half years of age at which point the family moved to Florida.

*Psychiatrist for the Defense

To this day, Bobby Joe Long holds a vivid and angry memory of one terrifying episode when Louella was absent—both physically and emotionally—causing him to nearly drown in the surf off Miami Beach. Neither can recall precisely how old Bobby Joe was at the time, probably four or five they say, but each has a radically different memory of what took place.

Louella remembers it as a typical day at the beach with little Bobby Joe, during a period when the two were living on Miami Beach in a boardinghouse where they shared a single room. They were within walking distance of the popular beach, which also attracted the hordes of retirees who streamed into Miami Beach to spend their last days sitting in the sun.

"Everyone on the beach—it was retired people and everyone knew us, and they were just older, good people, and that's the reason we went to that beach all the time," said Louella. "They knew him by sight and me, too. He was on a little raft and I was leaning back on the blanket and getting some sun, and I would lay back a little bit."

While his mother sunbathed, Bobby Joe dragged his little plastic floater down to the water's edge and launched himself into the breakers. Before he knew it, he was out too far to get back, and the tide was pushing him farther from shore. In a panic, Bobby Joe kicked too hard and tumbled off the floater. He managed to grab hold as he fell off, and his screams quickly attracted the attention of other swimmers and the beach lifeguard.

"I heard all this yelling and I had leaned back on my arm and was getting sun on my face, and I raised up and heard all the commotion and I looked out and it was Bobby," Louella continued. "I started running and trying to get to the water, and I was falling because, you know, you can't hardly run through water."

Bobby Joe was pulled to safety, but ever after he blamed his mother for letting him almost die. As an adult, that long- simmering resentment bubbled over into an angry letter he wrote to his mother.

"We didn't discuss it," she said. "But he wrote in a letter that I had been surrounded by men and that I wasn't paying any atten-

65

tion to him and couldn't care less. It just wasn't true but he believed it."

Meanwhile, Joe and Louella, as much as they fought when they were together, often found it harder to stay apart. There were periodic dashes back and forth between the Mountain State and the Sunshine State for both of them, and Bobby Joe was taken along because there was nothing else to do with him.

When it was time to start school, Louella enrolled Bobby Joe in a Miami-area elementary school. A little more than halfway through the term, she took him out of school and moved back to Kenova for another try at marriage with Joe Long. With only a few months left in the term, Bobby Joe was enrolled in the first grade at Kenova Elementary School.

He flunked.

A child must be mightily disturbed, withdrawn or slow to necessitate repeating the first grade. It was the first sign that school and Bobby Joe were a poor mix, a failure that he and his mother later attributed to the constant moving around from school to school.

It was while he was repeating the first grade in nearby Huntington that Bobby Joe suffered the first of two major head injuries, injuries that some psychiatrists would later point to as justification for his murderous ways.

TESTIMONY OF LOUELLA LONG

When Bobby was about six or seven he was involved in a car accident in West Virginia. He was coming home from school and there was a big snow on, and he and another little boy dashed in front of a car, and it hit him in the face and head. It threw him out of the road into a yard along an embankment, and they took him to the hospital and he had surgery that night.

He had a lot of facial injuries, especially around the jaw and the mouth, and his eyes and his

forehead. He was all bloody all over and a lot of
cuts and bruises. The headlights hit him in the
face. It did a lot of injury to his mouth especially, and his teeth, he had beautiful teeth, but after
that, his teeth protruded almost straight out, and
he suffered a great deal from that from humiliation,
the children teasing him and he came home almost
every day after that for years crying, and I tried
to get his braces on him sooner. They said that he
would have to wait until he was eleven or twelve,
and I kept pushing them to put them on him so he
could get his teeth straightened out, because it
hurt him so bad. The children would call him
Bucktooth and all kinds of names, the way children
do, and it upset him an awful lot. So he was around
eleven and a half or twelve when they put them on.

▲   ▲   ▲

The fact that the youngster was bundled up in a thick snowsuit
was probably the only thing that saved his life. It took a long time
for Bobby Joe to recover physically from those severe facial
injuries, longer still from the deep psychological wounds that were
inflicted on him as a result of his ugly scars and protruding teeth.
"He got a complex out of it, that's for sure," sighed Joe Long,
Bobby's absentee father. "He was self-conscious about his jaw and
teeth. He would come home crying from school because kids
would make fun and just teased him all the time. He sure wasn't
pretty."

As defense psychiatrist Dr. Helen Morrison later outlined for a
jury of Bobby Joe's peers, the accident that smashed his face was a
hammer blow that also shattered the youngster's fragile personality.
"Between the ages of four and seven, children become extremely
conscious of their bodies—a four year old child who has to have a
Band-Aid and you can't see a scratch on them, but they need that
as some reassurance that they are, indeed, intact. And between the
ages of four and eight, a child begins to be able to develop his body
image and picture himself as a whole individual, and in Mr. Long's

case it appears that this accident had severe outcome regarding his reaction to the injury. His statement was that he had never been as hurt or as disorganized, to use my words, as he had experienced at that period of time."

During the course of his long recuperation, Bobby Joe was hustled off to Florida again when Louella had once more had her fill of the cold, drab, small-town life Kenova offered and the boozy battles with Joe Long. Miami's bright lights, its warm sea breezes, and the supercharged night life continued to entice her.

In South Florida, mother and son resumed the nomadic apartment hopping, one single-occupancy motel room or boardinghouse after another. Whenever possible, the folks they rented from doubled as baby sitters for Bobby while Louella worked the hash joints or bars at night.

TESTIMONY OF LOUELLA LONG

There was two specifically I recall—this older lady, she was up in her seventies, Mrs. Burrell, but she was a very good lady, and she took very good care of him, I know. It was just a couple of blocks where I worked, and she would bring him down there sometimes at night when he was a little boy when he was about three or four. They would bring him down there at the end of the lot, and I would go over and hug him and talk to him a few minutes when I was working.

Then when he was about eight or nine and that was after his accident, and Joe and I had been married three times to each other. And, so, we only were together a few months that time, and then we [she and Bobby Joe] moved back to Miami and we lived with the Silverthornes for a couple of years. Between the time he was two and eight, oh, eight or ten different people took care of him, maybe more.

We would usually have a room, and Bob and I would stay in that room wherever we lived, and we, Bob

would, get his meals and they would take care of him, I would pay them like so much a week and I would eat out and, like I say, I was working as a car hop and I would work until two or three in the morning, from like five or six in the evening until two or three in the morning.

▲   ▲   ▲

Records indicate that during one period Bobby Joe attended Flamingo Elementary in Hialeah, although you couldn't prove it by his mother.

"It's so hard for me to remember that far," she said. "I can't recall the ones he went to in Miami. He went to so many of them. I remember some of when he was older, but I don't remember the grade schools, the real younger years."

With the constant moving from one cramped room to another, traveling back and forth between Miami and Kenova, Bobby Joe never really settled in one place long enough to put down any educational roots or form lasting friendships. Each move meant another new school, another painful attempt to fit in, another round of ridicule over his still-healing face, another bunch of kids to adjust to.

▲   ▲   ▲

I guess I have always had a pretty violent nature to a degree. Ahhhh, it was called for in a lot of instances because, you know, I moved around a lot as a kid and I changed schools a lot as a kid and ahhhh, you know, you either have to be a little violent, to be able to take care of yourself or, you know you would get picked on like I was the new guy in school. And ahhhh, so I guess to some point I have always had a pretty bad temper once it goes off. (Bobby Joe Long/CBS News Interview.)

▲   ▲   ▲

By the time he was ten years old, Bobby Joe had gone to schools twice in Miami and twice in West Virginia. After that, he and his mother remained in South Florida, but the constant uprooting from one school and replanting in another continued for years in Miami. One year, he attended four different schools, always the new kid on the block, always at risk of proving himself. Bobby Joe himself couldn't remember how many schools he attended during this period. When he was in the seventh grade, however, Louella found a small house in Hialeah, which allowed Bobby to settle down and spend some time in one school for the first time in his life. ("I went there for two years in a row, which was a record for me," he recalled.)

Soon after Louella and Bobby returned to South Florida, several members of Louella's clan, the Lucases, moved down to join them--Louella's mother, her two sisters, a half-sister and seven of Bobby Joe's cousins—thirteen in all. The whole family crowded together in a five-bedroom house. But for Bobby Joe, the situation really hadn't changed or improved. If anything, it was worse than before, because now his mother had her sisters and all their kids to occupy her attention, which meant that Bobby Joe was shoved even further into the background of his mother's affections. Not only that, but to his great embarrassment—since his cousins were now there to snicker and teased him—Bobby Joe was still sleeping in the same bed with his mother, same as before.

TESTIMONY OF LOUELLA LONG

    Q.   Now, you also mentioned that in the resi-
dences you would usually have one room.
    A.   Always.
    Q.   And you and Bob would share that room?   Sleep
together?
    A.   Yes.
    Q.   How old was he as far as sleeping with him--
how late in his age did you sleep with him?

A. Well, I couldn't remember, and I called my sister last night. I have such a bad memory and I was trying to remember. We slept in the same room, but the only thing is I was working until five o'clock in the morning. It's after I became a bar-maid when we lived in North Miami Beach. I wouldn't come home, you know, I wouldn't get off until five. And about the time we cleaned up it was daylight and by the time I got home from work he would be going to school, and we did sleep in the same room. He was about eleven or twelve then, and I just couldn't remember--I had to ask my family how did we sleep. And I was wondering, because there was twelve of us in the house.

▲   ▲   ▲

It was also during this erratic period in the boy's life that Louella started hustling drinks full time at one of the many Big Daddy Lounges that dotted South Florida in the Sixties and Seventies. And along with the new job came the "sexy little outfits" that Bobby Joe came to despise for the way they exposed his mother's body to strange men, a body that Bobby Joe had come to view as belonging to him alone.

"I had never mixed a drink in my life," Louella explained, "and the girl taught me and after I got off my other job as a waitress at two o'clock in the morning, I began working until five for nothing. Bob felt very bad about me working in the bars. It embarrassed him. I didn't know how much until lately. Back then, I know he didn't like it at all because of the way I had to dress.

"He started being very abusive to me verbally and treating me like I was filth," she continued. "I tried to explain how we needed the money, but he just had such disgust for me. He told me later he wanted me to dress like a mother, and it hurt him and embarrassed him to see me."

According to one psychologist's notes on the matter, "Mother was a barmaid. She quit being a waitress when he was about

eleven. It was mother and him. They didn't get along very well. He says, 'I just avoided her from age twelve on— never saw much of her, either working or going out. I grew up pretty much alone. Nothing I did was right. I was sick of listening to her.'

"Then again, a quote from him, 'I hated her. I thought of killing her a few times.' Mother got a boyfriend who scared him. There were lots of fights."

Years later, Bobby Joe Long was still blaming his mother for everything that had gone wrong in his life, from stale bread to slain hookers. Pinellas County Detective Terry Rhodes, in the course of investigating one of the vicious Ad Man rape cases, interviewed one of Long's former girlfriends who told him that Bobby Joe "...often complained...about how no one understood how tough he had it as a child. [He] had to get up and fix his own breakfast when he was just seven years old and alone. He was living on the streets while mom worked or entertained boyfriends in bed. He would get very angry when talking about his mother, build into a rage. [She] said she grew to be afraid of him at those times and urged him to get psychiatric help. He promised he would, but then always backed out."

Throughout his growing years, Long groused to anyone who would listen about the "unfair" way his mother treated him. "To be honest with you," Long's childhood sweetheart and former wife, Cindy, once testified, "Bob always hated his mother because of her behavior, because of the way she treated him...She neglected him. I can say that because she would buy steak for a dog and feed him hamburger. She was out late at night. He could pretty much come and go as he pleased, as a young teenager...He was fed and clothed, but he had nobody there to teach him right from wrong..."

Bobby Joe was, indeed, jealous of that pet pooch that often was fed prime filet mignon for dinner, while Bobby had to settle for greasy, fast-food cheeseburgers and fries. In fact, Long told others, he became so frustrated and resentful over the attention showered on the pet, attention he felt was being denied him, that he grabbed the little dog and shoved a .22 caliber bullet up the animal's vagina as a furious and symbolic protest over the perceived neglect. "She

wouldn't even bother to feed me. But she would cook steaks and stews for that dog to eat. I had to make my own dinner," he fumed.

Significantly, he chose the female animal's sex organ through which to express his rising anger and frustration at a time when his own confused sexual identity, precipitated by the bizarre sleeping arrangements with his mother, was lurching out of control and becoming more disturbing with each passing year.

Mother and son shared the intimacy of the bed well past the point when Bobby Joe, bombarded by the raging hormones of puberty, had learned what a hard-on was and how to use it. As he grew older, the unhealthy sleeping arrangment was a source of great shame and humiliation to the boy. While there may have been no sex between the two in the physical sense, there was, in the opinion of many shrinks who studied the case, strong evidence of "emotional incest." A sexually developing young male, forced to spend night after night pressed against a mature and sexually stimulating female body, even if it was his own mother's, is bound to be profoundly affected by the contact, especially on those nights when he was displaced by an adult male whose access to his mother's body was total—if such sexual couplings did in fact take place, as Bobby Joe insisted they did.

Moreover, since he was rarely in one place long enough to form friendships or bond with others, Bobby Joe was forced to rely on his mother for companionship as well as parenting. Thus, each time he was kicked out of bed in favor of grown and lusty men, more fuel was fed to the fire of his deeply buried but long smoldering rage. Long later described his mother as cruel in her disregard for his needs. He claimed she frequently manipulated conflicts between her son and her boyfriends that often resulted in the younger boy being beaten by the older men.

Even when Louella had some time off, Bobby Joe said he would often beg her to stay home with him or take him places so they could do things together. But usually, she dumped him with a sitter and took off with the boyfriend du jour.

"But she always had her dates. Her boyfriends. And I'd have to stay with one of the neighbors," he complained.

73

Later, during the long hours he spent with wife Cindy, she became a sounding board for all that hurt and bitterness which Bobby held toward his mother, pain that festered like an untreated boil on his soul.

Even after the Longs moved in down the street in Hialeah, Cindy said, "She [Louella] had different boyfriends at the house. She had one gentleman there that was living there for a while. When I first met Bob, she was married to a gentleman by the name of Ace Landon, I believe was his name. And they divorced. And then she had a gentleman by the name of Jim—I don't remember what his last name was—living there with her. And then after he left, there was other men that did come there."

The first significant relationship Louella says she had with a man other than Bobby Joe's father was when the boy was about eight years old. His name was Jerry and, according to Louella Long, Jerry and her son got along well, at least at first.

All three would often go places together, which was a change for Bobby Joe, who was accustomed to being left behind when Louella went out. But the brief honeymoon ended when Jerry disciplined Bobby Joe for going out to play with the neighbor's kids.

"Jerry spanked him one evening for not staying in the yard," Louella recalled. "He was watching him, keeping an eye on him. We lived on the side of this lady's house that was taking care of Bob and she had two boys and, Jerry came by and Bob had disobeyed him and gone out, and he didn't stay where Jerry told him to stay, in the house or something. I don't remember it that well, but I do remember that Jerry spanked him and Bobby didn't care for him after that."

It was during this period of growing frustration and resentment over his mother's love affairs that the seeds were planted that later blossomed into the savage rape and murder of those women who manipulated men with their bodies just as Bobby Joe believed his mother's did with him and other men in her life. Again, say the psychiatrists who sought to explain away Bobby Joe's murderous impulses, even if his mother were entirely innocent of such behavior, it wouldn't matter. As long as Bobby Joe grew up believing it

was so, than his perception transcended all reality.

Every adolescent boy has trouble coping with his evolving sexual maturity, especially someone like Bobby Joe Long. With no strong father figure to explain the natural facts of life, and only a sexually ditzy mother as a role model, Bobby Joe, was overwhelmed by the powerful and conflicting sex signals pounding his already fragile personality like howitzer shots.

Then, if that wasn't enough to screw up a young male's raw and raucous sex psyche, when Bobby Joe hit puberty he started growing breasts, just like a girl.

The condition is called gynecomastia, the development of female-type breast tissue in a man. Gynecomastia, say the medical experts, can develop in a male at any time, but is most likely to occur during puberty or senescence. Although gynecomastia is fairly common, it is rarely discussed because most men are too embarrassed to talk about it. The exact cause of gynecomastia isn't always clear. But it can result from a deficiency of the male hormone, testosterone, from the use of certain drugs or medications, from liver disease, tumors, or genetic malfunctions. Gynecomastia that occurs during puberty is thought to be related to hormonal changes in the body. Some believe a defective gene may be the culprit.

For the second time in less than a decade, Bobby Joe Long's self-image was shattered. The memories of the childhood taunting motivated by the damage to his face, were still painful. Now he had to endure the ridicule from other teenage boys, for whom a strong macho image is a ritualistic act of passage. Hey, look! Bobby Joe Long's got tits!

Thus at thirteen years of age, a pivotal turning point in an adolescent's developing sexual identity, Bobby Joe Long went under the surgeon's knife to have six pounds of excess tissue removed and to shed himself of the girlish breasts.

"He wouldn't wear a shirt that clung to him or anything, and he wouldn't take phys.ed., and I finally found out why," his mother explained. "He had a hormone imbalance, and he took shots for several months. We took him to a doctor in North Miami Beach, and they gave him the shots and they didn't seem to do any good. So

75

because it was affecting him mentally, they agreed to—well, my insurance covered it and if it had been cosmetic surgery, they wouldn't have, but they did. It was causing him trouble mentally, so he had the operation. They took several pounds of tissue out of his chest."

The operation may have been successful, the outer scars may have healed; but the unseen impact on the boy's personality was calamitous. In his study of serial killers (Walking Time Bomb) Dr. Joel Norris discussed the gynecomastia condition and its effect on the boy:

"Bobby Joe Long has said that he always had a problem with women. He has always been fearful that women would take him over. Even when he was a child he was afraid that he would turn into a woman, and that would have been the worst punishment of all because from the earliest times he could remember, Bobby Joe Long says, he hated women. That was why he became so petrified when he realized he was growing breasts.

"Eleven year old Bobby Joe Long didn't understand it, but when he reached puberty he began turning into a girl. At least that's what it seemed like. His breasts became abnormally large, swelling up and becoming tender, and he began to feel ashamed and foolish. He could look down in the mornings before school and see his enlarged nipples filling out his shirt right through the breast pockets. When he ran in gym, his breasts would shake up and down. Other children at school teased him about it. He was in a fury about that. His clothing became tight and looked ill-fitting as it stretched around his chest and spread at the seams over his enlarged buttocks...(The surgery) remedied his physical appearance, but it didn't keep him from experiencing a lunar protomenstrual cycle for the rest of his life.

"'Even now,' he recalls, 'I can always tell when it's the full moon, I get crazy when the moon is full. I can't sit still. I have to pace. Even the smallest thing sets me off.'"

Around 1966, in one of their frequent moves, Louella and

Bobby Joe landed at 6335 West 113th Terrace in West Hialeah, a suburb northwest of Miami. Much of Hialeah, except for its famous, flamingo-infested thoroughbred race track, is a bland and boring collection of cookie-cutter stucco houses with postage-stamp yards. Despite the growing estrangement between mother and son, there were still a few good days left, like the time when Louella took Bobby Joe over to the Hialeah Race Course, a few blocks from where they lived, and taught him to drive in the parking lot. He loved that, she sighed.

Soon after that move to Hialeah, what good relations still existed between him and his mother ended as abruptly as running head on into a brick wall. In Long's case the brick wall came in the form of a slight, squinty-eyed, sandy-haired little girl with a nose too large for her narrow face. Her name was Cynthia "Cindy" Jean Guthrie, and she lived down the street from the Longs. She was ten months older than Bobby Joe and looked an awful lot like Louella Long. The two went to Palm Springs Junior High together, and almost from the very first became inseparable soul mates.

Cindy's parents also were divorced, although she claims that the home she grew up in was loving and supportive compared to the empty shell that produced her boyfriend. However, as children of divorce, she and Bobby had something in common and became fiercely protective of each other. They went everywhere together, fixed meals together, and confided only in each other.

With few parental restraints on either of them, the two inevitably plunged into the hyperactive discovery of teenage sex. The first time was when Cindy was fifteen and Bobby Joe still fourteen. Following the timeless sexual ritual of generations of American youngsters before them, it happened in the back seat of a station wagon, parked in the furthest row of a drive-in theater. Both of them dove into sex like thirst-crazed pilgrims stumbling in from the desert. Many times, they romped the afternoon away at Bobby Joe's house, if not with Louella's explicit approval, at least with her tacit understanding that her boy and the girl down the street were busily screwing the day away in her own bed.

And almost from the very moment that he and Cindy became

77

intimate, Bobby Joe stopped sleeping with his mother. For a boy who had spent most of his life alone, friendless and the object of ridicule by other kids, finding a girlfriend who was crazy about him and would do anything he asked was a bombshell event in his young life.

As Bobby Joe entered his teens, Cindy couldn't help but notice the hostility he displayed toward women in general and particularly those whose "loose" dress reminded him of his mother's scanty barmaid costumes. "He would call them sluts, you know," she remarked. "Ones that were dressed pretty loosely. If we'd see somebody going down the street, you know, walking down the street or something, dressed loosely—short shorts, exposing portions of her body and stuff, he'd call her a slut. In my opinion, the women he called sluts, they resembled his mother."

Cindy insisted that the young Bobby Joe she fell in love with was a polite boy, considerate of her feelings and respectful toward adults. Although, she admitted, "...he had a quick temper when he got upset." But not everyone had as high an opinion of Bobby Joe as his lovesick teenage heartthrob. Helen Wandel was one of Cindy's best girlfriends in the West Hialeah neighborhood. Cindy was a frequent visitor at her home and Bobby Joe often tagged along. Helen found Bobby Joe's actions and attitudes strange, to say the least, such as the weird way he always found something funny to laugh about in tragic situations that normally upset most people. Like the time he laughed and joked when another boy they had grown up with in the neighborhood killed himself.

"Bobby Joe Long," Helen Wandel concluded, "was eerie to the point that whenever he came over to my parents' house, I locked my bedroom door."

Cindy's mother, Elsie Louise Moran, didn't think much of her daughter's boyfriend, either. Although she and Cindy lived apart due to the divorce (Cindy was raised mainly by her aunt), Elsie did run into the boy on visits to Hialeah.

She later told a Tampa homicide detective that she thought Bobby Joe Long was a "snotty kid." And although she didn't know

Louella Long very well, she described Bobby Joe's mother as "flighty." One time, Louella stopped in Georgia (where Elsie was living) to pick up their shared grandchildren and, "While enroute back to Florida [Louella] stopped in a park and took a picture of the kids bending over with their pants pulled down and buttocks showing," according to the police statement.

Elsie also recalled how the young Bobby Joe became very aggravated while talking about his mother, often referring to her as "Big Daddy's whore." Elsie also described Bobby Joe as a very temperamental kid who would go from "hot to cold" very quickly, especially if he was talking about his mother.

After all these years, Louella is barely able to conceal her dislike and resentment of the younger, mirror-image of herself, who took her Bobby Joe away and who, in Louella's mind, turned son against mother.

"Bobby was the perfect cute little boy," Louella recalled. "He was good and made good grades in school. About thirteen, that's when he met Cindy Guthrie. From then on, it was the two of them against the world. They were constantly together and they fought me at every turn. We just kind of drifted apart after that. I didn't see much of him—he didn't want to be around me and, you know, I was a barmaid then and when he did see me he just looked at me like I was dirt. And he had grown up so big. He was so strong that I was scared to death of him.

"Cindy was manipulative and one of the cruelest people I ever knew. She never really had a mother, or a family for that matter, and was jealous of the family that Bobby Joe had. I tried to be a mother to her and to help her with the children, but she never liked me.

"You have no idea how she changed him, and how what she did ruined his whole life."

The feeling was mutual, and to this day each woman blames the other for the twisted and tragic turn that Bobby Joe's life took.

"Louella always wants everything to be her way and only her way, Cindy recalled." As a child—or I should say as a teenager, and

into my early years of marriage with Bob—she was always trying to tell me how to raise my children, always telling me what to wear, what not to wear, the type of makeup, how to grocery shop, those type of things. That's how she was pushy with me."

As the highly charged sexual relationship deepened between Bobby Joe and Cindy, friends of the young couple couldn't help remarking on the similarity of the two women in his life. Not only did Louella and Cindy resemble each other physically, but they also sounded alike and even seemed to be cut from the same temperament cloth, which for Bobby Joe meant two shrewish, aggressive, dominating, manipulative women, perfectly willing to use the sex hammer they held over Bobby Joe's head in order to mold him like a lump of warm Play-Doh.

According to Dr. Joel Norris, "Bobby said that Cindy became his second mother. She took over where Louella left off. Friends of the two of them have described her as forceful, insistent, aggressive, and domineering. She appeared in Bobby Joe's life at precisely the time when his mother was getting married to her second husband. For thirteen year old Bobby, Jr., who was bursting through puberty to emerge with surgically altered breasts, meeting Cindy came at exactly the right moment. With his own mother now remarrying and effectively, in his mind at least, leaving him for another man, Bobby found his mother's 'body double' in the adolescent Cindy. Louella had established herself a new partner, and so did her son."

On December 13, 1970, Bobby Joe Long had his first recorded brush with the law when he was picked up with a couple of buddies and charged with stealing a car battery. The charges were dropped the next day. Just a few months later, on February 23, 1971, Bobby Joe again ran afoul of the law by resisting a Hialeah cop. One report was that he was running with a buddy who was caught stealing another car battery; Cindy said he was stopped while drag racing. Whatever the cause, the punishment was merely probation without conviction, which allowed Bobby Joe Long to walk out of the courthouse with his clean record still intact.

Louella Long complained that Bobby Joe was constantly

harassed by Hialeah police for no reason other than that he was a teenager out on the street. They hounded him, she said, at one point issuing him seven traffic tickets in one day.

When he was eighteen, Long was accused of raping a girl, but it turned out the girl was lying, his mother said. He had only picked her up and given her a ride home. Even so, the cops brought him in and fingerprinted him.

"He's been filled with hatred since then," Louella Long said.

In school, Bobby wasn't too interested in books, and that disinterest became more pronounced during his brief career at Hialeah High School. He dropped out twice and then returned. His third try ended only a few months after the start of his sophomore year. After his eighteenth birthday in October, 1971, Bobby Joe Long finally dropped out for good. But due to his inattention and sporadic attendance he was still in the tenth grade, three or four years older than his classmates and branded with yet another shameful label as the big, dumb kid in class.

"He always felt like an outsider." said Louella, always ready with an excuse. "He stayed out of school a lot. He would leave to go to school, but then he came back home. And when the school tried to call home, he wouldn't answer."

On the other hand, Cindy Guthrie Long insisted that Bobby Joe was "... pretty normal...an average student as far as grades. His problem was he had a hard time accepting the teachers, you know, telling him what to do. He just didn't feel like they should have the right to tell the kids what to do at school. He was bored in school. He just didn't enjoy studying or the social life of school."

Like most kids of his generation, Bobby Joe experimented with drugs—mainly hallucinogens such as THC and LSD, some pot and uppers, a little booze. Even as an adult Long was not known as a heavy drinker or drug user, although he told police he still used amphetamines occasionally.

After Long left school, his mother got him a job as an electrician with ARC Electric. Long worked with that company in Miami until the company went bankrupt. Working at ARC Electric, Bobby Joe felt he had found his niche as an electrician's helper. He

enjoyed the work, but since it was tough to move up in the trade without experience, he decided to enlist in the Army, where he could gain enough experience to become licensed as a master electrician when he came out. On September 19, 1972, at age nineteen, Bobby Joe Long was sworn in and shipped off to Fort Benning, Georgia for basic training. In accordance with the terms of a contract he signed with the Army upon enlistment, Long was sent back to serve his tour of duty at Homestead Air Force Base, just south of Miami. Perched on the edge of the Everglades and at the tip of the Florida mainland, Homestead served as the nation's primary air defense watchdog over any threat from Cuba, only ninety miles off the edge of Key West's Sundown Dock.

It was like he'd never left. Bobby Joe bought a motorcycle to shuttle back and forth between Homestead and Hialeah, only thirty miles away up the Florida Turnpike. Cindy was still in Hialeah, and the couple resumed their romance.

By the end of 1973, Cindy Guthrie was pregnant.

The year 1974 had to be one of the most turbulent and significant years in the life of Bobby Joe Long. It was a classic good news/bad news year, packed with enough drama and melodrama to send even the most serene psyche screaming for relief. And Bobby Joe Long was anything but serene.

On January 25, 1974, Private First Class Bobby Joe Long and Cynthia Jean Guthrie were married in the Homestead Air Force Base chapel, Captain Richard N. Donovan, Captain, USA, Protestant Chaplain, presiding. In addition to the bride and groom, six other friends and family members made up the wedding party. The wedding photo taken outside the base chapel speaks volumes in body language. It shows Bobby Joe Long, standing awkwardly in uniform, feet splayed, head turned away from his bride and leaning toward Louella Long, who stood by his other side. The bride, in a long white gown and veil, stares straight into the camera, her fingertips barely laced through her new husband's widespread fingers. All in all, it's a portrait of a wedding party stiff and uncomfortable in both their dress-up clothes and in the situation they find themselves in.

82

Following the ceremony, Bobby Joe and Cindy Long moved into a tiny mobile home on Lot No. 381 at 4955 N.W. 199th Street in Carol City, on the far northwest side of Miami.

Two months later, in mid-March, 1974, Bobby Joe Long picked up his paycheck at the base, leaped on his motorcycle and headed up U.S. 1 to cash the check.

"An eighty-three year old man turned in front of me with a car and I broadsided him," Bobby Joe told CBS reporter Victoria Corderi.

"They estimated fifty to fifty-five miles an hour but I know I was going faster, at least sixty-five or seventy. Aahhhh, I don't remember the accident. I guess when I hit the car, I flew over it."

When Cindy was notified that Bobby had been critically injured in an accident, she was told to get to the hospital as quickly as possible. He was unconscious and surgeons were standing by to take him into surgery.

"By the time I got to the hospital, he had come to and signed his own consent papers and was already in the operating room," she said. "And then they brought him out of the operating room. He had head injuries. He had a concussion, I should say. He almost lost, I believe it was his left foot. His bone—ankle bone—had come out of the skin. He had stitches in his leg, scrapes on his buttocks and on his hands.

"With all the different operations he had to have after that, I'd say it probably took about a year for him to recuperate."

After he was released from the hospital, Bobby Joe still had to wear a full leg cast for four months. Even so, he was left with a slight limp, long-term headaches, dizziness, and other complications.

▲   ▲   ▲

A LETTER FROM BOBBY

I'm gonna go ahead with the tests Friday (EEG) its one I know will show something abnormal, because since I flew over that car I broadsided on my bike

in seventy-four, the left side of my face has been
numb, and my pupil on the left was fixed and dialat-
ed at twice the size of the right, definite indications of brain trauma.   Man I was in another world
for a fuckin year.   Still get dizzy spells,
headaches, nerves twitching on side of my face...I
flew forty ft over the car and landed right on the
left side of my head. Busted a fuckin Bell safety
helmet all the way back to the neck. Its incredible
I didn't die.   The fuckin troopers picked me up by
the legs and arms and just laid me off the side of
the road.   They thought I was dead...All I remember
is thinking Oh shit, your dead, and a loud crash.   I
woke up a few days later in the fuckin hospital.
Busted my eardrum, and had fluid from my semi-circu-
lar canals (inner ear) leaking out of my ear.   Bout
lost my left foot, sliced my left knee halfway thru.
It was a good crash, wish I could have seen
it...I've had scars that would take a total of thousands of stitches to close, even had wire stitches
in my knee and ankles skin grafts, it was a mess.

▲   ▲   ▲

Even more than the extensive physical damage, the accident
apparently wrought some bizarre personality changes that manifested in increasing hostility and a sex urge that accelerated into
overdrive. First there were the violent and unexpected temper
tantrums, the flashes of irrational anger over nothing. The slightest
noise irritant that most people shrugged off would be enough to
drive him into a frenzy.

"After the accident," Cindy later testified, "he got real sensitive
to loud noises. If the children were crying, he'd get very irritated
with that. There was an occasion where I had Chris in the baby
swing, our son, the firstborn. And the swing was squeaking, and he
had—threw a temper tantrum, took the baby out of the swing and
threw the swing out the door, because the noise was irritating him.
He wouldn't listen to the TV very loud or the radio.

"You never really knew what was going to come out of him. If he was going to be in a good mood, or if he was going to be in a bad mood, his temper tantrums. It was day by day you'd have to take it. You didn't know what to expect out of him, if he was going to be in a good mood or if there was going to be a fight. Before the accident, he never got violent with me, but afterwards, it happened anywhere from six to ten times.

"And he complained of headaches all the time. He took Tylenol for them, used to go through bottles of it a week. His balance was off. At times he could sleep normal. At other times, he wouldn't be able to sleep at all for the entire night. Also, he had memory loss right after the accident and up till times quite a bit after the accident there would be minor things that he would forget and sometimes major things. For instance, if you'd send him to the store for three items, he'd come back with one or two of the three. At one point, somebody asked him when our daughter's birthday was, and he couldn't remember the year that she was born in."

Even Joe Long, who was seldom a factor in his son's life, was shocked by the behavioral changes and marked the motorcycle accident as the crucial turning point for Bobby Joe. "Since then, he's been more like a Jekyll and a Hyde. Sometimes he's so nice to us and sometimes he's just a terrible human being," Joe Long said.

"I was down visiting him which I did quite often," Louella testified. "I'd go down uninvited, and I would invite myself to stay there with my grandchildren and I loved to see them and be with them, all of them.

"One day I asked Bob, it was on a Sunday—we were all in there talking, and I asked Bob if I could use his car. Cindy and the children were going to the store, and he said, 'Sure.' And we were all just talking like we are, and I walked by him. He said, 'The keys are on the TV.' I went over and got them and I said, 'I'll probably just be a couple of hours.' I didn't went to take my car, because it had a U-Haul in the back, and he reached out and grabbed me and pulled me down. He was on a chaise lounge, and he just pulled me down, and I thought he was going to give me a kiss on the cheek or something, but he turned me over his knee and just started blister-

ing me and pounding me, and he did this for a long time. And I was screaming and crying, and he just dumped me, threw me on the floor, and then he just got up and left without saying a word. And then he came back later that night, and he acted like nothing had ever happened. I had a handprint on me for days on my rear.

"[Now] he just gets angry over the least little thing. If you disagree with him and you just didn't say what he wants you to say, like one day we had gone from the house when he was living with us, and we would go a few blocks—I don't know what the argument was over, but it was really nothing, and he just got out and slammed the door with all his might, and in a little while he was home and everything was fine. Mostly he was at home when he would just get so angry sometimes. I would go in my room, because I just didn't want to upset him, and sometimes he was as sweet as he could be— just talking and laughing and just as ordinary as could be and then other days he would stay in his room for days at a time, would never talk to either one of us. We couldn't approach him."

Then there was the other backlash from the accident. In retrospect, it was even more ominous that the illogical rages and violent temper tantrums. When he had recovered from his injuries, Bobby Joe Long discovered he had an insatiable hunger for sex, highlighted by wildly erotic sex fantasies about any woman who crossed his line of vision. Before the accident, Bobby Joe claimed, his sex life with Cindy was limited to two or three times a week. After the accident, that accelerated to a demand that she make love to him two or three times a day. And in between, Long said, he still had to masturbate at least five more times a day, so driven was he by the need for sexual relief. That hyperactive sex drive began to overwhelm him while he was still in the hospital.

"I started thinking about sex," he told Dr. Norris. "That's all I could think about day and night. I thought about it with my wife, with her friends, with people I knew from before. It started driving me crazy. I couldn't get these thoughts out of my mind, and Cindy and I had gone from having sex two or three times a week to at least two times a day. And I was still masturbating to get relief. I thought about having sex with just about every girl I met or got to know.

Questioned years later, Cindy Long confirmed the changes in her husband—the mood swings, the unexplained anger, the increased sexual appetite, although her memory of the frequency doesn't dovetail exactly with his.

Sometimes he would want to have sex three or four times a day, but that might happen only two or three times a week, not every day, she remembered. However, Cindy agreed that the increase in their frequency of their sex life was, to say the least, "dramatic." Bobby Joe had never been much of a reader, but during his recuperation, Cindy noticed how avidly he pursued such magazines as Playboy, Hustler, Oui, or Cheri. Louella Long, Cindy emphasized, was the one who kept her son supplied with the graphic skin magazines. There were also many times, after Bobby Joe was at home and unemployed, that he'd grab her the instant she walked in the door after work and want sex immediately.

"There was times that I would not," she said. "Sometimes he would get upset about it. I'd tell him I was just too tired, but he'd still get mad."

Cindy told Hillsborough County detectives that her sex life with Bobby Joe was "very good" when they were first married. She said he never asked her to engage in bondage or other such acts and that she did not considered him to be oversexed or kinky in any way. (A curious statement, which didn't square with her other accounts of Bobby Joe's wildly accelerated sex drive following the accident.) Once or twice when they were first married, she admitted, he may have taken a couple of nude photos of her, but they were just Polaroids and she didn't feel that was anything unusual. And he never tried to take pictures of them engaged in sexual activities.

On June 19, 1974, Christian Joseph Long was born. And, in August his father, still recovering from his massive injuries, was out of the Army and out of a job.

There's some confusion about that discharge. His family says it was a medical discharge. Rudy Machado, a family friend, told Tampa police that "...Long was dishonorably discharged..." Long claimed that the Army violated its contract with him, but Machado suspected that Long did not go his duties and failed to show up for

work. Long got an Army lawyer and contested the discharge, ending up with a general discharge.

The version Bobby Joe told CBS had a strange twist involving the teenage daughter of a Homestead officer, and carried an ugly foreshadowing of things to come. "Two months after the accident I was still in a cast, right? And I was coming back from ..., the Air Force Base in Homestead coming home and ..., I picked up a girl that was on her way to high school. And ..., that resulted in my first charge against me.

"It was a charge of attempted rape, but it ended up lewd and lascivious behavior and they put me on probation. You know, I really didn't think I did anything criminal at that time. I just left the base, I picked her up two blocks from the base in an Army uniform with my name on my chest and a cast on my leg, you know. Do you know what I'm saying? But they didn't see it that way. Then about two or three months after that I ended up with about five charges and a court-martial charge in the Army, ended up getting out of the Army on that. Not for rape. AWOL, and for striking a non-commissioned officer, ... whole bunch of crazy charges."

In yet another version, Long claimed the charges were reduced because he was able to convince authorities that the girl had willingly accompanied him out to the Everglades for a round of mutual oral sex. The reduced charge of lewd and lascivious was merely a face-saving move on the part of the Army, he insisted. Whatever the reason for the discharge, Bobby Joe Long left the service with a forty percent disability rating, due to injuries to his head, ankle, knee, and hearing. By 1984, his disability check amounted to $249 per month.

After he was released from the military, Bobby Joe embarked on a sporadic work career, hopping from one low-level, low-paying job to another. With Cindy and little Christian in tow, Bobby Joe resumed the nomadic lifestyle that had been implanted in his brain during his childhood with Louella. The new family moved about the crowded North Dade-South Broward County area, seldom staying in one place for long. And as they moved, as Cindy worked to support the small family and Bobby did not, as his sudden tem-

per surges and insatiable sexual demands escalated, the more the marriage deteriorated.

Early in 1975, with Cindy pregnant with their second child, the Longs moved from a small place in Plantation to a larger house in Ft. Lauderdale. Cindy recalled.

"We moved out there to have the extra room for the extra baby, "And he was not working, and we could not afford the place that we had purchased, and it became repossessed."

Bobbi Jo Long, obviously named after her father, was born October 18, 1975, only three days after his birthday. A few months later, shortly before Christmas, Bobby Joe took off for West Virginia, leaving wife, toddler son, and infant daughter behind. Bobby Joe told Cindy he was going to look for work as an electrician. He didn't find a job, claiming that his motorcycle injuries made that kind of work too difficult for him. But he spent a few weeks at home in Kenova with Joe and Louella, who were back together, this time apparently for good.

Early in 1976, the Longs moved again, this time back to the West Hialeah area where they'd started their married life. A few months later they rented a place in Miramar, a West Broward County subdivision stuck between a regional airport to the north and Calder Race Track to the south. Soon, they were on the move again for the third time in less than a year. The Longs bought a three-bedroom, cinder-block house (financed in part by Joe and Louella Long) at 4441 SW 40th Street, in the Lake Forest section of Hollywood.

Bobby Joe was still bouncing from job to job, none of which lasted more than a few weeks or months. "He worked off and on in convenience stores," Cindy said. "He worked for a photo-lab for a while. That was probably for about—maybe nine months to a year straight, he worked there. The rest of the time it was just convenience stores and odd jobs that he would pick up here and there. During the time he was working for the photo finishing company, he was working the night shift. And that was—like I said, somewhere on the average of nine—probably nine months to a year."

Cindy Long usually found work as an office secretary. And dur-

ing those occasions when Bobby Joe was also working, they left the children with neighbors. One baby sitter said Long gave her the creeps. "I was scared of him," recalled Joanne Clark. "He always liked to grab you and hug you and lay you down and stuff like that that wasn't right."

In 1977, Bobby Joe finally seemed to settle on a career that promised a stable future. He enrolled at Broward Community College in Ft. Lauderdale in a two-year course leading to an associate's degree in radiology. Following his day classes, Bobby Joe sometimes worked the part-time evening shifts in the radiology departments at Memorial and Broward Hospital. In November, 1979, Long got his first full-time X-ray technician's job, at the busy Parkway Regional Medical Center in North Miami Beach. On a later job application, Bobby Joe described his work at Parkway as "...evening shift, very busy E.R., with a lot of O.R. exams."

But by then it was too late for the marriage. Cindy had had her fill of his erratic work habits that did nothing to support the struggling household. With Cindy as the major breadwinner, the relationship deteriorated into running battles over money, or the lack of it. She started nagging him about his inability to hold a job. Sometimes, in the heat of the argument, Bobby Joe would slap her, and she'd slap him right back. But he would always apologize later, and Cindy never felt like he was a wife-beater, or that he abused her.

"I mean, we used to fight about all kinds of things," Cindy recalled. "Money—God, anything!"

When Cindy finally filed for divorce in June, 1980, the neighbors along 40th Street in Lake Forest weren't at all surprised. Bobby Joe and Cindy Long never did seem like the ideal "couple next door." After their inseparable teenage years, compatibility was no longer part of the Longs' vocabulary. More and more often, the neighbors noticed, Bobby Joe stayed home while Cindy took off for a night out with friends.

"I never saw them go out as a family," said neighbor Sandy Hamilton. "I thought that was weird. She went her way, he went his. Cindy liked to party a lot. He didn't seem like the type. He

stayed home while his wife was more outgoing." Baby sitter Joanne Clark said she often went over to their house with her sister, Lynn, but only when they were sure that Cindy was home. "He always talked dirty," she said of Bobby Joe. "Me and my sister would go over there and we'd always feel uncomfortable. We wouldn't stay there when he was alone."

The way Bobby Joe explained it to CBS's Victoria Corderi, his problems really started during this period, when he was often unemployed and things between he and Cindy were falling apart, mainly over their terrible financial situation. Being out of work, unable to find or hold a job, wasn't really his fault, though. There were plenty of excuses to go around.

"When the problems first started, when I got out of the Army I was a cripple. OK? I almost lost my left foot, my left knee was sliced in half and the only thing that I knew how to do, outside of the Army, was electrical work. That's all. I started working when I was fifteen, and I worked until I was eighteen and went in the Army...I didn't even have a high school education, I had to get a GED in the Army ... So you know, here I am, I'm out of the Army, I'm crippled, I don't know how to do anything. So I went through probably fifteen jobs in ahhh, maybe a two-year period, two, three-year period, yeah, about three years. It was just anything that I could get, to get some money coming in, you know. It was working in liquor stores, stocking liquor stores, installing dental equipment, working in convenience stores. Anything that I could get, right? But most of them involved being on my feet at least and all of them involved a lot of bending and stooping and things like that. And I couldn't take it— you know, I would come home at night and have to crawl in the door and crawl into bed I couldn't even walk on my foot.... I guess it was getting to me you know. And the problems really started, one time when I was unemployed. But I know when things started...It was these classified-ad things down in Miami."

Sixteen months after Cindy and Bobby Joe Long were divorced, she married again. Cindy and her second husband were divorced in July, 1983. She has since married for the third time.

A few months after Cindy sued for divorce, Bobby Joe, typical-

91

ly, lost his job at Parkway Regional Medical Center. Unable, or unwilling, to find other work in the South Florida area, he packed up and moved to Tampa late in November, 1980. According to a job application he filed at Tampa General Hospital, the reason he left the Parkway job was: "Divorce, left area."

However, Bobby Joe Long may have had a hidden agenda in getting out of South Florida. The activities of the Ad Man Rapist, who was growing more brazen and active by the week, were attracting too much heat. Even in a sprawling metropolitan area, patrolled by scores of separate law-enforcement agencies, detectives from sex-crime units were meeting in sit-downs to compare notes on the well-dressed, smooth-talking predator who had developed a sophisticated scheme for stalking his victims in their own homes. There were dozens of cases piling up in which the identical M.O. was used. But, as the experienced cops knew only too well, for every reported case they had to work on, there were probably three more victims who out of fear, shame or both did not report an attack by the Ad Man Rapist.

In the booming Tampa Bay area, Bobby Joe Long saw an opportunity to start over.

▲   ▲   ▲

A LETTER FROM BOBBY

```
Do me a favor Man--
Call me Bob--
Only the fuckin hillbillys up in W. Va. call me
Bobby Joe.
```

▲   ▲   ▲

Northeastern University sociologist Jack Levin, the co-author of Mass Murder: America's Growing Menace, once observed: "True serial murderers often have a lifetime of frustration. And they have a need to dominate other people, but the point is, how different are they from anybody else?"

"We actually know very little about the origins of sociopathy; some psychiatrists think it's early childhood problems like abandonment or abuse, others think it's a genetic defect, still others think it's brain damage after birth. But, in fact, the evidence that it's any of these is flimsy. Millions of people in this country have terrible childhood problems and don't commit violent acts at all."

The baggage that Bobby Joe Long toted along with him from South Florida to Tampa Bay included all three of Levin's suspect characteristics. But at that point, in 1980, there was still nothing to indicate that the makings of a conscienceless serial killer were brewing behind the quiet, boyish facade that was maturing into a handsome man. The serial-rapist demon that had been pulling Bobby Joe's strings was, for the time being, placated by the move, and waited patiently deep in the dark and twisted labyrinth of Bobby Joe Long's psyche.

Or so it seemed.

With the move to Tampa, Long began leaving a long and clearly marked paper trail that homicide investigators later tracked in compiling their portrait of a killer. Their reports, painstakingly assembled, traced the wanderlust of Bobby Joe Long almost from the instant he hit Tampa, across the country to California, and back to Florida, right up to the moment they pounced and threw him face down on the pavement outside the Main Street Theater.

So it was that during Thanksgiving week, 1984, while other members of the Task Force were sorting through the mounds of evidence gathered in the searches of Long's car and apartment, several other detectives—Rick Duran, Greg Brown, Lee Baker, and Polly Goethe among them--set out to interview friends and colleagues of the killer, to try and put together the many scattered pieces of the puzzle of Bobby Joe Long. The State Attorney and the lead investigators in the case needed a clear picture of the suspect. Just who was this guy, anyway, and how had he managed to slip through the cracks in the system long enough to kill ten women and rape countless others?

Detective Brown began by driving over to the Ocala area, in the central part of the state, where Bobby Joe had spent time with

a couple of old boyhood chums from Hialeah, and where Elsie Louise Moran, Long's former mother-in-law, also lived.

According to Elsie Moran, Cindy sometimes brought the grandchildren to Ocala to visit. After Bobby Joe and Cindy were divorced, Bobby Joe was usually the one to come for the kids when it was time to take Chris and Bobbi Jo home. But she had to take the kids down to the convenience store on the corner to meet their daddy, because Bobby Joe and her husband, Joe Moran, despised each other. There was so much bad blood between the two men that Bobby Joe had more than once threatened to kill Joe.

Elsie described one particularly ugly incident, when she thought for sure Joe and Bobby Joe were going to shoot it out with the rest of them caught in the crossfire. It was a Fourth of July holiday. Bobby Joe had just collected the kids and was being especially nice to Elsie when little Chris innocently repeated a nasty remark that Joe Moran had made about Bobby Joe. That set him off. Bobby Joe started shouting about how he was going to kill the son of a bitch. When she pointed a finger at him and told him to shut his mouth, Bobby Joe slapped her hand away. Just about that time, Joe, who'd been staying back out of sight, came barreling in with his rifle, threatening to do some killing of his own.

Elsie said she put Chris in Joe's car and made them get out of there. She took little Bobbi Jo herself to keep her away from Bobby Joe, who was shouting and carrying on about how she'd never see her grandchildren again. Moran called the local police department. The cops wouldn't let Long take his kids because Cindy had legal custody of them, which enraged Bobby Joe even more. He tore out of there, and she didn't see him again until he was on the news about killing those girls.

From there, Brown drove over to Citra, just north of Ocala, to talk to Robert Frederick Fry, who had gone to school with Bobby Joe Long back in Hialeah. Over the years, Fry had stayed in touch with Long and with three other classmates, Rudy Machado and Rick and Buddy Marshall. Sometimes they still got together for hunting trips out in the South Florida boondocks.

Fry shrugged when asked if he had ever noticed anything

unusual about Bobby Joe. Well, he did like guns a lot; seemed almost obsessed with them sometimes. But nothing unusual about that.A lot of the good old boys Fry knew had guns around all the time, went hunting a lot. It was just part of that Southern macho tradition. And Bobby Joe liked to play the role of a tough guy from the streets of Miami who didn't take shit from nobody. He also talked all the time about women, about cunts, really. Liked to brag about the different ways he'd fuck `em or make `em suck his cock. Really got off on that, but talking about sex wasn't unusual either. All the guys Fry knew talked about fucking all the time. Most guys did.

Bobby Joe, Fry continued, was a friendly guy, a smooth talker, but sometimes he went through real sudden mood changes. He'd get violent with little or no provocation at all.

Fry said he moved to the Ocala area in 1982, and didn't have any contact with Bobby Joe until Long showed up around Christmas time, 1983, to see Rudy Machado, who had also moved up from Hialeah. Rudy told him then that Bobby Joe had been making frequent trips to Ocala to visit. At the time, Long said he'd just come back from New Jersey, where he spent a few months with a girl named Kathy.

Long told him about an unusual incident that took place while Long was living in West Virginia with his parents after his marriage broke up. He was alone in his bedroom one night when a couple of guys carrying guns came to the door and pushed their way inside. Bobby Joe said he overheard the men order his parents to lie on the floor while they tied them up. Bobby Joe said he hid in his bed-room while the bandits ransacked the house and got away with a small amount of cash the Longs had on hand.

Bobby Joe grumbled indignantly about the "scummy and low-life" assholes that would do such a thing. Strange sentiments coming from a man who bragged incessantly about his tough-guy street image, stranger still from a predator who had perfected his own home-invasion technique in which the consequences—rape, sexual terrorism, robbery—were far more destructive than anything those small-time West Virginia punks could imagine.

▲   ▲   ▲

A LETTER FROM BOBBY

I've had knives and guns pulled on me, and pulled a few myself. I have had to deal with and be around some really "bad" dudes, and I can do it. Pretty much I don't fuck with nobody, and they fuck with me just once! If it comes down to "even a doubt" about someone, they better make sure I don't get a shot at them first. I will take it.

▲   ▲   ▲

There was something else, Fred Fry told Detective Duran, something that his family had kept from him until Bobby Joe was arrested. In late May or early June, 1984, Long showed up at Fry's mother's house in Bellview, near Ocala. Fry's sixteen year old sister, Michelle, was alone at the time, and while he was there Bobby Joe made sexual advances toward her. It really pissed Fry off, too, since Bobby Joe was supposed to be his friend and he (Long) had known Michelle since she was a baby. Go see my mom, Fry advised. She's got the whole story.

Detective Duran did just that. He met with Joyce Imel, who told him that Bobby Joe had indeed shown up while Michelle was alone. Michelle told her mother that when Bobby Joe came in he grabbed her and hugged her in anything but a brotherly way, and made her very uneasy. He also made comments about how she was "really filling out," and the way he was looking her up and down and trying to hug her and staring at her and talking about her physical development, scared her.

Michelle said she called her boyfriend and asked him to come over right away, which seemed to upset Long. He tried to get her to leave with him and go to lunch, but Michelle refused, claiming that her mother would be home any minute and she couldn't leave without permission. Michelle said Bobby Joe kept after her to go

out with him, and kept staring at her in a peculiar way until her boyfriend showed up. Long left then, saying he would be back to see her soon.

He never returned, much to Mrs. Imel's relief. And when she read in the papers later that Bobby Joe had started killing women in May and June, right about the time he'd come to see Michelle, she almost collapsed in shock, realizing that Michelle might have been a victim.

"You know," Mrs. Imel added when she finished telling Duran the story, "there was something else that happened that was really odd. Just about a week ago, some people who said they were investigators from Tampa came by to talk to Michelle. Said they'd been tailing Bobby Joe Long for the last four months, and had followed him to this address back in June. They wanted to know what he was doing here, and when Michelle told them what happened they left." Duran assured her that the mysterious visitors had not come from any police agency in the Tampa Bay area. The identity of those "investigators" and why they had been watching Long months before he was arrested is still unknown.

Detective Polly Goethe conducted the interviews with Rudy Machado, Bobby Joe's one-time best friend, and Machado's wife, Lee Ann, at their home in Silver Springs.

Neither Rudy nor Lee Ann had seen Long since 1981. Lee Ann said that was about the time that Bobby Joe came on to her pretty strong. Rudy, a long-haul truck driver, was out on the road when Bobby Joe dropped in for an unexpected visit. I was lying on the couch, she told Detective Goethe, when he sat down beside me, started rubbing my leg and coming on to me. She said she told him to stop but didn't want to make a big scene, since he was her husband's best friend. But Bobby Joe kept making sexually suggestive remarks, and didn't stop until her sister-in-law walked in the room.

Back in Tampa, meanwhile, Detectives C.L. Nelms, Charlie Wolf and Deputy Gary Ganey from the Sheriff's Office drove over to Ted and Susie Gensel's place, a pleasant, oak-draped neighborhood in the Forest Hills section of north Tampa, bordering the Babe Zaharias Golf and Country Club.

Rudy started by talking about the teen years he and Bobby Joe had spent together in Hialeah. Long, he said, wasn't a good student, although he was bright enough and had good street smarts. But, Rudy added, he was really a "smartass" type who knew it all. Long didn't get in any real serious trouble with the law, as Rudy recalled, but like most of the guys they ran around with he did get into a lot of "general mischief." Bobby was never involved in any sports or extracurricular activities at school, but the two of them often went hunting, fishing, and snorkeling together.

As far as Rudy knew, Long was not abused as a child, never removed from his home by state authorities for neglect. But Bobby Joe would get terribly upset that his mother had many different boyfriends and was bringing home different men all the time. The Longs weren't too friendly with their neighbors, but Rudy figured that was just because they were a new family in an old, settled neighborhood, and because Long's mother worked a lot.

Bobby Joe Long, the Machados said, was their best man when they got married in Ocala in August, 1978. It was at the wedding that Long first met Suzette Rice*, Lee Ann's sister.

Bobby Joe was still living in Hollywood at the time and began visiting them on a regular basis, making the 300-mile drive from South Florida late Friday and staying the weekend. After Long moved to Tampa, the visits became more frequent. At times, Ted Gensel, another of the Machados' wedding guests who ended up rooming with Long in Tampa, came along.

Ted and Susie Gensel's place at 1515 Meadowbrook, a pleasant, oak-draped neighborhood in the Forest Hills section of north Tampa bordering the Babe Zaharias Golf and Country Club.

Gensel said he'd known Bobby Joe for about six years. Soon after they met at the Machados' wedding, Ted and Bobby Joe started rooming together. They were roommates for about six months.

Ted mentioned that he was dating Suzette Rice when he first met Long. Later, after Ted met Susie, his wife-to-be, he broke up with Suzette. Bobby Joe and Suzette then got together, but it didn't last long. She had him arrested for beating her up and "a bunch of other stuff," but Gensel was hazy on the details. Gensel also heard

that Bobby Joe had been arrested around that same time, on some kind of charge about making obscene phone calls to a doctor's office, but again, he wasn't clear on what that involved.

Bobby Joe liked guns and at one time had several, Gensel continued. He remembered that one was a .38 caliber, blue-steel revolver that Long carried under his car seat for protection.

Long was an avid racquetball player, a pretty good one at that, and spent a lot of time hanging around the racquetball courts at the University of South Florida, looking for a pickup game.

When he went out, Long favored Jerry's Tavern on Highway 60 in Brandon, or Babe's Pizza, also in Brandon. But he was a light drinker, usually only socially. Ted could remember only one time when he'd seen Bobby Joe drunk. In fact, Bobby Joe seemed to disapprove of heavy drinkers. "If he'd see somebody just totally wiped out, he'd say, 'What a waste of life,'" Gensel said. And as far as he knew, Long wasn't into drugs, either using or selling.

In a separate interview, Susie Gensel said that Bobby Joe had stayed with them for several months in the first part of 1984. Long moved out sometime in May, about the time, she now realized, that the killings started. "But he was my friend," she said. "When I needed somebody to talk to, he was there for me."

Even after he moved, Bobby Joe continued to drop by, maybe a few times a week. Sometimes he brought a woman he was dating along, as though he was showing her off. There were a few things about his old roommate that worried Ted Gensel, however. Bobby Joe had a hair-trigger temper, and little things could set him off like a short-fused firecracker. The other thing was that Bobby Joe kept some photo albums that were stuffed with pictures of nude women. Long spent a lot of time poring over those albums, and told Gensel that most of them were photos he had taken himself of all the girlfriends he'd had sex with in California.

And Bobby Joe had another odd little quirk, Gensel recalled. He liked to shop for household items through newspaper ads, and often spent hours studying the classified section of the paper. I figured he was just a frugal man, Gensel said.

As the detectives went about methodically collecting bits and

99

pieces of Bobby Joe Long's life, a clearer picture began to emerge. It appeared that, when Long first arrived in Tampa, he picked up right where he'd left off in South Florida, bouncing from apartment to apartment and from job to job. He worked in convenience stores and as an attendant in a funeral home before finally landing a full-time position at Centro Asturiano Hospital where he was able to apply his training as a radiology technician. Even then, in 1981, Centro Asturiano, on the fringes of Tampa's historic but decaying Ybor City section, was already an aging, decrepit relic. Now closed, the ancient, blond, brick mausoleum-like structure with its neo-Classical columns faced busy Nebraska Avenue. Bobby Joe Long, coming and going on the midnight shift, passed the gauntlet of hookers who patrolled the narrow north-south street that was soon to become Bobby Joe's favorite hunting ground as he trolled the Tampa night.

He worked at the cramped old Centro from January to October of 1981. Long later stated on another job application: "I was the only person in the Dept., so did all clerical work as well as exams (mostly E.R.)."

Gloria Delgado was the Centro Asturiano supervisor who hired Bobby Joe as an X-ray technician. Because of their conflicting hours, she had little personal contact with him. However, she told Detective Rick Duran, after he had been working there about five or six months, she started getting complaints from various hospital personnel about Bobby Joe and his poor job performance. By August, 1981, the complaints had reached such a level that she was ready to fire Bobby Joe, when he beat her to the punch and abruptly quit. The reason, he said, was because he had to go to West Virginia "on personal business."

Gloria thought she'd heard the last of the technician who had turned out to be so lackadaisical about his work that necessary X-rays often didn't get done on his shift. But then, out of the blue, a letter arrived from Long asking her for a job recommendation. Sure, she thought, in your dreams, and trashcanned the letter. Several weeks later, an angry and insistent Bobby Joe Long was on the phone, demanding that she provide him with the recommenda-

tion. The phone call set off warning bells in Gloria's head; something in the guy's menacing tone of voice told her instinctively that she'd better do as he demanded "...for fear of retribution towards her or the hospital," as Duran noted in his report.

She had good reason to be fearful. Marguerite Morales, an X-ray technician at the Centro hospital during Bobby Joe's employment, had experienced firsthand the very real threat Long poised. Shortly after Bobby Joe quit, he came back to the hospital to pick up his final paycheck. Marguerite was on duty. Gloria Delgado had left orders that, if Long showed up, he wasn't to be given his check until he'd turned in his hospital identification badge.

"Long did not return his badge and, upon learning of Mrs. Delgado's order, he became furious and began to shout obscenities and throw telephones and other exposed objects in the work area," Duran reported. It was only when a frightened Marguerite rushed to call the police that Bobby Joe left. But on his way out the door, he "...began shouting threats to return to the hospital with a shotgun or place a bomb somewhere in the building."

The episode was typical of Bobby Joe's inability to hold a job and his spotty work record. And the fact that he walked out on a steady job when he was sorely pressed for money is significant. When Bobby Joe and Cindy divorced, part of the agreement was that he pay her $263 a month in child support. By March, 1981, he was behind $626 in his support payments, while back in Broward County, officials were threatening to toss him in jail if he didn't cough up the cash.

An indignant Bobby Joe fired off a complaint letter to the judge who had granted the divorce, complaining, in typical fashion, that it wasn't his fault and that he was being beleaguered by an insensitive court system. The letter was a forerunner of things to come—Bobby Joe's penchant for long, whining, "poor me" letters to judges, prosecutors, cops, prison officials, and just about anyone else who would listen concerning his unfair treatment, his persecution (unconstitutional) by the justice system, and harassment (malicious) by a vindictive but vague "them." It worked as far as eliminating the threat of a contempt charge in the child-support

case. It would work later in a more serious case of assault. And it continues to this day, with Bobby Joe Long inundating the Florida Department of Correction with a blizzard of complaints from his Death Row cell.

In his letter to the Broward court, Long wrote: "At the time we came to the figure of $263.00 I was in the position to pay it and not cause too much of a problem. However, less than one month after the divorce was final I lost my position at Parkway General Hospital in N. Miami Beach, as a diagnostic Radiologic Technologist.

"I was unemployed for three months and unable to find a suitable position there in S. Florida, so relocated here to Tampa. When I first got here I took jobs as a convenience store clerk, and as a funeral home attendant, waiting for a position at one of the local hospitals.

"I am now working at Centro Asturiano Hospital as a Radiologic Tech, but at a rate of pay that is two dollars less an hour than I would have been making there.

"I make $5.10 an hour and bring home less than $160.00 a week. Also from being unemployed for so long I got in such a hole financially that I am only just recovering enough to live a fairly normal life.

"I think it is only fair that the amount I pay be based on what I make, since I am unable to pay the $263.00.

"I want to say that I fully intend and want to pay Cindy a fair amount of child support, but I have to live too. We went to a hearing on March seventeenth in front of a General Master named Methelis, and at that time we both thought that the amount I pay would be adjusted. I can tell you that I have never been treated in a manner in which the Assistant State Attorney treated me and it was all I could do to keep from getting up and walking out.

"I am not used to being treated in this manner, and even though this fellow is used to dealing with all types of deadbeats and every other type of low life, I think he ought to learn to differentiate between different types. Even Cindy said when we left the hearing that it was totally unbelievable, and she wondered how

someone with such an attitude could live as long as he has. I think it is a shame that these types act as they do and are allowed to get away with it. I fully intend to follow whatever course I can to try and see to it that this attitude is not allowed to continue, and although I am sure that my letters will not cause a lot of interest, at least someone will be made aware of what is going on. I cannot believe that the man was behaving in a manner condoned by the courts, at least I hope not."

Long managed to catch up on his payments, but by 1983 he was far behind again. Once in October and twice in December that year, he was ordered under pain of contempt to appear before the Grand Master. He never showed up, but before a warrant could be issued, Cindy wrote to the head of the Broward County Child Support Enforcement Department advising that, "I am in receipt of your summons for the hearing on December 22, 1983. I would like to inform you that it is not necessary at this time to continue this hearing, due to the fact that Mr. Long has paid the hospital bills that I have for the children and when he was down here on Monday, he gave me $4,000.00.

"Thank you for your continued cooperation in this matter. Have a happy holiday."

Bobby Joe had dodged another Go-to-Jail bullet. The question was how, based on his habitually low income and irregular work record, he managed to come up with such a sizeable chunk of cash. At least part of the source, say the cops who tracked him down, may have come from the sale of the loot he was hauling out of the homes he visited as the Ad Man Rapist, a career he was about to resume full-time.

As Detective Duran located other former employers and fellow workers, stories similar to those told at Centro Asturiano began accumulating, and revealed a troubled and troubling personality. One of Duran's main stops was at the huge Tampa General Hospital (TGH) for a chat with Dick Barcia, director of the hospital's radiology department. Barcia told Duran that Bobby Joe Long started working at TGH on June 14, 1984, and was terminated on September 27. (Curiously, his tenure at TGH came right in the

middle of the horrendous murder spree.) Bobby Joe's pay was $7.50 an hour, and he worked ten hours per day, Thursday through Saturday. Barcia called Long an "average" worker, and said he was let go because he lacked the advanced certification the job required. In those three months Bobby Joe was on the job, he made quite an impact, mostly negative, on an amazing number of TGH employees.

Eugene DiBetta, the shift supervisor in radiology on weekends, considered Long to be a good worker, a real nice guy. They talked about girls, diving, fishing, hunting, and football. Long told DiBetta stories of hunting in the often treacherous South Florida Everglades. Bobby Joe was fond of high-powered "muscle" cars, and liked to brag about his sleek Dodge Magnum.

The one thing that really bothered him, DiBetta told the detective, was the way Long talked about sex continuously. And he didn't think much of the smutty remarks and sexual innuendos he made to women working in the radiology department. One employee, Kim Anderson, complained about Bobby Joe's advances and the way he once picked her up in his arms in an overtly sexual manner.

When asked about the confrontation, Anderson described how he suddenly grabbed her from behind, picked her up and turned her around in his arms, and then let her slide down his body in a sexual manner. She said the only reason Long stopped was that she got angry and yelled at him to stop. She complained to Gene DiBetta about the incident, but that didn't stop Long from constantly pestering her for a date.

"We just never seemed to agree on anything," Kim told Detective Duran. "He was such a chauvinist. And lazy. Really had problems with authority figures, especially if they were women."

DiBetta said that Long came to him after he'd been at the hospital a few months to tell him that he (Long) had just been placed on probation for assault. Bobby Joe explained that he'd gotten into an argument with someone and ended up damaging that person's car. DiBetta didn't learn until much later that the charge actually involved a gun and an attempted kidnaping when Bobby Joe tried to hijack a woman in her car. Long was concerned about losing his

job over the incident. He also explained to DiBetta that he'd recently started dating a pious, born-again Christian woman, and although they'd had some differences, he was trying to work them out and get back together with the woman.

Kathleen Kelley, X-ray technician at Tampa General, also worked with Bobby Joe Long, but the association was far from pleasant. Long rattled on about sex nonstop. Almost every conversation they had, he somehow managed to turn the topic to sex, so much so that it made her feel uncomfortable. That, plus the way Bobby Joe pushed himself on her, made Kathleen feel nervous and intimidated, she told Duran.

Another thing that scared Kelly was how Long's disposition would suddenly go sour and sullen when a female supervisor told him to do something. He just didn't like women telling him what to do. Really resented it, she added.

Geraldine Marsicano, a supervisor in the radiology department, also described Long as lazy. He would come into work, she told Duran, do one X-ray and then sit down. He told me that he didn't have to help out other members of the department even if they were swamped with work and needed a hand. "You know," she continued, "he acted like a little kid who thought he was being picked on. And he really had a problem with women supervisors." She recalled one incident when she told him to learn a different X-ray technique. He really blew up, she said. He never did learn the procedure.

Geraldine was also disturbed over the way Bobby Joe treated her son when the boy dropped by the hospital to see her. He would taunt the boy with remarks like, "Do you love your mommy all the time?" Seemed like a pretty strange and inappropriate thing to ask a kid. And one time, Bobby Joe wrapped up her son mummy-style with adhesive tape. He laughed like it was a big joke, but Geraldine sensed there was really malicious intent behind the prank to get back at her personally.

"I had a lot of problems with him as a worker," she added. And the way he stared at her all the time was upsetting. He had cold, cold eyes, she said.

105

Another female supervisor, Margaret Wilson, had a similar opinion of Long—lazy, hostile towards women in authority, obsessed with sex, a smart-alecky macho man, and frustrated to the point of anger when things didn't go his way. There were times, she recalled when, he seemed to delight in taunting her with stories she found unpleasant. Like the time he was out hunting in the Everglades and found a part-chow puppy and took it home. The dog tried to bite him, he said, so he put it in the car, drove right back out to the Everglades and blew its head off.

Then there was the time a group of them was sitting around talking about the serial killer that was killing women in Tampa. The way things were going, any one of them could be next if they weren't careful. Bobby Joe, she said, just laughed and walked out of the room. They could hear him laughing all the way down the hall.

Bobby Joe Long told another male technician, David Dray, how he enjoyed hanging out at strip joints and topless bars. "Those cunts are a lot better at sex than nice girls," he told Dray, and then laughed like it was a secret joke and only he knew the punchline.

Noel Helle said Long also told him that he preferred bad girls over good girls, and that he liked to "fuck 'em in the ass," whenever he had the chance. "Bobby Joe used to talk about going over to Nebraska Avenue all the time and how much he liked the girls [prostitutes] over there," Helle recalled. "He also liked to go to the Sly Fox or the Library Lounge, places like that, and talk and flirt with the girls at those bars. But he was really a big bullshitter and always had sex on his mind. He was always staring at girls, and whenever some woman was around he'd put on his big macho-man image."

However, one TGH employee who dated Bobby Joe Long didn't think he was such a bad guy. Candy Ellis°, an emergency-room nurse, went to dinner and a movie with Long in September. They talked mainly about their jobs, his motorcycle accident, and where they'd come from. On the second date, Bobby Joe came by her apartment. They hung around the pool all day and went to dinner and a movie that night. On their third date, they rented a video

movie, *The Thing*, and watched it at her place. Afterward, he spent the night with her. She described the sex as vaginal and oral. Nothing unusual, nothing "kinky." Nothing that really made the earth move either. Shortly afterward, Bobby Joe lost his job at the hospital. He called her a few times after that. The last call was on November 13. The next time Candy saw Bobby Joe Long, it was on a television newscast announcing that her one-time lover was a serial sex killer who preyed on women.

Investigators also tracked down some former colleagues of Long's at the Humana Hospital in Brandon, where he'd worked when he returned from California and West Virginia. Susan Suttles described Long as "picky" about his X-ray assignments. He especially resented doing X-rays for G.I. exams.

He couldn't stand his ex-wife, but loved his kids. Long told Susan that they got divorced because his wife was screwing around and he caught her with another man. He complained that his ex-wife wanted to go out and party all the time, but that he was a homebody who liked to stay home with his kids. While he was still at Humana, Bobby Joe got a subpoena for unpaid child support, Susan recalled. He was furious about it, yelling about how his ex-wife wasn't fit to have custody of the kids.

"I knew he was dating this nurse at the hospital," Susan continued, "which really seemed strange. She was so religious, and Bobby Joe talked about how he was an atheist." She heard on the hospital grapevine that several doctors and patients had complained about Long personally or the quality of his work. One story was that he told a pregnant woman he was X-raying, "Your kids are going to look like frogs." Susan said the word was that Long hadn't actually been fired, but that he resigned when asked to do so.

Detectives found another piece of the Bobby Joe Long puzzle at Gulf Bay Electric Inc. on East Hillsborough Avenue in Tampa. Long work there from May 3 through May 22, 1984 and, according to Chad Harrison, a senior electrician who worked alongside Long, nobody was sorry to see him go. Everybody made cracks about women from time to time, Harrison said. After all, it was a "guy thing" to talk about girls. But not the way Bobby Joe Long did. He

even grossed out the grossest with his crude, almost cruel talk about girls. Bobby Joe used to brag about how he'd do some unnecessary X-raying of women when he was working out at Brandon Humana Hospital. Only the young, good-looking ones, of course. Got a lot of free looks at pussy that way.

Harrison said that Long also boasted about the times he had some fourteen and sixteen year old girls over to his place to watch some porno flicks. They got so hot and horny, Long claimed, that they insisted on re-enacting with him all the sex scenes from the movies. Long also like to pull out nude photos he carried around and show them off. Said they were all old girlfriends. There was one of a spread-legged Oriental girl that he was really proud of.

The worst was when they would be out in public on a job somewhere and a nice-looking woman happened by. Bobby Joe would make loud comments about her that embarrassed Harrison. One of Long's favorites, Harrison remembered, was, "How would you like to bend that over and make her squeal like a pig? I'd like to give it to her right up her ass."

Surprisingly, the investigators actually turned up some former friends, all women, who had nothing but good to say about Bobby Joe Long. Additional pieces to the puzzle, no matter how mismatched they might appear.

Sharon Silvers lived in Seminole, Florida, across the Bay in Pinellas County. She got to know Bobby Joe Long through Debbie Canterbury, a friend she'd grown up with in Huntington, West Virginia. Debbie and Bobby Joe had gotten acquainted when Long was working at a hospital in Huntington. The relationship, Sharon said, was strictly friendly, nothing sexual about it as far as she knew. Debbie had grown close to Long when she was going through a painful divorce, and Bobby had offered a strong, silent shoulder to lean on. About two years before, Silvers said that Canterbury and Long came to Florida looking for work. They were in Florida for six days, but Bobby Joe stayed at her house only one night. Part of the time, he was down in Ft. Lauderdale visiting his kids and ex-wife. After Debbie returned to Huntington and Long relocated to Tampa, he would call her occasionally to ask about Debbie and talk about

her own family. She described Bobby Joe as "...always very friendly and polite. He seemed intelligent, and was very well mannered." The last time she saw him was on July 11, 1984, when Debbie was visiting again and Long drove over from Tampa to see her.

Rona Satz, another woman from Seminole, bumped into Bobby Joe Long during a cruise aboard the Starship Royale, which sailed out of Port Canaveral on Monday, October 22, 1984, and returned Friday, October 26.

When they met on board, Long spun a long tale—which she believed—that he was employed as a diver on the Royale. Rona said she had no reason to question the story since Long seemed to be very friendly with everyone on board and seemed to know his way around. He was always extremely polite to her, mentioning that he lived in Tampa, was divorced, had worked in a hospital, and that he had just started working on the ship as the official diver.

When the cruise ended, Bobby Joe offered to drive her back to Seminole, since he was going that way anyway. She accepted, and during the drive Long was the soul of good manners and gentility. He drove her straight home and carried her luggage inside. Before parting, Long asked for her phone number, and said he would like to get together with her later. Rona said he did call once, but in the interim she'd had time to think about Long and his diving story. There was something vaguely disquieting about it, so when he called for a date she turned him down, saying he wasn't her type.

▲   ▲   ▲

A LETTER FROM BOBBY

I've led a real good life, probably not like a lot of guys in prison.

I mean I've done most of the things I always wanted, I've scuba dove most any where in the US Mexico and the Islands worth diving, I've seen both coasts of this country and a lot in between, I've known a lot of fucking pussy (not just victims) but

109

I mean good stuff.

   I just got something fucking screwed up somewhere, thats all.

   Fuck man I worked as a dive instructor on the SS
Royale Cruise ship, pussy pussy every night a new
one or two.

   It pisses me off to even think about it. I had it
fucking made, great food, sunshine, horny broads,
worked two days out of a seven day week, if you call
it work, we were to go two days to the island they
used to film Gilligans Island on, and just party and
dive.

   Its quite an island now, not like on the TV show!
Booze food, Vollyball, hammocks everywhere, shit,
when I think how I fucked up I need a shot in the
head.

▲   ▲   ▲

Less than a month later, Rona Satz was stunned to learn that
the polite, friendly man who drove her home had, only seven days
before embarking on the romantic cruise, kidnaped, raped, and
strangled two prostitutes, Karen Dinsfriend and Virginia Johnson.
Within days of their return from the cruise, he kidnaped and
assaulted Lisa McVey and murdered Kim Swann.

   Evelyn Cheresne was thirty-four years old when she met
Bobby Joe Long in May, 1984, at a popular Crystal Springs dive
spot. She was a little old for Long, whose usual tastes ran to
teenagers, but she had the looks of a much younger woman—
which she showed off as a topless dancer at the Sly Fox Lounge on
North Nebraska. They both loved scuba diving and talked a lot
about their common hobby. When they parted, they exchanged
phone numbers. Not long afterward, during the first week of June,
Evelyn found herself in a pile of trouble and needed a friend. She
thought of the "nice guy" she'd met diving, and called Bobby Joe at
the place he was staying, out in Brandon.

   Please, she pleaded, can you come into Tampa and pick me up.

She was downtown filing charges of battery against her boyfriend. She had her little boy with her, but no money or transportation to get out to Zephyrhills where her ex-husband was. Dutifully, Bobby Joe climbed into his maroon-colored Dodge Magnum and drove the twenty miles or so, through heavy crosstown traffic, to get her. Then he had to drive all the way back out to Zephyrhills, another thirty miles or so northeast of downtown Tampa.

Evelyn directed him to the Boathouse Pub on Highway 39, just outside of town. While Bobby Joe waited in the parking lot, Evelyn went inside to meet her ex-husband and a girlfriend, Linda Staab. The pair convinced her that she should spend the night with them and not go back home, where her boyfriend might be waiting to beat her again. Evelyn agreed, and sent Linda outside to tell the guy in the red Dodge she was going to stay there. The guy acted really pissed off, Linda told her, and took off in a big huff. Evelyn said Long called her a couple of times after that, but they never got together again.

She don't know how lucky she is, thought Detective Pops Baker as he finished taking the woman's statement. This happened in June, the same time Bobby Joe was getting into the murder business on a serious basis. And she certainly fit Long's "slut" profile, even if she wasn't a hooker—topless dancer, used her body to manipulate men, hung out along the Nebraska Avenue Strip. Baker shook his head. It was a wonder she didn't end up like some of the others.

Then there was Lisa Leonardo*, whose relationship with the killer wasn't necessarily bad. It just left her cold and empty and feeling used.

Lisa was eighteen years old when she met Bobby Joe at a Fourth of July party at Ted and Susie Gensel's place in Brandon. The pretty five-foot, seven-inch blond with the striking bluish/green eyes was mildly attracted to the quiet guy with the wavy brown hair. Good looking, she thought. Rugged was the word that came to mind.

After a few drinks, she left the party with him and went to his

111

apartment in Brandon. They talked mainly about snorkeling and scuba diving, about his job X-raying people at the hospital. Not much else. Small talk, mainly. But she was sort of attracted to the guy, and the drinks and the warm, lazy afternoon were making her feel sexy, so it didn't take much for them to end up in bed. It was a disappointment. Long was so unemotional and insensitive toward her sexual needs that it "really turned me off." When they were finished they went back to the party and separated. Later that year, Lisa lived with the Gensels for a few months, and occasionally bumped into Bobby Joe when he dropped in. He asked her out a few times, but the memory of that one afternoon in bed with him was so distasteful she refused to date him again.

▲   ▲   ▲

A LETTER FROM BOBBY

I didn't mean to confuse you--my kinky girl friend is named Lisa, no she won't ever come back here. She doesn't exist anymore--understand?

▲   ▲   ▲

Late in 1981, Bobby Joe Long was hit with a double whammy of legal problems, which apparently motivated him to pack up and head for the West Virginia hills until things cooled down. He thought that The Ad Man Rapes in South Florida were a thing of the past, but things were starting to spin out of control again and Bobby Joe was feeling that old, aching urge come alive.

The first trouble was a disturbing charge of mailing obscene photos and "very obscene letters" and making obscene phone calls to the twelve year old daughter of a Tampa physician.

Case number 81-13637 charged that Bobby Joe Long "...did unlawfully when knowing its content and character, exhibit obscene material, to wit: The defendant sent victim a letter which was addressed to witness Sandra Levitt°. The letter was obscene and

the same envelope also contained photos of oral, anal and mission-ary position intercourse..."

Since the victim was a minor, most of the official records of the case were closed, according to Florida state law. However, it seems that Long was caught when police traced the obscene phone calls to his home number. Apparently, the girl's father was a doctor at one of the hospitals where Long worked in the radiology department, and that's where the initial contact was made. Long pled "no contest" to the misdemeanor charges. He was ordered to pay $65.50 in fines and costs, sentenced to spend two days in confinement at the Salvation Army Corrections Department (but was credited with time already served), and placed on six months probation.

Only two days after the obscenity charge was filed, the second hit came, involving Suzette Rice. And therein lies a tangled tale.

Several weeks earlier, on August 25, 1981, Suzette had accused Long of raping her. But authorities who investigated the complaint felt the evidence was too flimsy to warrant an arrest. Bobby Joe's excuse was that the situation involved a messy love triangle that he was sucked into against his will.

This is the version of the incident that Bobby Joe related to Dr. Joel Norris (Walking Time Bombs): "He admits that the woman was able to manipulate him because he wanted and needed to have frequent sex. However, out of jealousy over her former boyfriend's new relationship and anger at his intervention in her life when she got too drunk to drive herself home, a former girlfriend charged Bobby with raping her after she had asked him to help her from his car to her apartment. 'This showed me what a real bitch could do when she didn't get her way,' Long explains. 'I've committed real rapes and I've murdered women. I know what happens inside of me when I get sexually violent. I know how I feel. I can tell you that I did not rape that girl. We had sex, but she was drunk, she invited me back to her place, and she announced in front of my friends before I drove her home that she wanted to have sex. Then, the next day, she told police that I raped her.'

Whatever the truth, there was an almost malevolent irony taint-ing the incident. For the third time in his life, Bobby Joe Long,

career rapist, managed to slither out of a rape charge by employing the same tactic—claiming consensual sex and painting the woman as a whorish schemer bent on entrapping him. This from the same man who was simultaneously ravaging women as the Ad Man Rapist, the same man who told CBS News: "All in all I guess I probably destroyed about 100 people. You know? In one way or another, classified ad rapes or whatever."

The Rice woman, Bobby Joe claimed, was still seething that her rape accusation didn't stick when she showed up at the Gensels' residence on November 17, 1981. Complaint #81-13807, which Suzette filed two days later, alleged that a simple battery occurred when the "Defendant grabbed victim and threw her out of the door of the residence and struck her on the face with his fist causing a large bruise and swelling."

According to police and press interviews, this is the story leading up to that squabble as told by Suzette Rice:

She met Long in August, 1978, when he was best man at her sister's wedding in Ocala. Her new brother-in-law, Rudy Machado, said he had gone to school with Long in Hialeah. She learned that Bobby Joe was married and had two small children, although they did not attend the wedding. He returned to Hialeah and she lived in Ocala until January, 1980, when she moved to Tampa with her live-in boyfriend, Ted Gensel. About a month after they moved to Tampa, Bobby Joe showed up saying that his wife, Cynthia, ("the only girl he ever loved") had walked out on him, and he'd come to Tampa hoping to make a new life for himself.

Because she felt sorry for him, Suzette agreed to let him move in with her and Ted. They split the rent on a three-bedroom, white-cinderblock house in Forest Hills.

"We all palled around together," Suzette told a Tampa Tribune reporter. Waterskiing on Tampa Bay. Hanging out on weekends at the Dallas Bull or Faces Lounge. "Bob didn't drink much. Didn't smoke. Didn't do drugs," she continued. What he did do a lot was stare at women in a really scary way. "He would mentally undress a woman just standing there."

Once, after several teenage girls bitched that Bobby Joe was

coming on too strong, he laughed and told Suzette: "If they're going to play and flirt—they're fair game."

In her opinion, Bobby Joe was the type of person who couldn't stand rejection. Yet, at the same time he could be very intimidating. "I was scared of him," she admitted.

Gensel, Rice, and Long lived together until late spring of 1981, when Suzette and Ted broke up and she moved out. About the same time, Bobby Joe moved into a small efficiency apartment in Sulphur Springs, one of the older, deteriorating neighborhoods of North Tampa bisected by Nebraska Avenue. Some time later, Suzette called Bobby Joe to come to her apartment because of problems she'd been having with a new boyfriend and the threats he'd been making. Long, she added, had often bragged about his boxing and karate prowess, so she hoped that having a tough guy around would discourage the boyfriend from harassing her. Macho man Bobby Joe Long came riding to the rescue, playing the role of the good guy in the white hat to the hilt.

Bobby Joe was working the graveyard shift—midnight to 8:30 a.m.—at Centro Austriano Hospital and living in a crummy, one-room efficiency; Suzette had a day job and a place with lots of room. Why not, she suggested, move in with her. They were friends and were already used to rooming together. But, Suzette insisted, the relationship had to be strictly platonic. So in March, 1981, Long did move in with Suzette and her six year old daughter.

The strictly platonic crap lasted about three weeks. He started coming onto me sexually, Suzette complained. I wasn't interested, so I told him this wasn't going to work and asked him to move out. He did, and went back to the house where Ted Gensel still lived.

A few months passed and in August, 1981, Suzette stopped by to talk to Ted. He wasn't home, but Bobby Joe was and, according to her story, he threw her down and raped her. She said she called the cops, but due to her past relationship with Bobby Joe and the fact that she'd come to the house willingly, authorities were reluctant to press charges, and the case was dropped. But it wasn't forgotten. On November 17, Suzette went back to the house. As before, she claimed she just wanted to talk to Ted Gensel. But

again, Bobby Joe was home alone. This time the bad blood between the two erupted into a shouting and shoving match that ended, Suzette complained, with Long punching her in the face and throwing her out the front door. The woman marched right down to the Tampa Police Department, filed a charge of simple battery, and had Bobby Joe arrested. That was the last contact she had with him until they met later in court.

Due to the clogged court calendar, that meeting didn't take place until nearly two years later, on September 20, 1983. By then, Bobby Joe was working at Brandon Humana Hospital. Ted and Susan Gensel had gotten married, and Long was rooming with them in Brandon, just east of Tampa.

The first court date was a quickie affair. Bobby Joe defended himself in the non-jury hearing, and quickly learned the truth of the adage that he who defends himself has a fool for a client. The judge found him guilty of beating Suzette Rice,and sentenced him to thirty days in jail, six months probation, and fifty hours of community service.

That shock was followed a month later, when he was ordered to come up with $4,000 in overdue child support or go directly to jail. As 1983 wound down, and `84 dawned, things were definitely coming unraveled in Bobby Joe Long's life.

However, the ink on the assault case was barely dry before Bobby Joe Long began bombarding the Hillsborough County courts with letters, demanding that he be granted a new hearing on the grounds that he'd been railroaded into opting for a non-jury trial without proper legal representation. The tactic he employed to clear his name was to attack the other person's reputation. He was, he complained, the brunt of a spurned woman's revengeful false accusation. She'd done it once before in accusing him of raping her; now she was trying to get him again on the assault charge.

Although it wasn't his intention, the series of letters provided a revealing peek inside the dark and twisted recesses of Bobby Joe's mind— manipulative, vindictive, paranoid, a master at rationalization, and adroit at shifting blame from himself back onto his accuser. The classic "poor me" defense again, first cousin to the

"devil-made-me-do-it" theory of criminal behavior.

"The woman charging me with Battery (Rice) is the same woman who less than a month earlier had tried to set me up for a Rape charge," one twelve-page, handwritten harangue began.

"This whole Battery thing came about as a result of her coming to my place of residence, and then refusing to leave, after I asked her several times to do just that, for obvious reasons.

"The last time she was at my house I was accused of Raping her and I certainly didn't want her there alone with me again...

"But she refused to leave, even though my room-mate, (the person she had come to see) was just across the street.

"So after asking her twice, the third time I told her 'I wanted her out and I would give her to ten, then put her out.'

"Again she refused to leave...

"Keep in mind, here I am alone in my own place, with the woman who had just tried to have me arrested for Rape. As soon as I touched her arm she started pulling my hair, scratching my face, and hitting me.

"As I pulled her to the door, it was quite a scrap...

"At the time all this was going on Rice was abusing both alcohol and drugs (Valiums).

"Myself I've seen her take four or five Valiums at a time, and also just before this Battery incident she had admitted herself to a psychologic unit of a hospital as attempted suicide...

"It was a Monday night and I was laying in my room watching a Monday night football game when there was a knock on the door.

"Answering I said who is it? and a voice I assumed to be my room-mate's steady girl friend Suzanne, said 'Me.'

"Thinking it was Suzanne I yelled for her to come in and expected her to come by and say hello, as she usually did.

"After a few minutes of nobody coming to say hello, I came out into the living room and who is sitting on my couch but Rice, the woman who the last time she was in my house, had tried to have me arrested for Raping her.

"Need I say that had I known it was her at the door, there is no way she ever would have gotten into the house...

117

"The reasons Rice was so hot to get me out of her way...are that she was trying to break up Ted and his girl friend so she (Rice) could get back with Ted, who she (Rice) had lived with before.

"Rice and I too, were room-mates for about five weeks until I found out for myself that the warnings I had received about her being 'bad news' were true.

"At the time I moved in with Ted, Rice was also trying to get Ted to allow her brother...to move in with him, instead of me.

"Since this didn't work allowing Rice to establish a good foothold by having her brother living with Ted, and giving her access any time she pleased; I'm sure she saw me as an obstacle to her getting back with Ted, so decided to eliminate me, one way or another.

"To be honest I would much rather this be settled without having to go to court.

"I'm working full time and attending H.C.C. (Hillsborough Community College) and I have a very important National Registry Test (Radiology) in October that I need to give my full attention."

In another letter addressed to the presiding judge, Don Castor, Long poured out his vitriol on the justice system in general and Suzette Rice in particular.

"I want to say that I feel really taken advantage of by the judicial system...It's not fair and I'm sure you have to agree I did all I could do...and it was up to the system to do their part.

"They did not!

"To be honest, I am very angry about this whole thing.

"You were wrong, and this whole thing is just another of Rices schemes like her 'Rape' charge.

"She may have looked very sweet in court, but this girl takes three to four and five Valiums at a time, has O.D.'d at least twice that I know of, and worked for quite a while as a topless dancer.

"She's not the little quiet sweetheart she can appear to be.

"I want to know how to go about appealing this thing to get it in front of a jury?

"I'm no shirker and I accept responsibility for my actions, but you are wrong to believe that I purposely

hurt Rice. I didn't!...Would there be any way to maybe put us both on a polygraph?"

Apparently, the letters touched a nerve in Judge Castor.

It was an otherwise forgettable misdemeanor case, like thousands of others that came before him, but on September 26, Castor responded to Long:

"Although you do not appear to specifically request that I do so, I have treated your letter as a Motion for a New Trial, and scheduled a hearing on the motion for October 7."

Bobby Joe didn't make it to the hearing. He informed Judge Castor that "...I was hospitalized Oct 6th thru Oct 22nd for a slipped disc in my back. Surgery was performed at this time. When it rains it pours."

In a letter to the new judge assigned to the retrial, Bobby Joe continued to rail against Suzette Rice's character and to protest his own innocence:

"I want to emphasize that I committed no crime, and was completely within my rights, both legally and morally, when I went to remove this person from my house, after they refused to leave, several times, and then started attacking me as I was putting them out...the only reason they refused to leave was that they 'were not going to be bullied by me...'

"The woman was desperate to get back together with my room-mate, who was at that time very serious about another woman...and she saw me as a barrier that had to be removed...

"I lived with this woman, even after being warned about her by her brother in law and sister...and shortly after I moved out she started dancing at a local topless club, and only just recently had a court appearance for lewd & lascivious behavior after being arrested for nude dancing.

"Okay, maybe legally all this doesn't really count, but when she appeared before Judge Castor and looked so sweet, and talked so sweet, I know how it looked to the judge.

"But that's not the case, and I really got the short end. I'm no angel, but as I said before, I did nothing criminal, and I want a chance to clear myself in this matter."

Bobby Joe Long did get his day in court—February 6, 1984—and, as he predicted, was cleared of the charge. With a lawyer from the public defender's office representing him, Long convinced the jury to acquit him. Among the witnesses appearing on behalf of Suzette Rice were Hugh and Susan Connor from across the street. Hugh Connor testified that, yes, he did see Long strike the woman. The jury didn't believe him.

In amazement, the Connors watched as Bobby Joe stopped to laugh in Suzette Rice's face as he swagger from the courtroom. "I watched that man walk out of court and thought, what kind of justice is this?" Susan Connor recalled. She said she turned to some members of the jury as they exited the courtroom and warned: "The next time you see this man, it'll be for murder. You don't know what you're turning loose."

Years later, while twisting the truth to shade his version of the events, Bobby Joe boasted to Dr. Norris about how effective his letter-writing campaign had been. "The judge took it as a motion," Long told Norris. "and he granted it. The charges were later dropped because I had witnesses who told the police that the woman had asked me to take her back home and had come over in the first place looking for sex. She was a whore anyway, and once that came out, the whole charge was thrown out of court."

Even though he convinced the jury that he was innocent of the assault charge, Bobby Joe Long continued to harbor a deep and bitter rage against Suzette Rice. If the murder task force hadn't caught up with him when it did, there's a real possibility, police believed, that Suzette Rice, would have wound up raped, strangled, and tossed in a roadside ditch along with the other "cunts, sluts, and whores" Bobby Joe Long hated so passionately.

But that still wasn't the end of the Rice affair. On November 19, 1984, three days after Bobby Joe was picked up for murder, Suzette went back to civil court and slapped a $5,000 personal-damage suit against Long, citing both the alleged rape and the simple assault for which he was found innocent as grounds.

▲   ▲   ▲

Then I was living with a girl for about three weeks in Tampa and it turned out to be a real pig, And, its such a long complicated story. Three days after I was arrested (for murder) I got a summons from her. She was going to sue me for $5,000. I don't know, ha, ha, ha. What difference does it make. I'm worried about $5,000? Give me a break. But you know that just shows you what kind of a broad this was, ok. And, that happened just prior to my going to Los Angeles in `80, I guess. No, It was later, it was about `81. (Bobby Joe Long/CBS News Interview)

▲   ▲   ▲

On January 27, 1985, Hillsborough County homicide detective Lee "Pops Baker" met with the thirty-four-year-old Suzette Rice at her home on North Ola. "She has not had any contact with Long since 11/81," Baker noted in his report on the meeting. "Advised Suzette her name had been mentioned in some correspondence since Long's arrest and I gave her my business card with instructions to contact me, or our department, immediately if someone contacted her about Long or someone became suspicious in her surroundings. She advised she would contact her attorney..."

▲   ▲   ▲

A LETTER FROM BOBBY

There's one cunt here in Tampa I'd give my balls to "Do." Her times gonna come, some day, some how! Its Suzette Rice [Address and phone number.] She has a kid about ten or eleven, and if I know her a guy is living there. Details? SLOW — PAINFUL — and I want her to know who initiated it! This bitch fucked me over royal, and she was on my list. Hey, a year, two years, five years, she was on my list for sure.

121

Your people do her and I'll know this is for real. Shes about five feet, seven inches,and 125-130 lbs Black hair, Brown eyes. Has American Indian blood in her. She's my best buddies sister in law, and he warned me about her but I didn't listen. Remember that cunts name—Suzette Rice. It would make my day! I'll be checking the obituary, I just want her dead and to know I'm involved "before" she dies. Fuck her for a week, first tear her ass up; I don't care as long as she dies! SLOW!

This bitch has fucked me over every possible way, cost me a lot of money, a lot of agrevation and headaches. Even tried to set me up for a rape, one I didn't do... and about the third day I was in here I got served papers for a civil suit by her for an undisclosed amount, but over five grand. I've been thru two trials for battery, not guilty both times, though I did knock the fuck out of her throwing her out my house, and she did every thing she could to get them to go on the rape, but luckily other people were there & saw what really happened...If these guys do her ass "Great!" If I get out of here, one day, I will! Nobodys ever fucked me around like this bitch, I almost killed a guy because of her, and she pulls all this.

Reading that cunts obituary, man I'd be high for a month.

▲   ▲   ▲

Between the time he was charged with assault in 1981 and his acquittal in early 1984, Bobby Joe Long was not just sitting around. During that interim, he was on the move, from Florida to West Virginia to California and back again. In November, 1981, Long gathered up his belongings and headed for Kenova. Louella and Joe Long were there, married again—this time for good—and living in a modest L-shaped, one-story, frame house with black trim and black awnings near the Norfolk and Chesapeake Rail Yard. Now that she'd settled down for good, Louella was running a small

dress shop called Lou's Place; Joe, having seen the light, was managing a Christian book store. Back where it all began, Bobby Joe found temporary haven from the woes besetting him in Florida. It also gave him time to seriously pursue a lifelong ambition to become a commercial diver by signing up for a $9,000 course at the Commercial Diving Center operated by Oceaneering International, in Wilmington, California. This was heavy-duty stuff—a rugged, bell saturation mixed-gas course; six months of tough instruction, sometimes twelve-hour days, in the classroom, in the training tanks, in open water.

One of those enrolled at the school while Long was there was

Brad McCormick from Vancouver, British Columbia. After Bobby Joe was arrested for the murders, Detective David Reichert of Kings County, Washington, one of the manhunters whose experience with serial killers included two of America's most infamous, Ted Bundy and the Green River Killer, drove over to Vancouver to interview McCormick as a favor to his Florida counterparts.

"I met Bob Long on the first day [at the dive school]," McCormick told Reichert, "but about mid-April, he moved in with us in our apartment and I got to know him better.

"He had a strange habit of keeping a selection of knives in his room...about five or six knives. Some were just plain buck knives, but others were a switchblade and a stiletto and a big Bowie knife. He constantly carried this one stiletto on him all the time, ate his steak with it without a fork. Used to pick his teeth with it. Constantly playing with it.

"He also had another unusual habit. He was constantly writing letters to lonely girls through ads, pen-pal ads basically. On a normal day I think he'd receive four or five letters from girls. On good days, he'd get anywhere from ten to twelve. These letters, most were from inside the United States, but there was also a lot of Asian ones, Guam, maybe, but mostly from the Philippines and Hawaii...I thought it was a strange habit. After classes, he'd go back to his room and write letters or go out by himself and ride his bike, a Suzuki Three-Fifty. He never talked about where he went, but I think he stayed around the Long Beach area mostly. I knew

123

very little of his movements at night, cause I never encouraged him to hang around with us...He spent an awful lot of time locked in his room writing letters to his penpals. Writing letters and writing letters and writing more letters.

"I didn't know what his motive was, besides being lonely or wanting attention, but after seeing the report on him on CBS, I thought there might be a chance he was carrying on the homicides in California by contacting these lonely women as a way of finding his victims.

"He dated," McCormick said. "He was always on the hunt and stuff, I guess for girls. I only saw him with one or two, and they seemed to be very quick little romances. He dated a girl where we lived at ... in Long Beach. She was from New York. Her name was Janice but that was only for about a week. According to Bob there was always something that wasn't working out right, and he was constantly dumping them or they just weren't satisfactory, but there was always seemed to be a string of girls.

"He had a definite attraction to women, no doubt about that, but deep down I think he held a lot of contempt for them, just complete contempt. That was because of his wife. He couldn't have her back and that triggered a great amount of anger inside of him. He was always looking for conquests and after he was done, just called 'em bitches. He used to brag about picking up women, how he'd score. He was always trying to procure some, uh, sexual satisfaction. Sometimes he'd be happy about it, some new girl he'd met, but within forty-eight hours it had all fallen through. She was a bitch, or there was something wrong with her, some deficiency that didn't fit his, uh, needs. There was always, always someone sorta new, but we never saw them."

▲   ▲   ▲

A LETTER FROM BOBBY

The reason I'm not being charged with a lot more shit than I am four year statute of limitations. That leaves three or four in Pinellas, three in

124

Orange County they could hit me with, one in W. Va.—
she was something else, one in Kentucky, five in
California. I don't think they'll tie me in to the
ones out-of-state at all. I'll tell you about these
two— twelve-year-olds and the fourteen-year-old in
Cal some time. There was another one out there—what
a hot bitch, she practically raped me—closest I ever
came to getting caught. It was delicious though!

▲   ▲   ▲

Exactly how much truth and how much fancy there was in
Long's boasting about his sexual conquests, only Bobby Joe knows
for sure. He was secretive about his life away from school and
classmates, further evidence of his ability to compartmentalize different areas of his life and keep them separated. However, given
that a pattern of self-aggrandizing behavior was basic to his nature,
the odds favor fancy.

Brad McCormick continued: "There was only one time that I
saw any violent behavior, and that was when he was talking to his
parents in West Virginia. Someone was bothering him beside the
telephone booth and he said he was ready to pull his knife and do
the guy, 'til his mother on the other end of the telephone pleaded
with him to take it easy, Bob. And I know he really hated Spanish,
Hispanic people, especially coming from the Fort
Lauderdale/Miami area. He had a great hatred for Hispanics,
Cubans, Haitians, Puerto Ricans, and anyone with a combination of
black. He used racist terms all the time. He just figured they were
a threat because a lot of them carried knives, too.

"I tried to talk to Bob Long the least amount possible. I always
felt that I'd better be sleeping with one eye open because of his
knives, his mannerisms with his knives. It always left me a little
uncomfortable. He moved in during April and at the start of July,
me and this other guy who was sharing the apartment, we asked
him to leave. We found it was too uncomfortable living with Bob.
His habits of carrying knives made me very uncomfortable. [The

125

other roommate, Jeff Milton, a twenty-two-year-old Oregonian, shrugged off Long's odd behavior as "...typical redneck stuff."]

"I never saw him drunk, but he smoked pot occasionally, used to mellow him out a little bit if anything." McCormick continued. "He wasn't hyper, but he could get irate, especially at school when he figured people were targeting him...He was a real loner. He was not quick of the tongue, but if he thought people were trying to screw him up it would be sort of a vendetta with him, like really a hate mission would come out of him. Anybody came in his way, he was plotting one way or the other to get even with them even if it was the smallest little thing. Like if guys would get there before him to get the diving equipment, he'd get really pissed off and say how he's gonna get even with this guy or that guy.

"I don't believe he had any close friends. He never regarded people as friends, just as foes. Like he had a real persecution complex that people were always trying to take advantage of him.

I remember he was upset about being shafted or something at his old job as an X-ray technologist and wanted to get away from the U.S. scene, go overseas, something with a little excitement.

"I'm not sure if he completed school. I think he quit just one or two weeks before graduation. He didn't study very much at all. He sorta had a piss-on-it attitude. Also, on a lot of the diving, the basic projects, he didn't score too well and that got him frustrated. A lot of them were two-man projects and he tended to blame it on his partner when he (Bob) didn't do well. Turned it around, find someone else to blame all the time.

"He wanted to get into commercial diving, but with the recession and the glut in oil-field diving, there's thousands of people being pumped out by the diving schools, but not many jobs," McCormick concluded.

A reporter for the Tampa Tribune tracked down a fellow Floridian, from Indian River Shores, on the Gulf Coast, who attended the school at the same time Bobby Joe was there. The impression Long made on twenty-year-old Mark Nash was anything but flattering. Bobby Joe Long was arrogant, immature, bad tempered and a bullshitter who didn't fool anybody, especially

126

when he started blowing off about a teenage girlfriend who was a bondage freak and who had seduced him into tying her up and fucking her. "Bob Long, which was what he told us to call him, had what I'd call a caustic personality," Nash recalled. "He was the guy who was always playing jokes on other people, but nobody else thought they were funny. He used to talk all the time about a thirteen or fourteen year old girl he said he met in Long Beach. He said he tied her up and...that she was really kinky, begged him for sex. Everybody has their quirks and in a lot of ways, Bob didn't stand out that much. I never thought anything like this [the murders] would happen."

When Tampa and Hillsborough Country investigators retraced Bobby Joe Long's movements prior to the start of the murder spree, their attention naturally focused on the six months he spent in Southern California, where serial rapes and unsolved killings are indigenous to the scenery. Did Bobby Joe Long resume his unique persona as the Ad Man Rapist, with the vast metropolitan L.A. area spread out before him as a giant smorgasbord of potential victims? Were there raped and strangled bodies of street hookers left rotting in the California desert?

"We don't know and Bobby Joe isn't talking," commented one member of the Tampa Task Force. "It's possible there were other victims before ours, maybe in California, West Virginia, other places in Florida, maybe even in Kentucky. We always felt that the ligatures, the methods he used to kill our victims were too sophisticated to be the work of a beginner. He had to have learned all that somewhere, probably by trial and error."

From California, Bobby Joe journeyed back to Kenova for what he hoped would be a short stay. It stretched into a ten-month black hole of disappointment and frustration, into which all his dreams and ambitions of becoming a commercial diver vanished. Long eagerly looked forward to landing a job on an offshore oil rig, maybe in some far-off place like Saudi Arabia, where the pay was fantastic and the adventures unlimited. From the fall of 1982 through the spring of 1983, Bobby Joe cranked out application

after application. And, as the months dragged by, he watched with increasing dismay as his parents' mailbox filled up with rejection after rejection. As the disappointments mounted, Bobby Joe began to brood more than usual, spending hours alone in his small bedroom, or stretched out on the living-room sofa in front the television, lost in the banal fantasy of soaps and reruns.

"He hated this place," Joe Long later recalled. "He'd break your heart, not for the things he said, but for the things he didn't say. We tried to boost his spirits but we just couldn't reach him."

The gloomy West Virginia winter was the perfect backdrop for Long's morose moods. By nature, Bobby Joe had always been a loner; but now, isolated as he was in the one place in the world he loathed above all others, with his dream of commercial diving slowly fading like green leaves in fall, Long sank deeper and deeper into his angry blue funk. Cindy had remarried; his kids were growing more remote by the day; the warmth of Florida seemed far away; and he continued to be afflicted by the headaches, wild mood swings, and seething sex drive that had plagued him since the motorcycle crash.

In that frame of mind, a blowup was inevitable. And it came in mid-November, when Bobby Joe was arrested for destroying private property. A man whose wife had worked for Louella in the dress shop came to the Longs' home complaining that his wife was owed some back pay. Louella disagreed, and the two began shouting at each other. Bobby Joe jumped into the middle of the fracas. The confrontation moved from the house to the street, where Bobby Joe shoved the man and ripped a side mirror off his truck. Kenova police were soon knocking on the door with a warrant charging Bobby Joe with assault. About a month later, in a hearing before a judge, Bobby Joe was acquitted of assaulting the man, but convicted of destruction of private property. He was fined fifty dollars and paid eighteen [dollars] in costs.

Bobby Joe may have gotten off so lightly because the judge, Garland Wilson, was an old family friend of the Longs.

"He was a handsome-looking fellow, just the nicest-looking fellow you ever met in your life," Wilson said later in an interview.

"Just a gentleman. He had good manners. I've never tried anybody nicer."

In February, 1983, after trying unsuccessfully to land a commercial diving job, Bobby Joe reluctantly took a temporary job as a diagnostic radiologic technician at the Veterans Administration Hospital in nearby Huntington, a few miles upriver from Kenova.

Lea Ann Caines was Bobby Joe's supervisor in the X-ray department. Unlike the women who supervised Long in his other radiology jobs, Lea Ann reported the two enjoyed a good working relationship. "He was a good worker, a polite person," she recalled.

Sometimes Long joined his co-workers at a nearby tavern for a couple of drinks after their shift ended. The only thing that stood out about those social gatherings was that Bobby Joe often complained about how much he disliked Kenova. "In fact," she recalled, "he kind of hated the hills of West Virginia. He missed Florida."

One of the hospital workers he became chums with was Debbie Canterbury. More than anyone else, the mind-numbing news that Bobby Joe Long was a rapist and murderer hit her with the impact of a sledge hammer. "He was the best friend I ever had," she said. "He gave me confidence. He loved his children. He was good to my children. He gave me moral support."

It was during the difficult period that Debbie and Bobby Joe drove to Florida together with the idea of finding jobs and putting the painful past behind them. When the pair returned to West Virginia, Debbie went back to work at the Veterans Center. Bobby Joe landed a job in the radiology department of the 174-bed Huntington Hospital. He started work on May 16, 1983.

On June 20th, he was fired.

Within days after he reported for work, hospital officials started hearing some disturbing gossip about their new employee. The rumors soon escalated into outraged complaints lodged by nearly a dozen female patients, who questioned the procedures that the burly, bushy-haired technician was subjecting them to in the isolation of the X-ray room.

"He involved himself in some unethical professional practices," Tom Wetzel, a hospital administrative assistant at the time, deli-

cately put it.

Those unethical practices including having women disrobe entirely, explaining that it was necessary to get a good X-ray, and taking unneeded X-rays of anatomies that had nothing to do with the patients' disorders.

"There had been some allegations that he perhaps in X-rays of female patients was X-raying areas that might not be involved," Wetzel continued, adding that there was such a "wealth of evidence" that the charges were indeed true, that Long didn't protest his dismissal and left quietly. "He came here as an unknown and left as an unknown," Wetzel said.

Despite the cloud under which he left Huntington Hospital, Bobby Joe soon returned to Florida bearing a letter of recommendation from the Veterans Administration hospital in Huntington, dated April 11, 1983, stating that Long had shown a "good working relationship with his coworkers" and that his "cooperativeness was excellent." He pulled out of Kenova over the long Fourth of July holiday weekend, driving the red 1978 Dodge Magnum with the spotless white leather interior that Joe and Louella bought for him. On July 6, 1983, he reported for new employee orientation at the Humana Hospital in Brandon. His hours were parttime, filling in for the regular X-ray technicians on weekends, which meant working two double shifts. When he quit ten months later, on March 30, 1984, Bobby Joe listed as his reasons for leaving: "No chance for adv. (advancement), too exhausting."(Other than confirming Long's dates of employment there, officials at Humana would not disclose the circumstances of his leaving, nor any other details of his work record, when reporters contacted them after Long was arrested for the murders.)

The job at Humana marked a significant turning point for Bobby Joe. He fell in love but was rebuffed. And that rejection, he has since implied, was the match that lit the murder fuse. Or it may just have been an excuse he latched on to to justify the horror that spewed out of him. In any case, Bobby Joe insisted that he became romantically involved with an attractive, dark-haired nurse at the hospital--romantic, at least, from his point of view. The nurse

denied their relationship had advanced much beyond the hand-holding stage. But they did date and while they were together, Bobby Joe Long and Bonnie Switzer° formed what was certainly one of the oddest of odd couplings.

Bonnie was thirty years old, and a born-again Christian who was so devout in her religious beliefs that when Bobby Joe took her out to restaurants she would "witness" to fellow diners and pass out pamphlets that expounded her Christian beliefs, or so he told Louella in an excited phone call to Kenova announcing his new relationship. For people as irreligious as the Longs, such overt devoutness was unsettling. "Sometimes he didn't know how to handle it," Louella said. "But he was so crazy about her that he started going to services with her. It shocked me that he attended church with her." his mother said.

But the calls home to talk about his new-found love began to taper off. Finally, a somber-voiced Bobby Joe telephoned Louella to tell her that the relationship was finished. He said he caught Bonnie out with another man (the same reason he gave when he and Cindy divorced, Louella recalled,) which crushed him because he thought he found a loyal, devoted woman at last.

"He was brokenhearted and lost," Louella said. "He just felt life wasn't worth living. He told me, 'Mom, I can't find any decent girls in the world. They've all gone bad.' It just broke him up.

▲   ▲   ▲

When I went to LA, I was out there for about a year and then when I left there I went to West Virginia to stay with some family for a while trying to get, what I went to LA for, I went to go and do some diver training, some commercial and when I left there I went back to West Virginia to stay with my family I had resumes out all over the world for a diving job...unfortunately that was right when the oil glut was hitting... the rigs were closing down, there wasn't any diving jobs. If I wanted to get a job I had to go to Saudi Arabia or China or you know, I really didn't want to do that. So ... I was in West Virginia till about the middle of '83 then I moved back to

Tampa I got a job back in Tampa in a hospital--X-ray technician. And ahhh, I moved back down there for that. And things were going pretty good, you know I liked that job, it was a good schedule. I worked weekends and was off Monday through Fridays. And at that time my whole priority in things was just to kick back and relax...and just work on a suntan. A sun tan...and racquetball. That was my main priorities in life...And ahh, you know I was dating...quite a lot. And ..., you know, that brings me to something else--a lot of people think that I was doing these things (rapes and murders) cause I'm some kind of ..., freak who couldn't get a girlfriend or couldn't, you know what I'm saying? But, that's garbage, you know. Anybody that knows me knows just what garbage that is. So that has nothing to do with it, you know.... I hear how I hate women. Maybe something inside of me does, I don't know. But I know that the guy sitting here talking to you right now doesn't, you know. I don't have no problems sitting here talking to you. (Bobby Joe Long/CBS News Interview)

▲   ▲   ▲

By the time Bobby Joe was arrested for murder, Bonnie Switzer had taken a leave of absence from her Humana Hospital job and returned to her home in the Midwest, where she planned to undergo surgery. Detective David Wolf finally tracked her down for an interview, but not without surmounting roadblocks Bonnie's highly protective friends and colleagues threw in his way. She was in a panic that the press would learn about her and jump to the conclusion that she was the serial killer's lover. Such exposure would destroy her, she feared. Detective Wolf first spoke to Bonnie by phone and arranged for a more extensive interview when she returned to Florida. Wolf's initial report stated:

"Personal data on Switzer is in my files, such as her Tampa address and her phone number in [the Midwestern city].. She is still an employee of the Brandon Humana Hospital and is on a medical leave of absence. She has agreed to an in-depth interview upon her return as to personal data on suspect Long. Bonnie is

fearful of press exposure and her friends and family are very protective of her at this time...Bonnie was Long's girlfriend from
approximately August 1983 through August 1984 by her own
admission." When she returned to the Tampa area several weeks
later, Bonnie told Detective Wolf that when she first met Bobby
Joe Long, he was living in the Turks Cap Apartments in Brandon.
He then moved in with Ted and Susie Gensel in the Forest Hills
area of Tampa.

According to Detective Wolf's notes on the interview, Bonnie
Switzer was worried that she might have a dozen or more pieces of
stolen jewelry that Bobby Joe had showered on her during the
spring and summer months of 1984. She said she even questioned
him about how he could afford such obviously expensive items
when he didn't have a job. He never gave her a straight answer, and
always managed to change the subject whenever she brought it up.
Detective Wolf noted: "Bonnie was able to describe some of the
jewelry as follows: (1) diamond ring, size six or seven, small and thin
in appearance, approximately 1 carat stone—cut unknown, in yellow
gold ring flush mount. (2) earrings, pierced, small green stone in
yellow gold style mount. (3) earrings, diamond (small), in yellow
gold style mount. (4) wristwatch, ladies, "Armatron" brand quartz
style, yellow gold style band, no numbers on face, no second hand,
face is grayish-white in color, back of watch is silver or chrome steel,
two numbers inscribed on back are 25-2582 and 32002. (5) necklace, sterling silver, approximately sixteen inches in length,
turquoise cross charm in metallic mount. (6) necklace, gold chain
with heart-shaped charm has three chips in middle. (7) bracelet,
thick yellow gold band with cameo charm, cameo looks like clear
plastic, bracelet has safety chain."

Hillsborough County police speculated that the love gifts Bobby
Joe was bestowing on his deeply religious girlfriend were actually
the loot that, as the Ad Man Rapist, he'd stolen from women he
brutally assaulted and sexually abused with unspeakable cruelty.
That supposition became fact when Bonnie Switzer met with police
from neighboring Pinellas County in the State Attorney's Office on
April 12, 1985. Pinellas Sheriff's Detective Terry Rhodes was the

133

lead investigator on a particularly vile and bestial rape that occurred in the Palm Harbor community in March, 1984. Lynn Newell°, a young mother, had been raped and sodomized in front of her small children. The invader, who fit Bobby Joe Long's description and his signature classified-ad M.O., got away with household items and several valuable pieces of jewelry.

Bonnie Switzer told Detective Rhodes she broke-off the relationship, which, she insisted, was a casual one and never serious or romantic, at least on her part. Bobby Joe started bringing her gifts of jewelry in the early part of 1984. When she asked where he bought the items, he usually replied vaguely, "Here and there" or "At the store." She also noticed several new additions (paintings, figurines, and the like) to his apartment when she visited him, but got the same vague responses when she asked about them. Long was also very evasive when it came to talking about what he did with his time when they weren't together.

Of the twenty-one pieces of jewelry the woman turned over to investigators, Detective Rhodes was particularly interested in an unusual 14K yellow gold ring with a thin antique band. The ring—with a crescent moon setting of pearls, circled by a setting of opals with one opal missing—was a family heirloom, handed down from Lynn Newell's great-grandmother. Bonnie said that Bobby Joe came to her apartment in the spring of 1984 and presented the ring with a romantic flourish. She took the ring, but admitted she suspected that Long was stealing the jewelry from his ex-wife when he went to South Florida to visit his children.

Bonnie also mentioned that there were times before the breakup when they talked about the scary reports of murder victims, all women, who were turning up with alarming regularity throughout Hillsborough County. The newspapers and television were talking about a serial killer, some kind of sex fiend on the loose, and warning women to beware of strangers. The news usually left Bonnie shaken that such evil could exist in the world. At such times, Bobby Joe would put his arm around her shoulder and soothe her fears. "There are just a lot of sick people out there,"

he'd say, and advise her to be more careful when she was alone and not be so nice to strangers. She would never have dreamed that the boyfriend who held her so tenderly was, in fact, a modern-day Jack the Ripper who was busily butchering hookers in between their chaste dates and twice-weekly church services.

Bobby Joe Long's last official work day at Brandon Humana was March 30, 1984. (The previous month he had successfully defended himself in the retrial of the Suzette Rice assault case.) On April 3, he applied at Tampa General Hospital for a job as a licensed X-ray technician at a salary of $300 per week.

On April 5, Long was picked up and charged with aggravated battery in connection with an attempt to abduct a Tampa woman. The incident was so bizarre and reckless that police are convinced the woman involved clearly was a targeted rape/murder victim who was lucky to be alive. In hindsight, the message is as bright as neon at night: The monster locked up inside Bobby Joe Long was straining to be free. A breakout was looming.

▲   ▲   ▲

A LETTER FROM BOBBY

I was in a fuckin Jaguar with some cunt driving when she flipped it and we slid about one hundred feet down the road on the fuckin roof. Can I tell you I was out of that fucker before it stopped sliding. I've totalled two cars & one motorcycle, had three milder car wrecks. Just so much shit I always said I'd be lucky to reach thirty. Lots of the boys I grew up with aren't with us anymore. Okay I've made thirty-one, now I'm shooting for forty.

▲   ▲   ▲

Shortly after 11:30 p.m.on April 5, Hillsborough County deputies responded to calls from several citizens who had witnessed a car crash on Busch Boulevard, just west of Twin Lake in

135

the Carrollwood section of northwest Tampa. As they discovered when they arrived on the scene, they had much more on their hands than a routine traffic investigation. The dust was still settling around the demolished frame of a classic 1960 Jaguar roadster. Traffic was backed up on both sides of the road. The glare of headlights illuminated a knot of people gathered protectively around a bruised, hysterical woman lying on the grassy swale.

Deputy D.J. Whittemore was the first officer on the scene. He calmed the woman down enough to get her story.

A few minutes earlier, Mary Ann Hicks related, she had been enroute from a business meeting, northbound on Dale Mabry Highway, headed towards her home on White Trout Lane. It was late, but the forty year old woman still had one more stop to make— at Eckerd's Drug Store in the Carrollwood Shopping Center, to pick up school supplies for her daughter.

She was waiting for a light to change at Dale Mabry and Waters when a driver in the next lane motioned to her to roll down her window. "That's a great car," the man said admiringly. "What is it?" Mary Hicks smiled. The Jag was, in fact, in mint condition and she was very proud of it. People were always asking her about it when she took it out, so she wasn't surprised that the man in the red Dodge parked beside her asked if he could take a closer look. "I've got to stop at Eckerd's," she told the man. "Meet me up there."

The man followed her into the parking lot, got out and walked around the Jag a couple of times, asking what year it was and complimenting her on the amount of work that had obviously gone into restoring the car. Mary said that after a few minutes of conversation, she went inside, made her purchases, and returned to the parking lot. The man was still there. She recognized the signs. A real car nut. The Jag attracted them like flies.

"Look," he told her, "I'll probably never get another chance to ride in a car like this. Would you mind giving me a quick spin around the block?" Mary Hicks studied the man. He looked like a nice guy; well dressed in a brown leather jacket, tan jeans and boots; polite and friendly. The guy obviously was a car lover from the kinds of questions he asked about the Jag. He didn't look or act

136

threatening. What the hell, she thought. It'll only take a couple of minutes.

She told him to climb in, and pulled out of the parking lot, heading back south on Dale Mabry to the first major intersection.

The street running east from Dale Mabry was Busch Boulevard, but westbound from Dale Mabry the name changed to Gunn Highway as it angled northwest into Hillsborough County. Almost immediately after passing Dale Mabry, the landscape on either side of Gunn Highway changed drastically from heavily urbanized to rural countryside, covered by moss-draped live oaks. Isolated housing developments were beginning to spring up along Gunn Highway, but it was mostly dark woods and empty fields.

At the light, the man pointed west. "Let's go that way," he suggested. Mary Hicks shook her head. She knew how secluded it got the further west you went on Gunn Highway. So far the guy was no problem, but she didn't trust him that much. Instead, she turned east onto Busch Boulevard, drove for about a mile, then turned around and headed back. The man was still talking about cars as he reached inside his jacket and pulled out a long-barrel revolver and pointed it at her.

Oh god! she thought. He's going to rape me and steal the car. Instinctively, before the man could tell her what he wanted, she violently jerked the wheel to the right and then quickly whipped it back to the left. The speeding roadster skidded sideways on the pavement and flipped over, rolling three times before coming to rest in the middle of the eastbound lane. Incredibly, neither Mary nor her gun-toting passenger was seriously injured. When they crawled from the wreckage, the man stood up, still with the gun in his hand, pointing it at her. But other motorists were pulling over and jumping out to lend assistance. Mary started screaming, and the man turned and ran west on Busch.

By the time she finished telling her story, backup officers had arrived. This looks like maybe an attempted kidnaping, Deputy Whittemore told them. Deputies fanned out to search for the suspect, now on foot. Within minutes, Deputies Robert Mesa and John Lorenz spotted a man matching the description running north

on Dale Mabry from Busch Boulevard. Bobby Joe Long had made
it more than a mile from the accident site and was only yards away
from the safety of his Dodge, still parked at the Eckerd's store,
when the officers stopped him. Although he carried no identification, Long gave them his correct name and said he lived just a half
dozen blocks from the accident scene. After a few minutes of questioning, Long admitted that, yeah, he was in the car, but denied
pulling a gun. He said the women went crazy when he asked her
for a little pussy and flipped the Jag.

Bobby Joe added that his I.D. was in his wallet which he had
left under the front-seat carpet of his car. When Lorenz reached in
the car to get the wallet, he noticed an empty zipper-type gun case
stuck between the driver's seat and the console. Long acknowl-
edged that the case was his, but said he'd sold the gun a few days
earlier to help pay for his car. The deputies took Long back to the
accident site, where Mary Hicks positively identified him as the
gunman. The gun was never found, but Long was arrested and
charged with aggravated assault.

On June 14, 1984, two days after signing a loyalty oath and
receiving a hospital photo-identification badge, Bobby Joe started
work at Tampa General Hospital. He was assigned to work four
ten-hour shifts each Thursday through Sunday.

The following week, TGH officials asked the Hillsborough
County Sheriff's Office to run a records check on several new
hires, Long among them. The report that came back showed
Long's 1981 no-contest plea on the obscene materials charge, plus
the information that he was facing charges of assaulting Mary Ann
Hicks in April.

On July 17, 1984, three months after the aborted attack on
Mary Hicks, Circuit Judge J. Rogers Padgett sentenced Long to six
months probation and ordered him to pay $1,500 in restitution for
damage to the Jaguar. Padgett withheld adjudication of guilt, thus
approving terms which had been negotiated by the State Attorney's
Office. Ten days later, Padgett denied Long's motion to prohibit his
probation officer from informing Tampa General about his record.

"His performance had been satisfactory at the time when these

charges came to light," a hospital spokesman said. "His references were very positive. And termination is not routine when someone is charged and not convicted. We did not perceive it [the assault charge disposition] as a finding of guilt."

Despite the negative reports, Bobby Joe Long held onto his job at TGH until September 27, when he was let go. Hospital officials insisted Long was fired during his "probationary status period" because he did not possess an "advanced certificate" in X-ray technology from the state Department of Health and Rehabilitative Services. When he applied at TGH, it was for a position as "Diagnostic Radiologic Tech." But he was hired as "Senior Radiologic Technologist." His lack of the required advanced license was given as reason for his termination.

In early October, Long filed a protest against Tampa General Hospital with the Florida Department of Labor and Employment Security. In an order issued November second (less than two weeks before a score of cops grabbed Bobby Joe Long outside the theater) a hearing officer found that "no evidence was presented to show that [Long's] discharge was caused by any condition or circumstance which could be construed as misconduct connected with work."

The officer ordered that his unemployment benefits be reinstated. But before the state could cut the check, the issue of Bobby Joe Long's employment or unemployment became a moot point.

He was now a permanent "guest" of the State of Florida.

And Death Row inmates are not required to work.

▲ ▲ ▲

A LETTER FROM BOBBY

Like I said "Life" just don't cut it. twenty-five years mandatory—just one of those I don't think I could handle. I guess you know that Miami, Lauderdale, Orlando, Clearwater, and New Port Richy are all just waiting to see what happens before they

139

Bobby Joe: In The Mind of a Monster

even fuck with me.   They all have charges! There're
more in California and maybe even W.Va. and Kentucky
"if" they tied me to them, which I'm sure they have,
same M.O. & description.   There was a shooting down
in San Diego, the guy was ripping off some cunt I
know, Drugs. I don't know if he died or not, but I
know I got at least 2 .22 hollow points in him,
maybe more, never heard anything about it, I think
he lives in Mexico, got taken care of or died there.
Who cares. So you see even if some miracle came
along and I walked away from all this (aint never
gonna happen) they'd be waiting outside the door and
nail me on this other shit.   Which would easily add
up to the rest of my life behind bars.

▲   ▲   ▲

140

Part Three

THE AD MAN RAPIST

A LETTER FROM BOBBY

```
    I've done em all, white, black, Korean,
Vietnamese, Japanese, and mexican, oh—Cubans too,
same as mexicans.
    A few of them got into it and even asked me if I
minded if they enjoyed it? I said go for it. I usu-
ally made them fuck me and made em talk to me. Damn
theres a lot of married women out there that are
miserable about their sex lives.
```

▲   ▲   ▲

In the days following Bobby Joe Long's arrest in Tampa on multiple counts of kidnaping, sexual battery, and murder, members of the multi-agency Task Force assembled to run the killer to ground, tracked down hundreds of the accused murderer's family members, associates, fellow workers, and friends in an effort to fill in some of the baffling holes in the massive investigation.

When "Pops" Baker finished jotting down Ted Gensel's account of how Long often had expensive gifts for Gensel and his wife, Susan, Baker closed his notebook and prepared to leave. Then Gensel offhandedly mentioned that he frequently overheard his old roommate calling people on the telephone about ads they'd placed in the paper. Stuff for sale— bedroom furniture, TVs, an old couch. Frugal, that's what he was, shopping through the newspaper ads, looking to save a few bucks here and there.

"Bobby Joe," Gensel shrugged, "was always reading want ads."

141

▲   ▲   ▲

A LETTER FROM BOBBY

How it worked was the standard process I used in about thirty to forty of these things in three states. It was really foul-proof & if I'd just stuck with it & not gone this cunts way--killing people, I'd still be out there. It was like a hunt. Really!

I would pick certain ads in the local paper of wherever I'd driven, I never worked in the county I lived in, and go to the classified ads and look under furniture household items. Pick the ones with beds for sale or bedroom furniture for sale because in order to see the bed or the furniture, you would get a good chance to check the place out & and make sure it was just her, or her & very small kids & babies. This all started back in seventy-five or seventy-six and I'm telling you it was perfect. Never even came close to getting caught. For years I was referred to in the Miami Herald as the "Classified ad rapist," but I worked Dade, Broward, Palm Beach too, then moved up here & have hit Manatee, Pinellas & Orange counties. It worked in W. Va., California and Kentucky. It was so good I never should have switched! [To murder.]

Anyway it got to the point where I could scan the ads, and just by the way it was worded, know the approx age, naturally I wanted young ones, but sometimes the older ones would be good enough and they usually had nicer jewelry and more expensive shit. Mostly I did it for the "thrill," the "high."

So I'd go wherever I targeted, get a local paper, scan the ads, write down ten or fifteen numbers, go

142

to a pay phone, and start calling. If they sounded real old, fifty or more,I'd just hang up. If they were older but sounded good, (you can tell a lot about a woman on the phone by her voice & choice of words) I'd ask a lot of questions, get a little humor, see their reactions, their laughs—you can really tell a whole lot the way a woman laughs or doesn't laugh for that matter—and if they were "worthwhile" I'd get the address & make sure they were gonna be there.

I'd always hit early morning 9:30-10:00, husband & kids gone for hours, and eventually I worked up the routine to where I'd even know when the hubby was coming home, by saying "We really need this stuff fast." Lets say I like it and its what we're looking for, how soon would someone help me load it up?

By their answer (either my husband gets home around six, or well I'll be here all day) I knew pretty much what I was dealing with. So out of ten or fifteen numbers I'd have it narrowed down to three or four, usually "one" I'd put a star by, for the first & best sounding one. It was usually right on the money. This was one of three ways I used that were perfect. I'll tell you about the others some other time.

▲   ▲   ▲

Police throughout the three-county area of South Florida knew all about Bobby Joe Long's peculiar fascination with the want ads. What they didn't know, until after he was arrested, was his true identity. They had their own colorful monikers for him: Ad Man Rapist, the Classified Ad Rapist. Same guy. Same M.O. Same viciousness that left scores of women emotionally, and often physically, scarred for life.

Serial rapists are frequently identified by the peculiar, quirky M.O.s they ritualistically follow when committing their crimes. There was the Pillowcase Rapist, for instance, who always covered his victim's head with her own pillow case while raping her; the Cape Man, known by his flowing black Batman cape; and the Polite Rapist, who was so solicitous of his victims' well being that he often bathed their tears away and brought them something to drink when he finished ravaging them.

In the late 1970s, another rapist with a highly specialized, signature MO began terrorizing women and young girls in their homes throughout a wide area of South Florida. The man gained entry to homes by answering classified advertisements placed in local newspapers, offering furniture or other household items for sale. He telephoned first and if a woman answered, the caller would make an appointment to look at the item, usually at midday when the victims would likely be alone. Once inside the home, the rapist threatened the women with a knife, bound them, violently raped them, forced them to perform oral sex acts, and looted the home before fleeing.

Sometimes the rapist altered his approach. On several occasions women were attacked, tied up, and raped in homes they had posted for sale. Realtor signs in the front yards were the bait that attracted the roving predator to that particular residence, usually during the morning hours when the men were likely at work and the women home alone. Homeowners eager to sell, know that potential buyers may come knocking on the door unannounced, without first making an appointment with the realtors.

The attacks became progressively more vicious and sadistic.

At least fifty such rapes were attributed to the Ad Man, but police suspected that many more went unreported. Then, just as quickly as they began, the string of violent home invasions and sexual assaults ended in South Florida. That was the good news. The bad news was, they resumed in a wide arch across central Florida, from Ocala down through Orlando and over to the heavily populated resort/retirement communities stretching along the Gulf Coast from St. Petersburg into the Tarpon Springs-New Port Richey area.

Only after he was arrested and charged as a serial killer did authorities discover that Bobby Joe Long was, in fact, the Ad Man Rapist who had preyed on women in their homes all across the Sunshine State for years. It's impossible to know how many victims are still suffering night terrors, broken marriages and shattered lives because of the Ad Man's rampage of terror and rape. Bobby Joe Long lost count himself. As is true with the majority of rapes, most of his victims chose to keep silent, given the archaic stigma still attached to the victims of the crime— an attitude that was even more prevalent two decades ago when Bobby Joe Long began stalking his neighbors' wives and daughters. With the hodgepodge of competitive police agencies throughout south Florida, there was little, if any, coordination of effort that might have established a pattern. As it was, each agency worked its own cases, kept its own counsel and, inevitably, buried the evidence of a single rapist beneath its own bureaucratic paper blitz. Many who worked the rapes have retired or moved on. For those who remain, there have been too many rapes and murders since then to remember a single twenty-year-old rape case. Names of the victims who did report the attacks are shielded by law, and since no one was ever officially identified and charged in the series of South Florida rapes, there's no way to cross-reference those victims with a perpetrator.

But not all were forgotten, ignored, or misplaced.

Ft. Lauderdale Detective Vicky Russo Benoit was assigned to the sex-crimes unit when Bobby Joe Long was terrorizing South Florida housewives. After Long's arrest, she participated in the law-enforcement symposium at Tampa, a gathering of sex offense and homicide cops from all over the Southeastern United States called to compare notes on unsolved rapes and murders.

"When Bobby Joe Long was operating around here we obviously didn't know who he was. Those victims who did report the rapes couldn't identify him." recalled Detective Benoit. "There were no fingerprints, no physical evidence to tie him to the crimes. We didn't have stuff like DNA to go on back then.

"After he was arrested for the murders, Long alluded to the fact that he might have committed some rapes in Broward County

but never would talk about them after that, so he was never charged, although the cases we were investigating were identical to the ones in the Tampa area. Plus the statute of limitations had run out on most if not all of them. Even though the victims we were able to find felt pretty sure he was the guy when we showed them Long's mug shots, we couldn't charge him. He managed to slip away from us. Thank God, the people over there in Tampa got him and got him good."

One South Florida victim did positively identify Bobby Joe Long as the man who attacked her, but the identification came years after the assault and was too late to help all the other victims. For Patricia Gordon*, the satisfaction of pointing a finger at the man who invaded the sanctity of her home was small consolation for the emotional terror and physical pain she was subjected to. Her case was typical of those attributed to the Ad Man Rapist in the late 1970s and early 1980s. It illustrates the distinctive M.O. that Bobby Joe Long was in the process of perfecting and utterly refutes all his protestations that "I never caused them any physical pain or terrified them."

The date was Friday, October 10, 1980. Casa Del Mar, on West Palmetto Park Road, is among the many, upscale developments that in the 1980s transformed the, unincorporated western reaches of Boca Raton into one of the coveted locations for thousands of nouveau riche. Patricia Gordon was upstairs in her home on Palmetto Circle North, next door to the Casa Del Mar office, doing some paperwork at her typewriter. The Gordons had recently put their home up for sale, and there were a hundred and one things to do to get the house ready for market while preparing to move to their new place.

Shortly after 11 a.m., the doorbell rang.

The man at the door was young, dark-haired, and good-looking. He was dressed in a blue t-shirt and jeans, not the usual fashionable designer couture favored by residents, but he smiled pleasantly and said he was interested in looking at her house. "My parents," he explained, "are moving down from Atlanta. They wanted to live in the West Boca area and they don't have much time to shop for a

new place. This is the kind of place they're looking for. Mind if I come in and look around?"

The young man was so polite and cordial that she wasn't concerned at all about letting him in, Patricia Gordon later explained to Palm Beach County sheriff's investigators. She said she gave him a quick tour of the downstairs portion of the townhouse and then led him upstairs. In the master bedroom, the man pointed to the vertical blinds covering the sliding-glass doors that opened onto a balcony. "How dark does it get in here when you close the blinds?" he asked. Patricia said she closed the blinds to show him, but when she turned around the man was reaching for her and pointing a long hunting knife at her face.

"Get down on the floor," he snarled. The pleasant, friendly smile was gone, replaced by an ugly, menacing grimace.

Mrs. Gordon told officers that she was suddenly paralyzed by panic, but she realized that if she submitted to his demands she would probably be raped, maybe even killed.

"What do you want from me?" she demanded, backing towards the glass doors.

"Shut up! Get down on the fucking floor. Get on your hands and knees," the man ordered, jabbing at her with the knife.

The man pressed closer, seized her by the shoulder, and in one sudden move sliced off a double rope belt she wore around her waist. He drew back, and as she reached out to grab him, her hand closed on the knife blade. The man jerked it away, and the blade sliced deeply into the palm of her hand. Blood spurted everywhere, but when she started to scream the man grabbed her by the hair, punched her several times in the face, and threw her to the floor.

She either fainted or was knocked unconscious, because the next thing she knew she was facedown on the bed. The man was straddling her from behind, sitting on the small of her back to keep her from moving while he tried to stuff a pillowcase in her mouth as a gag. Her hands were already tied behind her back.

Groggy as she was, Patricia Gordon fought the man's advances. She was able to pull her right hand free from the bonds, because it was slick with her blood that flowed from the deep hand wound.

Suddenly, there was a knock on the front door and the man pinning her to the bed, froze. Patricia spit out the gag and warned the attacker, "That's the realtor coming in to check the house." The man ignored her and was struggling to retie her hand when there was a second knock on the door. This time, the man leaped off and ran toward the stairs. Mrs. Gordon was a few steps behind him. Whoever was at the door, she thought, had to know what was going on. She was afraid that the man would turn the caller away and resume his attack on her.

Jim Panczak was at the front door, answering a call to repair the Gordons' air conditioning. When he got no answer the first time, Panczak walked next door to the Casa Del Mar sales office. Go back and try again, he was told. We know she's at home.

The repairman returned to the Gordon town house and knocked again. This time he heard a commotion inside; seconds later, the door burst open and a tall, burly man rushed by him with a hysterical woman on his heels. "Help that woman," the man gesticulated. "She's dying.' He pushed on past Panczak, ran to a small, white, pickup truck parked nearby, and burned rubber out of the parking lot.

Panczak turned back just in time to catch Patricia Gordon as she fainted in his arms. For the first time he noticed the blood, lots of blood, all over the woman's body and trailing back up the stairs. A piece of rope (her belt) and a strand of speaker wire were tied around her left wrist. Panczak ran next door to summon help. Minutes later, sheriff's deputies and emergency personnel were on the scene. Mrs. Gordon was rushed to Boca Raton Hospital, and underwent emergency surgery to repair the severely damaged tendons and muscles in her hands. She was also treated for the blows to her face and an ugly red abrasion around her neck, which occurred when the man ripped an eighteen-inch gold serpentine necklace worth about $325 off her neck, she told Deputy Kevin Vislooky. Upon returning home, she also discovered that the man had taken a watch with a gold band and gold face that was on her dresser.

Back at the Gordon townhouse, lab technician Gary Green was

busy photographing and fingerprinting the crime scene. He discovered that the woman had put up a struggle even after being cut.
Blood stained the bedroom floor, one wall, and the dresser, and
had soaked through the bed coverings to the mattress. A trail of
blood from the bedroom led down the stairs and to the front foyer.
Green photographed one piece of the rope belt in the bedroom
and another in the foyer, where Mrs. Gordon had fainted. He also
noted that another piece of speaker wire lying on the bedroom
floor had been looped and knotted, but apparently the man had
fled before he put it to use. There were no latent fingerprints of
any value.

Palm Beach County sheriff's detective J.P. Rendell took over
the investigation. Something about the case troubled him from the
very beginning. With all his experience as a cop, Rendell couldn't
recall any cases in which a rapist had attacked his victim in this
manner. Rendell quickly learned, to his dismay, that this wasn't the
first time the rapist had struck in Palm Beach County. In fact, he
discovered, the man had attacked Mrs. Gordon less than an hour
after another botched attempt to rape a housewife, only a few
blocks from the Gordon's Casa Del Mar townhouse.

A Boca Raton police officer, Roy Turner, had picked up the
sheriff's "be on the lookout" broadcast for a rapist driving a white
pickup truck, and contacted Detective Rendell. "You're not going
to believe this," Turner began, "but I think the same guy just tried
the same thing a few minutes ago." Turner said that at 11:01 a.m.
he was dispatched to a residence about a mile from the Gordon
home, but within the Boca city limits. There he met a Joanne
Davis,° who was terribly shaken but otherwise uninjured following
an encounter with a man who fit the description of Patricia
Gordon's attacker, and who also was driving a small white truck.

According to Mrs. Davis, she had recently advertised in a local
paper that she had a couch for sale. That morning, about 10:30
a.m., a man called, saying that he was interested, and asked for
directions to her home. He arrived within minutes. In his report,
Detective Rendell described what happened next:

"The suspect entered the house and followed Mrs. Davis to the

149

garage where the couch was located...The man asked her to open the couch so he could see what it looked like opened as a bed. As she bent over to open the couch, the suspect attempted to strangle her with a piece of clear speaker wire and threw her to the ground. He also displayed a knife in a threatening manner...The victim's daughter heard the screams and came running to the garage...When the suspect saw the daughter, he fled from the garage to his vehicle...It appeared he had left the keys in the ignition for an immediate getaway."

The information that the same man had attempted to rape two women in their homes within minutes of each other sent chills down Rendell's back. Bad news, he thought. The guy's obviously out of control. No telling what he might do next.

Later that same day, Rendell had reason to be even more alarmed when he huddled with Boca Raton police detectives Raymond Bond and Dennis O'Hara to compare notes. It seemed that the dangerous home invader who came armed with a knife was already a familiar figure to Boca police. Back in May, another local woman had advertised in the Palm Beach Post that she had a couch for sale. A man called saying he was in Lake Worth, about twenty miles to the north, and asked for directions to her home. He showed up about an hour later. When she let him in, the man asked for a glass of water, and followed the woman into the kitchen. There, he pulled a knife, and tried to grab her around the throat. The woman screamed and started to run, but he tackled her from the rear and fell on her. Pressing the knife to her neck and threatening to cut her throat if she resisted, the man seized a handful of the woman's hair and started dragging her along a hallway toward the back bedroom. The family dog, tied outside in the carport, became frantic at the commotion inside and knocked something over. The noise seemed to unnerve the man. He hesitated, long enough for the woman to scream that it was her husband outside. With that, the intruder let her go, ran out the front door, jumped into a white pickup truck, and disappeared.

The Boca detectives then handed Rendell a second report, dated July 11, 1980. The same suspect had telephoned to inquire

about a television advertised for sale, again requesting directions to the woman's home. This time, as soon as the woman opened the door, the man grabbed her, held a knife to her throat, and demanded money. He pulled strips of white cloth (which turned out to be cut from athletic socks) from his pocket and began tying the woman's hands. However, as in the other case, her cries brought her daughter running from another part of the house, and the man fled.

Detective Rendell also got a call from Detective Jerry Zito, a member of the sexual-battery squad at the Dade Public Safety Department in Miami. In his report, Rendell noted: "He [Zito] has advised they have labelled their cases "Ad-Man," due to the fact that they have several in which the suspect was successful in his assaults, meaning that he sexually battered the victims. The suspect's description, the suspect's vehicle and the modus operandi is identical to the cases we are investigating."

For several months, Rendell and his Boca Raton counterparts continued to check out leads in the case, running down numerous tips, all of which turned out to be nothing but dead ends. If the Ad Man struck again in their jurisdictions, they didn't hear about it. As far as they knew, the guy had been caught, had quit, or, more likely, just moved on to other hunting grounds.

That's how the case languished for nearly a decade. Patricia Gordon's outer injuries healed, although she never recovered full use of her hand; but it was the inner, emotional wounds that continued to haunt her nightmares for years to come. Then in mid-June, 1989, another pair of Palm Beach County detectives, David Ferebee and Mark Murray, came knocking on her door. We think we know who attacked you, they told her. Would you mind looking at a photo lineup to see if you recognize any faces? They placed photographs of six different men on her dining-room table, and asked her to take her time and study the pictures. Mrs. Gordon didn't need time. She instantly stabbed a finger on number five, middle photo, second row. "That's him!" she exclaimed. Detective Murray turned the photo over. The name on the back was Bobby Joe Long.

In his report, Detective Murray stated that in May, 1989, he

151

and Ferebee had been assigned to review the unsolved 1983 homicide of Gayla Ann McNeil, a Palm Beach County woman who had been strangled, her body dumped along a rural road.

In reviving that investigation, Murray noted, "A suspect was identified as a Bobby Joe Long who may also have been a suspect in several sexual batteries and home invasions which occurred in the early portion of the 1980s in the south end of Palm Beach County. At that time, these cases were more popularly known as the 'Want Ad Rapes' where an individual seemed to locate the victim through the want ad section of the newspaper and upon contacting the victim at their residence would sexually batter the victim. "During the course of this investigation, myself and Det. Ferebee traveled to Hillsboro [sic] County and spoke with Corporal Lee Baker who was one of the lead investigators on the cases involving Bobby Joe Long...Long had committed several 'Want Ad' type rapes in the Hillsboro area & were similar to the Gordon case."

Murray and Ferebee returned to Palm Beach County and arranged for Mrs. Gordon to view the photo lineup. After she identified Long as her attacker, Murray continued, "I informed Mrs. Gordon that the statute of limitations on this case had expired and that our agency would be unable to pursue prosecution. Mrs. Gordon said she understood. However, she said she would be more than happy to assist us in our endeavors in convicting Long if possible on any other charges. She offered her cooperation at any time necessary in the future."

▲   ▲   ▲

A LETTER FROM BOBBY

Most women I'd cut all their clothes off! It was a turn on to me, and several times to them. Plus the intimidation factor of me using a very sharp, nasty looking blade. Psychology—and it worked, none of them ever tried anything after the thing was start-

ed. They believed I would use the knife! I don't think I ever would have, plus I always carried a gun in the back of my pants, under my sport jacket, in case a hubby or boy friend or whatever showed up. It never happened. This method was fool proof. If I ever get out of here, I'll go back to it. Its too good to pass up.

The most baffling questions, as the murder investigation unfolded, were questions that neither Long nor all the experts who have studied him have ever answered: Why did he leave the women he attacked in their homes alive? Why did he kill the women from the streets?

"The thing that was so unique about the guy was that he could separate the home rapes from the street kills," said "Pops" Baker. "I guess that in the homes tying them up, raping them, and leaving them in that condition was as far as he needed to go to get whatever satisfaction he was looking for. The rape and the humiliation took the place of the murder. Whereas out on the street, he had to complete the kill."

Former FBI agent Stan Jacobson, who worked up the psychological profile on the serial killer several weeks before Long was captured, observed that "Bobby Joe Long was very much the power assertive rapist when he tied up and attacked women in their homes. But why did he kill the street women and not the women in their homes?

"Probably because the risk was so much less, simple as that. You kill someone in the safety of their own home, the cops are going to be all over the place. There is a horrible murder in the supposed safety of one's own home and it's big headline news. But a prostitute is found dead out on a country road, well, it's too bad and they investigate it, but while most law enforcement jurisdictions take it seriously, there is a lot less public pressure and outcry to get the guy who did it.

"To not kill the rape victims in their homes, to me that was a

153

very cold, calculated decision on his part to avoid being caught. As long as he just raped and robbed them, Long knew the chances of the cops coming after him in full force would be a lot less than if he left the body of a prominent housewife behind."

Major Gary Terry, the Task Force commander who was as close to the case as anyone, has his own theories. "There was one occasion," Terry recalled, "when Long raped a victim in Pinellas County, didn't kill her and the next day committed a rape-homicide in Hillsborough County. That was the really strange quirk about this guy. From an investigative standpoint, years ago, I would have told you there's no way that you'll have a serial rapist in one county, and the same one committing serial homicides in another county, and not do them vice versa. Long was a serial rapist in Orange, Pinellas, Pasco counties, but a serial killer in Hillsborough.

"The big question was why didn't he kill housewives. Apparently, he perceived them as different victims. Maybe he killed the street women because he thought there wouldn't be as much heat on him as there would be if he killed the women in their homes. Maybe. But I think he left them alive for a very evil and sadistic reason. In one of his letters he talked about what a good feeling he got knowing that the rape victim would have to tell her husband about being raped in her own bed, or that the husband would come home and find his wife tied up like that. Part of his kick was knowing that it might ruin sex for them for the rest of their lives. He knew exactly what mental and emotional torment he was putting his victims and their families through.

"That pretty much sums up his character."

In a piece on America's increasing engrossment with serial murder, the Washington Post reported:

"In a sense, the serial killing phenomenon is an extension of the country's rape problem, which is growing even faster than the homicide rate. Per capita, the United States has fifteen times as many reported rapes as England, twenty-three times as many as Italy, and twenty-six times as many as Japan.

"But people don't like to think about rape. It is too low, too vulgar, too crass.

"'We are fascinated by murder. We are not fascinated by rape,' says James Alan Fox, co-author of the book Mass Murder: America's Growing Menace. 'Crime stories focus on murder, not on rape. Rape has never been fashionable, it's always been seen as disgusting and demented. We can be fascinated by murder, it's so extreme, it's so bizarre, but we're only sickened by rape.'"

Bobby Joe Long, on the contrary, was fascinated by rape. He was in love with rape. He indulged in rape. He was enthralled with the "foolproof" techniques he'd devised to locate his sexual targets and pursued his goals with all the zeal of a yuppie on Wall Street.

Like others of his type, when Bobby Joe Long wasn't shopping for a rape victim in the classified ads, he often became a night creature, a cruiser who trolls for his victims along the dim and darkened city streets.

Long himself said that he spent so much time and put on so many miles driving around in search of prey that he racked up 50,000 miles a year on his Magnum muscle car, and over one year's time had to buy a dozen new tires. New, that is, to him, but Long's excessive mileage made the cost of brand-new tires out of the question, so he habitually resorted to recaps and unmatched, used tires whenever an old one wore down to the threads and he had to change. And, ironically, that idiosyncrasy produced a piece of key physical evidence that, along with a few tiny, tell-tale fibers, tied Bobby Joe Long irrevocably to the scene of the crimes. Among the many used tires Long picked up was one oddity that not even the voluminous FBI reference files had a record of. Casts of the unusual tire markings were flown to an expert in Akron, Ohio, who identified the impression as being made by a Vogue tire, an expensive tire that comes only on Cadillacs. That peculiar tire track at some of the body dump sites became a crucial piece of physical evidence, just as damning as a killer's fingerprint.

For Bobby Joe Long, that pattern of cruising along mile after mile of urban hunting grounds began in the mid-1970s, when he roamed the Miami-Ft. Lauderdale streets, studying the suburban homes and lifestyles and polishing a scam that would gain him

155

entry. All those households, to Bobby Joe, represented the mother lode of free, rough sex for a horny guy with a velvety smooth gift of gab, the balls of steel to pull it off and the conscience of a goat.

▲   ▲   ▲

A LETTER FROM BOBBY

```
    I  had  a  fold  out  buck  knife,  just  for
effect...never hurt this kid, or any of the others.
The worst I ever did to any of them was one punch to
a couple who'd fight at first, after one punch, they
were resolved to it, and accepted it, and knew I was
for real & would hurt them. Give a bitch a choice
between getting dicked or getting hurt, you know
what shes gonna pick.
```

▲   ▲   ▲

After Long took up residence on Florida's Death Row, he talked to psychologist-author Joel Norris for Norris's study of serial killers, Walking Time Bombs. According to Norris:

"Once inside the house, he would pull out his knife, tie up the victim, rape her, and rob the house. He never committed any murders and was rarely violent.

"'I never beat anyone. I felt sorry for them, and I told them that I didn't want to hurt anybody. I didn't even like tying them up. I think they knew that I wasn't violent because many of them victims talked to me not like I was a criminal but like I was a person. They were pretty sad too because of the lives they had. If conditions had been different, we might have had a relationship.'"

Later, Bobby Joe ran the same con on CBS reporter Victoria Corderi: "I had never been violent with, you know...I mean up to this time I probably attacked a hundred women, but I never hurt any of them. They only one that got hurt was one that grabbed a knife by the blade and cut her hand, but I never had hurt any of

156

the...you know. I read about these clowns that carved their initials in people and cigarettes and coat hangers and broom handles and everything else, but you know I never did anything like that. And maybe it doesn't count for anything but... to the contrary, I, I tried to be as gentle as I could. And even about tying them up. You know, I'd make sure I wasn't hurting them or anything..."

Bobby Joe Long was either a champion dissembler or a flat-out liar, with a mean streak as wide as Tampa Bay. Authorities who have dealt with Bobby Joe prefer the latter explanation. Bobby Joe was violent. He did hurt his victims--slapping them, punching them, sometimes torturing them with his knife, sadistically slicing the clothing from their bodies, binding them with painfully tight ligatures and, of course, the agonizing acts of forcible vagina, anal and oral rape. That's just the physical side. There is also the mental and emotional torment those women and their families must endure for the rest of their days.

Incredibly, Long would have us believe that many victims succumbed, not to his force, but to his charms and sexual charisma. The illusion that his victims really enjoyed the sexual acts he forced on them is, psychologists say, a mind-set typical of rapists, a blind spot that prevents them from recognizing that the act of rape itself is a brutality beyond compare.

"The woman in Palm Harbor was raped in front of her kids," Gary Terry added. "He threatened to kill them if she didn't cooperate. She was totally shattered by the attack and has never fully recovered. She got divorced and spent a long time under psychiatric care. Maybe she still is. One of the other victims he choked so bad that he left her with permanent damage to her vocal cords. If all that isn't hurting people then I don't know what is, but Bobby Joe Long still brags that he never hurt those women and that most of them enjoyed it. Disgusting!"

In her study of sex crimes against women titled simply, Rape, author Carol Horos observed: "On the basis of detailed interrogations with convicted rapists, Kinsey's Institute for Sex Research arrived at five categories of offenders.

"The first type is what the Institute called the 'assaultive vari-

ety.' Twenty-five to thirty-three per cent of rapists questioned were in this group.

"These rapists use unnecessary violence and strong threats when they rape. They are sadistic men who are often compelled to punish and hurt the victim. The assaultive rapist gets his kicks through the use of force, not from the sexual intercourse. The women are generally strangers and the rapists may carry a weapon of some kind. Brandishing a gun or knife adds to their feelings of 'machismo,' the self-image of a dominant, aggressive, brutal male.

"The assaultive rapist hates women, all women, and typically steals something, no matter how trivial, from the victim after the rape. A sixty-three year old California woman, raped at gunpoint by a twenty-four year old man, was robbed of two dollars after the rape. His parting words were, 'I bet I made your day.' He then threw her a kiss and ran away.

"According to the Institute, these men delude themselves into believing that they are actually wanted and desired by their victims and 'they seem to find it difficult to believe that the women bear them any ill will.'"

▲   ▲   ▲

A LETTER FROM BOBBY

    Glad you liked my novel. Yeah she was something
else, and yeah she'll never forget me. I gaurantee
you every time she gets dicked or plays with that
thing she'll think about me and what I did to her.
She loved it!
    Just one of dozens.

▲   ▲   ▲

By 1983, the Ad Man Rapist had perfected his technique. Profiting from his South Florida mistakes (and successes), Long had learned how to check out the house he was targeting before

grabbing his victim. Too many times he'd acted impulsively without first determining that the victim's family members weren't somewhere in a back room, as was the case on at least two occasions when he struck in Palm Beach County. When he resumed raping in the Central Florida and Tampa Bay areas, Long had the system down pat, and had cut the risk of being caught in the act to almost nothing.

Part of the reason the Ad Man was able to operate so long was Bobby Joe Long's chameleon-like ability to blend into his surroundings—an in-the-flesh Jekyll and Hyde who was quiet, mannerly, good-looking, well groomed, and nicely dressed. "Such a nice-looking boy," in the words of a courtroom spectator. Long relied on that All-American demeanor to throw his victims off their guard, particularly those women he attacked in their homes, all of whom knew better than to admit a total stranger when they were by themselves. But this was Mr. Nice Guy, in his neatly pressed three-piece suit, smiling shyly at the door. Funny, he doesn't look like a rapist. With that typical observation, all the traditional early warning systems cracked and crumbled. And the instant they threw open the door, Bobby Joe Long knew he had won another round.

During the initial interrogation following his arrest, Long bragged about his "foolproof" Ad Man scheme to Detectives Randy Latimer and Bob Price. Said Price: "He continued to talk about his MO, which was the classified section of the newspaper. He made a comment about how easy it was. He said, 'All you've got to do is put on a three-piece suit, comb your hair, and they'll open the door.'"

▲　　▲　　▲

A LETTER FROM BOBBY

You wanted a story of one of my victims, this was one of the top ten for sure. I'll tell you about the last rape that didn't end up with someone dead. I want to tell you about Jennifer--the thirteen-year-

159

old (there were two younger—twelve—in L.A.). I was
checking the Orlando paper and found this one ad--
canopy bed for sale. A bell went off as soon as I
read it. It was summer & school was out, I usually
worked these during school so the women would be
home alone. But I was getting the "urge" and when I
read this ad, I knew there was a young girl there,
who else sleeps in canopy beds, so it was just a
matter of getting her on the phone, she answered & I
asked for her Mom. She said her Mom was at work and
I said, 'well, when will she be home?' She said five
or six, it was like 8:45 or 9:00 in the morning. She
said her Mom usually came home for lunch at
twelve...So I said well I'm calling about your ad in
the paper, is there anyone around older I could talk
to? She said she was thirteen & could tell me whatever I wanted to know because it was her bed. To put
it in your terms—"Bingo"—she was mine! She had a
real sweet little teeny bopper voice and we bullshit
around on the phone a bit, yeah I can lay a line
when I need to, and she gave me very precise & accurate directions. I said I'll be there in about thirty minutes...She said, 'Okay!'

So I took off, figuring I'd get there by ten or
so and would have at least an hour to do what I was
gonna do to her. From there it was just a question
of what she looked like, and I was pretty sure by
her voice & the way she spoke, she wouldn't be too
bad.

I got there, went up (always wore a sport jacket,
women trust you much more) knocked on the door, nice
house in a nice suberb, no cars in driveway, no people—neighbors—out doing yard work or anything. It
looked good.

She opened the door, I was knocked out. This
thirteen-year-old had a body like—well—any woman
would be proud to be built like her about five feet,
five inches, 110 lbs, long reddish brown hair, pretty face, not beautiful, but pretty, the real clinch-
er was she had on a blue bikini top, nice tits, and

a pair of shorts. Just a very tasty little morsel all around. She just opened the door, I said hi I called about the bed she ran back to the phone telling me to come in, she would be right back. She got off the phone, while I was waiting, I was taking it all in. There was nobody else home. She was a sweet thing! Perfect!

She came over said something about her girlfriend on the phone and started down the hall to the bedrooms. The whole end of the house was bedrooms (three) and the other end was a garage. no concern there! I checked the rooms as we passed em, and she was chit chatting some shit about the bed, me following her.

She never even saw the knife. I just pushed her right onto the bed, face down as soon as we got near the bed. She didn't resist, at all, I told her don't worry, I'm not gonna hurt you. Then I showed her the knife and said, unless you make me hurt you! Same line I've used basically on all of em. I had her put her arms behind her, and untied her bikini top, she was going oh God oh God. I said "Baby, don't be scared, I promise you I'm not gonna hurt you!" It was true, it calmed her down.

I got her top off, she was like on her knees with her waist up on the bed, face down. She smelled good! She felt great! Theres nothing like a girl whose just turned woman—firm, tight, sweet. I know of what I speak!

I used her bikini to tie her hands, not behind her but so they would be at her sides, no further. It was something I learned from experience. It made them feel controlled, but I never tied them right tight, and I never tied their hands behind them. They got in the way if I did, and besides this way they could use one hand in front of them on me or on them, while the other hand was pulled behind them. Can you picture it? Then I picked her up and put her on her back on the bed, and started on her shorts...as I'm taking her shorts off, she says

Bobby Joe: In The Mind of a Monster

"Your not here for my bed, are you!" I said "no, what do you think I'm here for?" She said "Me!" I said "Thats right!" and then I saw the pussy and it was no little girl pussy, it had a lot of hair light brownish colored, but very hairy. She was firm and very muscular legs, but it was all firm, the tits were not huge but I'm tellin you no woman would be ashamed of them, firm, beautiful, big brown nipples. I mean the brown covered the whole end of the tit, and the nipples were hard! She knew what was coming!

I kissed her mouth, like I know she's never been kissed before—deep—hard, then I told her to kiss me, she didn't know what I meant at first as a lot of them didn't, but a lot of them did too! I told her again—stronger—KISS ME! YOU KISS ME! She got it then and gave me her tongue. I know she'd never been kissed like this, most women I have known and dated were amazed at what I'd do to their tongues, no shit, I've been told more than once that it was the first time they'd been kissed like that, these are women now twenty-five, thirty year olds, and I know after Jennifer was kissed by me like that, shes gonna be real disappointed in the way her little schoolboy boy friends kiss her for a long time.

She was getting into it!

Then I moved down to her tits, I told her they were beautiful, she thanked me, blew my mind! I told her to tell me all the things she was going to do for me. I did this to all of them, some of them would start the penis and vagina shit, Jennifer did, I said NO, not like that tell me like you'd tell one of your girlfriends, I don't want to hear penis, vagina or intercourse I want to hear cunt pussy cock prick suck fuck screw ball everything you can think of and don't stop telling me tell I say so!

Man I've seen some married women have a much harder time than this thirteen year old. She cut loose with some really good stuff. She watched me

on her tits. She liked it, she'd lift up the one
closest to my mouth by raising her shoulder, so I
could get at it better! She was really into it now.
Her story was getting real dirty, then when she
started to slow down, I told her I was going to
wait for her mom to come home from work, and I was
gonna do her while she watch, then do Jennifer
while her mom watched. I told her I was gonna make
them do things to each other, but for her to tell
me what! She did and she had a little problem at
first, then I started licking her belly, it was
tight and nice, then I started licking her thighs,
first from one knee, all the way up, just passing
over her cunt, breathing on it, and down the other
way. When I got right up to her pussy lips with my
tongue, I'd just rub thru her hair, wouldn't touch
her cunt, just breath on it. Her breathing
changed, when I got by where she thought my tongue
was gonna hit her pussy, she's tense, expecting it.
This was standard, did it to all of them, they were
never dry by this time, they were ready, Jennifer
was ready, she was telling me she would eat her
mothers pussy and her mother would eat hers, I
asked if she knew what sixty-nine was she said yes.
I told her I was gonna put her & her mother in
sixty-nine and then (with her on top) fuck her just
above her mothers face, so mom could see my cock
going in and out of her pussy, so mom could see her
baby wet and lubricating my cock as I put it in and
out of her real slow! Then I asked her what else I
could do to her in that position? She said "Butt
fuck me." I said tell me about it, then I went to
work on her pussy with my tongue. She was soaked,
her clit was like a little rock, I was running my
tongue up the lips, inside them up to her clit, but
wouldn't hit the clit itself. She was delicious!
She started about me butt fucking her while her mom
watched but by now I was ready & so was she. I slid
my pants down pulled her way up on the bed, and
pulled her legs up under the bends of my arms so I

had access to cunt, or ass, either one. I left her
ass alone, found out I couldn't get into her, too
tight, without hurting her. I didn't want to hurt
her. Some I did, not her. From prior experiences I
had with young virgin cunt, I knew the only way to
get her without tearing her apart was to put her on
her knees, legs spread real good, face down on the
bed, ass arched up, and high. Jennifer assumed the
position! I was used to it from a twelve year old
Korean girl I got in L.A. a twelve year old Mexican
girl (one of the most beautiful girls I've ever
seen) in L.A. and a fourteen year old Japanese girl
in Long Beach.   Maybe I'll tell you about em some
time. Totally different approach, and orientals &
latins are not the same as American girls. Another
time.

Pussy opens up to the max in this position—I
slipped right in! There was a little gasp from her,
I think she was one of those that thought it would
hurt worse than it does. I'm telling you, these
twelve, thirteen year old girls today are women.
They're ready to fuck.

It was tight, it was hot, and it was real wet,
when I pulled back out of her there was a little
blood on me as with all the other virgins.   Not
much, not real thick just like a pinkish red colored cum!

I made her move on me, fuck me! I usually did! I
liked them fucking me! All of em! Heres this guy
they don't even know and they're fucking him, not
him fucking them. Just a little personal prefer-
ence. I liked it like that.

The young ones like Jennifer would always say
"But I don't know how!" I'd "guide" them how, tell
em faster or slower, no matter what position. This
wasn't my favorite position!

It was sweet and this was when I'd get their
ass. I'd spit on it, right on the ass-hole, then
while I fucked em in the cunt, my finger would go
in the ass, usually thumb if its doggie style like

164

Jennifer. Something else I learned from all these girls. The young ones like Jennifer had no trouble when I'd start on their ass—a couple of times their pussy would be tighter than their ass anyway—but I like butt fuckin these bitches. Even if its just for a few minutes. A lot of the older (thirty to thirty-five) year old housewives had never had it up the ass. The way I did it they liked it. Not at first, but after a minute or so when the sphinctor muscle of the ass loosened up, theyd always like it. The young ones always took it much better, never questioned it, I think they "expected" it. I still can't figure the "older ones" would be so surprised at it sometimes. The young ones—never! And it never hurt them even at first! Very strange, I'd have thought it the other way around.

After a few minutes of this I was ready to blast off. This girl was sweet meat, and was into it real good! I had her start telling me about what her and her girlfriends said about fucking. She did! Then I asked how often she played with herself, and what she thought of to make her cum.

At first she said she never did that, I slapped her hard on the ass and told her not to lie to me again! A lot of them said that, then after one slap, they'd tell me! Man these girls think of some weird shit, and once they get the little slap to prod them they'd let it go. Brothers, fathers, niggers, getting raped, getting gang banged, fuckin a dog. I heard them all! Jennifer said she thought about her girlfriend licking her all over. No wonder she had such an easy time telling me about her & mom, I found out Mom was thirty-three, built real nice, big tits, blondish colored hair, black pussy hair. A little better than average looking, according to Jennifer.

I was still considering if I should wait for her and do this to both of them. I'll tell you now, I've had three chances this being one of them, and for one reason or another, I never got to do a

165

mother daughter.

I even would have settled for a brother.

Just something real weird, make some sweety go down on her brother & him on her, then make em fuck! Never got that either.

But back to Jennifer. I rolled her on her back and now she had no trouble slid right in. Man I was hot and sweaty, her too, I took my shirt off, so I could feel her tits & her sweat on me. I always did that too.

Then I had her kiss me, eyes open, looking in my eyes, while I pumped her. about four or five minutes, bam, that was it.

I sat her up on the side of the bed, had her lick and suck my dick clean. Her blood & pussy juice & my cum. I had to physically move her head & just told her to suck, suck hard. She did, and I was up again real fast. Most of the time once was it, then grab a few things and split, real fast!   These virgins, too good to pass up, had at all of them twice.

Now I took her in Moms room, mom kept a little Ruger 22 by her bed.   Ahh! paranoid of a stranger in the night!

Put Jennifer down on her knees, it was suckee time! Giving head was something practically all of them said they weren't to good at, or didn't know how, or even married bitches telling me they never did it.

Jennifer learned real fast, her eyes on my dick going in and out and growing on every stroke. I had her do ten real slow from the tip to the base, then ten as fast as she could tip to base, and just keep on like that.   I liked that.   I've had head like that driving down the road for an hour or more because just when I'd get ready to cum, they would go over to the real and I mean real slow. It would die down a bit, then fast, ready to blast, then slow. After a few minutes of this, (She had a great set of lips on her, natural made for fuckin.) I told her to get back down face to the ground, and now it

throat, I could see her struggling to swallow and as each spurt hit, her eyes would widen. Hey, I don't have to tell you or any guy about the intensity & length of a second cum like that!

And she stayed just like that, didn't move her lips, didn't take her eyes off mine or mine hers, for a good twenty or thirty seconds till the very last little spasm and drop came out. I told her to come off me real slow, and try to suck me as clean as she could on the way out. She did! Then I rubbed my wet cock all over her face, I put it right up in front of her and let her look at it, I knew at her age she never had seen a real one close up, and where she could really look at it. She looked, then I rubbed it all over her face, her nose, her eyes, the last bit of wetness being wiped off onto her face.

That was it! As much as I'd have loved to have waited for mom, and do what we talked about, I didn't know if I could handle another one. These were two real good blasts. But I told Jennifer I was going to wait for mom, and we were going to do all the things we talked about, and she was going to taste her mothers cunt, and see me fuck her in every way possible, and that then I was going to make mom watch me do her all over again, and Mom was going to have her little girl stick her tongue up her cunt too.

Then I stood her up, & spread her legs while she stood there and just kissed all of her. She was fantastic, what a body. I got a towel and put it over her head and tied her feet together and sat her on the toilet in her moms bathroom, it was connected to the bedroom. Then I told her not to move not to make a sound, and I'd be back in a few minutes with Mom, and we'd all have a little fun. I turned the shower on so she couldn't hear real good then pulled the door almost closed, and I got in my car and hauled ass home.

Destroy this fucker! For sure!

▲   ▲   ▲

"Bobby Joe Long had absolutely no concept that rape is a vicious, violent act," "Pops" Baker mused. "Barbaric. To me it is the most violent act. Murder, while violent, is final. But rape leaves those women scarred for life. That's why I don't think that the 'Jennifer' letter was made up. It was all true. He was writing like she enjoyed it. It was all his way. Everything he did to her, he made it sound like he was doing her a favor."

According to Bobby Joe's own accounts, he rarely, if ever, committed the classified-ad rapes in the same county where he lived. It was a precaution he'd worked out while still living in South Florida. Long may have been motivated by a frenzied, deeply buried rage that drove him to rape, defile, and dehumanize his victims, but he remained cagey enough at the conscious level to recognize the risk of operating too close to home. Heeding his predator instincts, Bobby Joe roamed far afield in search of prey, to other communities or quiet, secluded neighborhoods where he seemed to find the most vulnerable quarry with uncanny ease.

So it was that on January 26, 1984, he showered, carefully shaved around his well-groomed mustache, brushed back his thick, dark-brown, wavy hair and donned his hunting togs--a spiffy tan suit, carefully knotted and subtly contrasting tie, well-polished shoes--and set out in search of game.

It was the start of a very busy year for Long—and for scores of police. It was to be a year of death for at least ten young women who fully expected to live much longer than the time Bobby Joe Long allotted them.

Following his usual routine, he headed east out of Tampa on I-4, crossed the Hillsborough-Orange County line, and pulled into Orlando's booming outskirts.

Long's hunger led him to a moderately expensive home on Skyview Drive in Orlando. Twenty-year-old Carol Bellini° had been sleeping late, but was awakened by a knock on the door. Drowsily, she looked at the clock as she threw on a robe—12:30 , lunch time.

When she opened the door, Carol was confronted by white male she described as five-feet, ten-inches tall, medium build, with brown hair and a brown mustache, and wearing a tan three-piece suit. He smiled and pointed to the "For Sale" sign in the front yard. "I'm house hunting," he said. "Sure would like to take a look at your place. Just the kind of place I'm looking for."

Slightly irritated at being awakened, Carol shook her head. This wasn't the way it worked. Buyers were supposed to make an appointment through the realtor to see the house. She told the man so, and suggested he call the number posted on the sign after 4 p.m.

"Aw, come on," the man cajoled. "Just let me take a quick look around, as long as I'm here."

"No," Carol insisted, "you have to make an appointment first." She started to close the door, but the stranger suddenly pushed her into the house, slammed the door behind him, and drew a knife from the waistband of his trousers. The woman started screaming, but her attacker wrapped a powerful arm around her neck and squeezed tight enough to almost make her pass out. He held the knife against her throat and hissed in her ear, "Shut up! Don't make any fucking noise and you won't get hurt."

The man pushed Carol ahead of him into the bedroom, and forced her to lie on her back on the bed. Still holding her with one hand, he pulled a roll of adhesive tape out of his coat pocket, jammed two nickels against her eyes and secured them with strips of tape wound around her head. Then, slowly, as though he were enjoying exposing her, the man began slicing Carol's robe away from her body with his knife.

He got off the bed and she heard the rustling of clothing. The next time he touched her, she felt his bare flesh against hers. An erect penis pushed roughly against her mouth. "Suck it!' the man commanded. When she didn't respond as quickly as he thought she should, the man slapped her several times. "Now,' he repeated. "Suck me off!" Terrified that she might be killed if she disobeyed, Carol later told police that she then fellated the intruder.

Afterward, the man tied her hands and feet with pieces of rope he apparently had brought with him. He also looped a rope around

her neck, nooselike, and tied one end to the bed. Investigators who later examined the crime scene were struck by that length of rope. You know, said one, it looks like a leash. While she lay bound on the bed, Carol could hear the man rummaging through her belongings. After going through everything in the bedroom, the man moved through the other rooms in the house, opening and slamming shut drawers and cabinets.

She lost track of how long she remained tied to the bed. But it was long enough for the man to return and sexually assault her twice more. Once, he untied her feet, roughly shoved her legs apart and brutally raped her. Another time he flipped her over on her stomach and assaulted her anally, tearing into her like a battering ram without benefit of lubrication or consideration of her cries of agony, muffled by the pillow he pushed her face into. And all through the ordeal, when she cried too loudly or failed to respond promptly to the man's orders, she was slapped and punched on the head and face.

Finally, the man left. Carol heard the front door close and a car start up and drive away. When she was sure he was gone, she struggled free and called police. Much later, when Carol felt strong enough to re-enter the house without being seized by a panic attack, she drew up a list of some thirty items the man had taken. They included a .38 special, two television sets, a 35mm camera, a stereo, jewelry, and her wallet. The estimated value was more than $1000.

Detective Karen LaForte, working with the Orange County Sheriff's sex-crimes division, was assigned to the Bellini case. As usual, she filed the information about the crime, including the intruder's description with the Florida Department of Law Enforcement. The information would be included in the next Criminal Activities Bulletin, an advisory distributed to the state's police agencies.

More than a month later and one hundred miles from Orlando, Bobby Joe Long stopped to look at another house for sale. The paired communities of Port Richey and New Port Richey embroider the white beaches between Boggy Bay and Big Bayou on the

171

Gulf Coast, just north of touristy Tarpon Springs. But Port Richey and New Port Richey, while exploding with new growth like most of the Gulf region, remained mainly "local" with the vacationers and the snowbirds heading south to Clearwater, St. Pete, or Sarasota, or north to Florida's sparkling clear natural springs—the Weeki Wachee or the Homosassa.

Cruising aimlessly, his senses alert to any prime game hidden in the suburban cover, Bobby Joe Long wandered off U.S. 19 and into the Palm Terrace Estates, a somewhat pretentious name for an otherwise unremarkable subdivision of average two-bedroom, middle-class houses in Port Richey. On First Avenue, Long spotted a "For Sale" sign in the front yard of one of the homes. He slowed and, instead of turning around, backed the car into the driveway. Less chance of some nosy neighbor getting the tag number that way.

Inside, Shelly Jennine Janke°, a twenty year old divorcee and mother of a four year old daughter, was getting ready for her shift at a nearby McDonald's, where she'd worked for the past two and a half years. Shelly was drying her hair when she heard someone knocking on the door. She glanced at the clock: 10:30 a.m. She was due at work at 11 a.m. and still had to pick up a fellow employee on the way in. Her first thought was that it was her dad stopping by as he often did after dropping Shelly's daughter off at day care in New Port Richey. At the time, the young woman was living a complicated life. She and Bruce Janke° had been divorced for almost a year. The previous fall, she'd rented the house on First Avenue from one of the other girls at McDonald's and, shortly afterward, Shelly and Bruce got back together. They worked out an arrangement of living together part-time on weekends. During the week, Bruce returned to Orlando, where he worked and had a place of his own. While Bruce was gone, Shelly and her daughter usually stayed at her parents' place in Hudson, a tiny hamlet a few miles north of Port Richey on Highway 19. In the morning, she returned to the house she was renting to get ready for work, while her dad took the child to day care.

Shelly Janke's account of what transpired that morning in March is taken from the testimony she later gave in depositions

and during Bobby Joe Long's April, 1985, trial for sexual battery and robbery.

"I was drying my hair and someone knocked on the door," she began. "I went and looked out the window and I saw a car backed into my driveway, but I didn't see anybody at the door. When I opened the door he was walking around to the back of the house. And when he heard me open the door, he turned around and said that he was looking to buy a house and just asked me some questions...how big it was or how many feet by how many feet, and I didn't know."

(When Pasco County detectives questioned Shelly later that day, she told them that while she was standing in the doorway talking to the man she had a good look at his car, and was able to describe it with pinpoint accuracy: 1977-79 Dodge, two-door, hardtop, maroon in color, spoke-type wheels. And it had the word "Magnum" in chrome script on the right rear of the trunk.She also described the man as five-feet ten-inches tall, 160-170 pounds, with brown hair and mustache, "nicely" dressed in a brown suit and tie. He spoke with a Southern accent.)

"I told him I didn't know anything about it because it was my girlfriend's and that he should call [the realtor]. I had the screen door open while I was talking to him and he just walked in the door and said he was going to take a look around and he started looking in the garage and the bedrooms and the bathroom. He looked in all the rooms in the house and I was still standing by the door...I didn't invite him in...he just walked by me and walked in.

"I didn't try to stop him. He was too big and I was in a hurry and my hair was wet. I was trying to leave to pick up my girlfriend before I went to work...I was getting nervous [but] I just thought he was being pushy."

After the man checked all the rooms in the house, he returned to where Shelly was still standing at the open front door, tapping her foot impatiently, anxious for the jerk to leave so she could get to work.

"Then he walked up behind me and pushed the door closed, and he grabbed me around the neck with his left arm and he had a

173

gun in his right hand that he put up to my head...I don't know much about guns and I didn't get a good look at it... it was black and I think it had brown handgrips...He said he wouldn't hurt me if I did what he said.

"Then he took me into the bedroom, but he didn't stay there. He turned around and went out into the living room...He said, `You got a nice stereo.' He turned it on and turned it up real loud....."

The man continued to hold her with one arm around her neck while he pulled a roll of white surgical tape from his jacket pocket. He began winding the two-inch-wide tape around her head, blind-folding her. (At one point during her trial testimony, Assistant State Attorney Michael Halkitis asked Shelly why she didn't scream or try to fight off her attacker before he tied her up. The woman broke into tears. "Because," she sobbed, "I was scared. I was afraid he'd kill me." In fact, she added, the rapist did strike her on the side of the face with the gun to emphasize that he meant business.)

As he wrapped the tape around her head, the man prodded the terrified young woman with questions: "Do you know what I'm going to do to you? What do you think I'm going to do?"

"I didn't say anything at first. He got mad and he kept asking me, what am I going to do to you. He kept asking me till I said he was going to rape me...That seemed to be what he wanted to hear...He didn't say anything after that...

"Then he took me back to the bedroom...he kneeled me on the floor in front of the bed and he unzipped his pants and he pulled out his penis. He told me that he wanted me to suck it. He pushed my head towards him and he was moving my head back and forth with his hands...It wasn't hard, really, a little bit maybe...that went on about a minute. He didn't ejaculate."

Either just before this or immediately afterwards, the intruder bound her hands behind her back with a length of clothesline rope, which he apparently brought with him, since Shelly did not recall any such rope being in the house.

"Then he put me on the bed," she continued. "I asked him, because I was afraid—my dad usually came back on his way from dropping off my little girl. She went to preschool. I asked him if he

was going to hurt my little girl and my dad if they came back. He said he wouldn't, he wasn't going to hurt me, but I'd better hope that he [her father] didn't come back, or something like that. He ripped all my—I had chains on and I had bracelets on and he ripped them off. He yanked them off my neck and ripped them off my wrist and put them in his pocket. Then he ripped my uniform...He ripped it off with the knife he had. It was shredded, ripped off of me...I was wearing a bra and nylons. He pulled my nylons off. He must have cut the bra off. I don't remember him taking it off. He didn't unhook it or nothing.

"Then he got on top of me and he stuck it inside of me. Well, he pulled—I was on my period and he pulled my Tampax out and threw it on the floor...He wasn't—it still wasn't real hard, though. I could feel it, that it wasn't real hard." (Shelly said the man did not ejaculate during the rape. However, a medical examiner later testified that a vaginal washing showed the presence of sperm.) The penetration, she said, continued for about two minutes while the man grew progressively more frustrated and angry.

"He got mad," she testified. "I assume because it wouldn't get hard, I guess. I'm not sure. I'm not sure what he said but I know he cursed. He wasn't cussing at me. Like I said, he was frustrated.

"He got off me and my hands came untied from where he tied them underneath, behind my back [during the rape]. He tied them to the bedpost on my bed...It was like a brass headboard, a full-size bed...and my hands were tied at each corner of the bed...He tied them tight. I had rope burns on my wrists...I'm not sure if my feet were tied up then or afterward. I know he tied my feet up. I don't know if it was before he got on top of the bed or not...

"When he was doing that, he noticed the rings on my fingers. I had this one on my right hand and I had a marquise with eight diamonds on each side on my left hand, and he took that one off but he couldn't get the one off my right hand, and tried to pull it off and I didn't—he had my mouth taped up too and he taped my face. I think that's when he noticed my hands were untied, because he sat me up to tape up the rest of my face...He went to my drawer and he got a pair of nylons and he stuck them in my mouth and then he taped over them."

175

After taping her face, mummy-like, the man bound her feet at the ankles and began rummaging through Shelly's belongings. She heard him pawing through the closet, the dresser drawers, the nightstand. Buried in one of the dresser drawers were several Polaroid shots that Shelly's former husband had taken of her in the nude.

"I knew he found them because he said, 'Nice pictures.' And he dumped out my jewelry box and took all my jewelry. After he went all through the house he came back in the bedroom and he opened up my legs and he started sucking on my legs. He put like a hickey like. Between my legs, up toward my vagina. There was two of them, one on each side. Then he grabbed a hold of my chest and he was squeezing my boobs real hard. He left bruises on them. He then stuck his finger in my vagina and in my anus.

"Then he put a pillow over my face like he was going to smother me, and I struggled and I tried to get up...and he pulled the pillow off my face and said that I was starting to piss him off and he ran the knife like down my neck...started at my neck and ran it down to my chest.

"Then he put the pillow next to my head and he just left it there and walked out of the room. I don't think he came back in after that. I heard him going through the house still, then I heard the door open and he went out. He was walking to his car. He came in a couple times and then I had a cold and I couldn't breathe because he had—I started to smother. I was getting dizzy. I laid there for as long as I could, because I didn't know if he was still there or not. I didn't hear the car start up or anything, but it was either try to get untied or smother to death, so somehow I got my hands untied...Then I pulled the thing [tape] off my face. I couldn't get the tape out of my hair. I just pulled it down. Then I untied my feet and I got my robe out of the closet and I went across the street to the neighbor...I was embarrassed to go over there, because I never met them before, but she didn't even recognize who I was because I had the tape in my hair. She said it looked like I had a neck brace on my neck. I told them that some man came into my house and raped me and robbed me."

Nancy Lee Yarry was the neighbor Shelly Janke ran to for help. About 11:00 on an otherwise quiet morning, she suddenly heard a woman screaming hysterically, "Help me! Help me!" Nancy looked out her window and saw a young woman clad only in a bathrobe, her head swathed in a thick layer of white tape, stumbling across the street.

Nancy called to her husband, and they ran to help the sobbing woman, half-carrying her into their home. The Yarrys listened in horror as the distraught victim blurted out that she'd been raped and asked them to call her dad. Mr.Yarry leaped for the phone. "I'm calling the police first," he said. That threw the girl into an even greater panic. "No! No!" she screamed. "He said he'd come back and kill me!" The Yarrys ignored her plea and called the Pasco County sheriff's office, and then notified her father. While they waited, the Yarrys gently cut the tape from Shelly's hair, washed her face and tried to calm her hysterics.

Deputy Joseph Paez was first to arrive and found "...this lady very emotional, crying, uncontrollably hysterical...just blurting out bits and pieces." Paez called for detectives from the Crimes Against Persons section, and asked that a female officer come to the scene to assist the victim. Deputy Debbie Floyd arrived within minutes, followed by paramedics and Shelly's father, but it was hours before she calmed down enough to give a full account of her ordeal.

Although she thought she could never do it, Shelly steeled herself, after Bobby Joe Long was arrested, to put herself through the long, painfully embarrassing crucible of a public trial. She took the stand in a Pasco County courtroom, and defiantly pointed an accusatory finger in the glaring face of the man who had so savagely molested her. Later, she sat crying softly in the gallery as she heard the judge sentence Long to 693 years in prison for the awful things he had done to her. But even that wasn't enough to heal her deeply wounded spirit. Shelly Janke later changed her name and moved to a Midwestern state, far from the nightmare that Florida had become for her.

Immediately after the rape was reported, Pasco County Detective Charles Troy, Jr. was assigned to the case. When Shelly

was able, he sat down with her and compiled an inventory of items stolen during the attack. The list included Shelly's engagement and wedding rings, bracelets, necklaces, earrings, crystal salt-pepper-shakers, and her purse. Not included on the list were the photographs of a teen-age Shelly Janke posing in the nude for her husband, pictures never intended for the eyes of a rapist who had already shattered her fragile sense of privacy and security. To think that somewhere out there that same animal had those pictures to fondle and gloat over made her sick to her stomach. It was as though every time he took them out to look at, he was forcing her to relive the horrifying and humiliating experience.

For the next eight months, Detective Troy kept moving the Janke rape/robbery file to the top of his to-do stack, as he searched for clues that would lead him to the home invader. The things that rotten bastard had done to that little girl, the sadistic way he'd ruined her life, really got to Troy. Someday, he promised himself, he'd see the guy hang.

Then came November, and the hasty formation of the Task Force to catch the serial killer who had been terrorizing the Bay area. Detective Troy was picked to represent the Pasco County sheriff's office. All the work he'd done up to then on the Shelly Janke case was shoved to the background, for the moment at least.

Events moved quickly after that. Bobby Joe Long was picked up by Task Force members on November 16, and hustled to the Hillsborough County sheriff's office for questioning. Excited Task Force members, gathered at the sheriff's compound, pounding each other on the back, eager for a peek at this guy they'd heard so much about in Task Force briefings. Detective Troy was among them when someone handed him a mug shot of the man in custody, along with a description of the suspect's car.

Skyrockets went off in his head. Dumbfounded, Troy found himself staring at the very face Shelly Janke had so painfully described. And the vehicle! Shelly said it was a maroon Dodge. And she especially recalled the word "Magnum" on the trunk.

My God! Was this the same guy who had raped and robbed Shelly Janke? It had to be—but why had he left her alive?

Troy pushed his way down the crowded hallway to the interview room, where Hillsborough and Tampa officers were grilling the suspect. He waited until Sgt. Randy Latimer stepped out of the room, and pulled him aside. "Look," Troy explained, "I think Long is good for a rape we had over in Port Richey." He briefly outlined the incident, providing Latimer with details only Shelly and the rapist could know. A few minutes later, Latimer re-emerged from the interview room. He caught Troy's eye, smiled, and nodded. "Yeah," Latimer said. "He copped to it. You got your guy."

Three days later, Troy obtained a search warrant for Bobby Joe Long's still heavily guarded apartment on Fowler. Inside, he found what he was looking for. "In plain view," Troy reported, "were two cassette tape holders containing cassette tapes, all of which were listed on the face of the search warrant as belonging to Shelly Janke, many of them in her own handwriting. Crystal salt and pepper with silver tops were located; jewelry box that had diamonds that matched the description of Shelly Janke's diamonds..."

Also in plain sight, Troy found a photo album containing dozens of photographs of women, many of them nude. Among them were the pictures of Shelly Janke. Next to catching the guy who did this, recovering those pictures and returning them to Shelly was the best part of all, Troy thought.

In retrospect, the chronology of Bobby Joe Long's movements during the early months of 1984, and the crimes he committed, takes on a clearer meaning.

Between the March 6 rape of Shelly Janke in Port Richey and the April 5 attempt to abduct Mary Ann Hicks in her classic Jaguar automobile, Artiss Ann Wick, a twenty year old bride-to-be, vanished at high noon on March 27 from a northeast Tampa street corner. Only after Long admitted to killing Wick did authorities revise their original supposition that Lana Long was the first to die at Bobby Joe's hands. Now they knew she was at least the second. Eventually, the record was revised to make Artiss Wick the first killed and last found, although police to this day are still not convinced she was, in reality, the first victim in Long's killing skein. The failed attempt on Mary Ann Hicks is only one incident that

makes them wonder who was first, and how many woman Bobby Joe really murdered. Had he been successful in his attempt to kidnap the Jaguar owner, she undoubtedly would have been included in the murder list probably coming in at number two. But were there others before Artiss Wick? After all, Bobby Joe was constantly on the prowl throughout the Bay area and across the state, leaving the police with the nagging, unanswered question: Are there other bodies out there whose identity may never be known?

As it was, the bizarre and ominous incident involving Mary Ann Hicks, a victim in waiting, which should have set off warning bells, slipped through the cracks in the system. Bobby Joe Long walked away, smirking, pleased with the fact that the slap on the wrist he got for attempting to abduct the forty-year-old woman at gunpoint barely stung. And before he again saw the inside of a jail cell, at least nine more young women died and several more were raped and brutalized in what they assumed was the safety of their own homes. By the time Bobby Joe appeared in court on the attempted-kidnaping charge, the killing spree had gained momentum. Authorities rushed from one isolated spot in Hillsborough County to another, frantically picking up the pieces of strangled Tampa night walkers.

Meanwhile, the Ad Man rapes continued.

It was May 29, 1984. Lana Long had been dead two weeks, her horrible death little noted except by weathered cops who came away from the dump site aghast by what they'd found there, and scared that it was only the beginning.

The sun was just burning the early-morning haze off the flat, turquoise waters of Tampa Bay when Bobby Joe Long pulled off the I-275 causeway connecting the city of Tampa with the Clearwater-St. Pete metroplex on the Gulf side of the Bay. He swung into a Denny's restaurant parking lot, picked up a copy of the Clearwater Sun from the rack outside the door, settled into a booth, and ordered a cup of coffee. As he sipped, Long spread the classified-ads section out before him and went to work. Within minutes, he had a list of a dozen telephone numbers to call. With a handful of quarters, Bobby Joe hit the pay phone and began

methodically eliminating those that didn't sound right. Finally, as he always did, Bobby Joe found one. With the address in hand and a rising excitement that started in his groin and worked its way up to his brain like a slow-moving electrical current, Long headed north on U.S. 19 to the affluent, hilly, seaside village of Palm Harbor.

Since the middle of May, Lynn Newell,° a thirty-three-year-old homemaker and mother living in the expensive Autumn Wood division of Palm Harbor, had been running an advertisement in the Clearwater Sun:

"Bedroom set, triple dresser w/mirror, chest of drawers, night stand, double headboard. Excellent condition: $350.00."

Her home telephone number accompanied the ad, which hadn't been too successful. Only one prospective buyer had called. About 9:30 the next morning, when Lynn Newell was busy tending to her active three year old son, the phone rang. The caller said he'd seen the ad and was interested in buying the bedroom set, and asked for the address. Lynn Newell asked if he was familiar with Palm Harbor. "No," he told her, "I live in South St. Pete. I'm a sales rep for IBM, but I usually work in Tampa."

He added that he was calling from a phone booth at Ulmerton and U.S. 19, several miles south of Palm Harbor. At his request, Lynn gave him explicit directions on how to find her home. Barely thirty minutes later, the doorbell rang at the Newells' new and expensive Spanish-style home. From the outside, it appeared that the Newells had it made. Kenneth Newell was on a fast career track, headed straight up. His success in sales allowed the young couple, still in their early thirties, to buy this big, beautiful dream home in one of the lushest subdivisions of Palm Harbor. Autumn Woods featured only large, expensive homes, individually constructed to blend naturally into the thick woods of tall pine trees and live oak.

Secluded as it was, deep in the shaded hills, the Newell home was still only a short hop to some of the finest beaches along the Gulf Coast. The house was one of two on a cul-de-sac backing into

181

a barrier of thick woods and, beyond that, the rolling expanse of the exclusive Innisbrook Resort.

The Newells believed they'd found the perfect spot for raising a family—quiet, far enough from the booming urban centers of Tampa-St. Pete to be safe, yet close enough to be convenient to the benefits of city life. They never dreamed that a horror few could imagine would come crawling right to their doorstep in such an idyllic setting.

Now, the polite furniture buyer was standing in Lynn Newell's doorway. Nice looking, well groomed, with a soft, surprisingly high-pitched voice.

"You give good directions," he smiled.

Despite his appearance and his friendly demeanor, there was something vaguely troubling about the man that Lynn Newell couldn't quite put her finger on. "Even when I was letting him in," Lynn Newell recalled, "I didn't feel right about him."

But this was home. Here she was safe, far away from the daily dangers of muggers and rapists and killers. Besides, she'd never heard of the Ad Man Rapist.

"The furniture sounds just like what I'm looking for," the visitor told her. "Mind if I take a quick look at it?" Lynn nodded and invited the man in. It's back here in the back bedroom, she indicated, walking ahead of the man down the hallway. As she stepped through the doorway of the master bedroom at the rear of the house, the man pushed Lynn against the wall, pulled a vicious-looking knife from his waistband, and waved it inches from her face. The pleasant, smiling face at the front door had dropped away like a mask. Snarling at her now was a real-life Mr. Hyde, his deep brown eyes glazed over with an icy cold cruelty that she'd never seen in another person.

Instinctively, Lynn Newell threw up her hands to protect her face and started to scream. As if he were anticipating the action, the man punched her on the side of her face. "Shut up," he growled. "You know what I want."

Numb from the sudden pain and paralyzed with fear, Lynn

barely nodded. God, she told herself, try to stay calm. Don't fight back. Three year old Trent° was playing in his room, and the Newells' infant daughter was asleep in the nursery. Don't do anything to make him mad, Lynn thought. Don't give him any trouble, or he might hurt the kids.

She tried to explain to the man that she'd do what he asked and to please not hurt her. "My husband," she sobbed, "he's going to be home for lunch any minute." But every time she opened her mouth to speak, he hit her again. Once he struck her with his hand holding the knife, and the blade opened a small cut on her cheek.

Holding Lynn by the throat with one hand, the intruder began to slice off her blouse and bra with the knife, slowly, taunting her as he did so. "I want a little pussy. I want a good head job." The man then ripped off her shorts and panties and pushed her onto the bed, while repeatedly threatening to kill her if she didn't obey.

He covered her head with pillows and told her to lie still. Stifling her sobs, Lynn could hear the man shredding a bed sheet with his knife. He then used the strips of cloth to tie her hands behind her back and bind her ankles. He used another strip to blindfold her, and roughly shoved another into her mouth as a gag. Once she was secured, the man turned his attention to the Newells' belongings. Dimly, she heard the man rummaging through her jewelry box; he moved a portable television set to one side to open a hope chest at the foot of the bed. Next, he grabbed her hand and started to pull off her wedding rings. When they stuck, he spit on her fingers and forcibly jerked them off, ignoring Lynn's whimpers of pain.

She heard him leave the bedroom, and prayed that now that he had her jewelry he would go away. But then she heard doors slamming elsewhere in the house and realized he was only searching the other rooms. Once she heard him open the side door, when it sounded as though a car had pulled into the driveway. The phone also rang several times while the assailant was there, but the man ignored it.

The man returned to the bedroom and pulled Lynn to her feet.

Pushing her ahead of him, he forced her, ankles still bound, to hobble to the combination den and office at the front of the house. As they passed Trent's room, the youngster stood at the door, his eyes wide, watching the strange man with his mother who was all tied up and nude. The man waved his hand at the boy. "Get back in there and don't come out," he growled menacingly. The youngster stepped back into his room and shut the door.

In the den, the man shoved Lynn to the floor beside the desk, pulled down his pants and fell on her. The violent sexual assault continued for several minutes until the man ejaculated. Numb, unable to scream or fight back, Lynn lay in agony and shock for several minutes. Vaguely, she heard the man going through her husband's desk. Then, just when she thought the horror might be over, that he couldn't do anything more to hurt her, the man returned, forced her to her knees, jerked the gag from her mouth and replaced it with his penis. He moved back and forth in her mouth until he was hard again, then slapped her away, threw her back on the floor and raped her anally.

Lynn Newell blacked out from the pain and revulsion of what was being done to her. Some time later, she became aware of the quiet and realized the rapist had left at last. She dragged herself along the hallway to the back bedroom, where she knew there was a pair of scissors. Lynn managed to cut the cloth binding her wrist, then stumbled to the sliding glass doors, pushed through the screen, and fell into the backyard, screaming, "Help me! I've been raped!"

Her terrified cries startled three lawn maintenance workers doing some landscaping behind the Newell home. Looking up, they saw a nude woman, blindfolded, with her feet tied together, trying to crawl away from the house. They ran to her aid. "Please, somebody!" she cried. "Get my children out of there!" Two of the men picked her up and helped her reach the house next door. The third worker, Sandra Bennett, ignoring the possibility that the assailant might still be inside, dashed into the Newell home. She grabbed the phone and dialed 911, left the phone off the hook, and ran to search the house. The first room she entered was the nurs-

ery. Sandra picked up the still-sleeping infant and ran next door, where the Newells' neighbor had wrapped the hysterical victim in a blanket and was frantically calling Kenneth Newell at work. Sandra Bennett handed the baby over and ran back to the Newell home. On the second trip, she found the frightened little boy cowering in his room and gently led him out.

Detective Terry Rhodes and Victims' Advocate Laura White were quickly on the scene, followed shortly by Lynn Newell's distraught husband. He'd been trying to call home all morning, he explained, and was concerned when he didn't get an answer. Worried that something was wrong, he was leaving his office to check on his family when the neighbor caught with the awful news that his wife had been attacked. After emergency personnel checked her over, Laura White accompanied the Newells to the medical examiner's office for a complete examination.

Later, the Newells checked through home and gave Rhodes a list of items the rapist had stolen. These included an antique opal ring that had belonged to Lynn's great-grandmother, several other items of jewelry, and a Krugerrand coin.

Detective Rhodes, following procedure, issued a BOLO (Be On Lookout) alert to law-enforcement agencies in surrounding counties, which struck pay dirt instantly. Later that same day, replies landed on Rhodes' desk describing cases in both Pasco and Orange Counties in which a similar M.O. was used, and whose suspects matched the description of Lynn Newell's attacker. Both had occurred within the past five months.

The information on the Orange County attack came from the FDLE's "Criminal Activity Bulletin" for March, 1984.

An Identi-Kit composite of the suspect accompanied the Bulletin. The suspect was described as a white male, approximately twenty-five years of age, brown hair, brown mustache, medium build. Neat, clean-cut appearance. He was last seen wearing a brown suit and driving a 1974-1976 white over fire-engine red Chrysler Cordoba or Mercury Cougar (models that at a quick glance might easily be mistaken for a Dodge Magnum).

The instant he read the description, Rhodes sat up straight.

Has to be the same son of a bitch, he thought. But as glad as he was that there were solid leads on the guy, the ominous pattern disturbed Rhodes. One up in Port Richey. One in Orlando. One here. How many are there we don't know about? And where is he now? Rhodes's cop sense told him the rapist was probably still in the area. It was obvious the guy was spreading himself around, making sure that he didn't strike in the same community twice.

Bobby Joe Long has never fully explained to anyone what motivated him to rape; how he devised the unusual Ad Man M.O.; what, in his mind, distinguished those who lived from those who died. Perhaps the closest Long ever came to any sort of reason was in the following exchange, during his interview with CBS News:

BOBBY: You're not familiar with those?...This was back in seventy-seven, seventy-eight.
REPORTER: All right, what happened?
BOBBY: (sigh) I really don't like to talk about it, ... It's a matter of public record.
REPORTER: I know...I'm trying to get at what you felt and...what drove you. In other words, did you feel that you needed to find somebody to rape them? Did you feel, you know, what drove you to do the violent acts that you ended up doing? What did you feel? What—did you just go out one night and try to find somebody?
BOBBY: No, no, nothing like that. It wasn't at night, in the first place. ... I don't really know how to explain how it started or why it started. I really don't, you know, I have been trying to figure that out. And what I did was, I would call these classified ads in the newspaper that were selling furniture or something in the daytime. And if it was a woman and she sounded like she was, you know, within a certain age group or whatever, I would make an appointment and go see her furniture and I would rape her, I would attack her. But I didn't hurt any of them. You know, I think that's important, you know, a lot of people probably don't 'cause, I know rape's a terrible, terrible thing and blah, blah,

186

blah. But none of these women were hurt. And I think
that's important. This went on for a long, long
time.

REPORTER: Did you feel better afterwards?

BOBBY: (sigh) What it was--when I would start
thinking about this I couldn't sleep. I lost interest in everything. I didn't want to eat. I would
wake up at five o'clock in the morning. As soon as
I'd wake up I'd start thinking about it, ok.

REPORTER: Thinking about rape?

BOBBY: Yeah, about doing one of these classified
ad things. And if I didn't do it, if I tried not to
do it, I'd be okay for a day, two, but it wouldn't
stop, you know. This would go on until I did it.
Then when I would do it I'd be okay for a month, two
months, three months sometimes longer. Sometimes a
couple of weeks, sometimes a week. And then it would
hit again. ... this went on for a long time...All in
all, I guess I probably destroyed about a hundred
people. You know? In one way or another, classified-
ad rapes or whatever.

REPORTER: And how did it all start to escalate;
you were keeping all of this inside?

BOBBY: It didn't escalate, It didn't escalate
for a long, long time. You know, like I said this
started about seventy-seven, seventy-eight, okay.
(sigh) I got divorced in seventy-nine and I moved to
Tampa, Things pretty much evened out there.

REPORTER: What do you think about the victims?

BOBBY: I think that it is really just, it's sad
what happened to them. And that I can do something
like that, to somebody. All the victims, all of
them. You know? You're talking about a lot of them,
lots. A lot of lives have just gone right down the
tubes because of me. In one way or another. And it's
not a good feeling, it's not a pleasant feeling, I'm
not proud of anything that I have done. And the
worse thing is, I don't understand why. I don't
understand why— when the rapes started, I was married to a very cute little girl. We had no problems
with sex or anything like that. Why? I don't know

why. I know after the first one, I was driving home
and I was thinking to myself, you got to be nuts.
What are you doing? What did you just do? You got a
wife and two kids and a nice house. You know? I was
getting ready to go to school, back to college. And
... you know, I remember that as plain, or plainer
than any other aspect of all of that. Is that first
drive home after that first one and what I was
thinking. The first rape. And thinking that, if, if,
it makes no sense. You know? I don't even remember
the second one. I remember the first one clear as a
bell. But I don't remember the second one or the
third. After the first one it's all just jumbled.

▲   ▲   ▲

One of the rapes attributed to Bobby Joe Long didn't fit his
usual "ad man" pattern, and still has investigators puzzled as to why
the victim was allowed to live. It occurred during one of Long's trips
to Miami to visit his ex-wife and children, and fell right in the middle of what appeared to be a hiatus in the killings—between the
June murder of Elizabeth Loudenback and the September disappearance and slaying of Vicki Elliott. Police still haven't figured out
the reason for that mysterious gap—unless, they say, there was really no gap at all, and there are still some unknown, unaccounted-for
victims out there somewhere.

Someone like Evelyn Moore°.

One quirk that's fairly common among serial killers, and to some
extent, serial rapists, is their penchant for collecting trophies of their
victims. Later, they use these souvenirs to jump-start their fantasies,
as they relive that murderous instant or that fleeting moment of
gratification when they held the victim in their power. Some take
pieces of clothing or an item of jewelry. Many take body parts.

According to Dr. Park Elliott Dietz, a forensic psychiatrist and
consultant to the FBI's Behavioral Science Unit, "Over fifty percent
of [serial killers] record the offense in some way, such as video or
audio tape or diaries." Forty percent of them "...keep personal items

188

belonging to their victims...jewelry, shoes, photo IDs, and the occasional body parts for memento value."

Bobby Joe Long didn't take body parts, but he did take just about everything else. The trophies he carried from the homes of his rape victims included salt and pepper shakers, wall hangings, toasters, expensive jewelry worth thousands of dollars and, in a surprising number of cases, nude photos of his victims taken by their partners in intimate moments. Many of the stolen items were recovered during a search of his apartment after he was arrested on the Hillsborough murder charges.

But Bobby Joe Long's favorite trophies did more than just remind. They recreated.

Bobby Joe took pictures—in at least one instance clear, explicitly detailed 35mm photos that he snapped of himself in the very act of rape, his penis penetrating his victim in various positions, his finger spreading wide the woman's vagina, or forcing her to do the same. In that, he may be unique among serial killers. Members of the Task Force came to believe, and the evidence bears out their suspicions, that an entire collection of Bobby Joe Long's photos may still exist—a collection now in the hands of others once close to Long, or former members of his defense team.

There's a belief that arose among many Native Americans encountering the westward expansion in the 1800s, that to take a photograph was to steal a piece of that person's soul. If true, then Bobby Joe Long was not only raping and murdering.

He was stealing souls.

Bobby Joe Long was heading back to Tampa following a visit with his kids, when he detoured off I-95, headed east on 79th Street, and turned right on Miami's famed Biscayne Boulevard-- not the portion made famous to millions of television viewers every New Year's as the spectacular setting of the city's colorful King Orange Parade. Bobby Joe Long favored that portion of Biscayne that hosted its own tawdry nightly parade of whores. He was looking for a hooker to keep him company on the long drive back to Hillsborough County—even if she didn't want to go. Somebody to relieve the monotony with the kind of free, rough sex he liked. This

was an old stomping ground for Bobby Joe. Back when he lived in Miami, he'd come over to Biscayne a lot to get blown. There was something exciting about sitting in your car, parked on a side street with people passing by, while some bitch cunt went down on you. Ordinarily, there was plenty to pick from along this corridor. All the weirdos roaming around make hooking a risky occupation, but with a drug habit to feed and a mean pimp to keep happy, girls like Evelyn Moore had to take their chances on the street or face even worse consequences from their main man. Besides, a quick blow job in an air-conditioned car meant a few minutes of blessed relief from the heat of a relentless South Florida summer night.

Evelyn Moore fit the ticket. White. Young. So ripe in her short hot pants and tight tube top, she looked about to pop. Prime-time stuff for any guy cruising Biscayne Boulevard with twenty bucks in his sweaty hand and a hard on in his pants.

August 29, 1984, was an unusual night for Evelyn Moore. A Miami woman with a record as a street hooker, Evelyn was taking a rare night off. It was Tuesday, a slow, middle-of-the-week night with not much happening on the streets, so she decided to catch a bus up to an old club on 82nd Street in North Miami where she used to hang out. Besides, Evelyn like to tell people, she really wasn't a whore. Prostituting was more or less a sideline, just something that sort of happened now and then. She had a real job at a record shop on the beach, but because she didn't make much, the only place she could afford to live was in one of the cheap, one-story, hot-sheet motels that cluttered Biscayne. Evelyn didn't have a car, so she sometimes hitched back and forth to work to save bus fare. Lots of guys picked her up. And if he was a nice guy and wanted to fuck her, well, sure, she'd do it. But she didn't give it away. That was how Evelyn hooked, she insisted. Friendly like; picked up some grocery money at the same time. But it also got her busted half a dozen times or more—often enough to make her a regular among the vice dicks who went out to sweep the streets periodically, when the politicians started complaining about drugs and prostitution driving away the tourist trade.

This hot August night, she was sitting on a bench at 55th and

Biscayne waiting for a bus when a guy in a maroon car started cruising her. She knew the signs. Slow down. Look her over. Around the corner and hit the brakes to see if she'd come running. Then drive around the block and do the mating dance of the horny male all over again. About the third time around, he stopped in front of the bus bench and rolled down the window. "You partying?" he called. Evelyn shook her head and the man left. A few minutes later he was back again, smiling nice. "Hey, I'm really not looking for anything," he said. "I'll be glad to just give you a ride where you want to go."

Evelyn shrugged. Why not? The driver wasn't bad looking. Dark hair. Hawaiian print shirt and white shorts. She'd gotten in cars with weirder-looking dudes than this. They drove north on Biscayne, chatting like old buddies. At the corner of 82nd Street, she motioned for him to pull over. The man turned off Biscayne into a darkened parking lot, and before Evelyn could open the door, he whipped out a pistol and jammed it up under her chin. "Don't scream, cunt, and you won't get hurt," he warned. The man reached down beside the passenger's seat and flipped a lever, and the seat back flopped down backwards. Evelyn was suddenly looking at the roof of the car, with the gun now pressed hard against her ribs. Shit! she thought to herself. A fucking weirdo! Every girl who'd spent more than five minutes on the street could tell you stories about the johns who turned out to be a bondage freaks. But it hadn't happened to her. Until now. Best thing to do with a john with a bad attitude, she knew from experience, was just humor him. Play along with his little game, and maybe he wouldn't beat her or cut her up too bad.

The man pulled back out on Biscayne and continued north. Many blocks later he turned off onto a dirt road with a lot of trees and bushes on each side, turned off the car lights, and stripped off Evelyn's clothing. The man pulled some pieces of rope out from under the seat and tied her feet and hands. The rope was cut into the right lengths, like he had it all ready just for this. He also tied another rope around her neck, and left one long end dangling. That he held onto, and used it to jerk her around— like a leash on a dog.

After Evelyn was securely bound, the man drove on. Somewhere up around Hollywood, she figured, he turned west and continued for several miles. Gradually, she noticed, there were fewer and fewer streetlights, so she guessed they were out in the country somewhere, maybe almost out to the Everglades. A half-hour passed before the man again turned north. Now there were no outside lights at all, so Evelyn knew she must be a long way away from Biscayne Boulevard. But she was confused about just where she was. (Later, she learned that the man had driven west to catch U.S. 27, the two-lane highway that cuts diagonally across the Everglades Wildlife Management District from west of Miami-Ft. Lauderdale to the southern tip of Lake Okeechobee. Lots of cane trucks and vans packed to overflowing with migrant workers used U.S.27. But at night, there wasn't much traffic. Just long, dark, empty stretches of blacktop. Monotonous. Boring.

Which is precisely why Bobby Joe Long brought Evelyn Moore along for the ride. To liven things up. Out of the corner of her eye, she saw the man unzip his fly and push his trousers down around his knees. He jerked the leash hard, pulling her head down to his lap. "Suck it, you goddamn cunt," he ordered. Awkwardly, Evelyn twisted her bound body around until she could get the man's penis in her mouth. They drove that way for miles. While she sucked, the man kept up a steady stream of "fuck" talk. Evelyn had heard it before. Some guys had to talk their way into getting off. Once in a while, he pulled her head up with the leash, slapped and punched her, and demanded, "Talk dirty to me. Talk your whore talk."

That went on for an hour or more. Evelyn sucked until she thought her jaw would fall off, and all the while man kept driving down the road. Somewhere he came to a crossroads gas station and pulled over. He made her sit up, took out a knife and, to her surprise, cut the ropes that bound her wrists and ankles. The man handed her some change. "Go get some sodas," he ordered, pointing to a soft-drink machine sitting on the sidewalk. Evelyn pushed open and slowly stepped out, looking to see who was around. Not a soul in sight, but it still felt really weird, getting out without any clothes on to buy sodas, even if it was way out in the boondocks.

When she returned to the car, the man didn't bother to tie her up again. He drove on, drinking his soda, until he came to a dirt road leading off into the middle of a cane field. The thick sugar cane rose up on either side of the road, cutting off everything except the star-speckled sky above. The man drove a mile or two and stopped. He got out and walked around to the passenger side of the car, stripped off his clothes, and threw them in the back seat. "Okay, cunt," he growled. "Fuck me." He pushed the woman onto her back on the front seat with her legs sticking out the open door, stepped in close and shoved his penis into her. So maybe she was a hooker, Evelyn thought, but it still hurt like hell. And the guy liked rough sex, slapping her breasts and her face while he raped her. Pretty soon, the man reached into the glove compartment and removed a 35mm camera with a flash attachment. Holding the camera above his shoulder and to the side of his head, he began snapping pictures. He pulled out and made Evelyn turn over on her hands and knees. She felt his fingers roughly open her vagina. The camera flashed again. Then he made her reach back and do the same thing to herself while he took more pictures. After that, with the woman still on her hands and knees on the car seat, the man pushed into her from behind, snapped a few more photos and ejaculayed.

As the man dressed, Evelyn sat up in the seat and, despite the August heat, began shivering. Now he's going to kill me, she thought. On the long drive up from Miami, he'd threatened repeatedly to blow her brains out and toss her in some roadside ditch. The man climbed back into the driver's seat, glanced at her once, and shoved her out of the car. He slammed the door and spun the car around on the narrow dirt road. The last Evelyn Moore saw of him was when the taillights winked on at the stop sign back at the highway, turned left, and disappeared, headed north on U.S. 27.

Stunned, barely able to believe that she was still alive, Evelyn Moore stumbled barefoot toward the highway, crying and tripping in the inky blackness, slapping at the hords of mosquitos that swarmed out of the cane fields. When she reached the highway, distant headlights were approaching. The nude woman threw up

193

her arms and waved frantically. Now, she didn't care who saw her naked, just so it wasn't that pervert coming back for more.

To her relief, the driver was a schoolteacher returning to Palm Beach County from Florida's west coast. The man gave Evelyn a small towel to cover herself as best she could, and drove to the Hendry General Hospital in Clewiston, the closest medical facility. Hospital officials called the Glades County Sheriff's Office in Moore Haven, a small agricultural community on the west side of the lake. Deputy Tommy Herne responded to the call.

By the time Herne arrived, the woman had been treated and someone had donated clothing for her to wear. He drove her back to the sheriff's office to take her statement.

"She admitted that she was a hooker from Miami," Herne recalled, "but I told her I didn't care about any of that. All I was interested in was getting the son of a bitch who did this to her. Later that day, her boyfriend came and picked her up.

"I remember asking her why she didn't run when he made her get out of the car to get the drinks. She said she was scared to death, and from the way the guy acted she knew he'd shoot her or run her down with the car if she tried to get away."

Herne filed the incident away as one of those oddball cases every cop runs into from time to time, and forgot about it—until one night in November when he arrived for his shift and found a teletype issued by Hillsborough County. The sheriff there had arrested a guy for a bunch of murders, and wanted any information others might have on him or his car.

"When I saw the description on the teletype, the lights went off in my head because she described that car to a T," Herne recalled. Herne notified Hillsborough officials of the connection, and was invited to Tampa to join other cops from all over the southeastern United States who were gathering to compare notes on unsolved crimes that might be tied to the Tampa serial killer.

During that symposium, Task Force commander Gary Terry reviewed the case for the scores of lawmen, and described the evidence collected in searches of the suspect's apartment. He project-

ed on an overhead screen one set of lewd slides which graphically displayed a male, photographed from the chest down, performing intercourse on a woman whose face was out of camera range. "We think," Terry announced, "that this was a rape in progress. But we know who did it. The bastard outsmarted himself this time." Terry pointed to a white smudge on the car seat beside the woman. We had this portion blown up, and guess what? It's an envelope addressed to Robert J. Long, 5802 East Fowler Avenue, Tampa, Florida.

"In common police terms," Terry laughed, "we call that a clue."

Tommy Herne held up his hand. "That sounds like it might be mine," he told Terry. "Our victim said that the guy was taking pictures when he was raping her. She should be able to identify the pictures." It took some time to get it done, however. Detectives didn't locate Evelyn Moore until January 15, 1985, when they found her in a South Florida hospital "beat half to death" by a man believed to be her pimp. She identified herself as the person in the photos being raped by Bobby Joe Long.

"The only reason I could come up with for him not killing her was that she did everything he told her to do," Deputy Herne reflected. "She never defied him in any way. I think that's what keyed him to kill all those other women. They resisted him, and he'd come unglued. He kept the gun on her most of the time and kept telling her he was going to kill her if she didn't do what he said.

"When he finished with her, he was out on a dirt road dead end. Pushed her out, told her 'Don't look at me,' and drove off. I told her, 'Lady, I don't know why you're alive.' And that was before I even knew who he was. After I found out about him killing all those women, most of them hookers just like she was, I was even more amazed that he didn't kill her. She sure fit the profile of all the others."

Gary Terry definitely believes there are more Bobby Joe trophy pictures. Somewhere.

"Some of the photos of nude women we recovered from his

apartment and the dumpster when he was cleaning out his place were of victims that he found during the home-invasion rapes and took with him when he left. Some we never identified," Terry said. "We found receipts and cancelled checks made out to a photo processing plant in New York where he sent his film and that developed just about anything except sex with kids and animals.

"The number of photos we recovered don't match the amount he spent on processing, which makes me feel that there were some photographs we didn't get to. He may have gotten rid of them before we closed in on him.

"Or," he added cryptically, "they may be in another location today."

The question of missing photographs became the focus of an exchange between William Eble, a Pasco County assistant public defender, and Corporal "Pops" Baker when Baker was being deposed prior to Long's second trail for the slaying of Virginia Johnson:

Q *All right. So you were—on December third, nineteen eighty-four you're talking to Cindy [Long's former wife]...*

A *We talked about the keys that I gave her from the search warrant. She requested a bunch of those keys. I gave them to her. We talked about that. I requested them back. She said she had given them back to the Public Defender's Office. And the reason I requested them back...is we thought there was a key to his post office box. We had information...[we learned] from his checking account that there would be some photographs coming. And I hope to this day that you have those now since you're representing him and--because Mister whatever his name down there in Miami had them last.*

Q *What photographs?*

A *It's believed that Mr. Long photographed his victims as he killed them and he has those photographs either in Mr. Ellis Rubin's possession or in your possession or in Mr. O'Connor's possession. [Charles O'Connor, from the Hillsborough County Public Defenders' office, was assigned to represent Long after he was arrested. O'Connor is deceased. Ellis Rubin, a Miami attorney*

famous for taking on controversial, high-profile, or flamboyant cases, volunteered to represent Long during the Supreme Court-ordered retrial in 1986 for the murder of Michelle Simms.] The last time I knew I was invited to go down to Mr. Rubin's office. Have you ever been to Mr. Rubin's office?

MR. EBLE: *No.*

DEPONENT: *Some day when you get rich you'll see Mr. Rubin's office. I was invited down there to look at these photographs which we know were received or mailed in around August of nineteen eighty-four, around sixty/seventy dollars worth of photographs out of...New York. There's an agency there that will produce photographs...*

Q   *Okay. Tell me about the photographs now.*

A   *See, we have the photographs of the girl from Glades County indicating she was being raped. You can see a ligature mark on her wrists. We got identification and it showed Bobby Joe Long's car and it shows an envelope with his name on it and it showed parts of his body penetrating her in various stages. I feel the possibility that those photographs, sixty to seventy dollars worth of them, contain possible victims. If he photographed this girl that day from Miami and brought her all the way to Glades and photographed her, why not photograph other victims. Why that one?*

Q   *Where are those pictures?*

A   *I have those pictures...*

Q   *What other photos are you aware of, sir, regarding any victims?*

A   *That's the only ones that I'm aware of that we believe are victims. There's other females but they're just regular photographs and I think we have established who those are.*

Q   *Any of them connected to rapes?*

A   *No.*

Q   *Or homicides?*

A   *Not to my knowledge.*

Q   *Of the sixty to seventy dollars worth of photos, those photos were never recovered?*

A *Oh, yes, they were recovered all right*

Q *To your knowledge they were recovered.*

A *You're the people who have them.*

Q *I'm not the people who have them.*

A *You're representing that man and they have been passed on from lawyer to lawyer...Mr. Rubin down there I'm sure has them and if you can get them out of him, fine and dandy, but I know he's got them because he invited me down there and I thought I was going to get to look at these photographs and the man gave me the courtesy of inviting me into his big, plush office and sitting my butt down and showing me one photograph of a female nude, similar to what I had seen and he let me see her face. Is she one of your victims in these murders? And it didn't look like any of our victims so that was the end of it. He showed me one facial shot of a female and that's all. There's the totality of sixty to seventy dollars worth of photographs and he didn't feel that I needed to look at the rest of them.*

Q *But there were other nude photographs somewhere?*

A *The only one I got is the one I received and we have identified her and she's a victim.*

Q *Where is the source of the information indicating that these are, in fact, maybe photos of people that he killed...*

A *I don't know. That source of information comes from our feeling that why aren't...they being showed to us.*

Q *What it was is you believe that--the rumor is based upon the fact that there were photos taken of this girl from--*

A *Miami to Glades.*

Q *To Glades County and that's why you think there's others?*

A *If he did that one, the totality and the intricacies, the way he did it—that's a bad choice of words, I suppose—but he's in that vehicle. He's actually penetrating this girl. You can see ligature marks on her arm apparently where she had been seized like these other girls at one time or another, homicide victims where there have been ligatures...And her own story is that she was bound, unbound, told she's going to be let loose, not let loose, finally let loose but she was raped numerous times, all the way up from*

198

Miami to that location in Glades County where she was let go and photographed with a thirty-five millimeter apparently while this was going on...

Q Okay...Photos of the girl. You're unable to get those photos. You believe his attorney has them somewhere.

A I know that your buddy down in Miami has got one of them. He even made it sound like he's got the rest of them...

Elsewhere, the former Cindy Long added to the mystery of the photographs, when she told authorities that she found several photos of nude women in Bobby Joe's belongings that were returned to her by Hillsborough County. She said she sent them back. Asked if the women depicted were dead or alive, Cindy replied that she couldn't tell for sure but some had very blank looks in their eyes.

A week after Bobby Joe Long was arrested and confessed, the November 23, 1984 edition of the Tampa Tribune reported that:

"Accused murderer Robert J. Long is a suspect in an unsolved murder and a burglary-sexual battery case under investigation by the Orange County Sheriff's Office, a spokeswoman said Thursday.

"In both cases, the method used during the crimes matched the way Long allegedly operated, said Joyce Drazen, public information officer for the Orange County Sheriff's Office. She said she could not elaborate. The victim in each case was a young woman.

"'Everything is looking good now. We have enough circumstantial evidence to list him as a suspect,' Drazen said.

"The murder of the young woman occurred earlier this year. Her body was recovered in April lying in a trash pile in a rural part of the county. Drazen said she could not provide further information.

"'He's the only suspect we have,' she said of the murder case. 'We've already investigated all the leads.'

"The Orange County Sheriff's Office in Orlando has about five unsolved murders, but Long is a suspect in just one, she said.

"But, it was the burglary and sexual battery case that led Orange County investigators to consider Long as a suspect. The

assailant entered the house, sexually assaulted the woman and stole some household items before he left.

"The list of stolen items was given to detectives who searched Long's apartment Wednesday night. Drazen said she did not know if the search turned up any direct links.

"'We began looking at him a few days after his arrest. There probably isn't a detective in the state that isn't doing the same thing.'

"It was during an apartment search that investigators said they turned up evidence connecting Long to the sexual assault of a Pinellas County woman in May. Investigators also found evidence allegedly from the rape and robbery of a Pasco County woman in March, including silver salt and pepper shakers, belonging to the victim...

"Long is being held in protective custody in the Hillsborough County jail."

Nothing more was said about the Orange County homicide in which Long was a suspect, nor the two home-invasion cases, in one of which he was positively identified by Carol Bellini (the second one in Orange County may have been the thirteen-year-old "Jennifer" Long described in his lurid letter.) But Pasco and Pinellas Counties still had plenty to say about the Ad Man Rapist and what his fate should be.

From April 15 through April 17, 1985, Bobby Joe Long stood trial in Pasco County for the barbarous attack on Shelly Janke in her Port Richey home the previous year. He faced seven charges--armed burglary, armed robbery, kidnaping, and four counts of sexual battery. The jury was sequestered in a local hotel during the trial and received the case at 12:10 p.m. on the seventeenth. It returned with its guilty verdict at 1:42 p.m.— and that included time out for lunch.

Following the conviction, Pasco County Circuit Judge Lawrence E. Keough wasted no time in imposing the maximum. He sentenced Long to ninety-nine years on each of the seven counts, for a total of 693 years.

In pronouncing sentence, Judge Keough castigated Bobby Joe Long, who stood before the bench with a smirk on his face. "The

cruelty inflicted upon the victim was dehumanizing and outrageously traumatic, loathsome and sadistic. No one but the victim knows the extent of the suffering that you inflicted because none of us can fully empathize, none of us can completely understand or accurately reconstruct in our minds the extent of the living hell that you fashioned for her in her own home. And her suffering will continue for as long as she lives."

The sentence far exceeded the normal guidelines the state recommends for such crimes. In justifying the sentences plainly intended to keep Bobby Joe Long behind bars until he dies, Judge Keough, angrily and in often non-judicial terms, declared that Long's conduct in commission of the crimes "...was particularly cruel and sadistic...He bound the victim, gagged her, covered her eyes and repeatedly raped her. At one point during the hell-like episode, the Defendant placed a pillow on the victim's face, while she was gagged and bound, and walked out of the room, leaving the victim unable to properly breathe, and the victim feared that she would suffocate...He also used a gun and a knife and at one point placed the point of the knife to the victim's skin and moved it as a simulation of gross immolation.

"[His] conduct...caused the victim to sustain great fear for her safety and the safety of her family members, and the victim was grossly dehumanized and caused to suffer great emotional trauma which will likely persist to some substantial degree for the remainder of her life.

"...Society must be spared the risk of future exposure to the Defendant's evil designs and his obvious uncontrolled hatred of young women. Rehabilitation...is unrealistic...During the pronouncement of the sentences, the Defendant repeatedly broadly smiled, and his inappropriate demeanor was a further reflection of his disdain for the rule of law. He discernably possesses not a scintilla of remorse. He is palpably extremely dangerous and should remain incarcerated for the remainder of his life."

This was the same Bobby Joe Long who continued to protest all the way to his Death Row cell that: "I didn't hurt any of them."

Three months after his conviction for raping Shelly Janke in Port Richey, Long decided it was pointless to fight the similar charges he

faced for the attack on Lynn Newell in Palm Harbor. He plead guilty to the following crimes:

COUNT I: Sexual battery, penis in mouth. Threat with knife, deadly weapon

COUNT II: Sexual battery, penis in vagina

COUNT III: Sexual battery, finger in rectum

COUNT IV: Kidnapping

COUNT V: Armed robbery

COUNT VI: Armed burglary

On July 15, 1985 Pinellas County Circut Court Judge John T. Ware accepted Long's guilty plea and sentenced him to six life terms, one for each of the six charges, another sentence far in excess of the state's guidelines. As did Judge Keough in Pasco County, Judge Ware also attached to Long's file an explanation of "Factors Justifying the Court's Departure From the Sentencing Guidelines" which stated:

The defendant used a high degree of sophistication and planning in carrying out the offence.

The defendant used a deadly weapon at the time of the commission of the crime.

The defendant used more force than was necessary to commit the offense.

The offense was committed in the presence of the victim's minor child.

The defendant, at knife point, struck, cut, bound, gagged and terrorized the victim.

As a result of the defendant's actions, the victim has suffered extreme emotional as well as physical trauma.

The defendant has engaged in an extremely violent pattern of criminal conduct which indicates he poses a serious danger to society. Should he ever be released, there is a substantial likelihood he would again commit crimes and his continued incarceration is necessary for the protection of the community.

Unfortunately, that portion of the community most in need of protection was most vulnerable. Too late for the girls of the street and his other victims— living prey for a sadistic hunter. And if Bobby Joe ever walked in society again, he'd pick up the scent, and the hunt would continue.

Sgt. Tom Hail with the Pasco County Sheriff's Office secures the crime scene off Morris Bridge Road where body of Virginia Lee Johnson was discovered on November 6, 1984.

Major Gary Terry. Headed Task Force.

Bobby Joe Long listens to court testimony during hearing in Tampa.

Corporal Lee "Pops" Baker. Lead investigator.

203

Ngeun Thi (Peggy) Long, 20. First found. Second killed? Body discovered May 13, 1984.

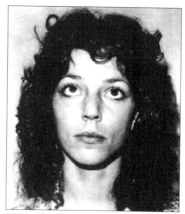

Michell Denise Simms, 22, found May 27, 1984. Beaten, strangled, throat cut.

Elizabeth Loudenback, 22. Missing, June 8, 1984. Found June 24, 1984.

Chanel Devon Williams, 18, found October 7, 1984. Only victim shot.

Karen Beth Dinsfriend, 28, murdered October 13, 1984. Asphyxiation.

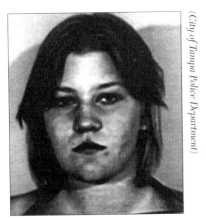

Virginia Lee Johnson, 18. Pasco
County victim.

Kimberly Kyle Hopps, 22. Mummified
remains found October 31, 1984.

Kim Marie Swann, 21. Strangled body
found in Tampa, November 12, 1984.

Vicky Elliott, 21. Vanished September 7,
1984. Remains found November 16, 1984.

Artiss Ann Wick, 17. Last victim
found. First killed?

Louella Long, mother of defendant Robert J. Long, takes in jury selection during Pasco County trial.

Bobby Joe Long escorted out of the Pasco County Courthouse in Dade City after being removed from a pre-trial hearing.

Miami defense attorney Ellis Rubin, right, confers with his client, serial killer Robert J. Long during re-trial in July, 1986.

Part Four

THE MURDERS

A LETTER FROM BOBBY

```
Once the killing started, it was just part of it.
None of the cunts suffered long...I'm not sadistic
to that point. After the first one was killed it
became necessary to kill the others for obvious rea-
sons. They were all sluts. Really!
```

▲   ▲   ▲

In one of those curious ironies of life, the first of Bobby Joe Long's victims—or more precisely the first known victim and the first body found—was also named Long. Peggy Long was the stage name she was known by among the regulars who came to gape at her tiny, taut breasts as she teased her way among the gropers at the Starlight Bar and the Sly Fox Lounge up on North Nebraska Avenue. Closer friends, including the boyfriend who'd lured her east from California, called her Lana. But she was Ngeun Thi Long to her Laotian family, who had settled in California with its rich promise of a new life. But for the restless Lana, what California offered wasn't good enough, so she kept moving east— where she found, rather than a rainbow, a gruesome and lonely death in a Florida ditch.

Mother's Day, May 13, 1984. The Hillsborough County community of Gibsonton lies a dozen miles southeast of Tampa. Here the Alafia River and the smaller Bullfrog Creek empty into eastern Hillsborough Bay, a landward extension of the broader and more

207

famous Tampa Bay. In 1984, the north–south portion of I–75 was under construction. The area around Old East Bay Road and Symmes Road was still mainly rural, although the construction of I–75 was already altering the rustic, Old Florida character as developers, anticipating a suburban boom sparked by the completion of the new superhighway, rushed to stake claims in the quiet countryside.

Signs of new developments were going up everywhere, but there was still plenty of room for a couple of kids to roam and explore and, as country kids have always done, make their own fun, which is what Jason Westerman and Greg Adams were doing that Sunday afternoon. After spending Mother's Day morning with their moms, the two friends wandered out late in the afternoon, looking for something to do. About 500 yards from the Westerman home, Old East Bay Road dead–ended at the I–75 construction site. The piles of dirt and rocks were just the things to attract exuberant teenage boys. The pair picked up a couple of discarded plastic bags and, using stones as weights improvised parachutes that they tossed up and chased around the mounds of dirt. It was while they were chasing one of the parachutes that the boys noticed a bad smell in the air. The closer they got to the construction site, the worse it got.

Then they saw it. Something black, off to the side in a field of low grass and weeds that looked like they'd been tramped down. "At first we thought it was just a dead cow or something," Jason explained. "But then we got closer and saw it was a person, so that's when we ran home and told my dad."

Jerry and Kay Westerman didn't want to believe there was a body practically in their own backyard, but the boys were too worked up to brush off. The Westermans followed Jason and Greg back to the site, took one quick look, and rushed home to call the sheriff's department. Deputy Dan Aggers arrived about 6:30 p.m. His initial handwritten report noted: "Was shown the scene by Mr. Westerman, immediately backing off the area and securing the same. Writer observed a female body lying face down, nude, with both hands bound behind her back with a white material. Also

208

observed the body to have shiny black hair & maggots covering the facial area, which was down into the grass."

Within the next hour, other uniformed units arrived in response to Aggers call, followed by detectives from the Major Crimes Unit, crime-scene technicians, and Dr. Charles Diggs from the Medical Examiner's Office. Major John Cacciatore showed up, along with Captain Bill Miller. The brass was out, which made the younger, uniformed deputies working the perimeter of the crime scene nervous. Top ranks didn't make the crime scenes very often, especially not on a Mother's Day Sunday afternoon.

Lt. Gary Terry was also on hand as the newly appointed head of the Major Crimes Unit. It was the first of what was to become a very bad string of Sunday afternoons for the young commander. A cop with thirteen years of experience, Terry had the wisdom to defer to the judgements of the old hands under his command, some of whom had twenty or thirty years of investigating hundreds of murders behind them. With that kind of experience, you develop a sixth sense about a murder scene. Sometimes your gut tells you as much as your eyes. A good homicide detective learned to listen to his gut and not be misled by appearances..Besides Terry, Detectives Lee "Pops" Baker and Randy Latimer were soon on the scene. At that time, in 1984, the Hillsborough County sheriff's office had 1,052 square miles to cover, but only eight detectives, who worked everything from assaults to murders. To have half the squad, plus the top brass, show up at one crime scene, was unusual, to say the least.

"This one," Terry recalled, "just didn't feel right.

"I knew as soon as I looked at that first body, we had something bad on our hands," "Pops" Baker" added.

"I'll remember that first one vividly for the rest of my life," Baker said. "It was Mother's Day. I'd seen many, many bodies over the years but this one here was unique due to the way she was displayed. No one could just throw her out and have her land that way in that position. She definitely had to be posed on purpose. Her legs were pulled further apart than she was tall and I don't think that's possible unless somebody did it on purpose."

Lt. Terry had an identical reaction. "When we arrived at the first crime scene, it scared the hell out of us the instant we saw it. It just didn't set right.

"I've got a captain there who'd been with the Sheriff's Office almost twenty-five years, a major who'd been there longer than that. I was a young homicide lieutenant and I see these guys scratching their heads. They tell me that in over a quarter of a century of investigating homicides, they'd never seen a body displayed like that. Of course, we didn't know what we were facing at the time. What we found there totally changed how Hillsborough County conducts murder investigations. We're still feeling the impact more than ten years later."

The woman was face down, with her feet spread unnaturally far apart to expose her genitals. The spread measured five–feet, two–inches from heel to heel. It seemed obvious to anyone at the scene that the woman had been posed deliberately by the killer to shock whoever found her. A layer of brownish maggots blanketed her midsection and neck. The skin of her buttocks, back, and legs was mottled with ugly black and reddish marks that resembled deep bruises, while portions of her thighs and upper arms seemed to be covered by massive blisters. The area around her anus and vagina was a blackened, crusted blob of oozing body fluids. The remains were covered with insect bites; clouds of flies, swarming the hot, muggy space around the body, had to be shooed away before crime—scene technicians could begin their work.

The victim's wrists were bound with rope and a length of white cloth, with her right hand resting palm up on her buttocks and her left at her side. The approximately eight–inch gap between her wrists apparently was intended to allow for some movement, presumably making it easier for the guy to have sex with her while she was tied up. There was a ligature around her neck, but what struck the investigators as they examined it was how much the trailing rope resembled a leash that the killer could use to control the victim.

Lt. Terry walked in a wide arch around the crime scene, shaking his head. "Oh shit!" he muttered to himself. "This is not good!" At the time, the sheriff's office routinely investigated twenty-five to

thirty murders a year. A few of the victims were bound, but no one could recall anything even close to this horror. There was a gnawing feeling deep in Terry's gut that he and his investigators were in for some bad times.

But at that point, there was only one victim and one crime scene to process, so the top priorities, as darkness glided over the lonely, brutalized corpse that Sunday evening, were to identify the victim and determine how she had died. Most murder victims, veteran investigators knew, are killed by someone close to them—spouse, lover, relative, friend. That's the place most homicide investigations start. Also, the method of murder can tell a sharp-eyed cop a lot. Was she shot, stabbed, strangled? Beaten? Raped? Killed elsewhere and dumped where she was found? What about forensic evidence? What pieces of himself did the killer unwittingly leave behind? So Lt. Terry and his squad, while tuning in to their gut reactions, started where every good investigation must begin: With the evidence.

"Pops" Baker got the assignment as lead investigator on the case. His initial report reflects his Sherlock Holmesian eye for detail and the painstaking steps that were devoted to gathering crucial evidence from that initial site. Later, as other bodies turned up and investigators learned to recognize the handiwork of the same killer, the job was quicker and simpler. Now, working under powerful portable lights set up to illuminate the scene, Baker began picking at the pieces of what was left:

"Writer entered the crime scene from the north along with CST (Crime Scene Technician) Judy Swann," Baker's report began. *"We both stayed to the extreme westerly direction following the fence line. CST Swann obtained photographs while walking towards the body...The body was laying face down, the head to the north with the face pointing in an easterly direction. The victim's feet were in a southerly direction, but both were pulled apart to an extreme. The feet were almost facing east and west. The victim was nude, but a light colored cloth material was observed under the head area. The victim's hands were bound behind her back with both cloth materi-*

al and a rope. The victim was not wearing any jewelry. The victim had dark hair approx. shoulder length. The victim had a rope around her neck three times. This rope was different from the rope around her wrist. The rope around her neck appeared to have a slip–knot type.

"Writer examined the immediate area around the body and found the grass and weeds standing indicating very little or no activity at this immediate area...

"Writer moved to the east on the traveled portion of the dead end road and observed an area which indicated activity. This area contained a piece of cloth similar to the material found around the victim's hands and under her head. Also a piece of rope was found which was similar to the rope around the victim's wrist. This area indicated the victim's body was either being moved or possibly attacked by her assailant(s)...observed one set of tire tracks leading up to the area where the ground was disturbed and these tracks indicated the vehicle left in the same direction it came. The tracks indicate it backed up a short distance, turned around and drove out...

"At 2130 hours, Dr. [Charles] Diggs arrived and examined the maggot infested body and could only determine the victim was female and the possible cause of death being strangulation. Dr. Diggs estimated the time of death to be within the last two or three days. He also estimated the age being in her teens. The race was not determined. Dr. Diggs ordered the body removed intact by Professional Services. He advised he would do the autopsy that evening. Writer observed the body being removed and requested ropes and cloth remain on the victim during transportation. The body was placed in a body bag due to the putrefaction stage and removed at 2250 hours.

"Due to the late hour, Lt. Terry requested that the area be secured and a Patrol Deputy left at the scene until we could return the following AM to do a more extensive search...

"At 2330 hours, writer arrived at the MEO...Dr. Diggs advised X–rays showed no projectiles within the body nor any broken bones....

Dr. Diggs examined the neck area and found bruising from the ropes, but the hyoid bone was intact. Dr. Diggs ruled cause of death tentatively as strangulation.

"At this point in our investigation we only knew the victim was female, possibly a teenager, race unknown, and died of possible strangulation....

"At 1600 hours, writer called FBI Agent Mike Malone to assist in the identification of our victims...He advised we needed to send the entire hands severing them at the wrist. He suggested we place each hand in a plastic container with lids and send them via express mail.

"At 1800 hours, writer met with Dr. Diggs...The hands were severed, placed in a container and taken into custody by CST Swann. We also learned the victim had pierced ears...This area of the lobe was cut off and taken into evidence..."

The steps Baker followed in gathering crime-scene and forensic evidence were routine police procedure. What followed was anything but routine.

"We were very concerned, because the condition of the body was so out of the ordinary, that we took some unusual steps right then which set the tone for the entire investigation and which turned out to be vitally important as we went along," Terry explained. "We decided on the spot that every bit of evidence we collected was going straight to the FBI lab in Quantico. Not by regular channels either. We put a detective on a plane with a bagful of evidence and flew him straight into the FBI lab, hand—carried it in, which is totally out of the ordinary. Beginning with that first body, we had couriers going back and forth between Tampa and Quantico constantly.

"And the FBI lab report came back with something totally unexpected—the discovery of cheap, red fibers found on the body. It was our first fiber evidence, but at the time it only meant a single piece of evidence relating to that one homicide. The fibers didn't become relevant until later, but, fortunately, we made a command decision as soon as we were informed that fibers had been found, to keep any information about such evidence secret.

"We didn't know at the time we had the first stirrings of a serial killer on our hands. I'm not sure we even knew what a serial killer was. This was still at a time when the huge publicity flap about serial killers hadn't really gotten started. The Green River Killer, the Atlanta Child Murders, Bundy, those were about the only ones the public knew about when our first body was found. Certainly, there wasn't any textbook available on how to investigate serial homicides. There is now, because we helped write it, but back then we were just feeling our way along and most of the time we did the right things," Terry said.

The FBI's initial involvement in the case and the vital role it was to play in the critical fiber evidence was recounted in an

FBI Law Enforcement Bulletin:

The first body, nude and bound, of a young Oriental female was discovered by young boys late in the afternoon in a remote area of southern Hillsborough County...The fibers which were removed from the items in this case were also examined and this evidence would provide the first important lead in the case. Eventually, it would prove to be the most critical evidence of the entire case. The equipment used for the fiber examinations consisted of a stereoscopic microscope, a comparison microscope, a polarized light microscope, a microspectrophotometer, a melting point apparatus, and eventually, an infrared spectrophotometer. A single lustrous red trilobal nylon fiber was found on a piece of fabric found near the victim. Because of the size, type, and cross sectional shape of this fiber, it was determined that this fiber was probably a carpet fiber. Because the body had been exposed to the elements for a substantial period of time, and fibers which have been transferred are very transient in nature, it was surmised that most of the carpet fibers which had originally been transferred to the victim's body had been lost. Since the victim's body was found in a remote area, she had probably been transported in a vehicle, and the carpet-

214

ing of this vehicle is probably the last item she had been in contact with. Furthermore, since there is normally a transference of trace materials [i.e., fibers] when two objects come into close contact, it was also surmised that the killer was probably driving a vehicle with a red carpet. Vehicular carpets readily shed their fibers, and these types of fibers are commonly found on the bodies of victims at crime scenes. These fibers could then provide a critical "link" in determining whether a serial murderer was operating in the Tampa Bay area.

The above information was provided to the HCSO, with the caution that the fiber information should be kept confidential. Experience has shown that if the existence of fiber evidence is publicized, serial killers might change their pattern and start disposing of the bodies in such a manner that this fiber evidence is either lost or destroyed. The most famous example of this is the Wayne Williams case [the Atlanta Child Murders]. The possibility also existed that if the killer knew of the existence of the red carpet fibers, he would probably get rid of the vehicle that was the source of this evidence.

"A single lustrous red trilobal nylon fiber..."

Hardly bigger than a breath, but there it was. A microscopic speck of red powerful enough to snare a killer. The fact that the fiber even made it all the way to the FBI's microscopes is a minor miracle in itself. In the years since the conclusion of the case, Gary Terry has put together a slide presentation of the Bobby Joe Long serial murder case, which he presents to law-enforcement groups around the country. During the presentation, Terry emphasizes the fact that fiber evidence is extremely fragile and ephemeral. The fiber formula investigators go by is this: In four hours, you lose eighty percent of fiber evidence. Within forty-eight hours, ninety-six percent of that evidence may be lost.

To find even a single fiber after three days exposure to the harsh Florida elements was incredible good luck. But, in the end, one was all it took.

For Lt. Terry, "Pops" Baker, and the others on the murder squad, the most pressing problem was identifying the victim. Until they knew who she was, they had no place to start their search for her killer. The day after the body was discovered, the still–unidentified remains piqued the curiosity of a roving Tampa Tribune reporter:

"The teen-age girl was five-feet-two-inches tall, about eighty-eight pounds, and had long dark hair.

"That's about all investigators working Monday had to go on in their search for the name of a girl whose nude body was found face down in a Gibsonton ditch on Sunday evening.

"A Hillsborough County sheriff's official said, 'We don't have any clothing. There was no jewelry. I wish there would have been a scar, a tattoo, something.'

"Sheriff's Lt. Gary Terry said the body appeared to have been in the ditch between two and three days. The ditch is beyond a part of Interstate 75 that is under construction near Symmes and East Bay roads, in the eastern part of the county.

"Terry said investigators are awaiting test results from the medical examiner before releasing the cause of death.

"But he said, 'We are confident it was a homicide.'

'Tests also should reveal whether the girl was sexually assaulted...

"Some Hillsborough County residents had called the Sheriff's Office Monday morning with information about missing girls, but so far the information has not been useful, Terry said.

"Also, law enforcement authorities in Georgia and across Florida have inquired about the discovery."

About 7:30 that same evening, after reading the item in the paper, and at the urging of friends, thirty-five year old John Michael Corcoran walked into the sheriff's office. He brought photos of his girlfriend, who left following an argument over money

216

the previous Thursday, May 10, and hadn't been seen since. Corcoran said he thought the woman, a nineteen year old Laotian named Ngeun Thi Long (Corcoran called her Lana), had just taken off for a while because she was pissed at him, which is why he hadn't reported her missing until now. He still didn't believe the dead woman was his girlfriend, but some of his friends did—and they said if he didn't come in and report her missing, they would, so here he was.

"Pops" Baker listened to the man's story and studied the pretty, dark–eyed, dark–haired, smiling young woman in Corcoran's photos. The teeth were what tipped him off. "Pops" recalled the straight, white, well–kept teeth of the corpse on the slab in the morgue. Just like the teeth of the woman in the photo. Corcoran signed a consent-to-search form, and drove with Baker back to his apartment in the Shadow Oaks complex. Crime—scene technician Racey Wilson met Baker there, and began dusting items for fingerprints. He picked up three good prints, two from a glass in the bathroom and one from a metal box in the bedroom that Corcoran said belonged to Lana. About an hour after he'd started, Wilson came up with a positive match: The dead woman was, indeed, Ngeun Thi "Lana" Long. But how she got all the way from the North Tampa apartment she shared with Corcoran to the rural dump site in southeastern Hillsborough County—and who took her there—remained a mystery.

The following day, the Tampa Tribune reported that the woman found in the ditch had been identified, and added: "Sheriff's Lt. Gary Terry said Long was a dancer at the Sly Fox Lounge. She was last seen alive in the vicinity of Fletcher Avenue and 15th Street, leaving a local lounge with an unidentified white male."

Now, at least, Terry's men had a place to start. Half a dozen investigators turned their full attention to learning all there was to know about Lana Long—and what there might be about her that got her strangled, and left for the bugs to devour. Naturally, their suspicions focused first on John Corcoran and then on Lana's job as an topless dancer at some of the shadier joints along the North

Nebraska flesh strip. Either one provided ample reason to suspect that something about Lana Long's lifestyle may have been a motive for murder.

John Corcoran was invited in for a session with Lt. Terry, "Pops" Baker, and a few of the detectives. Lana Long was his fiancee, Corcoran began. They'd met in L.A. about a year and a half ago, around September or October of 1982, and had gotten engaged in November, 1983. When they met, he was in the process of writing a book, something he'd been working on for eight years. For six or eight months while he was finishing the book, he'd been without a job or any income. That's when he met Lana and moved in with her. She supported him while he wrote. But by February, 1983, they were broke, and were evicted from their apartment. Corcoran moved in with a friend, and a few months later Lana returned and stayed with him while he scraped away at a "penny—ante" job he'd landed.

Corcoran said that he was friendly with members of the Southern California Asian community because of his long involvement in the martial arts, and through those contacts he became associated with the owners of several Los Angeles area clubs, lounges, and strip joints owned by Asians. He dated several of the dancers in the clubs, and one of them had introduced him to Lana, who was dancing in the Cameo Room on Sunset Boulevard. (Later, in a memo to file, Detective Greg Ganey noted: "The owner [of the Cameo Room] used to be a LCN [La Cosa Nostra] figure, Eddie Nash, who is involved with prostitution, narcotics and pornography. It appears Nash sold the Cameo Room in February, 1981...This information came from CIU Det. Lou Graham, Los Angeles PD.")

Late in 1983, Corcoran continued, he was offered a job he couldn't refuse. Gil Reneau°, his first karate instructor in Pittsburgh, Pennsylvania, had formed a film company, Reneau Productions. He'd set up shop in Tampa, and planned to make movies in Florida. When Reneau offered him a job as unit publicist, Corcoran jumped at the chance. Lana agreed to come with him, and they drove cross-country in Corcoran's Trans Am, stop-

ping off in Houston to visit some of Lana's Laotian relatives before arriving in Tampa on January 1, 1984. For the first few weeks, they stayed with Reneau at his luxurious condo on Davis Island, an exclusive waterfront enclave where the Hillsborough River empties into Tampa Bay, just across a short bridge from downtown Tampa.

Later, Corcoran and Lana moved into the one–bath, one–bedroom Shadow Oaks apartment on the city's far north side—a major comedown from his new boss's pricey condo, but it was all they could afford. Coming to Florida meant a new start, and Corcoran didn't want to see his pretty, sexy and, he felt, overly friendly girlfriend go back to dancing in the bars, even though she usually ended up with more tips stuck down her thread–thin G–string than any of the other dancers. But within a month, Lana was so bored that she threatened to go back to California if she didn't get back into the nightlife. Lana, Corcoran told the cops, was the original party girl, and working the topless joints was where the partying was. Corcoran said he didn't want to lose her, so he started checking out the bars himself. He found her a job at the Starlite, but the hours didn't suit her, so Corcoran helped her get on at the Sly Fox. He felt that was the best of the string of topless joints around town, because the Sly Fox management seemed to take care of the girls better than most. Also, the owner arranged for Lana to dance only four nights a week, and put her right to work on the 4 p.m. to 12 a.m. shift, the big-tipper hours. Most girls have to work hard to get those prime hours when they can make the big bucks, but Lana walked right into it. Lana Long started dancing at the Sly Fox the last week in February, and dove headfirst into the party life she craved. She started coming home drunk a lot, Corcoran recalled. Started calling in sick and then hitting the other bars looking for a party, meeting a lot of other men, although, Corcoran insisted, he wasn't the jealous type and Lana wasn't the cheating type. That's just the way Lana was. Friendly with everybody; loved a good party. And, lately, she had developed a healthy appetite for cocaine. But it got to the point where sometimes she didn't come home until morning.

219

In fact, a few days before she vanished for good, Lana had stayed out all night. About 7:30 a.m. on Wednesday, May 7, while Corcoran was getting ready for work, she'd finally wandered in and surprised him with the news that she'd quit her job at the Sly Fox. Corcoran said he was upset, since he'd gone out of his way to get her the job because they really needed the cash she was bringing in. His job, while he was excited about the potential it offered, just didn't pay enough. The quarrel over jobs and money resumed that evening after he got home, and continued most of the night.

The next morning, Thursday, May 10, Lana was still in bed when Corcoran left for work. He spoke to her once ,by phone, during the day, and urged her to call the people at the Sly Fox and try to patch things up. When he got home that evening, Lana was watching television, and the argument picked right up where it had left off. She said she wanted to go back to L.A. on vacation, or maybe get a job doing volunteer work at one of the Tampa hospitals, something that she'd done in California. Corcoran pointed out that they barely had money for food, much less airfare to California, and stormed out of the house. As he slammed the door behind him, he heard Lana call out, "Well, if you're going out, so am I.' Corcoran said he spent the next several hours hanging around the Sly Fox and Cheeks and a couple of other bars, trying to find out how deep Lana was getting into drugs and who she was staying out all night with. He went home sometime after midnight, and Lana, as he expected, was gone. Friday morning, he went to work as usual. He tried calling home several times during the day, but got no answer. That night, when Lana still hadn't returned, Corcoran drove around North Tampa, visiting the bars she liked, looking for her. When she didn't show up again that night, Corcoran said he assumed she was just trying to punish him by staying away longer than usual. It didn't occur to him to report her missing, he added. Coming from a place like L.A., he figured the cops would just laugh at him, since Lana was a consenting adult and could do what she wanted.

On Saturday he loafed around the apartment waiting to hear from Lana. That evening, he went to a spaghetti dinner the apart-

ment management was hosting for tenants and talked to a woman named Debbie, who worked in the rental office. She told him that two nights ago she'd bumped into Lana, who complained that Corcoran had locked her out of their apartment after a fight. Debbie said she loaned Lana ten dollars and watched her walk out to street. Corcoran said he slept late Sunday, but when he still hadn't heard from Lana by that afternoon, he began to worry. He spent most of Sunday evening calling all the numbers listed in Lana's phone book, but no one had seen her. By Monday evening, that concern had escalated into a real fear that something bad had happened. In fact, Corcoran said, he was looking up the telephone number for the police department when a friend called to tell him that a woman's body had been found south of Tampa. Sounds a lot like Lana, the friend said, adding "...if you don't get your butt down to the police right now, I'm going."

When Corcoran finished telling his story, the detectives had some hard questions of their own. What about drugs? Are you using? Did Lana? Yes, Corcoran readily admitted, he had used drugs in the past, but not now. Lana did bring drugs home from work from time to time. Some pot, a little coke, but never enough that he worried about it. Corcoran did say he often warned Lana to be careful about mixing booze and the street drugs that were always floating around the joints where she liked to party.

As for their sex life, Corcoran said that Lana was pretty straight, nothing that he'd consider "abnormal'— although lately, since they'd moved to Tampa, it seemed that her sex drive had gone way up while his had dropped off. He attributed that to the pressures of the new job. His boss demanded a lot out of him, and maybe the stress and fear of losing his job had watered him down a little bit, Corcoran conceded. But that didn't mean Lana would go out on the prowl. "She would have talked to me first and tried to iron out any problems if she wanted sex and I wasn't in the mood," Corcoran insisted. But she did enjoy teasing him about how guys were always trying to get in her pants, like she was hinting that if he couldn't take care of her there were plenty of others out there who could and would. He knew that she liked to go drinking with

221

guys she met at the Sly Fox, sometimes even stay out all night partying, but he really didn't think she was screwing around on him. She just wasn't the type.

Another thing that bothered him was Lana's habit of bumming rides back and forth to the Sly Fox or Cheeks or C.C.'s with guys she didn't know. It could be that somebody lured her out to the country on the promise of booze and drugs and then killed her, Corcoran said. In fact, just a few weeks earlier, she was out drinking at C.C.'s when some stranger offered her a ride. Somewhere around Sligh and Nebraska Avenue, the guy pulled over and tried to tie her up, but Lana jumped out of the car and got away. It was about 3 a.m., and Lana walked the streets for an hour before she flagged down a cabbie who took her home—and then started dropping in to see her all the time like he was a boyfriend.

"Lana was just too prone to party," Corcoran concluded, breaking into sobs. "And now some motherfucker took advantage of her."

Neither Terry nor Baker were convinced that John Corcoran's tears were for real, but so far he'd told them everything they wanted to know, and although he remained high on their list of suspects they had no reason to doubt his story. Plus, talking to Lana's other friends and associates gave them reason to believe that something or someone else might be involved in her murder. Every available Hillsborough County sheriff's detective hit the streets, canvassing the bars and lounges of North Tampa, concentrating on those along Nebraska Avenue where Lana Long either worked or played. They showed her photograph, talked to scores of dancers, waitresses, bartenders, and regulars. Do you know her? When was the last time you saw her? Who'd she hang around with? Who did she leave with? Notice anybody suspicious messing around her lately? Any idea who might want to kill her? Was she dealing drugs? Was she hooking? The more the detectives heard, the more interested they became in a possible drug connection.

Susan Jenkins, a bartender at the Sly Fox, told them that the last day Lana had danced there was on May 9, and although she was supposed to work the next couple of days, she never showed

up. Susan had the impression that Lana was turning into a coke-head. Big user, probably every day at least. Just the other day, Susan had walked into the ladies' room and Lana was in there, taking big hits off a cigarette laced with cocaine.

Robert Howard said he met Lana during her brief stint as a dancer at the Starlite Lounge, and sort of fell for her. "But we never had sex," he insisted. She told me she was living with this guy named John and another girl, but that John wasn't really her boyfriend. In fact, Lana really didn't seem all that interested in sex, even though she could get up there on the runway and put on one hell of a sexy show.

Howard gave her a ride home from work a few of times, drove her to a job interview, and took her to lunch once or twice. He got the impression that she wasn't too happy. She was having really bad nightmares, she told him one time, and often complained that she didn't have any friends in Tampa because her roommate (John) didn't want her to have any. The girls she worked with weren't friendly, and she didn't get along with her family, although she talked a lot about going back to California where she belonged.

Lana (or Peggy, the name Howard knew her by) drank pepper-mint schnapps, and while she could pour them down, he never saw her really blasted. But she did like her pot and coke. She'd called him a couple of times, asking him to score some grass for her. And she was really pissed off over a drug deal gone bad at the Sly Fox. Lana said she'd given a guy fifty dollars for some coke, but he ripped her off and never came back. Another thing Howard noticed about the young dancer was that she was pretty careless about who she left the bar with. She'd get in the car with just about anybody, but he doubted that she was hooking.

And, he added curiously and without prompting, she never talked about doing any porno flicks.

The subject of movies also popped up in an interview with another dancer at the Sly Fox. Pat Gray said she remembered one slow evening when she and Lana started talking with a guy named Howard, who was doing some electrical work in the bar and liked to sit around with the girls after work. This time, right before Lana

disappeared, Howard warned them about getting offers to do modeling work. Said he'd heard some guys were going around the joints trying to entice the girls into nude modeling, when what they were really doing was recruiting victims for "snuff" movies, really sick porno flicks where the girl ended up actually getting killed right there on film. Howard was afraid the girls at the Sly Fox might fall into the trap, since most of them had a tough time making ends meet and were always looking to make an extra buck.

Lois Alvarez, another dancer at the Sly Fox, also mentioned that Lana/Peggy definitely was a heavy drinker and "tooted lots of coke." Lana always seemed to get along with the customers, and was really good at teasing them along while they stuck folding money down inside—way down inside—her G–string. One thing that struck her as kind of odd was that Lana always seemed to have bruises all over her body, and in their line of work it's pretty hard to hide that sort of thing. Matter of fact, the last time she saw Lana, just a day or two before she disappeared, there were big, ugly bruises across her buttocks. Somehow, Lois added, she had the feeling the Lana might be involved in prostitution, but she didn't know for sure.

Richard Parr was a DJ at the Sly Fox while Lana danced there. He described her as a "classic type of chick" and, despite her youth, a regular user—coke, bootleg speed, whatever happened to be filtering through the clubs. The speed, he added, came from a biker who dated one of the other dancers. The rumor going around at the time was that this guy's biker buddies, besides dealing killer speed, were running a shakedown scam on the girls working the North Side topless joints—selling the girls "protection" for a cut of their nightly tips. According to the story Parr heard, Lana told them to fuck off, which wasn't the smartest thing to do when you're dealing with outlaw bikers. The cops had also heard rumors of a biker gang setting up an underground meth lab. Names like Pappy, Goofy, Roto Rooter, Cowboy, No Dope, and Shit for Brains kept popping up.

Valerie Gentry started dancing at the Sly Fox about the same time Lana did. When questioned, she told "Pops" Baker that, yeah,

she knew a biker named Pappy who lived up in Pasco County and had done time in Florida's Santa Fe Pen. Yeah, she had lived with Pappy and had sex with him. Valerie said Pappy could get violent when he didn't get sex when he wanted it, but he'd never used ropes or none of that bondage stuff on her. Lana/Peggy told her that Pappy was trying to run the protection scam on her, but she just laughed in his face and told him to fuck off. Peggy, Valerie recalled, used to bring her own bottle to work with her and drink from it all night. Used to smoke a lot of pot in between dances, too.

When "Pops" Baker found Pappy, the biker, who called himself a self-employed carpenter, he admitted that he did a little pimping on the side. Had three chicks working for him up at Cheeks, another at the Sly Fox. When Baker pressed him, Pappy also admitted that he and some other bikers were running a protection "business" for the girls in the north-end clubs—charged them twenty-five bucks a week for transportation to and from work, another twenty-five to take care of any "problems" the girls might encounter in the clubs. But, Pappy insisted, he never tried to sell his "business services" to Peggy. Matter of fact, he most always made "donations" to Peggy to "encourage" her to keep dancing. Pappy was down in Abilene, Texas when Peggy vanished, and had the alibi to prove it.

Until some strands of innocuous red fiber changed their minds, Terry and his men pursued the theory that Lana Long, as one of the most popular dancers along the Nebraska Strip, may have been kidnaped and killed as an example that the bikers meant business with their protection racket.

But that promising lead petered out— just another red herring, one of many in the early stages of the Lana Long investigation.

One thing they did learn that made them wonder even more was that, in the last hours of her life, Lana Long was desperately trying to raise money to get out of town and return to her immigrant family in California. On the Wednesday and Thursday before she vanished, Lana had made a dozen or more calls to several numbers in both L.A. and the San Francisco area. In tracing the numbers, cops spoke to sixteen year old Mary Ann Dong, who said she was Lana's niece. Lana told her she had been trying to reach Mary

225

Ann's father, Melvin Dong, in San Francisco, to get money together to come home. Lana said she and John were fighting, and she wanted to come back to California.

In the end, none of that mattered—not the outlaw bikers, not a spurned boyfriend, not a possible drug deal gone bad. The police were doing their job, conducting a routine homicide investigation by the book. Unfortunately, the killer they were after was busy writing a whole new book, about which Terry and his men, for all their good intentions and hard work, knew next to nothing. They were about to get a crash course in the bizarre nature of a serial killer:

BOBBY: *The first one started when I was, we [the nurse at Brandon Humana Hospital] broke up again, and I went to a topless bar and had a few drinks. Uhhh, I don't think I am really what you call a drunk or anything, but you know I was feeling them...'cause I'm not a drinker. You know, so two or three drinks hits me. But when I left, I was on my way home. I wasn't thinking about doing anything bad to anybody. I wasn't in a real good frame of mind. But I wasn't thinking of attacking nobody or hurting nobody or anything like that. Okay? I was just going to go home and go to bed and go to sleep. And on the way home I saw a girl walking. This was about one/two o'clock in the morning. I saw a girl walking down the street in a mini skirt, tube top and a French beret and high heels on Nebraska Avenue in Tampa which is the meat market in Tampa. It's like U.S. One in Miami. So uhhh, I picked her up and she was going to a bar that was right on the way to my apartment. And uhhh, when I got by the bar instead of turning left to go to the bar I turned right and went into some unincorporated area and I don't know why, but it was a very violent...I don't know what it was about this girl. But it was very violent and I wanted to scare her and I don't know why. I don't know why!*

And that's how it started. But after that, then it was just like clockwork. It wasn't a matter of going out and prowling and...and you know, I'm going to get one and you know maybe I ought to check here...check there...God, a couple of them happened on my way to and from the racquetball court. Uhhh, to the grocery store. I

almost burned my apartment down one time cause I had a TV din-
ner in the oven cooking and went out to get milk and saw one walk-
ing down the street when I went out to get the milk...So when I
came back and my apartment was almost burned down, ended up
that I was gone so long, you know.

REPORTER: *So you'd be doing the most normal things in the*
world, racquetball, cooking yourself dinner, going to the grocery
store. And you would have something come over you?

BOBBY: *When I saw them walking around the street it was*
like ABCD. I pull over, they'd get in, I'd drive a little ways, stop,
pull a knife, a gun, whatever, tie them up, take them out and that
would be it. And they all went exactly the same way until McVey
came along. (CBS News Interview)

That's one account of the Lana Long murder. However, Bobby
Joe told Dr. Joel Norris a completely different story of his fateful
meeting with the young Laotian immigrant and why he killed her.
In this obviously self–serving, less-than-truthful version, which
appeared in *Walking Time Bombs*, Bobby Joe shifts the blame for
the killing to the victim herself, and portrays himself as the "poor
me" dupe of a scheming, flesh–peddling whore:

"Long recalls feeling an escalating sense of revulsion with each
rape–murder. He had no feeling of remorse for the victims at first,
because in his own mind he had categorized them as whores,
women who, he said, used, manipulated, exploited, and tricked
men. They aroused a visceral hate in him that he claims he was
never able to control after the [motorcycle] accident. 'I know what
I did. I raped and murdered them. But they were the ones who
offered the invitation.' He remembers that the first murder began
when Ngeun Long, the victim, picked him up in a bar on Nebraska
Avenue. 'She picked me up, really, I didn't go after her. She was a
whore. She cruised over to me selling everything she had for any-
thing I had. She knew how to seduce anything that walked. She
manipulated men and was after me. Once I had her in the car, I
tied her up and raped her. Then I strangled her and dumped her
body alongside the highway. I knew what I was doing, but I just

couldn't stop myself. It was like there was a dream me doing what I really wanted to do even though I knew I shouldn't be doing it. I hated her. I hated her from the time she picked me up, but I didn't plan to murder her. I don't even think I planned to rape her either. She was just sitting there in the front seat of the car staring at me, waiting for me to show that I needed to have her, and I grabbed her, covered her mouth, and tied her up. I couldn't believe what I'd done the next morning. I was sick. I threw up. I knew I was in real trouble. Then a few days later I met the Simms girl, and it was the same thing all over again. She was just a barfly. She really picked me up, and I just turned on her in the car.'"

Lana Long, said Lt. Terry, was not a hooker, at least not as far as his men could determine in scores of interviews with people who should know. But she was a dancer in a topless bar, and was most often described as a "tease" who got customers to buy her drinks, which put her in a highly vulnerable category. Walking the streets or hitching rides didn't bother her, which increased her vulnerability. So for those last two weeks in May her death was handled for what it appeared to be—a single homicide, albeit one with sexual connotations, by person or persons unknown. Police attention focused on Lana Long's boyfriend, who seemed like the logical suspect, but Terry shrugged, "...that just showed us that you can't always count on the obvious to be the truth." The real kink in the boyfriend–did–it theory was the matter of the ligatures—not at all what you'd expect to find at ninety-nine percent of the murder scenes, particularly in domestic disputes that ended violently. The standard was take them out and shoot them, stab them, bash them on the head, and dump them. No messing around with tying their hands and strangling them with leash–like pieces of rope. So, in addition to checking out the usual tips and leads, Terry's men were very interested in why the killer had tied up Lana Long like he did. That was the freaky part. That and the obscene way she was posed.

Nearly two weeks after Lana Long's trussed-up body was found, Gary Terry got another call. Like before, it came on a peaceful Sunday at home with the family. A passerby had spotted a

woman's body in a clump of brush and trees out by Plant City. Terry jumped in his car, and on the drive to the crime scene, twenty miles straight east of Tampa and just north of the Plant City exit off I–4, Terry said a silent prayer: Please, please don't let her be bound.

"But the instant I saw her I thought, 'Oh no! Just like Lana Long. Only worse,'" Terry recalled. "Those of us who responded to the scene knew immediately we were in deep trouble. She had been bound like Lana, with her hands at her side and loose enough to allow some movement. The victim had fought for her life. She had a broken finger that apparently was a defense wound. There was a rope around her neck tied in a reverse hangman's noose and again with a trailing end that looked like a leash. The body was still warm when found, which meant the killer didn't think we'd find her that soon, or didn't care. And she had been killed outside the car."

"Pops" Baker, who was already at the scene when Terry arrived, was thinking the same thing: "As soon as I saw the body, with the same knots and ligatures and the way the hands were tied with the 'come along' rope, the control, the leash, there was no question in my mind, we were dealing with the same person. After we sent the evidence off to the FBI Lab, that was confirmed."

Detective Steve Hawkins was the reporting officer on the case. According to his notes, the dump site was seventy yards west of Park Road and three-quarter of a mile north of the I–4 exit. He described the areas rural, isolated, and littered with dumping debris.

The body was that of a white female in her late teens or early twenties. She was nude and lying on her back in a shady knoll about eight feet off a narrow dirt trail. She was small–breasted with the still–firm, smooth body of youth. Her head was turned slightly to the side; her left hand and bent right leg covered her genitals as though, even in death, she was trying modestly to shield herself from the world's prying eyes. There was a gold ankle bracelet with three stones on her right ankle, and a pair of off–white round earrings adorned her pierced ears. Remnants of peach nail lacquer

lent a touch of color to her toenails. While still alive, the young woman had spent time sunning herself. The tanning pattern of a bikini-type, two–piece, high–cut bathing suit outlined her breasts and hips. The lateral edges of the pubic hair had been shaved and now showed slight regrowth stubble. Neither her vagina nor anus appeared to be injured, although a closer examination later revealed the presence of a pasty white fluid in the woman's vagina. The woman's lips were parted and her eyes slightly open, as if she was just waking up. Or dozing off.

The victim's arms were at her sides but bound with a quater-inch clothesline rope that stretched from wrist to wrist across her belly button.

"The length of rope passes behind the victim's back and then each end of the rope is wrapped around the victim's left and right wrists two times then secured with a loose knot similar to a half–hitch," Hawkins observed in his initial field report. "The two remaining loose ends of the rope are then tied in front of the victim with a square knot...to loosely hold the victim's hands to the sides of the body, but restrict forward and backward movements. Victim has what appears to be a green pull– over type T–shirt binding her upper arms. The shirt appears to have been ripped or cut up the front and pulled down across the victim's back with both arms still secured in their respective short sleeves."

Another piece of clothesline rope was tied around the woman's neck and secured with a hangman's knot. There were three deep ligature marks across the front of her neck, two across the back, and one ugly red rope burn or ligature abrasion across her chin. To the cops and the assistant medical examiner on the scene, that chin ligature meant only one thing— the dead girl had put up a fight before she died. There was a three–foot length of rope extending from the noose. A leash. Like before.

The woman's cropped dark hair was caked with drying blood. She had been beaten with some kind of blunt instrument so viciously that it left four large wounds across the front and top of her head; another blow had left a mark the size of a half-dollar on her right temple. There was also, the M.E. observed, "...a massive

blunt trauma shock to the left ear area, resulting in a severe hematoma to the left side of the brain."

But that wasn't even the worst. The girl's throat was slit, at least twice, diagonally from upper right to lower left. In his autopsy report, Dr. Lee Miller, the assistant medical examiner, described the awful, gaping wounds in clinical terms:

"On the anterior neck extending from three-inch to the right of the midline is a sharply incised wound which severs the posterior half of the right sternocleidomastoid muscle at the junction of the lower third with the upper two-thirds, passes across the right carotid sheath, severing the internal jugular vein, the ends of which are separated by a gap of approximately three-inch, half transecting the right carotid artery, transects the vagus nerve in the carotid sheath, passes across the larynx at the junction of the thyroid and cricoid cartilages half severing the larynx, passes across the front of the neck producing deep muscle damage, downward across the left clavicle, ending at approximately midpoint, with a linear transverse "Tail" measuring 4" extending across the uppermost left chest and anterior left upper arm. This wound is at its deepest at the right apical portion becoming shallower when crossing the chest and on the left side. The wound measures 11". Lateral to and below this wound is a four and one-half inch incised wound separated from the above by a one-half inch gap of skin beginning on the posterior lateral superclavicular area extending downward and medially ending at approximately the level of the sternoclavicular junction. Both wound tracks are undercut cephalad and to the right and the tracks converge at the right anterior base of the neck over the sternocleidomastoid muscle. The 2nd wound produces extensive deep muscle damage without severing named larger blood vessels."

The killer hadn't merely cut her throat—he'd ripped it open with less finesse than gutting a hog. One wound was almost a foot

231

long and three inches wide; the other four and a half inches long and almost as deep.

The woman had been so brutalized, in fact, that Dr. Miller, even after a lengthy autopsy, couldn't tell Lt. Terry exactly how she'd died. The postmortem report officially lists the cause of death as: "Exsanguination, asphyxiation and closed head injuries."

Put more simply, she was stabbed to death, strangled to death, and beaten to death.

After Dr. Miller made his cursory examination at the death scene, the forensic experts went to work. ID technician Don Hunt, stepping carefully so as not to disturb potential evidence, gently plucked a reddish-colored fiber he found near the victim's left breast. He also collected strands of hair he found on her lower right stomach and beneath her right hand. The body was photographed and fingerprinted, and hair samples and fingernail scrapings taken. Hunt and his fellow crime-scene technician, Art Picard, tried to lift any latent fingerprints from the body, using both Superglue and graphite powder, but without success.

Hanging on a bush, about seven feet from the woman's head, was a pair of bloodstained panty hose. On the other side of the body, officers found a bloody white jumpsuit draped over a tree limb. On the dirt tail leading off Park Road to the dump site, searchers spotted a single barefoot print in the dirt at the side of the road. Tire tracks indicated that someone had pulled in to the site and turned around to leave. The tracks stood out like bas-relief, which the cops considered a stroke of luck. This was the beginning of Florida's rainy season when heavy afternoon thunderstorms swept in almost daily across the coastline to soak the interior. Had the body not been found within hours after it was placed there, much of the valuable evidence gathered at the scene would have been washed away. As it was, police hurriedly erected a canvas cover over the tracks so they could get good plaster-cast impressions before the rains came. The thing about the tracks that puzzled Terry was that they were all different. Same car, four different tires. And one, in particularly, was an oddity. On the inside

of the impression, the letter "V" clearly stood out followed by other, indistinct letters.

To help with identification, authorities recruited local artist Debbie Banta. She was given photos of the woman taken in the morgue, and asked to produced a rendering that would show what the woman looked like while still alive. Armed with copies of that sketch, detectives fanned out across Hillsborough, Pinellas, Pasco, Polk, and Orange Counties, hitting scores of bars, lounges, and topless joints. They were banking on the possibility that similarities in the two murdered women's backgrounds contributed to the similarities of their deaths. Someone said she was a hooker named Tina who worked for a pimp named Shawn; other witnesses misidentified her as Tina, the nude dancer from Maitland, who worked Orlando's infamous Orange Blossom Trail sex market. They were wrong, but at least detectives believed they were looking in the right places.

Sheriff Walter Heinrich authorized the release of the drawing of the victim to the news media and on May 30, the Tampa Tribune carried the item on the front page of its Metro Section:

"The Hillsborough County sheriff's officials Tuesday released a composite of a young woman found Sunday in woods near Plant City. They describe her as in her late teens or early twenties, approximately five feet five inches tall, weighing 119 pounds, with dark brown shoulder length hair and brown eyes. The Sheriff's Office said she was wearing a size eight white polyester-type jumpsuit and white pantyhose. Anyone with information is asked to contact the Sheriff's Office Major Crimes Bureau..."

"We didn't talk among ourselves about the possibility that this might be the work of a serial killer, that I recall," Terry said. "We may have discussed the term, but it was still such a new concept at that time that it really wasn't in our everyday terminology. Back then, 'serial killer' was a media term that we didn't use. We'd say 'an individual responsible for multiple homicides.'

"Releasing the information and going public with a warning that a problem existed was a hard decision to make, but we were forced to face the fact that we had two related homicides. From an investigative standpoint, you don't want to say anything that will scare the guy away, put him on the run into somebody else's jurisdiction. You want to catch him. You have to balance different concerns, and the ultimate concern that rises to the top is public safety. There were some pretty strong feelings among our guys about not telling the public a damn thing. But the sheriff made the right call. 'You've got to tell them something,' he said. 'The next victim may be a housewife, a child. Maybe the killer will change his routine.'

"With the fiber evidence and the ligatures, we knew that one killer more than likely was responsible for both murders, while, we knew next to nothing about the phenomenon of serial killers. Still, Sheriff Heinrich strongly believed that we had the obligation to alert the public without causing panic or spooking the killer. By not releasing anything, we faced the consequence of another innocent victim being killed."

As a result of that decision, the June 2nd edition of the Tribune jumped the story from the Metro Section to a prominent position on the front page, accompanied by a map pinpointing the two dump sites, a photo of Lana Long, and the drawing of the still-unknown second victim. Under a headline reading "Links discovered in brutal slayings of two local women," the Tribune told its readers:

"The mid-May strangulation death of a topless dancer is being linked by Hillsborough County sheriff's investigators to the fatal stabbing two weeks later of another young woman, who is still unidentified.

"Sheriff Walter Heinrich said Friday there are at least five similarities between the killings, which he called 'brutal homicides' with 'sexual overtones.'

"There are no suspects in the slayings and Heinrich added, 'We desperately need information'...

"Sheriff's Maj. John Cacciatore identified

these as the similarities in the deaths:

"'Both were good-looking young women. Both nude. Both bound. Both appeared to have been out in places of entertainment. They (the slayings) were ten days apart.'

"Heinrich said 'We're concerned because of the similarities between the two homicides that it may be one man...'

Heinrich said that 'as many as thirty detectives were working' on the cases...

The publication of the composite drawing produced immediate results. A clerk at a convenience store on West Kennedy Boulevard called the Major Crimes Unit, saying that he might know something about the woman.

"We didn't notice it at the time, but for some reason the artist included tiny details of a neckline with a kind of latticework just to sort of dress up the sketch," Terry said. "She hadn't seen what the victim was wearing, but after the sketch appeared in the paper we got a call from a man asking if the victim was wearing a white jumpsuit, which she was. He said he recognized her from that neckline as someone who he'd seen outside his store."

The clerk, a man named Bob Temple, said that about three or four weeks prior to the finding of the body, several new faces had shown up among the regular contingent of prostitutes working West Kennedy. He became friendly with one of the young hookers, a pretty blond who called herself Shannon Gill. She frequently came in the store for food and drink while trolling for johns near Renee's Lounge, a popular hunting ground for hookers. The day the composite of the Jane Doe victim appeared in the paper, Shannon came in the store, took one look at the drawing and started to shake. Scared her to death, Temple said. She said it looked an awful lot like a new hooker friend who was working Kennedy Boulevard with her last Saturday night. The girl, Shannon continued, went by the street name of "Monique," but her real name was Michelle Denise Simms. Michelle told her that she'd just come over to Tampa from Fort Pierce on the east coast. She'd gone down in a recent drug bust over there, and she and her "group" had

come to Tampa to work the streets. The last time Shannon saw Monique/Michelle that Saturday night was while the new girl was trying to line up a couple of tricks driving a beat-up van parked in front of the Seven Seas Lounge. Shannon refused to go along because something made her "leery" of the tricks, who were acting weird. Temple added that Shannon worked for a black pimp named Nick, and that the last he knew they were staying at a motel up on Columbus Avenue, because he'd dropped her off there once after he got off work.

The information sounded solid to Terry—good enough, in fact, to put a couple of detectives on a plane to Fort Pierce bearing copies of the dead woman's fingerprints. A check with prints on file with the St. Lucie County sheriff's office confirmed the identity: Michelle Denise Simms, born May 9, 1962, near Santa Barbara, California. Her last known place of employment was a Fort Pierce massage parlor. She had an arrest record for drug violations. Her next of kin listed an uncle and aunt, Doc and Sharon Indermuehle of Cutler, California.

When contacted, Sharon Indermuehle expressed sadness, but not shock, over the news of Michelle's death.

"Michelle was a beautiful girl," said her aunt. "In fact, she was in a beauty contest out here when she was a teenager. Her mother died in 1972, and we took her in and raised her since then. Her dad wasn't around, because one time he held Michelle and a baby sitter at gunpoint in their apartment before the police got him." (California prison officials corroborated Indermuehle's account, saying the father served time from 1966 to 1977 on a false imprisonment charge.)

Michelle left California about 1980, and the Indermuehles had only occasional contact with her after that. The last time she called, Sharon said, was just this past Mother's Day. "She was very confused," the woman added. "She didn't know what she wanted to be from day to day. But one thing I know for sure—she wasn't a prostitute."

▲   ▲   ▲

A LETTER FROM BOBBY

Listen, I don't know much about your charges or what you've done. I do know when I look in your eyes I can see you're a killer. Yeah, its crazy, but for a long time now I've felt people could see that in my eyes. I've done some cold-blooded shit, both known and unknown. It doesn't bother me a bit to kill someone. If the boys from Columbia can get me out of this I'll owe em, and I pay my debts!

▲   ▲   ▲

According to authorities, Michelle Denise Simms left Fort Pierce on May 24, in the company of another woman with a record for prostitution.

She arrived in Tampa on May 25.

She turned her last trick late on May 26.

She died in the early hours of May 27.

St. Lucie police put the Hillsborough investigators in touch with Leo LaFlesh and Michael Starling, a couple of Fort Pierce characters who'd known Michelle better than anyone.

According to LaFlesh's story, Michelle came from California about three or four years earlier with Starling, but this past January, the two split up and Michelle, needing a place to stay, moved in with LaFlesh and his parents. She bunked in the crowded mobile home for about two months, but resented the restrictions that LaFlesh's mother put on her, and the complaints about Michelle coming and going all hours of the night. "Mostly, my folks couldn't cope with her drug habit," he told investigators. The last time LaFlesh had spoken with her was about three weeks before, when she called to say she wanted to come and pick up some clothing she'd left behind. She told him she was working at place on Highway 68, just outside of Fort Pierce, called Ricewood, which she described euphemistically as a "men's club." "Really," LaFlesh said, "the place was just a massage parlor." She also talked about

237

doing some modeling work somewhere in South Florida. "Michelle's problem," LaFlesh added, "is drugs. Very bad habit." She didn't have any place to live and was just sort of bouncing around from place to place. "Last I heard," he shrugged, "she was shacked up with some niggers downtown."

Michael Starling confirmed that the two traveled together from California, and lived in the Fort Pierce area for about four years. But because of their cocaine habits, their living situation had become "unbearable." Starling said he'd gone through what little money he had saved, and resorted to borrowing from acquaintances just to supply Michelle with the coke she demanded. He was spending $1,000 a week on coke just to satisfy her habit. Lately, she'd started freebasing, and was really spinning out of control fast. Starling claimed he finally kicked drugs himself (except for booze and a little reefer now and then), and told Michelle in January that she'd have to do the same or hit the road. That's when she moved in with Leo LaFlesh. After Leo's mom kicked her out, she roomed for a while with a woman she'd met on the streets somewhere, and then wound up living with a black guy named "Blue," who was a well-known coke dealer around town. The last Starling heard from her, Michelle was working at that Ricewood place and dealing drugs for Blue. "I still loved her," Starling insisted, "but when I heard she was sleeping with a nigger I didn't want nothing more to do with her."

When the investigators returned to Tampa with their positive identification of the victim, an alert was issued for information on the prostitute who had been cruising Kennedy Boulevard with Michelle Simms the night she vanished. Bob Temple knew her only by her street name, Shannon Gill. The Tampa Police Department's vice squad, however, kept a "moniker" file that listed Shannon's real name as Pamela Gwin.

Meanwhile, the processing of the forensic evidence collected at the Plant City dump site moved forward. Since the three separate tire impressions at the scene were so fresh and clear, Terry was especially interested in having those identified. Two were fairly easy to classify. The tire that carried the evidence marking of Q31

238

was a Tiempo look-alike that Goodyear produced by the thousands in 1977. Q28 was a fairly common, low–priced tire called a Viva, also made by Goodyear, but Q29 was a poser. The experts could say only that the impression was from a special tire that probably came on high-priced production cars at the original time of sale, and not one normally sold in retail tire stores. Even the FBI with its tens of thousands of tire impressions on record couldn't make a match. The tire specialist at Quantico suggested sending the impression to someone at the Goodyear plant in Akron, Ohio. They should know what it is. The following day, a detective, hand–carrying the delicate plaster casts and photographs of the tire imprints, flew off to Akron. The Goodyear people went to work on the impression and within days had the answer. The tire was a Goodyear Vogue, a specialty model with a gold rim on the outer wall that in 1984 sold for about $250 new—if you could get them new, since the tires were manufactured exclusively for top of the line Cadillacs. Moreover, the impression indicated that the tire was mounted with the gold wall turned inward. If you find the car this tire is on, the cops were told, that mounting will be as positive as a fingerprint.

The tire impressions were the kind of solid evidence that would conclusively place the killer at the scene of the crime—if and when they caught him. Just as valuable from an overall investigative standpoint was the FBI's report on the other physical evidence, particularly that reddish colored fiber lifted from the woman's body:

"The evidence collected from where Simms was found was immediately flown to the FBI Laboratory. Since this had been a 'fresh' site , the chances of recovering significant evidence would be tremendously improved...The fibers removed from the evidence revealed red lustrous trilobal nylon fibers, which matched the Lana Long fiber. In addition, a second type of fiber, a red trilobal delustered fiber, was found, indicating that the killer was driving a vehicle containing two different types of carpet fibers.

"Grouping tests conducted on semen stains identified on the clothing of Michelle Simms disclosed the

239

presence of the "8" and "H" blood group substances.

"The hairs from the body and clothing of Michelle Simms were examined. Brown, medium-length Caucasian head hairs were found that could have originated from the killer. Human hair is valuable evidence, and in addition to providing information on race, body area, artificial treatment, or other unusual characteristics, it can be strongly associated with a particular individual when matched with a known hair sample from the individual. With this information, the HCSO was able to build a 'physical evidence' profile of the killer, which was distributed to other law enforcement agencies; however, the information on the carpet fibers and cordage was kept confidential."

The confirmed presence of those "red lustrous trilobal nylon fibers" immediately changed the entire complexion of the investigation. Both Lana Long and Michelle Simms had been exposed to the same physical environment just before they were murdered. That meant only one thing: The same killer or killers had done both girls. Thus it was that the June 2nd edition of the Tribune reported that:

"It has become clear that investigators think one man sexually attacked and killed both Ngeun Thi Long, nineteen, and Michelle Denise Simms, twenty-two. It also has become clear that [Sheriff Walter] Heinrich's office considers the case a lot bigger than most.

"Hillsborough County sheriff's Maj. John Cacciatore said late last week, 'I don't know how I can emphasize how concerned we are.'

"'We are working just about around the clock.'"

"The sheriff has so far taken these measures:

"Vacations have been shortened or delayed for certain investigators so they could be assigned to the case.

"Information about the crimes has been furnished to the Florida Department of Law Enforcement for sharing with other police agencies across the state

and for comparison with unsolved murders in other counties.

"Plans have been discussed to call the FBI to prepare a profile of a suspect. `We have made inquiries,' said Cacciatore..."

"From the first homicide, we had the uncomfortable feeling that it was totally different from anything we'd handled before," Lt. Terry said. "Then with the second case, we were pretty confident that the same person was responsible. The fibers solidified it and helped us focus.

"After the second murder, we issued a patrol alert to all deputies telling them what we were looking for: White male, driving certain types of cars, mid–size, medium build, brown hair, armed with a knife, Lt. Terry said." Everything on the list came from a different piece of physical evidence. The alert advised them to take a close look at cars for tires that might be mounted in reverse with all the black walls facing out.

"We went around to all the roll calls, the meetings of different shifts coming on, telling them that on any car they stopped to tell us what's inside the car, what the dash looks like, the color of the carpet, the color of the seats, any women's shoes or clothing. What we did not include in that alert was the fact that we had fiber evidence. We were asking for carpet colors, but we didn't tell them what we were asking for."

Detective "Pops" Baker added: "From that point on, the nature of our investigation began to change drastically. When you see the Lana Long file, it's probably a foot thick, but as we went along it got down to the point where the folder would be a few photos, the deputies' face sheets, some trace evidence, and some background on the victim. We weren't investigating husbands, boyfriends, neighbors any longer. We just knew we had the same fellow."

One killer, two victims. That much seemed certain, but what the cops didn't know, and urgently needed to find out, were the links, if any, between Lana and Michelle. Given the lifestyles of the two women, it was logical to suspect that a disgruntled john or some guy with a weird sex kink had killed them both—which now

241

meant that just about every living male in Hillsborough and surrounding counties could be counted as a suspect. With that in mind, police went back to the basic homicide investigation textbook.

"Serial killings are the hardest and most heinous murders to investigate," Terry said. "There are few clues and little evidence. In most homicides, there's usually some correlation between the victim and the killer, so you start looking at the activities of the victim over the past twelve hours and that often leads to a suspect or suspects. In this case, that didn't work at all."

▲   ▲   ▲

A LETTER FROM BOBBY

So you'll know, the killings I did (except the shooting) were personal! I don't ever plan to let personal feelings interfere with my actions. But if its "necessary" in a business or money related way— you gotta know I wouldn't hesitate. Or in a matter of self preservation. No hesitation, no explanation, just bang bang & bye bye.

▲   ▲   ▲

Among the scores of prostitutes that were stopped for questioning along Nebraska Avenue and near the intersection where Michelle was last seen, Laney Mueller° provided police with their best lead yet. The twenty year old prostitute said she'd been working Kennedy Boulevard for the last two or three months. She hitchhiked back and forth, not really going anywhere— that was just her method of getting tricks to stop. About three weeks ago, on a slow night, this guy pulls up in small silver sports car. Italian looking guy. About twenty-five or thirty, six feet two–inches tall, well built short, wavy, black hair, small mustache, blue eyes, smooth, hairless chest, wearing a black leather outfit that looked like it cost a bundle. The

242

car had crushed-velvet upholstery and a digital radio, and smelled brand new.

Laney said she jumped right in when he pulled over, and right off the guy asks, "What can I get for a hundred dollars?" No small talk about "dating." None of that typical john bullshit. "Honey," she replied, "you can get anything you want for a hundred bucks, `long as there ain't no pain involved. But I don't have a place to go."

"It don't matter," the guy said. "I got a place but it's a little ways out of town."

Laney told the cops that the man drove west on Kennedy, then cut north on Eisenhower Highway and headed out to the Town `n Country area, just west of the airport and north of the Bay. Yuppie heaven. She'd had a few drinks and a couple of joints earlier in the evening, so she was pretty lost when the guy finally pulled up to this really expensive apartment complex. The inside of the place was beautiful for a single guy, she thought. Lots of real good leather furniture and stuff. Soft lights. Good music. The trick pulled out a wad of bills and peeled off a hundred bucks as easily as most guys peel off ten.

When Laney was putting the money away, the guy suddenly jumped her from behind, tore her clothes off, and tied her up with a rope that he must have had stashed right there by the couch. For the next three or four hours, he forced her to have vaginal and oral sex. He really didn't have to force her, since he was paying for it, but if this was his kink it was her job to play along. Up to a point. But the guy couldn't get off, and the longer he tried the more frustrated he got—and started taking it out on her. The jerk had broken fingernails and when she shoved his fingers up her vagina the jagged edges cut her, Laney complained. One time, while she was sucking on him, the guy held a big knife to her throat and kept yelling at her that if she didn't make him come she wouldn't be of any further use to him, and he might just kill her because he hated hustlers.

At one point during the ordeal, when the man left her hogtied alone in the bedroom, Laney was able to fish a knife, that she carried for protection, out of her purse and cut herself free. When he

returned, still threatening to kill her, Laney jumped up and slashed him with knife. "I cut him real bad," she admitted. "Got him on the face, the chest. Stuck him one in the stomach." While the man lay on the floor bleeding and moaning, Laney said she got dressed, wrapped some figurines in a towel, and took another seventy-five dollars she found. She said she threw the stuff in a dumpster outside the apartment. "I wanted to make it look like a robbery, because I thought for sure the motherfucker was going to die," Laney said. She ran to a nearby 7–11, called a cab, went home, and threw up, she was so scared.

She never heard anything more about the guy, but, now that she thought about it, all this happened around Mother's Day, just a few days after they found that dancer tied up and strangled.

Police were unable to find any record of the cutting incident, and there the investigation stalled. The "rich Italian" sounded like a good suspect, but there was nothing more to go on. Then, on June 15, Lt. Terry summoned Detective Hawkins to his office. "We just got word that police in Atlantic City have located our girl—Shannon or Pamela or whatever the hell her name is. She's scared to death after what happened to Michelle. Afraid she might be next and took off. But now she's ready to talk. Get up there and see what she has to say," Terry ordered. Hawkins flew to Atlantic City, where local detectives took him to meet the twenty-one year old, redheaded hooker where she was holed up in a cheap motel, within streetwalking distance of the city's casinos and abundant tourist trade. Pamela reluctantly agreed to return with him to Tampa, and they caught the next flight to Florida.

Pamela described herself as a "working girl," whose usual place of employment was several blocks of Kennedy Boulevard. She and a girl named Janet and a pimp named Nick had been working the area for five or six weeks. About the last week in May, the three drove over to Fort Pierce to pick up a car for Nick. While there, Pam and Janet relaxed with some freelance hooking in a joint called the Bronco Bar. Pam was sitting there working on a john when this Michelle chick walked in, sat right down, and started talking to the "date" like she knew him. "We hit it off okay," Pam

continued, "and when we got ready to leave town, Michelle asked if she could come along." From Fort Pierce, the four drove over to Orlando to turn some tricks on Orange Blossom Trail. But they no sooner hit the streets than Pam got picked up for prostitution. That was on Thursday night. On Friday, after she was bailed out, the four returned to Tampa and took a motel room, registering under Michelle's name.

They showered, got something to eat, and hit Kennedy Boulevard to work the Friday night trade. Friday was usually a busy night, but Michelle wasn't doing too well. Bitched about not making any money in Orlando, and here she was in Tampa with nothing to show for her hours on the street except sore feet." I got the feeling she didn't have a whole lot of experience as a 'working girl'," Pam said. But later that night, things started to pick up. Pam and Michelle got a "date" together with a short, stubby guy who lived with his mother down on South MacDill near the air base. Mom wasn't home, so the three of them had a sex party. The guy had a whole pile of good coke, so he and Michelle did a lot of lines. Pam said she didn't snort. When it came time to pay up, she said the guy just tossed her his wallet and told her to take it all "...'cause I know it's hard for you girls out on the streets." The man drove them back to the motel about 5 a.m., and made a date with Michelle for later that afternoon.

On Saturday, May 26, Michelle left about 10 a.m. to meet the guy. She called back later to say he hadn't shown, but she was going to stay out and work for awhile. Pam said Michelle returned to the motel about 3 p.m. with a hundred bucks she'd just made, and was in a much better mood about the Tampa "dating" scene. The girls rested and returned to Kennedy about 10 p.m. When they left the motel Michelle was wearing a white polyester jumpsuit, white pantyhose, light gray pumps, and was carrying a white vinyl handbag with a shoulder strap. Their first stop was at the ABC Lounge on Kennedy. Had a couple of warmup drinks and then hit the street. "I tried to kind of keep an eye on Michelle," Pam explained. "She was used to working in a massage parlor, but she didn't know shit about working the streets, in my opinion. She was ready to

jump in any car without checking them out first, looking to see if they might be undercover or what."

The two stayed together for about thirty minutes before Pam caught a date. Took her about fifteen minutes, and when the trick dropped her back off on Kennedy, Michelle was gone. A few minutes later, Michelle popped out from around the corner on a side street, spitting come out of her mouth. Got me a quickie, she explained. Over the next couple of hours, they each caught a few more dates before spotting two guys who'd been cruising around in a light-blue van, and now were parked in a lot next door to Rene's Lounge. Michelle walked over to talk to the guys, and Pam followed a few steps behind. "She was talking to the guy on the passenger side," Pam recalled, "and I walked around to check out the driver. Older than the passenger. Dark hair, probably wearing glasses. They were kind of hassling Michelle, and there was something about them I didn't like." Pam's streetwise hooker instincts told her to back off, and she pulled Michelle aside to whisper a warning. Just about then, a car horn beeped. Customer calling. Pam said she went to the darkened parking space behind the 7–11 on the corner to do her "date", and when she returned fifteen minutes later, Michelle and the van were gone.

"Never saw her again," Pam concluded. "I just figured she'd taken off and gone back to Fort Pierce." On June 17, Pam Gwin agreed to be hypnotized by the sheriff's resident hypnotist, Sgt. George Moore, to see if she could recall any more details about that Saturday night or the occupants of the van. According to Hawkins' report, three additional points emerged from the session:

"Pamela recalls talking to a subject named Ben in the ABC Lounge on Saturday night. Ben introduces them to an old man who Michelle was supposedly going to have a 'date' with, but does not know if anything ever came about as they left the bar together to go out and work together on Kennedy.

"The van parked next to the Life of Georgia Insurance building is still believed to be light blue, faded, bad (bald) tires, missing a hubcap on

the back, possible damage to the right front fender, mirror missing on the passenger side. Indicates front floorboard very dirty, covered with cigarette butts, old rags and so forth.

"Recalls approaching the van initially on the driver's side while Michelle was talking to the passenger, reaching in and feeling of the driver in an attempt to check for wires or weapons in her belief that it might be an undercover police unit. Did not like the looks of the subjects and encouraged Michelle not to 'date' them."

Police later tracked down the occupants of the van—a couple of guys from Lakeland who'd been barhopping in Tampa. They'd stopped in Renee's to check out a black "she-male" dancer there. They left around midnight and ran into the two hookers, one dressed in a white jumpsuit. The pair decided to have a little fun with the girls, and told the one in the jumpsuit they'd give her $100 to blow them. The woman turned to her friend and said, "I got me a couple of suckers here," and climbed in the van. The men said they drove around the block teasing the hooker, and when she saw they weren't serious she made them let her out again on Kennedy Boulevard. That was the last they saw of her. One of the men later took a polygraph examination that confirmed his story.

But the van brought up something bothersome about the Lana Long and Michelle Simms cases that grated at the back of Lt. Terry's mind like an itch you can't scratch. Both young women were found miles from where they were last seen alive. How did the killer get them all the way across the city without being seen?

"If you had told me," Terry said, "that some killer could drive all the way across Hillsborough County with a nude female tied up in the front seat beside him and not be noticed, I'd have said, no way! In the initial stages of the investigation it was just like the Wayne Williams thing in Atlanta—we thought it had to be a van. How can he take these people tied up, bound, across town without somebody seeing them? Had to be a van, motor home, something like that. That's why we were so interested in talking to the people

in the blue van, since it seemed to fit what we wanted to believe, which maybe blinded us a little bit at first. But it wasn't a van at all. It was that damn Dodge Magnum.

"He got control of the victims almost as soon as they got in his car. He picked up Lana Long outside of her apartment complex, drove right around the corner, and pulled a knife or a gun. When she started crying he slapped her around, told her to shut up. Reclined the passenger seat, stripped her, tied her up, drove her nude from that location all the way to East Bay Drive in southern Hillsborough County.

"Some fought back. Michelle Simms put up quite a struggle. You could tell from the defensive wounds on her hands. We later learned that she was taken from the west side of Tampa to Southeastern Hillsborough County, raped repeatedly, then driven several miles back north, pleading for her life all the way, raped again, and murdered.

"Unfortunately, I think some of the women just made a conscious decision that if I resist he may hurt me more, and if I go along he may let me live.

"They were scared to death, just too terrified to resist...

"Those of our victims who were prostitutes might have been exposed to similar situations in the past, johns who wanted to tie them up and so on, so they probably expected that if they just endured what the guy wanted, they'd come out of it okay. Wrong."

"Pops" Baker believed that Bobby Joe Long had deliberately rigged the passenger seat of his Magnum to drop into a reclining position when a victim fell into his trap. "He put a weapon on them and took control real quick. Snapped that seat down, threatened with a knife or gun, rolled them over and tied them. Of course, those who were prostitutes go through this sort of thing all the time. Get banged up, tied up. Ain't the first time somebody took a prostitute in a car, tied 'em up, did their thing and got rid of them but didn't kill them."

During a deposition he gave in connection with one of Bobby Joe Long's trials, Tampa psychiatrist Dr. Daniel J. Sprehe described how, according to Long, what started as a simple matter

of picking up a hooker evolved into rape and murder. And, as seemed to be the standard operating procedure with Bobby Joe Long, someone else was to blame—in this case, his old girlfriend, Suzette Rice.

"He said he was out cruising and she [Michelle Simms] was by Renee's," Dr. Sprehe began. "She caught his eye; she had a white jumpsuit. She said it would be fifty bucks, he said okay. She jumped in, she was very attractive. She was in her early twenties, dark hair. He took her to Plant City off the Interstate in a field, had straight intercourse."

Long told the doctor: "She had oral sex on me. Then, I felt some anger before and during this. She reminded me of a bitch I used to live with named Suzette. Suzette did me wrong, took advantage of me. I tried to have her killed when I got in jail...

"She was an American Indian, like Simms."

Long assumed Michelle Simms was an American Indian because of her features, Dr. Sprehe continued.Because of everything Suzette Rice had put him through, Bobby Joe harbored deep resentment. "And he wanted to kill her. He says that, 'If I get out on the street, now, she'd be dead, now.' He's talking about right now.

"So, back to Simms. He jumped her, hit her in the head with a club [because] he didn't want her to suffer. Then, choked her. Then, cut her throat. " And then, he went home and he had a long sleep afterwards. And he woke feeling great. Now, that was a little different than what he told me before.

"It was two weeks after the first killing, of Lana Long. He picked her [Simms] up on Kennedy, she was a whore. 'I liked her, I took her to Plant City, she was cooperative. Only afterwards...[now, he says she was cooperative, but the police report said she was tied up] ...only afterwards I decided to kill her. I hit her in the head with a club, then strangled her, then cut her throat.' So, the sequence is a little different.

"Afterwards he felt sorry, cleaned his car the next day, went to bed, went to sleep, slept fourteen to sixteen hours."

▲   ▲   ▲

REPORTER: *Do you think of yourself as the serial killer?*

BOBBY: *That's what I'm in here for. I tell you the truth, from what I know about serial killers, and I know quite a bit about them by now, 'cause I have talked to some of the best doctors in the country that specialize in it. It's when I hear the similarities between all of these guys and me, it's scary. It really is. And if you don't know about it maybe you should check into it 'cause it's frightening...I found out from [Dr. Joel] Norris yesterday, my...there is a...there is a sign of an enzyme imbalance in your body that all of these serial killer types have, right? Where the second toe is longer than the big toe and he used to ask me, out of the clear blue when he was talking...is your middle toe longer than your big toe...and I looked at him real weird and he says...you know I had to ask. And I said yeah, it is. And he says can you show me?*

REPORTER: *So how did you feel about that. You have all this stuff in common with all these other serial killers?*

BOBBY: *Well, it tells me that there is a certain type of person that this thing happens to. That you know, it's not like I just woke up one day and I said...ahhh, I'll go out and do this or that. It isn't like that. This is...you're talking about a life–long progression and a psychological development and ..., I'm telling you, it's scary, it's scary. If the people knew all the different things, I mean, I can't remember all of them, right? But Jesus, these people are telling me things that the similarities in all of these serial killer types, right? And it's scary, I'm telling you, it's scary. (CBS News Interview)*

▲   ▲   ▲

Scary indeed. In fact, one of the scariest things about Bobby Joe Long is that, while he's a classic loner, he's not alone.

He's part of a trend.

About the same time that Bobby Joe Long set out to hunt hookers, a new generation of modern murderers known as serial killers was just coming into vogue and Long was in the vanguard.

Among the bloodiest were Ted Bundy, John Wayne Gacy, Christopher Wilder, Edmund Kemper, Son of Sam, the Hillside Strangler, and Randy Kraft. Many of these "celebrity" killers have been endowed with an undeserved aura of perverted glamour. Ted Bundy received fan letters by the thousands, love letters by the hundreds—even marriage proposals, before being electrocuted in Florida's Old Sparky. Almost overnight, serial killer became a chic term—if your view of serial murder is the sanitized, neatly packaged Hollywood version, the version that rarely mentions, much less shows, sexual mutilation; sadistic, bloody rape; gnawed off nipples; butcher knives shoved up vaginas and broomsticks up rectums; ligatures that cut to the bone; defecating death throes; bodies grotesquely posed with heads ripped off; genitals lewdly displayed to achieve maximum shock effect; and maggotted, stinking, mummified remains. That's the real side of serial murder, the ugly, repulsive side—overshadowed only by the hell, deep horror that marks the victim's last moments of life as she stares into the cold, pitiless eyes of her thrusting executioner.

With the success of the hit movie "Silence of the Lambs," the serial-killer phenomenon grabbed the public's attention. Police, the FBI's special psych squad, and a few criminologists and psychologists had been studying this group of predators for more than a decade. But Hollywood elevated serial killers to pop-culture status, and sparked a spate of instant analyses seeking to explain the presence of these monsters in our midst.

"Something curious is going on in America," wrote Washington Post reporter Joel Achenbach. "Murder is a growth industry, particularly this special kind of murder, the bogeyman homicide, the sadistic slaying by a stranger who, without comprehensible motive, steps out of the shadows and savages.

"Before the 1970s, they were the rarest of creatures. In most countries, they still are. But in America, they have become so commonplace that criminologists estimate there are as many as twenty serial killers roaming the country at any given time."

Some FBI estimates tell us there may be as many as thirty-five wandering the U.S. On the other hand, John Douglas, chief of the

251

FBI's Investigative Support Unit (and the model for the supervising agent in Silence of the Lambs), was quoted in the July 12, 1992, edition of Parade Magazine: "Today, there are probably fifty serial killers in the U.S., one for each state—and that's a conservative estimate. We could cut them off early in their careers if we could track their crimes."

The serial killer, the Washington Post continued, has become "...an American Original, a romantic icon, like the cowboy.... Real life is not so gothic. When police bag a serial killer, he is usually a weak man, cowardly, not terribly savvy and a failure at most everything he's ever done in life. He's a loser. He manages to get away with multiple murders not because he's smart, but because he kills strangers and keeps moving...He's inept. He's uneducated. He's a zero".

And that just about sums up the real Bobby Joe Long, not the "Mad Dog" Long of his own imagination, not the macho man image Long fantasized to shield himself from the reality of his own zeroness, the otherwise powerless persona who found power only through the domination, humiliation and destruction of creatures even weaker than he.

The Boston Globe was another major newspaper that checked in with its own assessment of the serial killer phenomenon in America by quoting several "experts" who might have been describing Bobby Joe Long in their characterizations of serial killers. Ironically, a reprint of the Globe article appeared inside the Tampa Tribune on the very day that news of Bobby Joe Long's arrest dominated page one.

"They are virtually all male, usually white, often intelligent and older than most criminals--in their thirties. Their victims are almost always female," the Globe article began.

"But most important, they are 'bad'--that is, legally responsible for what they do--not 'mad,' or crazy, say a chorus of forensic psychiatrists and criminologists.

"Serial murderers 'can conform their behavior to

the law if they choose to,' notes Northeastern University criminologist James A. Fox. 'They are guilty because they can choose not to kill. They want to kill...'

"Like some rapists, serial murderers are often driven by intense hostility to women and as with rape, many serial murders involve sex, not for its own sake but for domination and control. "'They mutilate and have no remorse, but they are as rational as anybody in the courtroom,' says criminologist Robert Ressler at the FBI Academy in Quantico, Va.

"Dr. Helen Morrison, a psychiatrist who as director of The Evaluation Center in Chicago has spent 5,000 hours interviewing several serial murderers (Bobby Joe Long among them. She also testified on his behalf.)

"'On the surface,' she said, 'they are charming, helpful, almost nice. They're not bizarre. They don't foam at the mouth or have weird stares. They're not crazy or delusional. It's only when you regress them to a more childlike psychological state that you see how chaotic they are inside.'

"They know they've murdered, she says. They just don't care that what they have destroyed is a human life. 'They have a total lack of empathy for a human being.

"It's terrifying to deal with,' she mused. 'I don't go around shaking, but the terror I experience is that a human being has the capacity to be that disorganized psychologically. You begin to recognize how they could indeed commit murder after murder after murder.'

"Perhaps most disturbing is that such men are remarkably similar to one another, so much so, notes Morrison, that they are 'carbon copies' of each other.

"Serial murderers, said Morrison, are "powerfully built individuals...who strike one as having odd components of traditionally male and female attrib-

utes...soft facial features contrast with masculine torsos. (Bobby Joe Long's adolescent breasts come to mind.) Cooperative, helpful, confident, accommodating, easy-going and nearly jovial...' (Bobby Joe Long was all those things, according to his friends.)

"But if serial murderers are not crazy, why do they kill? 'They do it because they like it,' said Dr. Park Elliott Dietz, psychiatric consultant to the behavioral science unit at the FBI Academy in Quantico, Va. and associate professor of law and psychiatry at the University of Virginia.

"'Nobody understands that,' he added. 'These are people who love to kill. Most serial murderers don't shoot their victims; these sexual murders (expressing a need to dominate or control) are more often knife wounds or strangulation because these are more personal weapons.' (Strangulation was Bobby Joe Long's method of choice.)

"Many serial killers, says Dr. Richard Ratner, a forensic psychiatrist at George Washington University, are enraged at their mothers, yet they feel unconsciously so dependent on them that they are terrified of losing them. They kill--an act of 'displaced rage'--to achieve emotional relief from their conflicting emotions. (Given Bobby Joe Long's confused and bizarre relationship with his mother, some experts believe he was symbolically slaying her each time he murdered.)

"But the real clue to such men, say all the experts, is the overpowering need for dominance and control of a woman. And, added Dietz grimly, 'No one is more totally controlled than a dead person.'"

Another ugly fact of life about serial killers is that, like everyone else, they learn by doing, a hideous on–the–job training, so to speak. It's not easy to kidnap a strong, healthy young woman (even a prostitute who comes willingly on the promise of money) harder still to subdue and kill them. Such skills take practice and

trial–and–error learning. Over time, serial killers polish their techniques. What begins as a crude fumbling and usually sloppy murder gradually becomes more sophisticated—more cunning in its planning and more precise in its execution.

"They learn from their mistakes," observed Lt. Gary Terry. "Every time they commit a crime, they learn how to do it better the next time. They kill because once they get a taste of killing they find they enjoy it. And soon they become good at it!"

The detectives who had to clean up the messes Bobby Joe Long left behind were struck from the beginning by the obvious sophistication of the crime scenes, with the style of the ligatures, especially their signature leashes and with the efficiency of the garrotting. He didn't just start off that way, Terry told his men. He had to learn what methods work best, which means he had to learn on somebody or something. But who? And where?

And that theory—that the more he kills, the more sophisticated and efficient the serial killer becomes—was precisely why the Hillsborough investigation went off on a tangent when the third body turned up. The killer switched tactics, perhaps unintentionally, but just enough to temporarily throw the man hunters off the scent.

▲   ▲   ▲

A LETTER FROM BOBBY

You say how sick your buddies are and the "crazy" shit they've done. I have no trouble with that, and I'm not trying to outdo anyone or sound proud of the things I've done, but there is so much that nobody knows about or ever will (even in "My Story") that makes me feel a little "ill" just thinking about. Things its hard to comprehend anything worse than.

▲   ▲   ▲

At first glance, Elizabeth Loudenback didn't seem to have much in common with your typical street whore. She was a loner, quiet and shy, "mousy" was the term often used to describe the twenty-two year old child–like young woman, whose washed–out, sandy–blond hair hung limply on either side of a face accented by large horn–rim glasses with rose–tinted lenses. Liz wasn't a hooker, but she liked to hang out in bars a lot, mostly because she was lonely, anxious to find somebody who'd treat her nice. The place she favored most of the time was Grandpa's Pool Parlor, a beer joint on Skipper Road, just down the street from the Village Mobile Home Park where she shared a crowded trailer with her mom, step–dad, seventeen year old sister, and fourteen year old brother. She'd come into Grandpa's several evenings a week, drink beer, and watch the other regulars shoot Nine Ball and argue and get drunk. A few doors down from Grandpa's was Cheeks Lounge, but that was mainly a topless joint, and Liz knew she didn't have the looks or the body to compete in there.

But there were plenty of other North Tampa dives to hang out at besides Grandpa's and Cheeks—joints where undereducated, seldom employed, long–haired drifters congregated to spend their meager and irregular paychecks on beer and burgers, pot and pills. Liz and her small circle of rootless acquaintances, mainly guys who used her for sex when nothing else was available, were the forgotten back end of society's up-front dropout problem.

Elizabeth Loudenback was born in Huntington, Indiana. She wasn't a dropout, but Liz struggled until she was ninteen years old before finally squeaking through high school on marginal grades. As one of the barmaids at Grandpa's said, "She was slow, but not retarded."

Norma Hill, Liz's mother, said that part of her daughter's problem was epilepsy, which she'd had since she was eleven-years-old. Sometimes her seizures were brought on by flashing lights, or even sunlight glittering off a wet tree. The seizures had been pretty much under control the last three or four years, due to the medication Liz was taking—250 milligrams of Depakane and twenty milligrams of Tegretol three times a day. Liz was faithful

256

about taking her pills, too, and never went anywhere without them.

Norma moved to Tampa in 1982 with Liz and her younger siblings, after divorcing their father in Indiana. They settled into the mobile home in the Village Mobile Home Park in August, 1983, about the same time Norma married John Hill.

Norma Hill described her daughter as five–feet, four–inches tall, 110 pounds, with a thin build. Her shoulder–length blond hair was sun–bleached on top. She had no tattoos or scars, but her ears were double pierced. Liz had never been married, but, her mother admitted, she did have an abortion sometime in early 1983. She knew Liz drank beer occasionally, but didn't think she used drugs.

For the past year, Liz had worked with her mom at Astra Products, a light–manufacturing company near Oldsmar, between Tampa and Clearwater, on the northern tip of the Bay. Liz worked all day at a soldering table, putting together communication devices and junction boxes under federal contract. It was boring, repetitive work, but Liz didn't complain and was considered a reliable worker by the management. She worked the 8 a.m. to 4:30 p.m. shift, and her take-home pay was $131 per week. She banked most of her money, although she was secretive about her finances. When they went to the bank together, Liz always turned her back so her mother couldn't see how much she was depositing or withdrawing. Liz also paid her mother and John Hill thirty-five dollars a week for rent.

She and John, Norma continued, didn't try to hold Liz to a curfew since she was, after all, a grown woman, although still pretty childish in a lot of ways. She had her own key and sometimes stayed out until midnight or later, but there were a few nights when she didn't come home until morning. Lately, John had been complaining about her coming in late, and warned Liz that if he took away her key she'd "...have to sleep in the shed and see how you like that." The family almost always sat down to supper together at 6 p.m. Afterwards, they liked to lounge around the community swimming pool talking to the neighbors. Liz was getting so she stayed home at night less and less. After supper, she'd

head over to Grandpa's Pool Parlor and sometimes spent hours over there, especially on weekends.

Norma Hill didn't know many of Liz's friends. They never came around much, but Liz mentioned a few once in a while. One was another regular at Grandpa's named Tina. She knew Lee, who lived in the same trailer park, and then there was David, a kid who did yard work and lived in his 1973 Ford Torino. He came over to the trailer once and sat around playing video games with Liz, but one night Liz had come home from Grandpa's saying David got mean and beat up a couple of girls there, so she wasn't going back. Later, she heard that David had been banned from Grandpa's, so she started going back again.

The boy she'd been talking about lately was Eddie, and from what Norma and John Hill could figure out, since Liz didn't confide in them too much, Eddie had recently started slapping her around and taking money from her. The people around Grandpa's who knew Eddie said he did construction work, and ran with a pretty tough crowd from Rudy's Pub on Nebraska.

Eddie, who also went by the name of Clyde, was living at another trailer park on North Nebraska near Rudy's Pub. The Hills knew that Liz had withdrawn money from her savings account to give to Eddie, a couple of hundred dollars at a time, which they didn't approve of. Also, the last time Norma Hill saw her daughter on Friday, June 8, Liz told her mom that she and Eddie had fought the night before and she was breaking up with him. Hill added that Eddie had called on Saturday, June 23, asking if Liz was home yet. Eddie told Norma that Liz had left a message for him at Grandpa's on the 8th; she couldn't argue with him that day, because she was going away for ten days.

In fact, the family had planned an outing together— on Saturday, June 9, they were going to the condominium they had leased on the tip of Crystal Beach, a popular Gulfside resort area. John planned to come back Sunday night, but Norma and the three kids would stay the week. She and Liz would commute to work from the condo that week, since the plant at Oldsmar wasn't far from Crystal Beach. Friday, June 8, they all packed their bags so

they could get an early start on Saturday morning. Liz left hers on the bed in her tiny bedroom before going out for the evening.

Norma last saw Liz about 7 p.m., but Liz's brother Lincoln said he bumped into her at the entrance to the mobile home lot on Skipper Road shortly afterwards. He said Liz was sitting on the curb talking to a couple of men, and warned her, "You'd better be coming home." His sister ignored him, got up, and walked off in the direction of Grandpa's Pool Parlor. The next morning, Liz's bed hadn't been slept in. "Out again all night," John Hill grumbled. The family waited for her until mid–morning, and when Liz still failed to show, they left a note on her bed to call them at the condominium and left.

As planned, John returned home late Sunday evening. The trailer was just as they'd left it; the note and Liz's packed suitcase remained untouched on the bed. He and Norma spoke several times by phone and the next day, when Norma went to work and there was still no word from Liz, they decided to report her missing. Staying out all night was one thing, but a whole weekend, and then not showing up for work, was not like Liz at all. On Monday evening, June 11, the Hills called police and filled out a missing persons report on Liz. Nothing was heard from her all week, and by the time the Hills returned from Crystal Beach the following weekend, Norma was convinced something terrible had happened to her eldest daughter. Liz was so child–like, after all, that people easily took advantage of her. Somebody like that no-good Eddie.

What alarmed Norma even more was the earful she got at work from Sylvia Miller, Liz's production supervisor. Sylvia also gave Norma a disturbing note that Liz had left with her on June 6, two days before she vanished. In her jumbled handwriting, the note read: "Eddie, Clyde, lives on Nebraska, police, get in touch with Lee, van." And "Green–10, Chevy," to describe the van. When Sylvia asked Liz what the note was for she replied, "Well, I just think somebody should know this just in case."

Liz also had confided in the older woman because, Sylvia said, "I think I was about the only friend she had, at least here at work." During their conversations at coffee and lunch breaks, Liz had

259

mentioned three different men she hinted she was involved with: Lee, who talked about working with the cops or the DEA; David, who broke up with her because she didn't have a car; and this Eddie character, who Liz acted like she was in love with but was scared to death of at the same time.

Liz told Sylvia that she gave Eddie money several times. Once she withdrew $400 on her Honor Card so he could buy drugs, mainly cocaine. Liz admitted she smoked pot when she was with her friends, but didn't do other drugs— not like Eddie, who was a big user, according to Liz. She talked about how he would get upset and punch her and knock her down when he needed money from her. He said he needed it for his "stuff," Liz told her friend.

Sylvia said she knew Liz had become more and more jittery about Eddie in the past week or two. On Wednesday, June 6, she slipped Sylvia the note indicating the police should look for Eddie if anything happened to her. That Friday, when they were walking out to the parking lot after work, Liz turned to her and said, "I'm going over to Eddie's house to tell him its over. I don't want to see him any more." And those were the last words Sylvia heard from her.

After talking to the family and co–workers, police checking out the missing-persons report set out to track others who knew Liz. Tom Langan, the owner of Grandpa's Pool Parlor, nodded when shown a photo of Liz. "Yeah, she's one of the regulars comes in here. If I was looking for somebody who might have killed her," Langan advised the detectives, "I'd be looking for that guy, David. He used to work for me mowing the lawn, but I had to fire him 'cause of the way he hates women. The girls that come in here were scared to death of him and would take off when he came in. Three, four weeks back, he really beat up bad on a girl here, knocked her down on the ground outside. That's when I told him to get out and stay out."

Lee Darby, the neighbor in the mobile home park, confided that he was really a CI (confidential informant) for the Tampa narcotics squad. Others who knew him said Darby like to throw his weight around by bragging about his police connections. Darby

told the cops he'd met Liz over at Grandpa's seven or eight months earlier, and they'd gone out for pizza a couple of times. He knew that lately she'd been going out with Eddie, because he saw her get in Eddie's green van several times. Liz complained to him that Eddie beat her up a lot, and about a month ago he made her give him $200 to pay off somebody "...to keep from getting his legs broke." Also, Darby suggested, you ought to go talk to David. I introduced Liz to him and I think he was screwing her, too."

When located, David said he met Liz at Grandpa's and talked to her four or five times. Then, one day out of the blue, she just walked up to him and said, "Let's fuck." "I figured, why not," David shrugged. So, the first time, he took her out to Ben T. Davis Beach and they had sex in the car. The next time, he parked at 17th Street and 148th Avenue, and just got out and put Liz on the hood of the car and screwed her there. Once they went to Al's Motel on Nebraska and spent the night. A couple of times he'd gone over to her trailer when her parents were gone, and they'd fucked there. Liz once lent him ten dollars, but that was the only time he ever took any money from her. David also admitted to smoking pot and using speed whenever he got a job driving a truck someplace, but that was all the drugs he used. David agreed to take a polygraph test which "showed signs of deceptions," according to the operator. Baker read him his rights, and when "Pops" drove David back to the place he was staying on Leisure Street, he noticed some marijuana plants growing in the backyard. David denied they were his.

When they finally talked to Eddie, he said, Yeah, Liz had lent him some money to help pay for the party at the motel, but he never beat her up or forced her to give him money. He was going to pay her back, but she disappeared before he got the cash. Eddie reluctantly agreed to a polygraph test, which, like the others, "...showed signs of deception." Was this a case of several buddies involved in the murder? Baker wondered. But they all had solid alibis for the time Liz vanished, and although the results of the polygraphs didn't look good, there was no basis for charging the young men in her disappearance.

Even so, family members and several of Liz's co–workers and

acquaintances agreed on one thing: Whoever took Liz away had to be somebody she knew. She'd never get in a car with a stranger and wouldn't hitchhike, they insisted. Why, one time she walked all the way home from the University Square Mall, three or four miles, because she didn't have cab fare and didn't want to call anyone for a ride. Also, when Liz failed to come home, John Hill said he checked with the bank and learned that about $500 had been withdrawn on Liz's Honor Card that same weekend.

In the missing-persons report, Norma noted that the last time she saw her, Liz was wearing an aqua tube top with a white border; jeans; blue, tennis shoes with white stripes; a strapless 32A or 34A bra, and white booty socks.

A vice-president at Atlantic Bank checked the records, and told Baker that Liz's Honor Card was used on June 9, the day after Liz was last seen. The first time was at 1:42 a.m. that Saturday morning at an ATM in Carrollwood, but the card was rejected because the request was a withdrawal from checking and Liz didn't have a checking account. Next, the user inquired about a savings account, which showed a balance of four hundred seventy-eight dollars and eighty-two cents, at which time two hundred dollars was withdrawn. The card was used again at another Carrollwood branch at 1:44 a.m. and fifty dollars withdrawn. The user tried again almost immediately, only to have the request rejected since two hundred and fifty dollars was the maximum withdrawal amount allowed within a 24-hour period. But whoever was using the card didn't give up easily. From 1:46 a.m. to 1:47 a.m., attempts were made to withdraw two hundred, one hundred, fifty and twenty dollars, all of which were rejected. A final attempt to get money from Liz's account was made at 5:39 p.m. on June 9, but that, too, was unsuccessful. The bank official said an alert would be placed on Liz's card with special instructions, if confiscated, to handle it in such a way to preserve any fingerprints.

Meanwhile, Lt. Gary Terry worked on the set of massive homicide investigation files that seemed to be growing thicker by the hour. What was most troubling was the certain knowledge that the guy wasn't through killing. Two victims, both off the streets—

raped, strangled, and tied up, nude bodies dumped in rural Southeastern Hillsborough County. Matching nylon fibers. Even now, he might be out there dumping more bodies. Somewhere in that towering stack of investigative reports there had to be a key, something that connected everything and pointed to a suspect. Something that Terry and his men were overlooking. But what?

"The biggest thing in a serial homicide is recognition," Terry said. "Once you recognize what you have on your hands, you can do certain things, marshal your resources to be more focused and efficient. Unfortunately, what happens too often is that agencies don't recognize what they have until there are six, eight, ten bodies down. By then they may have lost some valuable evidence that by all rights should have been found at the first few crime scenes. But they may not have realized the significance of it in those first few cases. It was the fiber evidence that solidified for us that we did indeed have a serial killer in Hillsborough County. However, I have to say that we did have that feeling even without the fibers. When you take your gut feelings as an experienced investigator, look at the similarities in the crimes scenes and then suddenly tie it in forensically, that's when you really link things together."

That system, ideal in theory, broke down in practice when Ronnie Allen Barnes, a young grove worker, climbed aboard his John Deere tractor and went out to do some mowing in one of the grove. It was a Sunday, but the work had to be done and Barnes could use the overtime. He was working toward the rear of a forty–acre grove where thick, low–hanging citrus branches effectively concealed the site from passersby traveling north or south on Turkey Creek Road. On a northeast–to–southwest diagonal, the rural grove lay almost exactly midway between the Lana Long dump site and the spot were Michelle Simms' mutilated body was found near Plant City.

For young Ronnie Barnes, it was the smell that hit him first. The overpowering, sickening stench of something dead. Working out in the groves like he did, Barnes was always running into dead and decaying critters—possums, coons, armadillos. But this was worse than anything he'd run into before. He held his t-shirt over

his nose to block the stench and was turning the tractor–mower around to get out of there when he spotted the pair of blue tennis shoes sticking out from under an orange tree at the rear of the grove. That's all Ronnie Barnes needed to see. He hightailed it to the nearest phone and called the sheriff's office to report there was somebody dead out in the grove.

Ronnie Barnes stood by to guide the first deputies to arrive back to the site, but stayed far back when they approached. The two Hillsborough County deputies who responded to the call continued on through the trees until they were almost overcome by the terrible stench. As bad as the smell was, the condition of the body was even harder to take. Swarms of flies engulfed the remains— a body stretched out on its back, legs slightly apart, and arms straight out to the sides as though nailed to a cross. The body was fully dressed, the ground around it soaked black by a pool of fluids. There was an aqua-colored tube top with a an inch–wide white band around the bottom covering the top of the torso. The victim was wearing blue jeans, but between the top of the jeans and the bottom of the tube top, the exposed abdomen had caved in from decomposition so it looked like the jeans were several sizes too large. There were blue jogging shoes and white booties on the feet; around the neck was a necklace with a yellow, heart–shaped pendant. The nearly fleshless head was turned to the side, staring sightlessly over the left arm that now resembled a thin log blackened by fire.

It was another ruined Sunday for Terry and his harried squad, who were beginning to feel the inevitable heat that comes boiling down the line of command when the city-hall types get upset over important cases too long unsolved. But after taking a look at the Loudenback murder scene, the investigators breathed an almost unconscious sigh of relief—prematurely, as it turned out. Not our guy, they told each other. No ligatures. Victim fully clothed. Body found far from the other dump sites. One shoelace untied, which was about the only thing out of place. An autopsy later confirmed that damage to the delicate hyoid bone in the front of the throat indicated the victim died of strangulation, but that alone wasn't

264

enough to connect her to the other victims. The police were more convinced than ever that this murder was not linked to the earlier slayings when they identified the remains as Elizabeth Loudenback, and determined that she wasn't a prostitute.

The Monday, June 25th edition of the Tribune reported on the discovery of the unidentified body in the orange grove. That article, and one the following day, raised for the first time the frightening specter of a "copycat" killer taking advantage of the current murder spree to cover his own crimes:

"In a steamy orange grove east of Brandon Sunday morning, a man hired to cut grass found the badly decomposed body of a young female—the fourth such body discovered in Hillsborough County in six weeks.

"Lying fully clothed near unpaved Whitehead Road west of Turkey Creek Road and south of U.S. Highway 60, the body of a white female in her late twenties or early thirties was discovered at about 10:30 a.m., according to the Hillsborough County Sheriff's Office...

"Nothing initially discovered appears to link her death with the recent deaths of other young women in the county...

"The battered bodies of two women, (Lana Long and Michelle Simms) both found nude and bound, were discovered in May in eastern Hillsborough County...

"Two weeks after the discovery of Simms, the fully clothed body of a Bradenton day care worker was found asphyxiated in an isolated ditch in Riverview. Cynthia Ruth Wood was 33.

"[Sheriff Walter] Heinrich said last week that Wood's death is not linked with those of Long and Simms.

"The Sheriff's Office obtained an arrest warrant June 18 for Donald Santini, 26, a Texas fugitive who Wood's relatives said was seen with her before her death.

"Santini, who has a Texas arrest record, fled from Florida into Kentucky and Texas shortly after Wood's murder, Sheriff's deputies said...''

The latest murder victim was identified when a routine run–through of missing-persons reports quickly turned up the name of Elizabeth Loudenback. Her description and the clothing she wore when last seen enabled authorities to positively identify the decomposing remains. The following day, the Tribune announced that the dead woman had been identified, while reporting on yet another body added to the count:

"A 22 year old Tampa woman who lived with her parents near the University of South Florida was identified Monday as the latest victim in a series of murderous acts which have left five women dead in the rural stretches of eastern Hillsborough County.

"Sheriff's officials said the body found Sunday morning in an orange grove seven miles east of Brandon was that of Elizabeth Loudenback...

"'Since we lived here, she was more or less not that outgoing,' said Loudenback's stepfather John Hill. 'Ninety-nine percent of the time she was at home...'

"Being an epileptic, Loudenback had to take medication three times a day, her stepfather said. Although she usually carried a two-day supply with her, the rest of her medicine was at home, along with all her clothes.

"Before she disappeared, Loudenback went to the bank with her mother to either cash or deposit her paycheck, Hill said.

"'She turned her back to her mother during the transaction," Hill said. 'She could be sneaky.'

"Hill said Loudenback's purse was not found with her body.

"But Sheriff's Lt. Gary Terry said investigators do not know whether robbery was the motive in the killing...

"People who knew Loudenback agreed that she was not the kind of person who would have gotten into a car with a stranger.

'She's not one to hitchhike,' said Hill.

With all the bodies suddenly littering the landscape, investigators went back to their "cold file" to see if some recent killings might be connected. One case they looked at closely was that of twenty-one year old Betty Sue Foster. Her body, nude and bloodied, had been found on December 13, 1983, in the weeds beside a chain-link fence that surrounded the Progress Village sewage treatment plant. She had been stripped and shot through the chest with a small-caliber gun.

Terry's investigators never seriously considered the murder of the Foster woman to be part of the developing string of serial killings—wrong MO, and wrong part of the county. And the city police were already zeroing in on a suspect, who eventually was arrested and charged. The slaying of Cynthia Wood, however, was another matter. In Terry's words, "It bothered us tremendously."

When Cynthia Wood's body was found, Terry and his squad of detectives feared the worst—that the same killer had dumped another body on their turf. The site was in the Riverview section of southern Hillsborough County, only a mile or two north of where Lana Long's body had been found and about the same distance southeast of the Liz Loudenback crime scene. Two neighborhood women taking an afternoon bicycle ride discovered the woman lying in the ditch alongside Alsobrook Avenue. Unlike Long and Simms, the woman was fully clothed and had not been tied up. "Nevertheless," Terry recalled, "we couldn't close our eyes to the possibility that the deaths were related. We knew at the time, although we kept the information secret, that there were at least five similarities between the Lana Long and Michelle Simms killings. When we didn't find any of those similarities in the Wood case we felt pretty confident that this wasn't our guy.

"But the murder of Cynthia Wood was a perfect illustration of a copy-cat murder," Terry continued. "She was killed as a result of a contract placed on her life. The killer took it one step further when he saw we were having this problem in Hillsborough County, so when he murdered Cynthia he brought the body up here from Manatee County thinking it would be lumped in with ours."

To confuse the issue even more, yet another body of a nude

young woman, strangled and with her throat cut, was discovered early in July in Manatee County, bordering Hillsborough on the south. Again, the initial similarities were too striking to ignore, so Detective John Marsicano was told to drop whatever he was doing on the Loudenback investigation and coordinate with Manatee County authorities. Marsicano's report states:

"On 9 July 84, 0810 hours, writer called Manatee County SO and talked to Det. Richard Hough, Sr. reference the young w/f found in their county over the weekend...He advised that she had been identified as September Amanda Cabral, w/f, DOB 9/26/62, and they had two suspects reference this investigation...States Dr. Diggs examined the victim and commented their case looked similar to our cases. Writer made arrangements to meet with Hough at his office at 1530 hours this date.

"At 1530 hours, writer met with Det. Hough, Det. Betty Rominger and Sgt. M.J. Rominger at the Manatee County SO. Also present was Det. Ron Albritton from Sarasota County SO. They were interested in [the two suspects] reference a murder which occurred in their county over a year ago involving strangulation.

"Writer learned that the victim had died because her throat was slit. She also had been beaten and strangled. Writer observed the body and photos taken at the scene and did not observe any ropes or ligature marks. The victim was left nude from the waist down, her pants nearby and her panties on one leg. Motorcycle tire impressions were found at the crime scene as well as motorcycle parts. Writer learned that the victim had been in this area for the past three or four months with her boyfriend. Originally from Massachusetts. She was in front of a local convenience store on SR 41 south of Bradenton and was apparently picked up by [a suspect]. This was observed by a patrol deputy at approx. 0300 hrs. 8 July 84. She was apparently driven to the crime scene area near an orange grove

off a secondary road and killed. The suspects do not live far from the crime scene."

The death of September Amanda Cabral was close enough to attract serious attention from the Hillsborough investigators, but not close enough to warrant inclusion in the list of serial killings. It was possible, Terry conceded, that the Hillsborough victims were killed by two people working together like the Cabral woman, but he didn't think so. Too much about the Lana Long, Michelle Simms, and Liz Loudenback crime scenes pointed to one unknown perpetrator, or, as the FBI liked to call him, "Unsub."

Besides, there was one critical piece missing from the Cabral crime scene that pretty much ruled it out in Terry's mind: those red lustrous trilobal nylon fibers. Hillsborough authorities came to the conclusion that neither the Cabral murder nor that of Cynthia Wood was the work of the killer who was snatching women off Tampa streets, raping them, and strangling them. However, while several of the slayings were unrelated to the serial murders, media reports on the discovery of each new victim only fueled the growing public hysteria that a dangerously nightmarish New Age Jack the Ripper was loose in the community, killing at will. The dread that was spreading like a cancer throughout the law-enforcement agencies whose hands were dirtied by the killer's residue was that the guy was spinning more and more out of control. The next victim might well be Mrs. Middle-Class Housewife on her way to the store; a child grabbed off a playground; a nun on her knees in prayer.

Meanwhile, "Pops" Baker recalled, "We were about ready to arrest Elizabeth Loudenback's boyfriend because he looked like he'd had reason to kill her and had done so poorly on the polygraph. But then the fiber evidence came back from the FBI, and we dropped that plan real fast.

"The Loudenback girl was hanging around the area of Skipper and Nebraska when she was picked up. I've worked the streets when we've had other prostitute murders and went up on the Strip looking for information. I'd stop some girl and she'd say, 'I'm not a

prostitute. Why you asking me?' Well, she's in a prostitute area and looks like one. So I suppose the Loudenback girl looked like that."

Added Terry: "During the entire investigation we did a lot of things right and a lot of things wrong.

"The Loudenback investigation was one of the wrong things.

"We ID'd her initially as a missing person. Unlike the other victims, her missing bank card had been used.

"The big question was: Is this related to the others? Where was the continuity? That issue of continuity is why it's important to keep the same detectives, the same lab technicians on a case like this from beginning to end. They develop an instinctive feel for similarities and differences.

"Another thing that threw us off at first was that from the beginning, Elizabeth Loudenback's boyfriend was a top suspect. We found a note in her home that said something like, 'If something happens to me, Eddie did it.' Friends and family said she'd had trouble with him in the past, he was into the drug scene and apparently forced her to give him money. The boyfriend had an alibi but for some reason failed a polygraph. We looked at it as another routine—quote unquote—homicide and assigned another team of detectives to it. But then when we sent the forensic evidence from the crime scene to the FBI, they came back with those same tiny, red, lustrous trilobal nylon fibers.

"Suddenly, where we thought we had two related homicides, the fiber evidence proved we actually had three and didn't realize it.

"Now we really started to get worried."

The FBI Bulletin issued later—and in hindsight—mildly criticized the handling of the Loudenback investigation:

'On June 24, 1984, the body of another young white female was found, the third victim in this series of homicides, although this would not be known for a few months. The victim was found in an orange grove in southeastern Hillsborough County. The victim was found fully clothed, and the body was in an advanced stage of decomposition. The total body weight of the victim, including her

clothes, was only twenty-five pounds. There were no ligatures present, and the victim was not found near an interstate as the first two victims had been. During the initial stages of the investigation, the victim's boyfriend failed a polygraph examination and appeared to be an excellent suspect. Evidence from the case was sent to the FBI Laboratory; however, no request was made for this evidence to be compared to the evidence from the previous two homicides until much later.

"The victim was identified as Elizabeth B. Loudenback, twenty-two, of Tampa. Loudenback was employed as an assembly line worker and was last seen at approximately 7:00 p.m. on June 8, 1984. She was known to frequent the area of Nebraska Avenue and Skipper Road in northern Hillsborough County, but had no criminal history.

"The hairs from the Loudenback case were examined with negative results. Serology examinations were also negative due to the extensive decomposition of the body. The fibers, examined later, were determined to be both types of the red carpet fibers evidenced in the two previous cases. If this examination had been done initially, it would have been immediately known that Loudenback was, in fact, the third victim. When the evidence arrived at the FBI Laboratory, it was not assigned to the examiner who had worked the first two homicides. One of the most important aspects of handling a serial murder investigation is to have the same crime scene technician at all crime scenes and the same forensic examiners at the laboratory, so that one individual can become totally familiar with the forensic portion of the investigation, in order to recognize patterns and associations which might be present."

Unfortunately, the investigators were to repeat the same mistakes and faulty assumptions they made in the Elizabeth Loudenback case when the remains of a young black prostitute

271

were found by road workers in a ditch, just a few yards south of the Pasco County line in northern Hillsborough County, miles from the previous dump sites. But that didn't come until months later. And the mysterious, four–month gap between killings left police more baffled than ever. According to most theories on serial killers, the guy should have kept on killing with the bodies piling up at an ever-increasing rate. However, what appeared on the surface to be a gap may have been only an illusion. Perhaps the murders were continuing—only somewhere else. Bobby Joe Long was still prowling the Nebraska Strip, Terry said, while also moving back and forth between Tampa and Miami to visit his children. He didn't spend all his time in the Bay area, so it was possible that Hillsborough's relief from murder was some other jurisdiction's misfortune—except that nobody ever connected them.

"There was the prostitute from Miami he kidnaped and left alive in Glades County in August," said Terry, 'That led to the speculation there could have been other murders as well during this supposed gap between killings, possibly outside our jurisdiction that we never learned about. Or, what we thought was highly probable, the bodies were never found."

While circumstances did in fact combine to temporarily curtail the body count, the lust to rape and kill continued to possess Bobby Joe Long, although there were other matters occupying his attention during this summer of 1984. For example, on June 14, only six days after Liz Loudenback vanished and before her body was found, Long was hired at Tampa General Hospital. In July, Long was also preoccupied with court appearances involving the attempted kidnaping of Mary Ann Hicks and the wreckage of her classic Jaguar automobile the previous April. In a hearing before Judge J. Rogers Padgett on July 17, Long negotiated a plum plea bargain for himself. He agreed to six months probation and $1,500 in restitution for damages to the Jaguar. In exchange, Judge Padgett "withheld adjudication of guilt." The terms were negotiated by Assistant State Attorney Wes Pardue and approved by Padgett. Pardue's supervisor, Assistant State Attorney Mike Benito (who later won the battle to send Bobby Joe Long to the electric

chair), said the victim in the assault case "expressed she was satisfied with the way the case was handled with Mr. Pardue...It's obvious the case was extremely weak from a prosecution standpoint, for one reason because no gun was found. The trial probably would have ended up as a swearing match between the victim and Long, so the state negotiated a plea. She said she was satisfied with the way it was handled."

Also in July, Bobby Joe Long was busy apartment hunting and preparing to move from Brandon to Tampa. On July twenty-fourth, records show, he purchased furniture and began moving into his new apartment in the Temple Terrace section of far northeast Tampa. His second-floor apartment was located above the Klip Joint Salon and Hairdressers, and Long had no sooner settled in than he began firing off letters to the building manager, complaining about the noise and the strong chemical odors coming from the beauty shop.

A month later, in August, Long drove down to Miami for one of his regular visits with his two children. Before heading back to Tampa, he changed his plans long enough to pick up Evelyn Moore, tie her up, drive her into a remote area of south central Florida, sexually assault her, and photograph himself in the act of rape.

▲　　▲　　▲

A LETTER FROM BOBBY

Somewhere down the road I may take you up on your offer for a blade...

But I'll say again, my hands are all I need. I don't look it, but believe it!

Sometimes when you write you sound like you think I'm a babe in the woods.

Hey--I grew up in Miami, and I grew up in the street. I can handle myself, I'm not stupid.

I've lived all around the country including L.A.

You can survive in Miami and L.A. in the circles

I did, you survive anywhere! I boxed in the Army, Open Division Golden Gloves (the best). I can take care of myself.

I'm thirty-one and definitely have not led a sheltered life.

No prison, I was lucky enough to get away with a lot.

But don't let my happy go lucky exterior fool you, I fucked up once, and they caught me.

Really--I wanted to get caught, for all the shit to end.

But I won't fuck up again!

Keep in mind, I'm not just some fucking yokel who blew someone away in a Armed Robbery or something.

I'm "Mad Dog" Long!

▲   ▲   ▲

Late one night in June, between the disappearance of Liz Loudenback and the discovery of her body, a couple of bearded, blue–jeaned, grungy-looking characters were cruising Tampa's North Nebraska strip. Like Bobby Joe Long, they were also hunters—but with a license and badge to back them up. The pair were undercover narcotics detectives sniffing out dealers and making busts . They'd just turned off Fowler onto Nebraska, heading south, when they spotted a young, attractive, white female with her thumb out, hitching a ride. The two police picked her up. She was on her way to work at the Ramada Inn coffee shop, the woman said. Although she did wear a waitress uniform, the always suspicious, street–wise police wondered why such a pretty young thing was out alone hitchhiking late at night, unless she was peddling something. They struck up a conversation about drugs and hinted that they were in the market to buy. Might be a couple of bucks in it for her if she could set something up for them. The woman laughed and shook her head. "Sorry," she said. "I don't do drugs, and I really am on my way to work." When they reached the Ramada Inn, the detectives identified themselves and warned the

woman that she shouldn't be out hitchhiking this time of night—especially not along Nebraska Avenue, where it wasn't safe to be alone night or day. "I'm not afraid," the woman replied. "I've got my protection." She reached into her purse and pulled out a long pair of scissors. "See," she laughed. "If anybody tries to mess around with me, I've got these."

Three months later, on the evening of September 6, 1984. Vicky Marie Elliott, a twenty-one year old night waitress, was getting ready for work at the Ramada Inn coffee shop at the intersection of North Nebraska Avenue and Busch Boulevard, just a half–block from the Starlite Lounge. Vicky had specifically asked for the 11 p.m. to 7 a.m. shift, because it paid forty cents more per hour. And the tips were better from the half–drunk Starlite clientele, who stumbled in for coffee after the topless dancers quit and were more than happy to drop a big tip on the sexy, bubbly, freckle–faced young waitress who brought them free refills. None of them even came close to scoring. Vicky Elliott wasn't the type. And besides, she had higher goals than a dreary life spent with one of these sweaty beer guts. But they kept on trying.

Vicky lived in a small duplex apartment on a narrow, gravel street squeezed into an old neighborhood of North Tampa where small, two–bedroom houses and transient apartments were shaded by massive live oaks. Vicky didn't have a car, and although neighbors and co–workers often expressed concern about her welfare, she insisted on walking to work or to the big new University Square Mall that had opened up on Fowler. Sometimes she caught a ride with the other waitresses, or with regular customers from the coffee shop. She didn't even mind hitchhiking since that, Vicky felt, was just one more expression of her independence and ability to take care of herself. But what Vicky perceived as strength, some of her friends viewed as a dangerous flaw. She was too trusting of strangers, and that could get her in deep trouble.

That same independent, adventuresome spirit was what prompted Vicky Elliott to leave her home in Muskegon, Michigan, a few years before, and move to Florida to spend some time alone and decide what she wanted to do with her life. By late summer,

1984, Vicky had pretty well made up her mind. She'd proved to herself and her family that she could make it on her own, and now she planned to return home, go back to school, and study to be a paramedic. She'd already given two weeks' notice at the coffee shop, had bought her plane ticket home, and expected to be back in Michigan in time to start the fall semester.

Vicky left work at 7:05 a.m. the morning of September 6, and was scheduled to return at 11 p.m. In the months she'd worked at the Ramada, Vicky had forged a reputation as a good, dependable worker who was always on time, cordial to the customers, and willing to pitch in with an extra hand when something needed to be done. So when Vicky didn't show up for the start of her shift at 11 p.m. that evening, supervisor Joyce Culbertson was immediately concerned. If she couldn't make it, Vicky would have called. Since coming to work there in July, 1983, Vicky had never missed work without calling first.

By midnight, Joyce was flat-out scared. She arranged for someone to cover for her in the coffee shop, collected one of the Ramada security guards, and drove to Vicky's apartment. The lights were out and, when their knocking failed to arouse anyone, Joyce returned to the motel and phoned police to report Vicky as missing.

As police began checking on the missing woman's movements, they spoke first with Ramada co–workers. Joyce Culbertson said that Vicky routinely wore her yellow and brown uniform to work, along with the required nylons, and brown Topsider shoes with white soles. Vicky had three uniforms, but only two were found in her apartment the day after she vanished, so they knew she had at least dressed for work before she dropped out of sight.

Pat Mills, the waitress Vicky usually relieved at 11 p.m., recalled that, several weeks prior to her disappearance, Vicky had talked about getting her hair cut at a place out on Fowler called the Klip Joint. Pat remembered it, because she and Vicky had laughed about the name of the shop. Vicky mentioned that while she was there she'd met a guy—tall, dark, nice hair. "Vicky said he seemed like a nice guy, but she had to get to know him better before she'd go out with him," Pat added. (The report that Vicky may have been the

only victim to have met her killer prior to the murder later stirred considerable interest among the investigators. However, a check of records at the Klip Joint could not confirm that Vicky Elliott had been a customer there. For his part, Bobby Joe Long never let on that he might have known Vicky any time before her murder.

Janet Lowe, who worked the same shift with Vicky three nights a week, said that Vicky had recently purchased a new purse with lots of deep pockets, in which she carried a big pair of scissors with black handles. Vicky told her the scissors were for protection, ever since a guy she'd hitched a ride with gave her a bad time and wouldn't take no for an answer.

At Vicky's building, officers spoke with Beth Griffin, Vicky's neighbor in Apartment B. She said she saw Vicky walking home about 6 p.m. from the University Square Mall, where she'd just had her hair trimmed at the Mantrap salon. Beth asked Vicky to go back to the Mall with her and introduce her to the hairdresser so she could get her hair cut. After the trim, the two ate dinner at Wag's in the mall. Vicky offered to buy dinner, since Beth frequently gave her a lift when she needed to go somewhere. When Vicky opened her purse to pay the tab, Beth said she was shocked at what appeared to be several hundred dollars in cash. The two returned home about 8:30 p.m., and Beth offered to drive Vicky to work later. She said she heard her neighbor's shower about 9:30, but when Vicky didn't come over for the ride to work, Beth said she went to bed a little after 11 p.m. She was awakened at midnight when the Ramada security officer came to Vicky's door, and again about 3:30 a.m. when several young women wearing Ramada uniforms came around looking for Vicky. It wasn't until the next day, when police and the landlord came to open the apartment, that Beth learned her friend was missing.

On September 14, the Tampa Tribune carried a story about the missing twenty-one year old waitress, quoting Tampa police detective Jim Conklin as saying that while there is no physical evidence of foul play, he was concerned that something serious may have befallen Vicky Elliott, given the circumstances of her disappearance. The only things missing from her apartment when he

checked were one of her three work uniforms and her work shoes. Nothing else was disturbed, the door was locked, and Vicky had left her pet dog and cat alone, indicating she expected to return.

Contacted in Muskegon, Michigan, Vicky's mother, Lora Elliott, said she had no idea where her daughter might be, adding that "She's never, never done anything like that before. She's always been very responsible when it comes to home and school."

Mrs. Elliott told Detective Conklin that in recent weeks, her son, who once lived in Tampa, had received phone calls from a man who claimed the Elliott boy owed him money and threatened to collect it from Vicky.

"They called me," Lora Elliott said. "They wanted money from my son, and if I didn't give it to them they said they had no alternative but to rob her. Vicky was afraid to leave money in her apartment because of that, and sometimes carried hundreds of dollars around with her."

She added that her daughter planned to return to Michigan soon to attend school and become a paramedic. Vicky had already purchased a plane ticket for a flight home on October 5. The ticket was found on Vicky's bed when police entered her apartment.

According to the Tribune:

"Because she had been harassed by men on her way to work, Elliott recently started 'carrying a big pair of scissors with her,' Culbertson said.

"Recently, she began walking about a mile to her job along some railroad tracks parallel to Nebraska Avenue, according to Conklin.

"But a police search of the tracks and the surrounding woods turned up empty, he said.

"'I'm pretty well satisfied she didn't walk the tracks that night,' Conklin said. 'More than likely she got into a car with somebody.'

"Jim Wolfe, a former boyfriend of Elliott, said she recently told him about a Peeping Tom in the neighborhood, but didn't seem particularly worried.

"Wolfe said he offered to get Elliott a gun because he was afraid for her.

"'I sure hope she's alive, that's all,' he said.

"Elliott is described as five-foot two-inches tall, 100 pounds, with red, shoulder-length hair. Anyone who has seen her since Sept. 6 is asked to call the Tampa Police Department.'

On September 27, 1984, while the search for the missing waitress dragged on without success, Bobby Joe Long was summoned to his supervisor's office in the bowels of sprawling Tampa General Hospital. "We're going to have to let you go," he was informed. "You don't have the proper advanced certification that's called for in your job description." Losing jobs, quitting jobs, not getting jobs was the story of his life. Long could have wallpapered his living room with all the worthless job applications he'd filled out since he'd dropped out of high school. Besides, not working those weekend hours gave him time for more important things.

▲　　▲　　▲

A LETTER FROM BOBBY

Columbia, Peru, both sound great. Fucking Peru has some of the most beautiful Pussy in the world! I'm serious!

I'd work for these boys, do ANYTHING they wanted!

I know some guys in Miami from Columbia (should say I "knew") they're some bad cock suckers! Cocaine Cowboys. We're talkin Ingram sub machine guns, execution style killings. Bad Boys. That was a while back. Too fucking hairy back then. Trying to establish territories and shit.

Thats what I meant about some of the boys I grew up with being dead, or just vanishing from the face of the earth. Some shit that used to go down would make your show Miami Vice look like Mother Goose! Believe me!

▲　　▲　　▲

279

The last place Chanel Devon Williams wanted to be was out here on a hot, dirty street corner in the asshole of Tampa selling her body. But it was about the only option she had left this Sunday night, the last day of September, 1984. Only twenty-four hours out of jail on a prostitution bust, the thin, almost emaciated eighteen year old had just come over from Winter Haven a month ago, and no sooner had she hit town than she was set up by Tampa vice dicks, or so she believed. Not that it surprised her. As young as she was, Chanel was already a street–smart veteran of the neverending, often ferocious, four–way tug of war over cash and flesh among Hooker, John, Cop, and Pimp, in which Hooker always loses.

Chanel Williams was destined to become number four in the Hillsborough County Sheriff's reckoning of serial murder victims. Or, as Lt. Terry and his men came to affectionately refer to this lost, doomed soul from the rural ghettos of Central Florida, "Chanel No. 4" Chanel Devon Williams was among the nameless legions who lost.

Morris Bridge Road, or County Highway 579, runs on a north-west diagonal out of Tampa, across the boundaries of Hillsborough State Park and into southern Pasco County. A half-mile before 579 crosses the county line, on the west side of the narrow, two–lane blacktop highway, there's a gravel side road leading to the K–Bar Ranch. A locked gate closes off the sprawling horse and cattle ranch from casual traffic that might wander in from 579. About 7:30 on the morning of October 1, ranch hand Les Wilkins stopped to open the gate on his way into the property, and was surprised to find a woman's bra hanging on the fence, just to the right of the gate's padlock. A knot was tied in the bra. Somebody must've had a good time, Wilkins grinned to himself. He removed the bra, tossed it aside, and thought no more about it. During the week, several other ranch employees passed back and forth through the gate numerous times. It wasn't until the following Sunday, October 7, that ranch foreman Clarence Hale finally spotted the decomposing, choco-late–brown body lying a few yards north of the road, partially con-cealed by a clump of shrubbery. Hale was leaving the K–Bar about

7:30 p.m. and was closing the pasture gate behind him when some clothing clinging to a bush at the side of the road caught his eye. The bra that he and the other K–Bar boys must have run over a dozen times or more on their way to and from work was still there, ground into the dirt. Now, Hale wondered if that bra might be connected to the other clothing in the bushes. Scattered about were a pair of grey jeans, a yellow sweater, and white, flip–flop sandals.

Hale stepped closer to investigate. The nude body was face down, and from the legs to the shoulders it looked like the person had just stretched out for an afternoon nap. The head, on the other hand, was a nightmare, something ghastly out of a Stephen King horror novel, writhing and slithering with an unnatural life of its own. What appeared at first glance to be a sandy–colored burlap bag sheathing the head turned out to be a living shroud of maggots and other feasting insects.

Clarence Hale rushed to the nearest phone to notify the sheriff's office, and as darkness settled over the empty pasture land, dozens of uniformed deputies arrived and began setting up perimeters with their yellow crime-scene streamers. Homicide detectives were not far behind, headed by Sgt. Randy Latimer, "Pops" Baker, and Detective Steve Cribb, already burdened down with at least four other unsolved murders—and dreading that this latest discovery would boost the tally even more.

Cribb's description of the scene reads:

"At 2220 hours, 7 Oct. 84, writer arrived at the crime scene...victim was laying on her stomach. She was totally nude. Her head was pointed in a southerly direction. It was totally covered with maggots and body fluids, preventing the face from being visible. The victim's left hand was extended and bent at the elbow. The forearm lay underneath the victim's head. Her hand was visible to the right of the victim's head area. The victim's right arm was extended out from her body. Both legs were extended from the body in a normal position. Decomposition was setting in.

"When the victim was moved...it was noted that the victim's head was decomposed nearly to the bone. The face was completely gone and the eyes were deteriorated.   A gold tooth with the letter 'C' was visible in the victim's mouth. This tooth was on the upper portion in the right front position...victim's hands and feet were bagged for later processing."

At 8:00 the following morning, the detectives reconvened at the medical examiner's office for the postmortem by associate ME Dr. Lee Miller. CST Art Picard was also on hand to take the victim's fingerprints. Dr. Miller's autopsy report states:

"This is the unembalmed body of a five foot nine inch black female weighing eighty-two pounds.   The body is received in a white bed sheet inside a body bag. The sheet is extensively soiled with products of decomposition. There are pieces of plant material and large numbers of maggots and red ants as well...There are extensive skin defects of the upper extremities and anterior trunk and head which are seething with maggots. The anus and the external vaginal orifice also seeth with maggots and these structures are partially eaten away."

The official cause of death, Dr. Miller ruled, was "Gunshot Wound of Neck." Significantly, he included the observation that "The hyoid bone and larynx are extensively cartilaginous. Fractures are absent. The styloid processes are intact." In other words, Dr. Miller was double–checking to see if Chanel Williams, like the other victims, might have been strangled before she was shot. The autopsy evidence indicated she was choked, but not enough to kill her. Bobby Joe Long said that he did try to strangle her first, only she wouldn't die easily, same as Michelle Simms. Choke out, is the way he termed it. So he dragged Chanel out of the car, walked off the road and shot her in the back of the head.

Later that same day, Latimer, Baker, and Cribb were back at the dump site using the daylight to search for more clues, when

they were notified that the victim had been identified through her finger-prints: Chanel Devon Williams, born March 26, 1966, in Bartow, Florida.

The quick identification was made through a check of local police records. The Tampa Police Department came up with a rap sheet on the victim that showed she'd been arrested on a prostitu-tion charge at 2015 hours on September 11, 1984, by city vice detectives Bob Weiderman and Ken Brouwer. Weiderman said the Williams girl was busted when she tried to hustle the two detec-tives at the intersection of Kennedy Boulevard and Howard Street. On the way to jail, Chanel said that she'd just hit town on a bus from Miami and was living on the streets. On the booking sheet, Chanel listed her occupation as "College" and said her next of kin was her mother, Lula Williams of Bartow. Bond was set at twenty-five hundred dollars, which kind of tickled Chanel since she didn't even have twenty-five cents to her name. She plead guilty, and in lieu of bond was ordered to serve out her thirty days in the Hillsborough County Stockade. Records show that she was released the morning of Friday, September 28. About 9:00 that same night, Weiderman and Brouwer were out cruising the hooker zone when they came upon the painfully thin, shy young Chanel walking on Nebraska near 26th Avenue, still wearing the same clothes she'd been arrested in on the 11th. Brouwer again tried to "engage her service" but Chanel either recognized them or just wasn't interested, because she didn't take the bait and wasn't arrested.

On October 9, Detective John Marsicano drove over to Polk County to notify Lula Williams of her daughter's death, and to learn what he could about the young victim's childhood in the drab rows of crowded shanty houses lining the colorless, dusty streets. He found Lula Williams on North Street in the Gordonville community of Winter Haven. She said her daughter was born in Bartow, but lived much of her life in Lake Wales with an uncle while Lula Williams worked in one of the small factories in the area.

Mrs. Williams said that Chanel's formal schooling ended at Dennison Junior High, when she and another girl were charged with stealing a television set. In October, 1983, she was sent to the

283

Alyce D. McPherson School, an Ocala reformatory. Chanel stayed there until June, 1984, and earned her high-school equivalency certificate before she left.

Since then, mother and daughter had little contact with each other. Chanel wanted to be on her own, and her mother told her that as long as she insisted on running with the crowd of no–goods she'd taken up with, then Chanel wasn't welcome to stay in her home. The last time Lula Williams saw her daughter was sometime in September, when Chanel came by to pick up some of her belongings. At the time, Chanel was with a black male driving a large car, but since Mrs. Williams was leaving for work, she and Chanel did not have much of a conversation. The last she'd heard, Chanel was hanging around Lake Wales with a girlfriend named Tara.

Other relatives helped Marsicano fill in the blanks.

"She was good and she was loved," said Chanel's great–aunt, Mabel Tyler. "She didn't leave home because nobody loved her, but Chanel was a quiet child and easily led. She would just go. She was an easy kid. That's what I attribute her death to."

"You know how young kids are," added Chanel's uncle Anton Williams. "They want to be grown before their time, and Chanel just didn't like living by anybody else's rules. When she left here to go to Tampa back in August, she told us she was living with friends over there, since she didn't have any kin in Tampa. She was talking about some white girl named 'Nance,' and said she was living with the woman at a motel."

"We didn't know anything about her being involved in prostitution," Mabel Tyler continued. "She could've been—I'm not saying she wasn't—but we didn't know anything about it. But she was kind of on the wild side, smoking that marijuana sometimes. She just got in with the wrong company."

When the detective located Tara, a full–time cokehead and part–time hooker, the twenty-six year old woman hinted that she had some good information about Chanel's disappearance, but she was too high on coke at the time to make much sense. Tara agreed to go back to Tampa with Marsicano where she was put up in a local motel until she was straight enough to talk. She also offered to take

Marsicano, on a tour of Nebraska Avenue, pointing out where she and Chanel did most of their hooking.

The picture Tara painted of Chanel was quite different from that provided by the dead woman's estranged family.

For one thing, she said, Chanel was gay. Of course, that didn't stop her from hooking, although Tara believed that Chanel was forced into prostitution, either against her will or as a means to survive.

She told Marsicano a confusing story of her last contact with Chanel that couldn't be verified, and with dates that didn't jibe with other accounts, but which illustrated the hazards of hooking when a pimp is calling the shots. Tara claimed she bumped into Chanel on Lincoln Street in Lake Wales on September 27. Chanel said she was having trouble with her family and needed a place to stay, and Tara offered to let Chanel crash with her and a guy name Silas at the Lakeside Motel for a few days. (Silas later verified that Chanel was at the motel.) On Sunday afternoon, September 30, Tara and Chanel were again on Lincoln Street when a customized, cream–colored Cadillac limousine pulled up. The limo sported four antennas, jump seats, a wet bar, color TV, and a personalized licensed plate on the front with the initials "TT" in gold letters on a silver glitter background. Tara knew all about TT. Everybody on the street did, since he was said to work for one of the biggest coke and heroin dealers in Central Florida.

As the limo stopped, TT himself got out and grabbed Chanel by the arm, shoved her into the back seat, and drove away. If the description Tara gave of TT was accurate, it would be hard to miss the guy. She said he was six feet tall, 180 pounds, "very good look-ing," and with a scar on the left side of his face. She called him a "slick dresser," adding that TT usually wore a tight diamond neck-lace. And his mouth was a miniature Fort Knox—his bottom teeth were capped with gold, and a diamond had been inserted between his two top front teeth, both of which were also gold-capped with a question mark etched in the right tooth and the letter "T" etched in the left.

A second man Tara described as deeply scarred and carrying a weapon in a shoulder holster accompanied TT, as did another

known prostitute with the street name of "Lil Bit."

Tara said she knew all these people because she'd been to Tampa with Chanel once before when both were whoring for TT on Nebraska Avenue, mostly between Powhattan and Hendry Streets. Chanel usually hung around Mike's Lounge at Nebraska and Lake, trying to score johns. Tara added that a guy called "Slick' who worked at a service station at Nebraska and Osborne often put johns who were looking for a "date" in touch with TT, who then pimped out the whores. After that last time they were in Tampa together, Chanel told her that she didn't want to work for TT any more and was leaving town to get away from him.

Finally, Tara admitted that she herself was a mule, frequently running dope between Tampa and Lake Wales. But she was such a heavy coke user herself, she didn't always remember everything or in the right order. In fact, Marsicano diligently noted in his report that "...when this interview was conducted writer was aware that [Tara] stated she had utilized cocaine prior to this interview."

Meanwhile, back in Tampa, detectives where having better luck getting information from their hometown hookers. Lt. Terry ordered his men to track down other prostitutes who were housed in the Stockade when Chanel Williams was serving her time, to see if they could shed more light on the victim. Had she mentioned a pimp or a weird john who had reason to see her dead?

Susan Holmes° said Chanel told her she was from Winter Haven, but had just come up from Miami a couple of weeks before she was busted, apparently with a couple of other lesbians who also did some hooking to support themselves. All three were staying at a motel near Renee's Lounge out on West Kennedy Boulevard. When Chanel was released, she left the Stockade with a white prostitute who worked Nebraska Avenue. Susan thought the woman's name was Nancy, and said she had one tooth missing in front.

Mae Belle Porter° said she felt sorry for Chanel, who told her this was her first bust for prostitution. She said she was shooting up, and had just left Renee's and was walking off her high when the Tampa vice dicks picked her up. Chanel was concerned that

her mother would find out about her prostitution arrest, and swore that as soon as she got out of jail she was going to save up money for a bus ticket home. She was a nice girl, Mae Belle recalled. Not an old whore like the rest of us. When she got out, Chanel left with another tough hooker named Nancy from up on Nebraska. I didn't think it was such a cool idea, her hanging with the Nancy bitch, but Chanel didn't know Tampa and didn't have anyplace else to go, Mae Belle said.

Back on the street, the investigators talked to another recently released prostitute, Doreen Schweiner°, at the Royal Palm Motel on Nebraska. Doreen had nothing to add about Chanel Williams, but she did tell them a bizarre story about one of her recent "dates" that held their interest. About three weeks before, Doreen claimed, she caught a trick at Mike's Lounge, a guy about thirty with a tattoo of a butterfly on his left forearm. Drove a `69 Ford pickup with a lot of empty beer bottles on the floorboard. From Mike's, Doreen's date headed out I–4 and, somewhere around Lakeland, pulled off the interstate and stopped in a grove of trees.

The guy showed a badge that Doreen said looked like a police shield, God knows she'd seen enough of the real thing. He took her out of the truck and tied her up with rope, tape, and a set of hand-cuffs. Doreen said the trick told her, "I'm sorry I have to do this. Nobody can stop me. I'm a policeman." He also seemed to enjoy calling her a dirty whore and other names. "Liked to torment, too," Doreen said. "He burned my pussy hair with a cigarette lighter and shoved a cucumber up my ass." The only reason he stopped was because he heard someone coming through the woods and that scared him off. Doreen said the passersby took her to the hospital for a checkup, and she later filed a report of the incident with the Tampa police.

For a few days, the prostitute's story stirred up considerable excitement among Terry's detectives. Sounds just like our guy, they told each other. But the bubble burst when they pulled the Tampa police report, and learned Doreen had wildly exaggerated the story she told the sheriff's investigators. A postscript on the bottom of the report dismissing Doreen's tale noted, "Writer checked

Doreen's arms and observed heavy needle marks. She advised that she is a coke user."

Another promising lead to the killer, another deadend. Only one of hundreds that contributed to the growing level of stress and frustration fraying the nerves of the Major Crimes Squad.

Meanwhile, Detective Steve Cribb finally tracked down Nancy, the hooker with whom Chanel left the Stockade. She was holed up in room 7 of the Oasis Motel on Nebraska, where she took most of her tricks to conduct business. High on coke most of the time, Nancy gave a long, rambling account of meeting Chanel in the Stockade and of the dead girl's final hours.

Nancy began by telling Cribb that she'd worked the Nebraska strip for several years. Her turf generally encompassed the rich, three–mile stretch between Columbus Drive on the south and Sligh Avenue on the north, that at times carried bumper–to–bumper john traffic. She used to work for a pimp known as Tampa Red, but got away from the guy and now was on her own.

When they met in the Stockade, Chanel indicated she'd been working Kennedy Boulevard for about a week before she was arrested, and was looking to do a trick when she was busted. The girl really didn't know much about tricking, the veteran whore told Cribb. All she wanted to talk about was hooking. Find out how to get the johns' money without giving up anything in return. Tricks of the trade.

Both were released the afternoon of September 28, and hitched a ride to Nebraska and Columbus. From there, they walked to Nancy's sister's place on West Keys Street. Chanel waited outside while Nancy went in to change her clothes. From there they caught a ride with another hooker to the Lindell Motel at Nebraska and 22nd Street, one of the scores of small motels on the Strip that didn't ask questions when they rented out rooms to single girls who came in the night without luggage. Nancy only had twenty-eight cents to her name and Chanel twelve cents, so they started walking Nebraska doing tricks to earn money for a room. They were standing outside Mike's Lounge with another hooker

named Candy when Nancy caught a date. Nancy said she told Chanel to stay with Candy, but when she returned a few minutes later, both were gone. Nancy did another trick, came back, and still no Chanel. She told Cribb she didn't see the victim again until Sunday, September 30. (Cribb added this note to his report: "At first Nancy said Saturday, 29 Sept., but my investigation has determined it was Sunday. Nancy does cocaine (shoots up) and worked all night Friday and into Saturday a.m. She went to bed and slept right through to Sunday a.m. Nancy sometimes loses track of the days and sleeps twenty-four hours around the clock.")

Chanel, Nancy continued, finally showed up at the Oasis Motel, where Nancy had previously told her she took her tricks, about 10 a.m. that Sunday. A Spanish-looking guy, about thirty, curly hair, drove Chanel there in an orange compact car. "I really jumped in her shit about not letting me know where she was," Nancy said. Chanel claimed that the guy in the compact car had picked her up and driven her all the way down to Miami and back, just so Chanel could get some of her clothes. She wanted to leave her stuff with Nancy at the motel, but Nancy had a trick in bed waiting for her, so she told Chanel to come back later.

Chanel returned early that evening. The same guy dropped her off. Shortly afterward, the two women hit Nebraska again, concentrating on the area around the Alamo Motel. Over the next couple of hours, Nancy said she turned five tricks, but Chanel didn't do any. She acted like she was a new "hole" and was scared of getting fucked, Nancy said. I knew she was gay, which may be why she didn't want to do tricks. By 9 p.m., Nancy had one hundred dollars in her jeans pocket. They went back to the Oasis, and called a cab to take them down to 22nd and Columbus in Ybor City to score some coke. Nancy said she copped a half-gram for forty dollars, and Chanel waited in the cab while she did the deal. They went back to the motel and shot up together. About 10:30 p.m., still riding a pretty good high, Nancy and Chanel were back on the street. Nancy said she gave Chanel five dollars to buy some douche. Around 11 p.m., they were standing outside the Swann Motel near the Sulphur Springs Post Office when Nancy flagged down a trick.

289

Chanel went back to the Oasis with her, but waited outside while Nancy did her business.

When she was finished, the two women returned to the area of the Swann Motel where Nancy almost immediately hailed down another cruising john. The guy was paranoid, Nancy told Cribb, and didn't want both of us in his car at the same time. I told Chanel to start walking back to the Oasis, and I'd be done by the time she got there. (The distance between the Swann and the Oasis Motels, both on Nebraska, is two-tenths of a mile, Cribb noted.)

Nancy said she finished her trick in about ten or fifteen minutes and returned to the Strip. Chanel, she said, was nowhere in sight. "I figured at first that she'd probably gone ahead and finally caught a trick," Nancy explained, "But she never came back and I never saw her again."

Based on the information Nancy provided, police were able to locate the driver of the orange compact car who had dropped Chanel off at the Oasis. He was Ben Stanley°, a twenty-eight year old man who still lived with his parents on Faulkenburg Road on the far east side of Tampa.

Stanley told officers that he met Chanel at Renee's Lounge on Kennedy the night of September 28. They sat at the bar and drank and talked for two or three hours. After midnight, they drove to the new El Goya Club in Ybor City, but the place was crowded and so loud that they couldn't talk. Stanley said they left and drove all the way back out west to a motel on the Courtney Campbell Causeway. He said they lay in bed and talked most of the night. Chanel told him she was from Winter Haven originally, but had just come from Miami where she'd been living with a lesbian girlfriend who was half black and half Puerto Rican.

"She told me," Stanley continued, "that she hadn't been with a man for three years." Stanley believed her. In fact, she was built so much like a little girl and acted so young at times, that he worried about getting arrested for statutory rape. He asked her several times how old she was, and Chanel insisted she was eighteen. He even doubted she was a prostitute because she never asked him for money.

Sometime during the night they had intercourse, or tried to. "She had a real small and tight vagina," Stanley said, "and fucking was just too painful for her, so we stopped and I didn't try to have vaginal intercourse with her again after that."

The following day, Saturday, September 29, Stanley drove Chanel over to Winter Haven to her mother's house, and returned that night to pick her up. They drove back to the Bay area, had drinks at Whiskey Joe's and dinner at Crawdaddy's, and then hit Renee's Lounge again until after midnight. From there, they went to a motel at 50th and Columbus where they engaged in "...a very, very long period of oral sex." After breakfast the next morning, Stanley dropped Chanel at the East Lake Square Mall while he went home to change clothes. "I explained to her," he told police, "that I had to do it that way because my father would never allow a black person in his house." He returned to the Mall later, and they spent most of the afternoon riding around talking. Chanel asked to be dropped off at the Oasis Motel, but didn't stay because her friend inside, a hooker, was doing a trick. Sometime after 6 p.m., Stanley took Chanel back to the motel. The last time he saw her, she was standing in the doorway waving as he drove away.

Stanley admitted that he hung out at Renee's (known for its underground homosexual trade) because he was a bisexual who liked the "challenge and dangerous situation" gay bars presented. Since it appeared that Stanley was Chanel Williams' last known sexual contact, he was asked to provide samples of his pubic hair to match one found on the body. He also agreed to a car search. To their disappointment, officers discovered that all four tires on Stanley's car were new Bridgestones. Since they didn't match the carefully guarded casts from the other crime scenes, Stanley was eliminated as a suspect.

When word of the discovery of Chanel Williams' body reached Lt. Terry, he sent members of the Major Crimes Squad rushing to the scene, fearing the worst, but hoping this would not be "another one of those." Randy Latimer and "Pops" Baker did, in fact, report some encouraging news. A preliminary examination of the

291

maggot–covered body, convinced them that this was not the latest in the series of strangulation murders. Like the slaying of Liz Loudenback, the conditions didn't fit the pattern, or so they assumed. Yes, Chanel Williams was a prostitute, last seen working an area the killer was known to frequent. And, yes, she was dumped nude in rural Hillsborough County. But, no, she was neither bound nor strangled with that odd, leash–like garrotte. And she was black. The first (and only) African-American victim of the Tampa strangler.

"Usually," Terry explained, "serial homicides are within racial boundaries. White on white, black on black. Not always, but usually. So suddenly a black female surfaces, off the streets of the city, along Nebraska Avenue, you think it must be her pimp or something like that. Also, this was the first body found in the north part of the county. The head was encased in insects and maggots, which meant there was probably some kind of head wound or trauma to the head where the insects could gain entry. And, as the autopsy revealed, the Williams girl had been shot in the back of the neck. The slug had splintered and fragmented.

"Again the priority question was: Is this related to the others? Some investigators didn't think so, because of those several differences. "Pops" Baker was one of those who argued that this looked like the work of the same guy. In any event, based on the evidence we had on hand at the moment, we first disregarded the Williams murder as unrelated.

"But then Mike Malone at the FBI lab called to tell us what he'd found on Chanel Williams' body: Red, lustrous trilobal nylon fibers. And as soon as that forensic evidence came back showing the red fibers, all our old assumptions went out the window—for the second time in a row. You would have thought we'd have learned from the Liz Loudenback case not to assume. So now we knew without a doubt that we had four related homicides, and the pressure was really starting to build at that point. We also knew that there would be more."

Later, "Pops" Baker explained why his gut told him the Williams girl was a victim of the same killer when everything else

said otherwise: "With Bobby Joe Long's bodies, it got to the point that most of them had been there for a while so they didn't look the same as they would have if we had gotten there shortly after he dumped them. By the time we found them, they'd lost their display shock value. I believe there were certain things he did, especially with Chanel Williams. The display there, I've always thought, was the bra that was tied on the fence so somebody would see it and find the body. Of course, a farmer came along, untied it and threw it by the road. To me, that bra was almost like the killer was leaving a note for us saying 'I'm back!'"

Because Williams did not appear at first connected to the murders of Lana Long, Michelle Simms, or Liz Loudenback, the forensic material collected at the crime scene did not go to Quantico for analysis by courier, as was done in previous cases. Rather, detectives boxed up the evidence and shipped it off via UPS, an oversight that they later realized may have cost them precious time in their hunt for the killer.

The discovery of those tiny specs of red fiber at the Chanel Williams crime scene, where no one expected them to be, demolished any lingering doubt that the police were confronting a full-blown serial killer, or "...an individual responsible for multiple homicides in the county"—the euphemism employed in news releases in the vain hope of alerting the public without touching off panic. There was also an unspoken concern among some of the detectives that they might be in over their heads against a sophisticated, shrewd killer, who knew precisely what he was doing and believed he was too smart to be caught. Or, the other equally disturbing possibility—that the killer was just incredibly lucky and didn't care who saw him.

The question of whether—and how much—to tell the public sparked a fierce debate within the ranks. Some detectives held to the traditional theory that the less said about a murder investigation the better. But the other view, championed by Sheriff Heinrich, held that if the public was kept in the dark and the wife or daughter of some prominent citizen was the next to die, than all hell would break loose. The best way to protect was to forewarn,

Sheriff Heinrich declared. We'll tell them what we've got, we just won't talk about the evidence. The people deserve to know what's going on in their community.

As a result, the sheriff's office issued an understated press release expressing "concern of a possible pattern" in three of four recent homicides in the County.

▲   ▲   ▲

A LETTER FROM BOBBY

Tell me about this Tammy bitch, she sounds like I should know her, catch my drift? Maybe I use the wrong "tense" should I say, Sounds like I should have "known" her! Yuk yuk Joke. I'm harmless, wouldn't hurt a fly, just misunderstood as a child, thats all.

▲   ▲   ▲

The announcement that a serial killer was on the loose and apparently targeting the city's "night life" kicked over Tampa's rock of complacency, and out into the light came the seamy, drugged–out, dead–end life of the hookers on the streets. Rarely does the public get a glimpse of what really goes on when the sun goes down on the world of the twenty dollar hooker. Even in those pre–AIDS days of the early 1980s, the life expectancy of these prostitutes was tragically short.   Venereal diseases... tuberculosis...one dose of a bad drug, or too much of the good stuff...greedy, ruthless pimps...the psychotic john who got carried away with his sadistic sex games, leaving his partner for hire bleeding to death of a ripped uterus on some cheap, urine–scented motel bed.

Although most straight citizens chose not to look at the street-corner sordidness, this was the awful reality that the Tampa murders dredged up. Not that many people cared even if they did look.

After all, what could a street whore expect other than a violent death at the hands of some maniac. Or, as Bobby Joe said himself,"...the girls... were all dope addicts and whores. Not that anybody really deserves to be killed, but they weren't saints."

Certainly, the police knew they weren't walking on holy ground when they attempted to track the victims' final hours, in search of connections and associations that might spell out motives for murder. Like the time Detective R.E. Spiller set out with the composite drawing seeking to learn the identity of the second victim. Spiller's visits included the bars out on West Kennedy, where Bobby Joe and others like him commonly trolled. Tampa took pride in its reputation as a booming international port and a gleaming city by the Bay. But much of Tampa, the part shoved out of sight when visitors come to town, is a rusty, worn-out remnant of a once-booming industrial city, left to wallow in the backwaters of the yesterday's glory while time rushes on.

It was that decaying underbelly of the city that the murders exposed, much to the chagrin of the Chamber of Commerce and the high–profile Visitors and Conventions Bureau, which were so eager to attract big–bucks tourism but embarrassed by the headlines of a serial killer stalking the streets.

What made tracking the killer even more difficult was the randomness of the killing. Everyone on the street was a target, and no one was a target. The Tampa strangler was ecumenical in his selection of victims—neither blond nor brunette, neither short nor tall, neither black nor white preferred. That total lack of pattern confounded the already frustrated detectives. The only link they could pin down was that the killer seemed to favor weekends. The dump sites demolished whatever geographic theory the police may be have been working on. In the end, there was some relief when investigators learned there wasn't much they could have done to change the outcome. As Bobby Joe Long himself related, there was little rhyme or reason to his hunt, no pre-planning, and hardly any long term stalking. His targets were almost entirely victims of opportunity, the ones whose trails he happened to cross in his incessant nighttime trolling.

Once word leaked out that the city's prostitutes were under siege by a vicious killer, Tampa's news media swooped down on the already beleaguered, foot–sore whores like an avenging vice squad in an election year. It was tough enough working the streets, without having to deal without all the strobe lights and TV cameras that were guaranteed to scare off every john between here and St. Pete. Bad enough looking over your shoulder for some maniac with a knife, without all these news hounds running around ruining business.

The Tribune told its readers that, "The fear is palpable. It stretches from the jukebox go–go clubs of North Nebraska Avenue to Kennedy Boulevard's pathetic `meat market.'"

Reporters suddenly found themselves in the uncomfortable position of approaching young women on street corners and asking if they were prostitutes—and then getting them to talk about what it felt like to be living prey.

A woman who called herself Yvonne reluctantly admitted that she was a hooker and told of an incident a couple of weeks earlier when the driver of a brown station wagon, stopped, leaned out the window, and leeringly told her, "I'm the Angel of Death, and I want to kill you."

"The petite, twenty-one year old Tampa native, who is visibly pregnant and hustling to make enough money to pay for her soon-to-be-born child, did not accept the offer to get in the car," the Tribune article continued.

"After four years of prostitution, Yvonne has seen her share of bizarre customers. She accepts the constant fear of being beat up or worse as part of a job that pays $200 to $300 a day for a series of brief encounters with the men who cruise Kennedy Boulevard looking to buy sex.

"Now, for the women who hang around the bus stops and street corners in the afternoon and evening, there is an added edge to their fear...

"Nonetheless, the prostitutes have not stopped working. The money, they say, is too good and they

need it to pay for their attorney fees, for their rent and hotel rooms and for alcohol and drugs.

"Danger is always part of their lives. 'Every car you get in could be some freak that wants to kill you or severely hurt you,' one woman said.

"However, since the killings began...they have been wary of getting into cars with men who are not regular customers. 'I'm becoming a lot poorer than I was before this started happening,' said a woman whose street name is 'Cat.'

"Becky knew one of the four victims, Chanel Devon Williams...Like Williams, who came from Winter Haven, Becky is the product of a small town. Becky said she grew up in Plant City and has been turning tricks since she was fifteen. She does not appear to be much older than that now...

"The attraction of earning fifty dollars for a five-minute encounter keeps her working despite the constant danger, despite being constantly stopped by police for 'I.D. checks,' despite the small humiliation of being barred from the convenience store on the corner where she works.

"Nonetheless, every time she gets into a car Becky thinks 'Is this a cop, or is this the killer...?'"

The girls who entertained at the topless bars along Nebraska and Kennedy and Skipper were just as apprehensive. "I've probably looked right at him and not even known it was him," said a twenty-one year old dancer, glancing over her shoulder at the customers at the runway bar. "He's been here. Probably a regular customer. And I'm damn scared"

Bar owners began warning their dancers against going out with customers they didn't know. Some even posted news stories of the latest killing in the women's dressing rooms and rest rooms, as a not-so-subtle reminder that a killer was out there stalking dancers or "nightlife" girls—and any one of them could be next if they didn't watch their step.

If the hookers were nervous, the police were riding the fine

line between fear and anger. Unlike the general public, experience had conditioned them to expect more bodies—one, two, five, twenty. Lt. Terry was working around the clock to counteract the negative publicity, by keeping as much as possible about the slayings out of the media. Common sense told him that the killer was probably following the police investigation closely, maybe even keeping a scrapbook of newspaper stories of his handiwork, since these psychos feed off the panic their atrocities generate. The more the killer was kept in the dark, the less likely he would be to change his tactics and throw the hunters off the track. And if he continued to kill the same way, the likelihood was that he'd become more complacent and, sooner or later, make a mistake.

As the murder score mounted, so did the mountain of reports and rumors and suspicions that inundated the detectives working the case. Ivestigators spent hours running down leads and interviewing hundreds of witnesses, possible witnesses, suspects, and potential victims. It was at this stage in the investigation that the police found themselves caught in an grotesque Catch-22, one that police in other communities cursed by serial murders have experienced, but rarely want to talk about.

"I don't like the way it sounds, but it's almost as if you can't wait for the next body to show up," "Pops" Baker explained. "That sounds barbaric, but you kept hoping that on the next one he'll make the mistake we were hoping for. On one hand you pray that the killings are over, that no more innocent people will die. On the other hand, you find yourself praying for the next body to show up."

With four bodies down and the almost certain knowledge that more would follow, the investigators made a decision that, at that time, was a gigantic leap of faith: They decided to call in the FBI's brand new psych squad, the Bureau's largely untested cadre of experts in the new art of psychological profiling. Traditional gumshoes tended to look askance at the theory of personality profiling as some kind of New Age psychobabble that the Ivory Tower boys cooked up in classrooms, far from the gory reality of the streets that local police waded through daily. But there had been

some good cooperation between the Sheriff's Office and the guys in the Bureau's Tampa field offices, especially when it came to tracking the red fibers that had been collected at each of the crime scenes. Might as well try this new profiling thing.

About the same time that Bobby Joe Long was beginning to stalk women in their homes in South Florida, a new discipline focusing on criminal behavior was finding its way into the dark, dangerous, and largely unknown world of the serial rapist–serial killer. Before the 1970s, murder in America was a fairly predictable thing. Police knew that the majority of murders are solved, often with hours or days, simply because most murder victims die at the hands of someone close to them. Only a relatively small portion were "stranger" murders.

But as the decade progressed, that picture began to change horribly. For one thing, the murder rate soared to more than 20,000 (more in the neighborhood of 25,000 in the 1990s), and at least 5,000 of those are unsolved killings. It's still impossible to know how many of those 5,000 murders are the work of roving serial killers, but it's safe to say the number is in the hundreds. Such an extraordinary shift in murder demographics demanded equally dramatic crime-fighting techniques. One of those techniques came to be known as the Criminal Personality Profile, as conceived and refined by the specialists assigned to the FBI's Behavioral Science Unit (BSU). At the heart of the system is the separation of killers into two camps—the organized and the disorganized.

An early proponent of the profiling system that has since become a standard law enforcement tool was Agent Robert K. Ressler, since retired and the author of Whoever Fights Monsters: My Twenty Years Hunting Serial Killers For The FBI. In his book, Ressler goes into detail about the importance of clues found at the crime scenes, which tell the profiler whether he's dealing with an organized or a disorganized killer. The attributes of the organized killer Ressler describes are like pieces of a jigsaw puzzle that, when fitted together, reveal the face of Bobby Joe Long.

Ressler begins by pointing out that few people, local police officers included, ever confront grisly murders that may include

mutilations, disembowelments, or cannibalism. But by the late 1970s, the BSU had accumulated a mass of information about such crimes, and enough experience in assessing the crime scenes that analysts could begin deducing clues to behavior (perhaps even identity) that not even the killer himself was aware of.

"Amassing this knowledge was one thing," Ressler writes. "Communicating it to our audience—those police officers who sought our help in tracking down violent criminals—was another. To characterize the types of offenders for police and other local law–enforcement people, we needed to have a terminology that was not based in psychiatric jargon. It wouldn't do much good to say to a police officer that he was looking for a psychotic personality if that police officer had no training in psychology; we needed to speak to the police in terms that they could understand and that would assist them in their searches for killers, rapists, and other violent criminals. Instead of saying that a crime scene showed evidence of a psychopathic personality, we began to tell the police officer that such a particular crime scene was 'organized,' and so was the likely offender, while another and its perpetrator might be 'disorganized,' when mental disorder was present.

"The organized versus disorganized distinction became the great divide, a fundamental way of separating two quite different types of personalities who commit multiple murders..."

The factor that distinguishes the organized criminal more than any other is the planning required to commit a crime of such magnitude. Organized crimes are premeditated; disorganized are generally spur of the moment. And the planning is an outgrowth of the fantasies the killer/rapist has been nurturing for years, long before they spill over into action.

"Most victims of organized offenders are targeted strangers; that is, the offender stakes out or patrols an area, hunting someone who fits a certain type of victim that he has in mind. Age, appearance, occupation, hairstyle, and lifestyle may be elements in the choice..." Ressler advises.

"The organized offender often uses a ruse or con to gain control over his victim. This is a man who has good verbal skills and a high

degree of intelligence, enough to lure the victim into a vulnerable area. Control is of the essence for the organized offender, and law enforcement personnel learn to look for control as an element in every facet of the crime. An organized offender might offer a prostitute a fifty–dollar bill, give a hitchhiker a ride, assist a disabled motorist, tell a child that he's taking him to his mother. Since the crime has been planned, the offender has devoted time to figuring out how to obtain victims, and may have perfected the ruse..."

Organized criminals are both mobile and adaptable, able to change their behavior or alter their plans depending on the exigencies of the moment. Another measure of their adaptability is their ability to learn as they go along. The fact that they become "better" at what they do displays a high level of organization. (This is precisely the point that continued to trouble Gary Terry, "Pops" Baker, and the others who pursued Bobby Joe Long. The first murder scene found, that of Lana Long, indicated the work of an experienced, sophisticated killer. It never showed the signs of a "first kill" site, which begs the question: Where did Bobby Joe learn how to kill? Furthermore, Ressler tells local police who are investigating a series of homicides to pay particular attention to the first slaying, "...for it will most likely have 'gone down' closest to the place where the killer lived or worked or hung out. As he becomes more experienced, the killer will move the bodies farther and farther away from the places where he abducts his victims. Often that first crime is not thoroughly planned, but succeeding ones will display greater forethought..."

The use of restraints by organized killers is common—"rape kits" containing ropes, handcuffs, or, in the case of Bobby Joe Long, shoelaces, provisions they carry along when they go hunting. The same is generally true of weapons. Organized offenders bring the knife or gun to the killing and take it away once the deed is done. They may be knowledgeable about forensic or ballistic evidence, so may wipe away blood or fingerprints to prevent identification—of themselves or their victims. The longer a body goes unidentified, the less the risk to the killer, so the bodies are often nude when found. Some killers go so far as to sever heads and dispose of them

away from the torso to frustrate identification. They will transport the bodies, often great distances, from where the initial crime (murder or kidnaping) occurred in an effort to hide the remains and thwart early identification.

"The organized offender," Ressler adds, "often takes personal items belonging to his victims as trophies, or to deny the police the possibility of identifying the victim. Wallets, jewelry, class rings, articles of clothing, photograph albums—all of these, once belonging to victims, have been found in the dwelling places of organized killers after their arrests. Usually, these are not items of intrinsic value, such as expensive jewelry, but, rather, items that are used to recall the victim. These trophies are taken for incorporation in the offender's post–crime fantasies and as acknowledgment of his accomplishments. Just as the hunter looks at the head of the bear mounted on the wall and takes satisfaction in having killed it, so the organized murderer looks at a necklace hanging in his closet and keeps alive the excitement of his crime. Many take photographs of their crimes for the same purpose. *Sometimes trophies of the crime, such as jewelry, are given to the killer's wife or girlfriend or mother, so that when she wears it, only the killer knows its significance...*" (Italics added.)

"All these crimes are sexual in nature, even when there is no completed sexual act with the victim. The truly organized killer generally completes a sexual act with a living victim, taking full advantage of the situation to rape and torture before murdering someone...Organized offenders are angry at their girlfriends, at themselves, at their families, and at society in general. They feel that they've been mistreated during their entire lives and that everything is stacked against them...In their murders, these men strike back not only at the individual victims but at society as a whole," Ressler concluded.

By the early 1980s, Ressler's pioneering work had moved out of the Quantico theory factory and into the FBI's field offices. Fifty–five agents were summoned to Quantico for some intensive training in profiling, and then returned to the field as the resident experts in this fascinating, but largely untried, method of prying open a killer's psyche to see what he might do next. Skepticism

over profiling's reliability at the local level, where it was intended to do the most good, was a major barrier that agents found difficult to overcome.

In Tampa, Stan Jacobson was the FBI agent trained in profiling. A bright, highly educated man, even he had his doubts about this new technique. Although not a street cop by trade, Jacobson nevertheless possessed the instincts of the street. Schooled in the classics, a lover of poetry, Jacobson's early career was spent battling organized and white-collar crime on the streets of New York. Later, before retiring to open his own Tampa–based security business, Jacobson was part of the federal team that apprehended Panamanian strongman Manuel Noriega.

When Hillsborough County officials came to Jacobson following the discovery of Chanel William's body, they were cautiously open to the idea of profiling, while still doubting its worth or effectiveness. But with four murdered women in the morgue, it was time to try anything—be it psychics or profilers—that might give them an edge on this creep who'd gone into the wholesale killing business.

Stan Jacobson just as cautiously agreed to put together a profile, although this would be only his second stab at divining the mind of a monster since his Academy training. Moreover, even Jacobson admitted he wasn't sure that a profile would be of much help to the cop on the beat.

But the results, as it turned out, were astonishing.

When Stan Jacobson finished sifting through the crime-scene photos, studying the forensic evidence, digging into the backgrounds of the victims, and talking to the homicide detectives working the cases, he came up with a portrait of the Tampa serial killer that looked like this:

FBI CRIMINAL PERSONALITY PROFILE

RACE	CAUCASIAN
AGE	MID 20'S
PERSONALITY	"MACHO" IMAGE, ASSAULTIVE WITH WEAKER INDIVIDUALS

EMPLOYMENT	DIFFICULTY IN HOLDING JOB
MARRIAGE	PROBABLY DIVORCED
VEHICLE	"FLASHY CAR"
WEAPONS	LIKELY TO CARRY WEAPONS
PERSONALITY	INCLINED TO MENTALLY AND
	PHYSICALLY TAUNT AND TORTURE
VICTIMS	RANDOMLY SELECTED
	SUSCEPTIBLE TO APPROACH
GEOGRAPHICS	CONFINES ACTIVITY TO GIVEN
	GEOGRAPHIC REGION

▲   ▲   ▲

A LETTER FROM BOBBY

Believe me, I've seen psychological profiles of me and Bundy and a few of the others. The similarities in our background and what we do and why is fuckin scary! No Shit!

▲   ▲   ▲

Now retired from the Bureau, Stan Jacobson discussed the criminal profile that pinned down Bobby Joe Long's personality like a moth on a specimen board.

"One of the first things I looked at were the ligatures he used and the similarities in the knots," Jacobson began. "These types of murderers frequently use ropes or other restraints because it gets them close in to the victim and gives them tight control. A lot of times serial murderers don't just simply shoot people. They play with them like a cat plays with a mouse before they actually kill them.

"And frequently the killing is through ligatures or strangulation or knifing as opposed to shooting, not that shooting doesn't happen. Long even used a gun on one victim that he apparently had

difficulty strangling. Strangling, especially, gives them the power to control. That's the whole thing as far as I'm concerned—one human being wanting absolute control over another.

"I also looked at similarities in the pattern—the times these women were picked up, where they were picked up, methods of death, although in his case they were somewhat varied. With all those factors, you become pretty sure you're dealing with the same person and not a copy-cat situation."

Profile: Race, Caucasian.

"Well, in this particular situation, and from my experience and from studying this types of cases, ninety percent of serial murderers are white Caucasians. You can pretty much come up with that as a conclusion."

Profile: Age, Mid–20s.

"Frequently, individuals in that age group commit this kind of crime. In other words, all the victims so far as we knew were locals here and we didn't see him traveling long distances around the country. Not that a person who was a serial murderer and traveling around the country would not be younger, but most often you'd look for someone a little older who would do a great deal of traveling, more affluent, a better job that allows them to travel. They might start killing in the area they were from and then broaden their base to other areas."

Profile: Personality, "Macho Image" Assaultive.

"More often than not, these killers are the macho type personalities, which is seen in the type of control he exhibits. This is the kind of conclusion that comes from dealing with a lot of known offenders and known crime scenes...The organized offender might ... take that body part, but would view it as a trophy. Again, that macho image of himself. If you see both hands, both feet and the head missing, you know you're dealing with an organized offender, because he took them not only for their souvenir value, or for some symbolic reason known only to him, but also to delay identification of the victim...the organized killer is like a chameleon, may be very appealing and likeable. He's the guy who does very well in jail

because he manipulates his jailer just like he manipulates the rest of the world around him. This type killer has no conscience essentially. They can be very social people, but they're anti–social in the sense they cannot function in society. Bobby Joe Long, bottom line, was an anti–social personality."

Profile: Trouble Holding Job.

"Sometimes his life revolves so much around his fantasy life that he has difficulty concentrating on the day–to–day work he's supposed to be doing. It's kind of like someone who chronically does drugs. Their whole life is devoted to getting the next high. Here, their whole life revolves around getting the next victim. They have difficulty adhering to discipline. They don't like people telling them what to do. They have a lot of difficulties with supervisory relationships. 'Who the hell are you to tell me what to do?'"

Profile: Probably Divorced.

"Given what we know about this type of personality, that person has great difficulty getting along with people in general, much less a wife to whom he's expected to give up some control. Most women would not want to live with this guy, although many get into these destructive relationships thinking they can 'fix' the guy. Most of the time, however, they come to the point that they can't tolerate him. He's usually out wandering around at night. Sometimes having sex with the victims before he kills them. He basically is not that interested in his wife, because to him she's just an object like the rest of society.

"The world exists for this individual as a place for him to play out fantasies. People, other human beings, are merely objects to be used. They have no sense of compassion, of feeling, of empathy for the victims or their families. That's why they so often refer to their female victims as 'cunts,' or 'bitches.' They depersonalize them, make them objects."

Profile: "Flashy" Car.

"Same thing. Look at the personality you've got so far—a controlling person, a macho–man image of himself. So this person frequently identifies himself with his car. Typically, he drives that big, flashy, muscle car as an extension of himself."

Profile: Likely To Carry Weapons.

"That's another hallmark of the whole macho image.

"Guns are another kind of extension of themselves, although a lot of guys who aren't killers are like that. And even though they project a macho image on the surface, deep down they may have a sense of insecurity, which they cover up with a big display of guns or other weapons. It's like the power–assertive rapist who doesn't go to the point of killing women, but he wants control of them. This is the date-rape guy. He has all the macho shit, the flashy car, the guns, the tattoos. And frequently serial murderers are the same—but not in every case."

Profile: Personality Inclined To Taunt And Torture.

"They like to do that because it is part of the control issue. The disorganized person usually does his manipulating, his evisceration, his cutting, whatever he does to the body, once the victim is already dead, because this type offender is ill–equipped to handle himself with a live body.

"Whereas the organized offender, if you see a lot of knife or stab wounds, or the medical examiner's report shows you the offender did a lot of manipulating before death has occurred, then you're probably looking for an organized offender, depending on the bleeding, the amount of discoloration around the wound. Medical examiners and a lot of good homicide detectives can tell if wounds are inflicted before or after death and if they are inflicted before, the chances are you're dealing with an anti–social personality like Bobby Joe Long or a number of others.

"Bobby Joe used a leash. What more control do you have than when you can yank a person around with a leash? That's why the ligatures were so important in this case. And the knots. Sometimes there is a lot of detail in the knots and how they are tied, shows they are really into what they are doing. All part of the control element," Jacobson said.

Profile: Confined To A Geographic Region.

"You know pretty much where the victims hung out in high-risk areas even if you don't know specifically where they were picked up, particularly if they are prostitutes," Jacobson continued. "If the

victim is grabbed in one location and the body moved to another, you're dealing with an organized personality.

"Long was also a troller. He liked to travel. And like many of these kinds of people, he identified with his car. Drove hundreds of thousands of miles. He wanted to know as much as he could about the area he was going to work in. Number one, he had to troll to find the victims. And in that trolling he became more familiar with the area, thereby reducing the risk of getting caught. More of the organization thing. These guys don't want to be caught."

The personality profile, Jacobson added, may be no better than a good educated guess. In the case of Bobby Joe Long, it provided some solid investigative leads. Jacobson's recommendation to any local police who are stumped in their search for a serial killer: Take a hard look at the evidence. If the evidence tells you to go left and the profile says go right, go left first. Follow the evidence trail until all that information is exhausted, then go back to the profile.

▲   ▲   ▲

A LETTER FROM BOBBY

These fuckers have talked to a lot of people and know me (my psychiatric profile) thats why they have two guards out with me & four det. escorts. I grew up in Miami on my own. (Drugs) A lot of people have bled because of me and they know it! Haven't you noticed how much different they act when I'm out? Anyway, even if they get me the life instead of the chair--big fucking deal.

Man I wish I'd have kept my fucking mouth shut.

They tell me I'd be out of here by now if I'd shut up. That hurts! What the fuck I was in shock and really only about the last week have I been coming back to "thinking." They're trying to get my statement tossed, because I told em I didn't want to talk to em, I told em I wanted a lawyer, they still were at me for like seven or eight hours.

▲   ▲   ▲

Once Stan Jacobson and his profiling entered the picture, Lt. Terry and his men were handed a crash course in serial killers. For example, the failure to detect sperm in some of the victims didn't mean much. These were sexually motivated murders from first to last. Victims may be held captive for a day or more while being tortured and abused sexually—anal rape followed by oral sex followed by vaginal rape, and then a repeat of the cycle, is a typical scenario.

Said another FBI expert, "I have yet to see a serial killing that did not have some sexual motivation. I have never seen a serial killer who is a happily married man or who has a successful, long–term relationship with a woman."

A theory in vogue is to view rape and sexual serial murder as acts of power, domination, and control, not acts of sex. Maybe, said the FBI specialists. But not always. Those elements are usually part of the scenario, but rarely without an accompanying sexual climax. Acts of domination and control, yes, but acts with some form sexual deviation as motivation.

Meanwhile, the object of all that profiling and probing was going about business as usual—the killing of hookers—oblivious to the mounting political pressure the slayings were exerting on the sheriff's office and, ultimately, on Terry and his team of investigators. The politicians were coming down hard on Sheriff Heinrich over the continuing bad publicity that was making Tampa and the prospering Bay area look like a charnel house. "Have you got him yet?" Heinrich demanded almost daily. "When are you going to get him? Do whatever you need to do, but get the son of a bitch! Fast!"

▲   ▲   ▲

REPORTER: *When you were reading those articles that no one is safe on the street, you knew that was ridiculous?*

BOBBY: *Yeah, I thought that was absurd...cause I didn't think that it could happen to anybody other than the types that it was happening to. So unless you were some street walker, or you know, whatever, it was absurd.*

309

REPORTER: *Well, a couple of people characterize it as a violent flame burning in you...Is there a violent flame burning inside you?*

BOBBY: *I don't guess there's any way to deny that. Is there?*

Reporter: *But outside, when you used to get that feeling you feel, what would happen?*

BOBBY: *I'd get in fights... you know what happens. A lot of crazy things happened. It was getting to the point see, where ... do you know about the girl that I let go?...She was different. The whole thing was different, that whole episode was different. That's when it really became clear to me that I was losing control...*

REPORTER: *How did you feel when you woke up in the morning?*

BOBBY: *I'd feel all right, I'd feel great. You know? Cause I'd be in a coma for like twelve or fourteen hours so I'd wake up feeling, feeling, you know, pretty good. (sigh) And it wasn't until several of these things had happened that I knew that I didn't have to have it reinforced any more, it was real. You know what I mean?...I was starting to understand that this was really happening and it was starting to get closer together. Just like it was saying in the newspapers was going to happen. It said that these things were going to start happening more and more frequently up till this guy is off the street. And there was nobody...no woman in Tampa safe.*

REPORTER: *Did you feel like a killer? I mean, could you reconcile yourself to that person in the newspapers was...*

BOBBY: *No, I'll tell you the truth. I used to stand in front of the mirror for an hour looking at myself, trying to see it.*

REPORTER: *Trying to see what?*

BOBBY: *The difference. And I didn't see it.*

REPORTER: *The difference between Bobby Joe the person and Bobby Joe the killer?*

BOBBY: *Yeah. And it got to the point where when I would meet, you know, a girl or something, I thought they could see it when they looked at me. And it was really, it was starting to be a real problem. And I was starting to see these predictions that I was reading about in the newspaper coming true. Happening more and*

*more frequently...and when the McVey girl happened I knew that
they were right. You know? That it was going to get a lot worse. It
had got to the point where (sigh) if I was driving and stopped at a
red light and somebody in the car next to me looked at me wrong
and I didn't like the way that they looked at me, twice I had the
gun out. I was ready to shoot these people. I mean cocked and
aimed at their head, and if they hadn't of took off, I would have
shot them. There is no doubt in my mind...and for no reason. And I
realized that things were just getting completely out of hand, completely. I tell you I'm really leery of talking about it, you know. You
got to understand my position, right. I have appeals going on, these
people are dead serious about strapping me in a chair and blowing
my eye balls out of my head, right. So, ahhh, I'm a little leery about
talking about certain things. (CBS News Interview)*

▲   ▲   ▲

Her real name was Kimberly Kyle Hopps. Her street name was
Sugar. She was twenty-two years old, and a native of Toledo, Ohio.
Her mother last saw her when she was seventeen and on her way
out of town with some black dude.She was five feet, three inches
tall with shoulder–length strawberry–blond hair, hazel eyes, and
bad teeth. She listed her occupation as "Professional Escort."

She was a whore.

And other than the fact that her body was nothing but a dried-
up mummy when they found her, that's about the sum total of what
Lt. Terry and his detectives knew of Kimberly Kyle Hopps.

That, and the fact that she was listed as Number Six on the list
of victims.

About 9:00 on the evening of October 4, 1984, Kimberly
Hopps got into an argument with thirty-one year-old Donald
Jones on the corner of Sitka Street and North Nebraska, in the
parking lot of the Orange Motel. Jones said he was Kimberly's
boyfriend and fiance. People in the neighborhood where the couple once lived said he did the pimping, while she did the whoring.
Did a lot of drugs, too, the neighbors complained. As usual, the two

were quarrelling over money, or the lack of it. Both were facing some hard jail time on recent busts, and they needed cash to get out of town. Move west somewhere. Texas, probably. The dispute centered on the fact that Sugar wasn't contributing to the cash flow the way Donald thought she was capable of doing. It ended abruptly with Sugar telling him to fuck off.

She stalked around the corner of the motel, stiletto heels clicking angrily on the sidewalk, and headed north on Nebraska. Almost instantly a car pulled to the curb. Sugar hopped in and took off. Didn't surprise Donald that she caught a trick so quick, dressed for work like she was in her tightest pink hot pants, pink blouse with the string straps, black scarf, and black, blue, and red open–toed high heels. The pickup spot was just across the street from the Tampa Greyhound Track, considered to be prime territory for regular hookers. Sugar staked out the area in the fall, when the dogs were running. The neighborhood around the track was ideal for doing business with customers heading home after an evening racing bill.

What did surprise Donald Jones, however, was that Sugar didn't come back after doing the john. Sure, she was pissed off at him, but she always came back. Jones waited three days, until October 7, before going down to the police headquarters on Tampa Street and filing a missing-persons report. The bored officer who filled out the form at the information counter in the lobby had heard it all before, and was the soul of brevity when it came to taking down the facts that would just end up buried in some bureaucratic landfill anyway.

"A known w/f has been missing for three days at the time of this report taken at the infor. counter.
"Interview: Compl. had a domestic dispute with his girlfriend (w/f Hopps) while at the area of Sitka St. and Nebraska. She jumped into the suspect veh. which traveled north on Nebraska. During these three days he has attempted to find her but with negative results. He stated they have lived togeth-

er for seven years and she has never been gone for
over a few hours. The veh. listed is not familiar
to compl. and he did not see the occupants and cannot positively ID the car.

"Investigation: Limited to interview via information counter. Also pickup placed."

On the form, Jones listed the address where he lived with
Kimberly. A Tampa detective later dropped by to check it out, and
learned from neighbors that the couple hadn't lived at that address
for over three months. "Glad to see them go," said the neighbor.
"She was a prostitute, he was a pimp, and they were both on
drugs."

A routine records check showed that Kimberly Hopps had
been busted by Tampa cops on April 23, 1984, on charges of grand
theft and burglary. Those charges were still pending when she disappeared. Exactly one month later, she was picked up again, this
time on two counts of offering to commit prostitution. For those
offenses, she was assessed a three hundred dollar fine and ordered
to serve thirty days in the county jail.

In hindsight, there was one highly significant portion of Donald
Jones' original missing-persons report that slipped through the
cracks. He described the car that carried Sugar off as a 1977–78
maroon-colored Chrysler Cordova with spoke chrome wheels—a
flashy automobile similar to, and easily mistaken for, a red Dodge
Magnum.

On October 31, Paul Both, a self–employed contractor, was
digging a ditch in northern Hillsborough County, on a portion of
Two River Ranch that runs parallel to Highway 301. It was
mid–morning on this Halloween day, and Both was about to get the
fright of his life.

A new road had been bulldozed alongside the ditch the day
before, and Both's job was to clear out the thick brush and under-
growth that filled the ditch. As he cleared away one large patch of
weeds, he exposed something that looked sort of human. Like a
body, maybe, but too hideous and ugly to be real. Both climbed
down from his yellow backhoe to get a better look. It was a

body—but like no body Both had ever seen. Indeed, the grotesque remains in the weedy ditch were far more horrifying than any Halloween ghoul he'd encountered in all his seventy-one years.

The body lay on its back, knees bent and legs spread in the missionary position. The arms were extended on either side of the mummified remains. The leathery skin had tanned to a dirty brown, so it blended in with the ground on which the body sprawled. But it was the head that sent Paul Both scrambling in terror up the crumbling wall of the ditch. Somehow the head had become detached from the body and was facing in the opposite direction, almost as if it had been deliberately pulled off and set back down in reverse. The mouth gaped open, as if interrupted in its dying scream. Jagged, crooked teeth, gleaming white in the morning sun, only magnified the horror of the silent, shrieking skull. Matted, reddish–blond hair had fallen away from the scalp forming a tossled pillow upon which the scull rested.

William Cannon, the foreman of the 16,000–acre Two River Ranch, told officers that people had been working in the area for the past several days putting in the new road, but no one smelled anything bad or spotted the remains until Both started clearing away the brush. The road was brand new. Until then, it would have taken a four–wheel drive vehicle to get down to the area where the body was found. But, he admitted, a regular car could have been driven pretty close to the dump site and the body carried the rest of the way to the ditch.

Thirty minutes after the report came in, "Pops" Baker and Steve Cribb reached the scene. According to Baker's report:

"We approached the victim via the dirt road on the east side of the ditch being dug out and then down a five or six foot incline to the body. It was apparent that the body had been in this position for several days or weeks. We found the body to be a W/F. We did not observe any clothing, jewelry or ligatures of any sort upon the body. The body was mummified and was being consumed by animals. The head had been disconnected and pulled away from the

body a short distance. [It was later determined this was probably due to animals disturbing the remains and not the result of a deliberate decapitation by the killer.] The victim had long, heavy reddish-blond hair, pubic hair also the same color and hairy legs of the same nature. Her teeth were missing in places and we observed one on the ground beside the head area. The body was face up and the head to the south. He hands were extended out; right to the east and left to the west. The right palm was down and the left palm was up. A large branch was bent towards the west and was under the body. It was apparent the body would have to have been rolled over the branch, versus someone just laying it down in that position. The right leg was extended out to the north and the left leg was bent up slightly and also facing in a northern direction. The vaginal area had been consumed by animals."

Baker and Cribb took note that the site was three miles straight east of where Chanel Williams' body was found, not far from the Hillsborough River State Park, and a mere 222 feet south of the Pasco County line. Couldn't be a coincidence. If this was the same guy, and Baker felt sure it was, that meant he'd now shifted his dump sites to the rural countryside of northern Hillsborough County.

Baker later added to his report that he "...found one lower tooth mixed in with the victim's head hair and we placed it into her lower jaw and found it to be very unusual. The tooth extended back into the mouth and would have been very noticeable to a dentist." The tooth was significant in the identification process. He asked Dr. Vickie Lindauer, a forensic dentist, to examine the remains when they were taken to the Medical Examiner's office. She compared the teeth remaining in the cadaver with a dental chart provided by Vicky Elliott's family, and determined that the dead woman was not the Ramada Inn waitress who'd been missing since September.

For the time being, the victim would remain a Jane Doe. The next day Dr. Peter Lardizabal conducted the autopsy:

"The body is that of a well developed, unclothed, markedly decomposed white female with varying degrees of mummification of the skin surfaces throughout. This body measures approximately five foot three inches from crown to heel. It only weighs twenty-nine pounds."

He went on to describe in detail the varying degrees of mummification and skeletonization of the rest of the body. But the remains were in such poor condition and had been exposed to the elements for so long, that he could only guess at the cause of death: "Nonspecific Violent Injury (probably asphyxial type)."

"There were no ligatures or any other kind of physical evidence found at the scene," Terry recalled. "Due to the time the body was exposed and the fact that the victim was left nude, any forensic evidence such as foreign hairs, fibers, or semen had long since been destroyed. There was absolutely nothing to go on— except Baker's instincts. The minute he saw the body he knew it was our guy somehow. He was right, and, as it turned out there was physical evidence after all. After we had Bobby Joe in custody we went over his car with—if there's anything finer than a fine tooth comb then that's what we used. We found some head hairs in the car that matched Kimberly Hopps, so we were able to physically place her in the company of the killer.

"Pops" Baker also regrets that no one made the connection between the missing hooker and the car she was last seen entering until too late. "Bobby Joe Long did more planning than a lot of people want to give him credit for," Baker said, "I'm sure he prowled and scoured the area before he actually made a pickup, but you don't have to be very lucky to pick up a street prostitute. Nobody cares when these girls get in cars. It happens every hour on the hour.

"What bothers me is that we did have one lead. We did have an excellent witness. Her pimp, the Hopps girl, saw her get in the car. Described the vehicle and a little bit of the driver. But when we found her skeleton remains we were unable to get her identified

316

very quick, so we never came across that missing persons report. So in that respect Long got a break. Otherwise, we would have had a vehicle to look for a lot sooner than we did."

That positive identification of the mummified remains as those of Kimberly Kyle Hopps didn't come until mid–November, when Bobby Joe Long was behind a massive security lockup system and under a twenty-four hour death watch.

Before he reached that point, however, there was much more killing to be done.

On October 14, 1984, Bobby Joe Long celebrated his 31st birthday. He marked the occasion with a nightmarish orgy of rape and murder.

In the early hours of October 14, Bobby Joe picked up Karen Dinsfriend, a drug–ravaged hooker, near North Nebraska and Hillsborough Boulevard, raped her, strangled her, and deposited her body under an orange tree opposite Lake Thonotosassa.

And within the same twenty-four hour span, another young prostitute with a long history of severe alcoholism and drug abuse, eighteen year old Virginia Lee Johnson, left a friend's home where she was crashing temporarily and walked the half–block to North Nebraska Avenue to pick up some cigarettes. Somewhere along the way, Ginny Johnson bumped into the birthday boy, out on the prowl again. She never returned. Johnson's bones were found scattered across a couple of acres of Pasco County pasture in early November. The rest of the body had been consumed by wild animals and dogs in the neighborhood. The telltale ligature with the come–along leash was still attached to the severed head and neck.

Later that October 15, the same day Bobby Joe Long picked up and strangled Virginia Lee Johnson, he dropped into Humana Med– First Walk–In Clinic near Zephyrhills, northeast of Tampa, and filled out an application for a job as a radiology technician. Lonna Watts, an official at the clinic, interviewed Long. She noticed that he'd trained at the Broward County Community College in Pompano Beach, and they chatted for several minutes about life in South Florida compared to the Gulf Coast.

317

Lonna Watts told Detective "Pops" Baker that she had the uncomfortable feeling when talking to him that Long really didn't like women. Nothing specific. Just a feeling. He was cordial enough to her, but she felt like he was putting on a nice–guy act just to get the job.

The Zephyrhills Clinic is a handful of miles from the pasture where, only hours earlier, Bobby Joe Long had tossed the garrotted body of Virginia Johnson. In retrospect, it was almost as if the killer decided, 'Well, since I'm in the neighborhood, I might as well kill two birds with one stone—get rid of this whore's body and go apply for a new job.'

▲   ▲   ▲

A LETTER FROM BOBBY

When you hear from these guys, you tell em about me. Even if they do know about me, they don't know the things that would be of interest to them as to my being an assett to them and their "business." First, I'm not stupid. Second, I learned about leaving "live" witnesses. Third, I'm good with anything from a .22 to a 50 caliber machine gun, that includes rocket launchers, M-79 grenade launchers, and even Claymore mines and hand grenades.

▲   ▲   ▲

Karen Beth Dinsfriend caught her last trick on Hillsborough Avenue sometime around 1:00 a.m. or 2:00 a.m. on October 14. Her body was found fewer than twelve hours after it was dumped in an orange grove near a small country settlement on the west shore of Lake Thonotosassa, northeast of Tampa.

Another Sunday morning. Another slaughtered hooker.

Shortly before 11:00 a.m., Jim Singleton and Carl Nehring pulled into the orange grove just north of Florence Road and started unloading their metal detection gear from the back of Nehring's

318

VW bus. They spread out an old map to check their bearings before beginning a grid sweep of the area. The two were treasure-hunting hobbyists and amateur archaeologists, and had come to search for buried artifacts left from the remains of old Fort King, that once stood on the site of the orchard.

But instead of keepsakes of the dead, they found the dead itself.

The body of the young woman with reddish, wavy hair was curled up in fetal position on its left side, as though asleep beneath the sheltering arms of an orange tree. A rust-colored blanket was wrapped around the feet and ankles; a torn piece of blue sweat shirt and sweat pants, each secured in a granny knot, were tied around the outside of the blanket. The pants carried a Montgomery Ward label. The lower legs inside the blanket were tied with a double loop of long, white, obviously brand-new shoelace, the kind ordinarily used with high–top athletic shoes. The ankles were also bound with multiple knots of white cord that appeared to be the drawstring from the sweat pants. The dead woman's hands were tied in front of her, the wrists crossed and secured by a red bandanna, again tied in a granny knot. One end of another long white shoelace was looped around the woman's neck with the other end tied to her right wrist. A yellow, short–sleeved sweatshirt was bunched up around her shoulders. She wore a yellow metal bracelet on her right wrist.

Her exposed left hip, leg, and buttocks were covered with scrapes, as if she'd been dragged through the dirt. On her right shoulder was the tattoo of a butterfly. There was a line of small puncture wounds running up and down the woman's right arm, some scarred, some freshly crusted over. More of the same on the back of her left hand. Needle tracks. Lots of them. You didn't need the trained eye of a street cop to instantly spot this as a hard–core junkie.

In contrast to the shocking, fish–belly white color of the woman's fleshy body, her face was the face of strangulation, of someone who'd died gasping to breathe until there was no breath left. Her lips were parted and swollen; her once–pretty face bloated and stained purple from the lack of oxygen.

The autopsy completed that day by Dr. Lee Miller revealed severe ligature abrasions of the neck, and hemorrhages of the tongue and cervical strap (neck) muscles. Vaginal, anal, and oral swabs for the presence of sperm were negative. There was no blood alcohol detected, but a urine drug screen revealed the presence of cocaine metabolite, quinine or quinidine, opiate, dramamine or benadryl, and nicotine.

The cause of death: Strangulation.

Fingerprints taken from the body quickly produced a dog–eared police record on file with the Tampa PD. The victim was identified as Karen Beth Dinsfriend, DOB 9/3/56, five–feet, five–inches tall, 125 pounds, brown hair, green eyes, medium build.

The FBI Law Enforcement Bulletin account of the Dinsfriend murder relates:

"...Upon arriving at the scene, the detectives strongly suspected that Dinsfriend's death was related to the previous homicides. The ligatures were almost a 'signature' of the offender. Red fibers were found when the body was examined at the medical examiner's office.

"By this time, all homicide detectives of the HCSO were assigned to the case. Other assaults, suicides, and unrelated homicides were assigned to property detectives. Six tactical deputies were assigned to do night surveillance in the suspect's 'hunting grounds', the area of Nebraska Avenue and West Kennedy Boulevard in North Tampa. The patrol divisions were again given alerts and were continually sending in field interrogation reports (FIR), which were checked. A personal computer was purchased specifically for this investigation and was used to record information on vehicles, vehicular tags, information gathered from talking to prostitutes, and information derived from the FIRs. At this point, the HCSO again went "public" to warn the community about these related homicides. However, the fiber information was kept confidential.

"The evidence from the Dinsfriend disposal site

was sent directly to the FBI Laboratory, and it
yielded valuable evidence. The knots in the ligatures were similar to the knots from the previous
cases; a brown Caucasian pubic hair, eventually
associated with Robert Long, was found on the bedspread; and semen was found on the bedspread and
sweat shirt and tests again disclosed the "A" and
"H" blood group substances. The bedspread was tested
and found to be composed of gold delustered acrylic
fibers. These fibers would also provide a link to
Long's vehicle.

"Both types of red nylon carpet fibers were again
found on most of the items and were microscopically
compared to the previous carpet fibers. The color
produced by the dyes from the red carpet fibers was
also compared using the microspectrophotometer. The
microspectrophotometer is one of the most discrimi-
nating techniques which can be used in the comparison of fibers. Since these carpet fibers both
microscopically and optically matched the red carpet
fibers from the previous five cases, it was strongly
believed that all of these fibers were consistent
with having originated from the same source, and
therefore, all of the cases were related."

▲   ▲   ▲

The photo of Karen Dinsfriend that police passed out to the
news media was a copy of a Polaroid taken during one of her many
busts. It shows an appealing, dark–haired young woman, still young
enough looking to be called a girl, whose girlishness and
fresh–faced innocence had long since been sandpapered away by
heavy-duty drugs and by the hard, dehumanizing, childhood–robbing life on the street. In the photo, Karen, wearing a grey t–shirt,
is looking to her right, a hunted and fearful look in the sunken eyes.
The look is one of deep, deep sadness and despair.

Within hours of the discovery of Karen Dinsfriend's body,
police had a pretty good idea of where she'd come from and the

321

circumstances that had brought her to such a violent and lonely death. They were surprised. Unlike most of the hookers and addicts and lowlifes they were accustomed to dealing with, Karen Dinsfriend had started out with every advantage a "good Jewish girl" from a solid, upper–middle-class family could expect. All–American girl. All–American home. All–American life. But at death, nothing but a gutter junkie.

"This girl," said "Pops" Baker, shaking his head, "was heavy into cocaine and prostitution. No question about it. She comes from a very nice family, well–to–do family, but she's into the drug scene and that's her demise.

"The last we know of her she was working off from Hillsborough and Nebraska, hooking, but her bag was she was a feisty girl. She was a rip–off artist. She would get a john, get his money and then split. In fact, we found some people that weren't unhappy she was dead. She was not the cooperative type prostitute. She really didn't like to get involved in the sex part of it. She just liked to get the guy set up and then run off with his money. She'd live with anybody that would take her in. Had an awful cocaine habit and would do anything to get money to support it."

But that's not how her loving and despairing family wanted to remembered Karen Beth Dinsfriend.

She grew up just across the Bay in the sheltered, affluent enclave of Gulfport, carved out of the southwestern corner of staid old St. Petersburg. Karen's father, Mel, was the well–known, successful owner of a business-supply firm. Karen and her sister, Judi, attended Boca Ciega High School, whose property line bumps up to Al Lang Field, one of the area's oldest and most treasured spring-training complexes.

But Karen didn't stay long in school. In 1972, she dropped out, still only a sophomore but already trapped on the remorseless treadmill of drugs. For her father, any attempt to explain Karen's descent into the maelstrom of drugs was beyond words. "I can't tell you the whole story," Mel Dinsfriend said when a reporter appeared on his doorstep. "It's emotionally impossible and chronologically impossible. I can tell you that when she was off drugs, she was a beautiful girl."

It began with one little hit of windowpane acid in the girls' bathroom.

"She just never came out of it and got worse and worse," Judi Dinsfriend told the Tribune. "She was smart, and that's what hurts me the most, being her younger sister. I think she probably wanted death without pain. She didn't like pain, emotional or physical. That's why she tried to mask it with drugs. It's difficult to say 'yeah, yeah, you love me' when you don't even believe it yourself."

After dropping out in 1972, Karen worked at several entry–level jobs around St. Pete, but her need for drugs increased, even as her ability to earn the money to buy them on the street decreased. The Tribune's investigation found that, in 1976, Karen faced grand larceny and fraud charges for skimming money from two bank customers while working as a teller. Over the next three years, Karen Dinsfriend was arrested and charged on four different occasions for forging prescriptions to obtain Dilaudid, a painkiller similar to morphine, that most addicts adore.

The Tribune reporter also learned that in February, 1978, Karen gave birth to a baby girl at a hospital in Bryn Mawr, Pennsylvania, while living with a woman friend. According to court documents, the state moved in and placed the infant in foster care before she was a year old.

"Three of Karen Dinsfriend's Pinellas County court files contain copies of a plaintive letter she sent a circuit judge in November 1978," the Tribune reported.

"'I love my baby,' she wrote. 'My heart is so heavy with grief from being without her now. Is there not a chance for me to take her and go where I can get the help I need and have my beloved baby?...I want to raise her and love her. If I lose her, it would not only hurt me, but how would she feel when she grew up?'"

Karen's pleas were in vain, and she continued her seesaw battle with drugs. At times she seemed to be winning, only to see her life tilt wildly out of control again as the addictive quicksand of coke and heroin sucked her down. During one drying-out period in jail, Karen settled down long enough to earn high-school equivalency degree. Later, she moved up to Tallahassee to escape the old con-

323

nections and to enroll in a computer training school. But it didn't last. In 1982, Karen Dinsfriend was sent back to prison for fraudulently obtaining prescription drugs. She was released in June, 1983.

Judi Dinsfriend told the Tribune that, after prison, her sister came home and got a job as a restaurant hostess in St. Petersburg. But, inevitably, needle freaks from the old days showed up, and overnight Karen was back in the life. "They gave her a freebie [heroin] and that was it," Judi Dinsfriend recalled.

On January 4, Karen was arrested for offering to perform sex acts on an undercover St. Pete cop. There was a cap of coke in her pocket; fresh red needle tracks marched along both arms. Only six months out of prison, and already Karen Dinsfriend was hustling on the street to support her habit.

The Tribune's reporter also spoke with Bob Neri, a director at Operation Parental Awareness and Responsibility (PAR), a drug-treatment center in nearby Largo.

"She liked heroin, Dilaudid—whatever was popular on the street," Neri told the reporter, adding that Karen had been in treatment at PAR as early as 1976. The last time counselors spoke with her was less than three months before she was killed. She left PAR without permission on June 2, after arriving six days earlier under court order. When Karen walked out and went back to the streets, the court issued an arrest warrant.

"When she left, she just dropped off the face of the earth—she just ceased contact with us, which is very unusual," the Tribune quoted Neri. "She was more desperate in her attitude. I think she understood the seriousness of the lifestyle she was involved in."

Apparently she didn't, because the next time the Dinsfriend family heard of Karen, was the news that she was the latest victim of Tampa's serial killer—but, in their minds, as much a victim of drugs and the street as she was of Bobby Joe's strangling shoelace.

"It surprised me the way that it happened," Judi Dinsfriend commented sadly. "But I knew she was going to die."

Karen Dinsfriend. Gary Terry nodded thoughtfully when her name was mentioned. "Her friends said she would do anything for drugs. And that got her killed. Bobby Joe said she asked for forty-

seven dollars for sex, which seemed like an odd amount, but she told him that was the amount she needed for a fix."

The significance of Karen Dinsfriend's murder, beyond the mindless destruction of another human being, lies in the fact that it marked a distinctive turning point in the intensity of the investigation and in the attitude of the police involved. Five bodies were five too many.

"We realized we were getting our teeth kicked in, so we decided it was time to take some proactive measures," Terry explained. "Instead of waiting for the phone to ring and sitting around waiting for the next body to come to us, we went out looking for the guy. We put undercover officers in different lounges, just hanging out and observing customers. We sent a lot more people out along Nebraska and Kennedy Boulevard to talk to and watch hookers. Didn't arrest them, but questioned them about weird customers, anybody that seemed suspicious to them. And we started taking down tag numbers of all the johns. We spent countless hours down on Kennedy Boulevard and Nebraska Avenue talking to prostitutes. They were helpful. Provided information on a lot of people who initially looked like good suspects but then just washed out completely.

"Next, we brought in detectives from other divisions and put them on the streets. We had officers sitting out watching key intersections and exits on I–Four all across the county. Two men in cars with orders to write down car and tag info. We couldn't figure out how in the hell he was finding all the remote dump sites, unless he was a lifelong resident of the county and did a lot of traveling around the county so he'd know where there were places to leave a body without being spotted.

"And we got a crime analyst. I quickly learned this is something that's absolutely necessary in a case of this magnitude. Information was pouring in on us, overwhelming us. I went to sheriff for help and he said get anything you need but get the guy. We bought one of the first PCs in the sheriff's office just to sort and control all this information we were getting, but that wasn't getting us anywhere.

"We Went to ROCIC [the Regional Organized Crime

Information Center] in Nashville, which targets traveling criminals and aids local law enforcement. They furnished special infrared lights that we install in our copters, really state of the art technology that picks up images of body heat which allows the operators to actually see in the dark without being seen. The helicopters were out cruising all over the county late at night and early in the morning. We actually hoped to find him in the process of dumping a body...

"Two female officers volunteered to go out on Nebraska Avenue as prostitute decoys. One of them dressed up in a very revealing and provocative outfit and wore a body bug. She was under strict orders not to get in any cars, just to check out the interiors, see what they were like. We told her cover that if she did get in a car, it's because she was made to get in and they must stop that car at all costs! I told all the officers assigned to that cover team surveillance that if we lose her, put your badge on the dash along with mine, because we'll all be out of here. Every time she hit the street, she attracted a crowd of would-be customers. At one point, the traffic was backed down the street and around the corner just trying to pick up this one young decoy officer. I've spoken with that officer since then, and she said it was the most frightening assignment she's ever had. Basically, it was like putting a worm on a hook and waiting for a strike.

"We were in the right areas, at the right times, but our guy just didn't show. I don't think he was sly enough to spot the setups or the decoys. I think he just didn't see them....

"By now we had established a locked and guarded war room in which only the detectives assigned to the case were allowed in. Any discussion of fiber evidence had to be done behind that closed door or over secured telephone lines. We were scared to death that the news of the fibers might leak out, which would cause the killer to change his tactics and clean up his act, maybe leave the area entirely. And as much as we would have liked that, we wanted to stop him here so he wouldn't go somewhere else and start the killing all over again.

"The tension and suspense were becoming unbearable. All of

us were working around the clock, almost. I'd go home at night after working sixteen to eighteen-hour days and lay awake thinking about the case, worrying about what little thing I might have missed. I used to have this constant dream about the killer as just a black, shadowy figure with no face. We just didn't have a name to go with all the evidence. We were building a terrific case based on the evidence but there was no face and no name.

"No one can understand the intense pressure that's suddenly on you, your detectives, your agency to catch the killer. It's unbelievable. And with each new body, it just gets more intense, buildsing like a crescendo, until everything seems to explode.

"Someone asked me who these victims were, because we were spending so much time and energy on them. Must really be somebody important. I said it's not a matter of who they are, but the fact that we are in the midst of a series of terrible homicides that are going to continue if we don't do something. It always bothered me, that idea that the victim has to be `someone' before they get this kind of attention and treatment. No one deserved to die the way these women died. I don't care what their background or business was....

▲   ▲   ▲

A LETTER FROM BOBBY

They have me in mind for at least a total of thirteen in Fla. They still think I'm the Green River killer [from Seattle] and won't give up that idea till they find some fresh cunt up there, and know I didn't do it, or they catch the guy! Which I don't think they will because he's not in the Seattle area anymore. I'd bet my life on it. Soon in some other state they'll have another series of dead cunts floating in a river, it will be him. Wanna bet? Wanna bet he hasn't read how they're trying to tie his bitches to me? and is taking advantage either by stopping or moving to a new area.

▲   ▲   ▲

327

While Lt.Terry was mounting a multi–front offensive following the Dinsfriend murder, fending off the rising chorus of raucous criticism in the press and trying to weather the heat being generated by the politicians, he was grimly aware that the killer was still out there roaming the streets. More than likely, additional bodies would soon turn up—despite all his well– meaning and "proactive" measures. Some, he feared, might even then be sprawled out there in the boonies, in some roadside ditch, cow pasture, or orange grove, waiting for someone to come along and stumble over the nude, strangled corpse.

And that's precisely what happened on November 6, just two days after Lisa McVey was freed from her harrowing experience with Bobby Joe Long.

Much of the rural area spreading landward from Tampa Bay is outstanding horse country. Numerous ranches, both large and small, are devoted to the siring and training of blue-ribbon thoroughbred horses, while Tampa itself annually plays host to major international horse shows, which attract the moneyed gentry and European royalty.

Linda Carol Phethean and her husband owned a ranch on Bromwell Road near Zephyrhills in Pasco County, with plenty of room for Linda to train horses for show and teach both the elegance and etiquette of riding to others.

The morning of November 6, one of her students, Candy Linville, arrived for her regular lesson. After spending some time in the stables grooming their horses, the two women mounted and set out across the pasture, expecting to return to the ranch house for a noon luncheon. About 11:30 a.m., they were riding along a dirt road leading from Highway 301 to the Phethean property when they smelled the odor of something rotting in the high grass alongside the road, and went to investigate. Linda was accustomed to coming across dead animals on her rides around the ranch. She knew what death smelled like, and this one, she later told police, "...had been there a long time."

A few weeks earlier, she continued, her dogs had come home sick. "We thought they had been poisoned," she told investigators,

328

"but when we took them to the vet, he found rotting flesh in their stomachs." The dogs often roamed the ranch and frequently carried home bones they'd found.

Linda told officers that when they smelled the odor, she and Candy "...teased each other that maybe it was another body. Really, all we expected to find was a dead armadillo.

"But then I looked down to see what my horse was looking at. It was definitely a leg bone, an entire leg bone, really. Then Candy called me over to look at something that, from a distance, she thought might be an armadillo or turtle shell. But it was a skull. I could make out the structure of a cheekbone of a skull with some cloth wrapped around it. Basically, it was an upper torso with the skull attached with some hair on it...I said, 'This is a human skeleton. Let's get out of here,' and we rushed home and called the police."

The first Pasco County deputy who responded to the call confirmed that the bones were indeed human and called for assistance. Captain George Mangrum was among the officers who responded to the call, followed by crime-scene technicians from the Florida Department of Law Enforcement (FDLE) and by Dr. Joan Wood, the medical examiner for Pinellas and Pasco Counties.

"We suspected it was probably a female," Mangrum reported, "and one of the first things we wanted to do was determine if it might be related to the recent string of discovered bodies in Hillsborough County. One of them was found just down the road a piece off Three-oh-one."

In addition to the bones Linda Phethean found, body parts had been scattered by animals over an area the size of a football field. For the next three hours, FDLE technicians carefully searched the surrounding pastureland, setting out some thirty small orange flags to mark bone placement. The tatters of a woman's blouse and panties, along with a floating heart pendant, dimly shining in the weeds, were found near the remains.

When the crime-scene technicians were satisfied they'd found all they were going to find, the remains were turned over to Dr. Wood. In her autopsy report, Dr. Wood said she observed a

shoelace "...running two times around the neck...It was tied in a double knot. At one end of the shoelace there was a portion tied into a small loop. The inner circumference of the shoelaces after their removal was 9–1/8 inches long. Appeared to be work [boot] lace because it was quite long...Another shoelace with two loops large enough for a person's wrists with the distance between the two loops being 8 1/2 inches."

When she testified at trial in April, 1985, Dr. Wood added that small hand and wrist bones also were found entangled in this second shoelace, which apparently had been used to bind the victim's hands eight inches apart. She believed that the woman had died of strangulation, since no other evidence of death was present. But she could not say, Dr. Wood added, if the victim had been strangled manually before the shoelace was tied around her neck.

"But the hands of a dead body would not have needed to be tied," she said pointedly.

In addition to his own personnel, Captain Mangrum also notified Hillsborough County authorities of the discovery, "...because we knew they were investigating similar types of cases."

Lt. Terry sent men speeding to the scene. "When they got there, they took one look and called me: 'It's him again.' All they needed to see were the ligatures that were still attached to know it was the same guy."

Once the bones were collected and Dr. Wood had finished piecing them back together in the ME's office, they were identified as those of a young, probably white, female who had appeared to be in reasonably good health before she died. However, the body remained a Jane Doe until three days after Bobby Joe Long was arrested. At that time, sheriff's detective Ken Hagin took a phone call from a distraught woman who identified herself as Sharon Martinez, thirty-four, who lived in Tampa. She had a friend, the woman said, who she hadn't seen since mid–October, and she was afraid that this serial killer guy might have got her.

Hagin drove out to a service station at Nebraska and Fletcher Avenue to meet the woman, who explained that her friend, Virginia "Ginny" Johnson, had a serious alcohol problem and was skin–pop-

ping heroin and coke and God knows what else. And she'd been hooking on Nebraska and Kennedy Boulevard to get money for drugs. Ginny, the Martinez woman continued, had been staying with a guy named Alvin Duggan, who lived about half block off Nebraska, just around the corner from the Alamo Lounge where Sharon worked and where Ginny often hung out, hoping to score a trick. While they were talking, Duggan drove by. The detective flagged him down, and followed Duggan to his home to get more details and to go through the belongings that Duggan said Ginny had left behind. In the pockets of the few articles of clothing that were stuffed in a cheap overnight bag, Hagin found $90 in cash and a slip of paper listing the young woman's Social Security number, date of birth, mother's name—Sonja Peters of Danbury, Connecticut—and how to get in touch with her in case of emergency.

Duggan said he last saw Ginny on October 15, when she said he was going over to the Alamo to buy cigarettes but never returned. Duggan speculated that Ginny might have strolled up Nebraska to a popular north-side attraction, the Malibu Grand Prix, a go–cart raceway and arcade room. It was the kind of place that teenagers like Ginny Johnson like to hang out. Liz Loudenback also used to meet her friends at the Grand Prix, which was just across Nebraska from the rear property line of the mobile-home park where Liz had lived with her mother and stepfather.

And besides, it didn't surprise Alvin Duggan if Ginny decided on the spur of the moment to go walking along Nebraska Avenue. After all, streetwalking was her trade, and Nebraska was where she did her business. It wasn't too unusual for her to leave without a word and be gone for days or weeks at a time.

Ginny, he recalled, was a little upset when she went out for cigarettes that evening of October 15. Earlier in the day Ginny had hitchhiked downtown to keep an appointment at the VD clinic in the Hillsborough County Health Department. She told the nurse on duty that she was overdue on her period, and complained of vaginal itching and burning. Ginny said her last sexual contact was the night before. Asked about the number of sex partners she'd had

in the past four weeks, she replied "Many!"

The pregnancy test was negative. However, Ginny tested positive for gonorrhea—for the fourth time in her young life. She was also carrying trichomoniasis, another sexually transmitted parasitic infection—neither of which stopped her from soliciting johns that same night, or, in a delicious irony, possibly passing on her venereal diseases to her killer.

Duggan and Martinez also confirmed that they'd seen Ginny wearing a floating heart pendant like the one found among the Pasco County bones. Hagin then called the Danbury telephone number listed in Ginny's effects and spoke with Robert Peters, Ginny's stepfather. He said the family hadn't seen her in three or four months, and assumed she was still living in the Tampa area. Peters gave Hagin the name of Ginny's Danbury dentist, who agreed to send his patient's dental charts.

On November 21, Hagin received the records, and handed them over to Dr. Ken Martin, a forensic dentist, to compare with the postmortem dental X–rays. "There's no question," Dr. Martin confirmed, "they're the same." Viirginia Johnson had been found.

Like so many of the others—Karen and Chanel and Michelle and Kimberly—Virginia Lee Johnson was a victim long before she became the victim. In death, as in life, few knew her name, not even the killer who looked into her eyes while he strangled her. To Bobby Joe Long, she was just another nameless, faceless,slut. She had it coming. Same as all the others. Or, as Bobby Joe explained it to Dr. Joel Norris: "I know what I did. I raped them and murdered them. But they were the ones who offered the invitation. [Starting with Lana Long.] She picked me up, really, I didn't go after her. She was a whore. She manipulated men, and she wanted to manipulate me. Once I had her in the car, I tied her up and raped her. Then I strangled her and dumped her body alongside the highway. I knew what I was doing, but I just couldn't stop myself. I hated her. I hated her from the time she picked me up..."

Ginny Johnson was born in Connecticut. Like the Dinsfriends, Ginny Johnson's family felt powerless to confront, much less combat, the demons that staked out their claim to the young girl's body

and soul long before the end of her life. During the two years she'd been in Hillsborough County, Ginny Johnson had managed to accumulate an impressive rap sheet of arrests for prostitution and drunk and disorderly conduct. She was a familiar street figure to the Tampa vice squad, a cagey eighteen year old who could spot an undercover detective by the way his jeans hung. After scoring a couple of johns, Ginny like to drink at the Sly Fox Lounge or at Crackers Lounge, another Nebraska Avenue dive, where a sign over the door warned patrons they weren't allowed to carry knives inside.

Sharon Martinez, in a pre–trial deposition, later painted a grim portrait of Ginny Johnson's short, sad, and sordid life:

I met Ginny year before last at Alamo Liquors, a little neighborhood bar in North Tampa that I used to work at. When I met her she was waitressing. She was cooking on a boat when I first met her and then she started waitressing, a food waitress. Then the last time that I saw her she was in a restaurant down the street from this bar I was telling you about, and she told me that she had hitchhiked downtown because she had got put on probation. She hitchhiked downtown to see her probation officer. I told her not to be hitchhiking because of some crazy guy out there killing all those girls. I said, "Have you heard about all the girls missing?" because she had just come back from Connecticut. She had been gone about maybe six months. I took her to my house where I live with my mom and my kids. She was only seventeen years old. She was an alcoholic, I mean bad, since she was ten years old, and her little sister was sixteen. She [Ginny's sister] got killed in Tampa last year also. She got run over, hit-and-run. They were both alcoholics since they were babies, and I felt sorry for her. I took her to my house...

She told me she had been an alcoholic since she was ten years old, and her sister was nine and her brother, I think he is a year older than her. All

three of those kids were alcoholics since they were little kids. Their stepfather was real mean to them and tried to sexually abuse them all their life and everything. That is why she was like that. She couldn't help it. It was her mother's fault for living with that man and letting him hurt those kids. She was a beautiful girl, not a violent person. She wouldn't hurt anybody. I mean, she didn't even talk bad to people, you know. If somebody said something to her she wouldn't even talk back to them. Just a really calm person. She didn't have a chance in life. I took her to my house and I made her dry out a little bit. Just little by little I cut her down. You know, she would get up early in the morning and tell me to go get her a bottle, I said, "No, get a shower and get something to eat because I'm not taking you to get a bottle."

She would get the shakes real bad and then I would have to get her a drink or something. I told her, "Why don't you go to a doctor and see if he can give you some nerve pills and get off the liquor?" She got almost completely off of it, and she started thinking straight. She said she was going to go back home and get a job and straighten herself out for awhile. She did. She went home and got a job in a factory up there and everything. She called me collect from Connecticut and said there was snow on the ground. She had sandals and a Florida coat. Her mom wouldn't even let her come spend the night there as soon as she got there. Her mom said she couldn't come there. She was crying and everything. She didn't know what to do, I said, "Don't you have any friends you can go to?" I guess she went to one of those houses. She had been in and out of homes all of her life. So, they took her in and she got a job. She straightened up for a while and then she came back down here when it started getting cold again up there.

The last time I saw her was at the Country Inn on Nebraska. She told me that she had hitchhiked down-

334

town to see the probation officer. She hitchhiked
over on Kennedy. She made some money. Prostitution.
I said, "Ginny, aren't you scared to do that? If you
want to do that you don't have to hitchhike around
and do it. You know enough people from that bar. If
you need money somebody will give you money in
there." I said, "And hitchhiking around, why would
you do that? This guy is killing all these girls.
Somebody is killing all these girls."

Ginny's mother and stepfather, Sonja and Robert Peters,
denied the abuse accusation, while admitting they felt helpless in
trying to save Ginny from her self–destructive lifestyle. They knew
she was a heavy drug and alcohol user, and for the past few years
had been supporting herself as a prostitute. During that period,
Ginny often traveled back and forth between Danbury and Tampa.

Sonja's daughters, the Peters admitted, started getting into
trouble at very early ages. Ginny probably wasn't more than ten
years old when she took her first drink and kept right on drinking.
The problem with booze only intensified when she added a steady
diet of drugs.

"Ginny and Margaret were in and out of all kinds of programs
here in Connecticut," Sonja Peters sighed. "But they never seemed
to help. Those places were too lenient with them."

Half drunk or high most of the time, Ginny Johnson was a lost
cause before she ever reached high school, and she soon dropped
out, to no one's surprise. She began running away from home
almost on a weekly basis, getting drunk, raising hell, being hauled
in by juvenile authorities. When she was barely sixteen, Ginny took
off for Florida for the first time, Margaret not far behind her, setting a pattern the young sisters followed for the rest of their
lives—south in the winter, north in the summer.

Sonja Peters told reporters that the news of her daughter's
murder shocked her, but it didn't faze her husband.

"Did it shock me? No, not really," Robert Peters said unsympa-
thetically. "I expected something like this to happen sooner or later.
I was in the Navy, so I know what goes on out there on the street.

And it's especially dangerous if you're a hooker, because you're nothing more than a piece of meat for all kinds of perverts and crazies, drug addicts and killers.

"She had been my stepdaughter since she was a little girl. I never had any problems with her until she started drinking and taking drugs and then got into prostituting. She tried to keep what she did a secret, but we eventually started to figure it out. Especially when she was in Florida in 1983, when she told us she was working on a tugboat—as a cook.

"She had a home here in Danbury, but she said she had to go back to Tampa because of her work. It killed her, like I tried to warn her it would. If you live that way, you die that way."

The FBI's account of Virginia Lee Johnson's murder states:

"On November 6, 1984, the remains of a female were discovered near Morris Bridge Road in Pasco County just north of the Hillsborough County Line. The bones of the victim were scattered about a large area; however, a ligature was found. Another ligature was discovered on an arm bone...

"The evidence from the Johnson site was sent by the PCSO to the FBI Laboratory. Again, due to the extensive decomposition, the body yielded very little physical evidence; however, in the victim's head hair from the crime scene a single red lustrous carpet fiber was found, relating this case to the others. Eventually, Virginia Johnson would also be associated with Robert Long's vehicle through a transfer of her head hairs."

▲   ▲   ▲

The police were stunned, none more than Agent Mike Malone and Lt. Gary Terry, when that single, but damning, red carpet fiber was found clinging to the remains of Ginny Johnson's scalp. All the forensic formulas told them that this tiny fiber should have been long gone. But there it was—another solid link in the chain of evidence from each crime scene that was inexorably lashing the killer to the electric chair.

A LETTER FROM BOBBY

When I told you about boxing and shit, I know
that stuff aint shit in here or in the
streets...I'm not a real "trusting soul" and when
it comes to man to man--"messing in their business"--I know what your talking about! Don't worry
about it! I'm careful enough, and I know I'll
probably have to make an example of someone somewhere down the line just so the word goes out.
Don't fuck with Long. He don't care! Cause I
don't! What are they gonna do give me the chair?
Ha!

▲   ▲   ▲

The weekend of November 10, Bobby Joe Long went out hunting for the last time, and left another trail clearly marked with
more of those incriminating little fibers. Less than a week had
passed since he'd released Lisa McVey. Less than a week of freedom remained before the Task Force swooped down on the surprised killer as he emerged from the Dale Mabry theater.

On Bobby Joe Long's last foray, he found twenty-one year old
Kim Marie Swann.

Near downtown Tampa, Kennedy Boulevard, a major thor-
oughfare on the west side, changes into Adamo Drive and parallels
the Crosstown Expressway as it carries traffic into eastern
Hillsborough County. Just before it leaves the city limits at the
Tampa Bypass Canal, Adamo sprouts an appendage, Orient Road,
that curves off and heads north through an area of railroad yards,
warehouses, and industrial complexes.

That's where Drake Reed reported for work on Monday morning, November 12, 1984. Drake, an employee of a St. Petersburg
sign company, had a work order for one of the elevated billboards
overlooking the heavily traveled Adamo–Orient Road cutoff. Reed
had been working for about thirty minutes when he glanced down
and noticed something "white and fleshy" looking, lying on the
eastern slope of a railroad overpass on Orient Road. From his high

337

perch, it appeared to be a dead animal. But it also looked human. Reed climbed down and walked up the steep embankment. When he was about four feet away, there was no doubt about what he was looking at—a dead woman, face down, legs spread grotesquely wide apart, both arms slightly extended at her sides.

Since the body was still within the city limits, Tampa police, rather than the Hillsborough County Sheriff's Office, responded to Drake Reed's frantic telephone call. Sgt. Bob Price and Detective Howard Smith were among the first officers to arrive after it was determined this was, in fact, a homicide. Close behind them came "Pops" Baker and Steve Cribb. Technically, it wasn't their case, but every officer present knew that this was probably the work of the same killer who'd been terrorizing the area for the past six months. The woman's body was a little above average size. She was sprawled about halfway down the 45-degree incline. A metal guardrail stretched the length of the overpass, so whoever left the woman here would have had to lift the dead weight over the rail before pushing her down the embankment. Not an easy task, especially considering it was done on a well–lighted, heavily–traveled street. In fact, Det. Smith discovered, scuff marks beneath the guardrail, at the point where the killer had struggled to heave the body over the side. Trampled vegetation from the top of the incline to the body indicated that the dead woman had slid down the embankment.

The body was nude, except for stockings that were rolled down around the ankles. Ants and other insects had already begun their attack on the remains. Price had seen photos of the County's homicide victims and recalled that one had been hideous displayed with her legs spread wide, apparently for shock value. At first, this appeared to be a replay of the Lana Long homicide, but on closer inspection, Price decided that the body had come to rest in that position as it tumbled down the hill.

Dried blood matted the woman's reddish–blond hair. When the body was turned over, officers were shocked at the bloodied mask that once had been a face. The nose was smashed, eyes black and swollen shut. The lips were bloated and puffy. Pooled blood

338

filled the nose and mouth. Whoever she was, the woman had taken a ferocious beating before she died. But the beating hadn't killed her. The body was not bound when discovered, but there were angry red ligature marks around the woman's neck, left and right wrists, and elbows. The woman had been tied up for some time before she was killed and, given the chafing and depth of the ligature marks, appeared to have struggled violently to free herself.

While Dr. Lee Miller from the Medical Examiner's office began his preliminary look at the body, detectives searched the surrounding area for clues. They didn't have to look far. Scattered about ten feet away were several items of women's apparel, including jeans and a dark-blue California Crush shirt, patterned with light blue and white flowers and green leaves. The shirt had been cut or ripped off the woman's body.

With all the experience they'd gained on previous cases, Baker and Cribb immediately spied something else stuck to the blue jeans—small, red fibers. A short, light-brown hair also was found on the jeans and carefully preserved.

In one pocket of the jeans, Smith found a driver's license issued to Kim Maria Swann, DOB 5/17/63, with an address on Countryside Drive in the Carrollwood section of Northwest Tampa. Fingerprints later confirmed the identification. There were also two traffic citations, one issued in connection with a fender bender accident that occurred November 1 on Dale Mabry, which showed Kim Swann as the owner of a 1979 two–door Toyota. A computer check later located the Toyota at International Body Works where it had been towed after being impounded on November 12. The car was parked in the lot of the LaPetite Academy, a day–care facility on Humphrey, just west of Dale Mabry Highway. The owner of the Academy had asked that the apparently abandoned Toyota be removed from his property, a good five miles from where Kim Swann was last seen alive and boozing it up with some friends.

An autopsy was performed at 7:00 that Monday evening. In addition to the ligature marks and the bruises from the beating administered before death, Dr. Miller also noted several superficial

vertical scuff marks on the breasts, abdomen, buttocks, lower back, and upper legs, all of which were postmortem, indicating the victim had been thrown down the embankment after she was dead.

The victim's blood-alcohol level tested at .175, meaning she was well over the legally drunk level of .10 when she was killed.

Kim Swann was a departure from Long's other victims, and represented a distinct shift in his stalking pattern—precisely what police feared might happen, as the murderous rage intensified and the killer became less selective about his targets.

Kim was not a hooker, and was driving her car, not walking the streets, when Bobby Joe Long came upon her late that Saturday night or early Sunday morning in November. However, Kim was no stranger to the Tampa nightlife that had produced most of Long's other victims. She enjoyed barhopping at the lounges along Nebraska and had worked as a topless dancer at the Sly Fox—where Lana Long also danced and Ginny Johnson liked to drink and pick up "dates." Kim lived in an apartment house four blocks west of Nebraska and across the street from the Tampa Greyhound Tracks, the area Long often prowled, searching for hookers to rape and kill.

After her death, the Tampa Tribune reported that Kim Swann "...had been seen in bars around the Nebraska Avenue strip since she was fifteen years old." A rather tender age, it seems, to be hanging out in some of Tampa's most notorious night spots, but an interview Detective Howard Smith conducted during the course of the murder investigation indicated that maybe the notion wasn't too farfetched.

Smith was contacted by a Ronald Timothy Edge, who claimed to have information about the victim that might aid the investigation. Edge insisted that he first met Kim Swann about eight years prior to her death, in a bar in North Tampa—which would have made her only thirteen or fourteen years old at the time. About five years before, Edge continued, he heard that Kim had turned to hooking and was working for a pimp named "Fat George" who lived across the street from her place. Edge claimed that, because he felt sorry for Kim, he talked her into leaving Fat George and

helped get her a job dancing topless at the Sly Fox. She still would have been underage, and few bar owners would put themselves at the risk of losing their license by hiring some jailbait teenybopper.

In August, 1982, Kim was issued a Tampa Alcohol Beverage Identification card, required of all bar and lounge employees. She listed her occupation as "Dancer" and was employed at the time at the Tanga Lounge. The card's ID photo is of five–foot, five–inch, 120-pound, healthy, athletic, attractive young woman, with sandy, shoulder length blond hair.

The month before the murder, police records show, Kim had reported two disturbances at her apartment in North Tampa. One involved a man throwing a motorcycle helmet through Swann's window, and the other report was of a man trying to break down her door. She filed a criminal-mischief report with Tampa police. A few days later, Kim and her one-year old son left the apartment and moved in with her parents.

Now, after some wild youthful years, Kim Swann seemed to be settling down and planning for the future. In September, she enrolled in the Erwin Area Vocational–Technical Center, hoping to land a career as a medical technician. Family and friends described Kim as someone with a sweet personality, who at one time had fallen in with the wrong crowd, but now was trying to turn her life around.

Once the dead woman's identification was confirmed, officers went to notify her parents, Louis and Bobbie Swann. In an interview with Detective Smith, family members told him that Kim had moved out of her apartment and in with them about a month ago. She was unemployed, but often went out at night.

The last time the Swanns saw Kim was the afternoon of Friday, November 9, when they passed her on Bearss Avenue, headed east. At home, they found a note saying Kim was going out to dinner and expected to be in early. When she did not return that night, the Swanns said they weren't concerned, since Kim often stayed out overnight. Even when she didn't show up all day Saturday, they didn't consider that unusual behavior for their free–spirited daughter.

But on Sunday, when Kim hadn't even bothered to call to

check on her child, the Swanns started to worry. But they still waited until Monday before calling the sheriff's office to report her missing.

Kim liked to go to bars, her parents said. One of her latest favorites was Michael's, which used to be the Junkyard Lounge on Nebraska. She also hung out at CC's Lounge on Fowler and at PJ Liquors on Dale Mabry. Kim had used drugs in the past. The Swanns thought she was off them, but lately they'd noticed a marked change in her personality—she was on edge, moody, losing weight—which made them worry that she'd started using again.

Kim's sister, Sandra Snyder, confirmed that Kim frequented bars and drank heavily at times. When she got drunk, it wasn't unusual for Kim to be gone all night, maybe two nights, while she crashed at a friend's home. Like her parents, Sandra had noticed the recent changes in Kim's behavior, and believed she was back on drugs. Two or three years ago, Sandra continued, she got a call from Kim to come pick her up at the emergency room at Tampa General Hospital. When she arrived, Kim told her that she'd been dancing at the Sly Fox when three men asked her to go to a party. The party turned out to be the three guys and Kim, and they took turns raping her for hours. (Detective Smith noted that a records check failed to turn up a report of the incident in either the city or county police files.)

However, Sandra added, even after that gang rape, Kim probably wouldn't hesitate to leave with some stranger she met in a bar, or allow herself to be picked up off the street—especially when she was on a toot.

Other detectives tracked down acquaintances who reported seeing Kim late Sunday afternoon, November 11— first at a convenience store a few blocks from her parents' home, and later that evening, drinking at the Bamboo Lounge in the West Village Commons Shopping Center.

One of the final entries in the FBI Law Enforcement Bulletin states that:

"On November 12, 1984, the nude body of a young

white female was found on an incline off of North
Orient Road in the City of Tampa, involving yet a
third jurisdiction in the homicides. The victim had
been at the scene less than twenty-four hours. A
wadded pair of blue jeans and a blue flowered top
were near the body. The victim was wearing knee high
nylons; the body was face down with the head at the
lower portion of the incline. Faint tire impressions
were observed in the grass next to the roadway, and
a piece of wood with possible tire impressions was
found. It appeared that the killer had pulled off
the road and had thrown the body over the edge and
onto the incline. Examination of the body revealed
that fecal matter was present on the inside of the
victim's legs and on the exterior of the clothing.
The body had a pronounced ligature mark on the front
portion of the neck. There were also ligature marks
on both wrists and on both arms; however, no ligatures were found.

"This victim was identified as Kim Marie Swann, a
21 year old female narcotics user, who worked as a
nude dancer. She was last seen walking out of a convenience store near her parent's home at approximately 3:00 p.m. on November 11, 1984.

"When the Tampa Police Department responded and
noted the ligature marks on the victim, they immediately called the HCSO and requested that they also
respond. This homicide was also believed to be
related to the previous seven homicides.

"The evidence from the Swann disposal site was
sent to the FBI Laboratory. The tire tread impressions on the board bore limited design similarities
to the tire impressions from the Lana Long and
Michelle Simms homicides. Again, red nylon carpet
fibers were found on the victim's clothing. The head
hair of the victim was examined and would eventually
be associated with the suspect's vehicle.

"Even though the three jurisdictions now directly
involved in the eight homicides continued to work
separately on their own cases, there was continual

exchange of information among these agencies, which enabled the HCSO to learn that the Tampa Police Department sex crimes detectives were working an abduction and rape of a seventeen year old white female. This exchange of information would ultimately lead to the big 'break' in the case, a case which had completely captivated the attention of the Tampa Bay area and one which was beginning to attract national attention as well."

Despite the witnesses who claimed to have seen Kim Swann on Sunday night, Bobby Joe told the two detectives who questioned him that he picked her up on Saturday night or early Sunday morning, about two days before the body was found.

Dr. Joel Norris's book, Walking Time Bombs, gives Bobby Joe's version of his last murder:

"Two days after he released his youngest victim, his compulsion came over him again. As he was driving along the outskirts of North Tampa late in the evening, he spotted a car swerving back and forth in front of him. He thought it was being driven by a woman and that she was drunk. He followed her. She almost swerved off the road, but then she noticed that she was being followed. She pulled over to the side. Bobby Long stopped his car directly behind hers, got out, walked over to her car, and the two of them began a conversation. In a few moments, she agreed to ride around with him, believing that he would drive her back to her car in the morning. Bobby noticed how big she was. He described her later as a hard-looking girl in cowboy boots. Not fat, but she had a large frame. She could stand up for herself, he could see, and he disliked her the minute he laid eyes on her. He almost thought he would enjoy killing her. Her name was Kim Swan (sic) and she would become Bobby Joe Long's final victim.

"As soon as she got in beside him in the front seat of the car, he attacked her. She screamed and fought back with a strength he hadn't expected, kicking him in the shins, forcing elbows and fore-

arms into his face, and putting her boots right through his dashboard. The two struggled until Long finally overpowered her and tied her hands. She kept on screaming, however, every time she caught sight of headlights approaching in the side view mirror. Finally Long squeezed her windpipe until she gasped for air and stopped fighting. Then he began cruising with her, promising her she wouldn't be hurt if she'd only cooperate. But she started to scream again until he forced her to stop by viciously tearing at her windpipe. Finally, he strangled her until she lost consciousness and slumped forward across the seat. He drove with her until she came to and started screaming again. Then he strangled her again until she passed out. While she was still unconscious, he undressed her. But he found, as he looked at the stirring figure on the floor of his car, that what had been a raging desire for sex had simply dried up. Now there was only hatred at what he'd become and hatred at the woman who, he believed, had enticed him into becoming a monster. When she came to for the last time, Long crushed the throat with such force that she died almost at once.

"He rode through North Tampa with the naked body of the dead Kim Swann beside him for hours. Nobody stopped him or noticed anything strange, even when he pulled into a secluded area outside the city and pushed her body out of the car. He had never even bothered to rape her."

Gary Terry, on the other hand, scoffs at the notion that Kim Swannn was not raped because Bobby Joe's sexual urge just suddenly dried up without reason. "Kim was the only victim he didn't rape because she defecated in his car, which made him instantly lose his taste of sex," Terry said. "Simple as that."

"He had the knife or gun out, stripped her, tied her up, and away they went. I think she was so frightened, just so scared to death, that her bowels let go and she defecated in his beautiful car, and that absolutely infuriated him because he loved that car. He just beat her unmercifully. Face and eyes swollen and blackened

almost beyond recognition. As he had with the other victims, he had her stripped and tied up and was heading out to the east side of the county where he was intended to rape her, kill her, and dump her. But before he got all the way out there she apparently defecated. That's when he pulled over, beat her, strangled her, and pushed her over the side of the overpass. We found a pair of her blue jeans he'd thrown out that he'd used to wipe off the seat trying to clean up the mess."

Whatever version is true, the fact is that Kim Swannn's body was found on Monday, November 12. Before the week was out, Bobby Joe Long was in custody and his horrific string of rapes and murders was over.

But while the killing may have ended, there were still more bodies to be counted.

Since September, Tampa police had felt instinctively that Vicky Elliott had fallen prey to the same killer who was stalking street hookers. When Ginny Johnson was found, they suspected that those remains might actually be the Elliott woman. But they had no proof that Vicky was even dead—not until Price and Latimer put the question to Bobby Joe Long near the end of the hours–long interrogation:

PRICE: *Well, uh, Vicky Elliott is the girl from the Ramada Inn...How'd you come across her?*

LONG: *Walking...walking down Nebraska.*

PRICE: *Did you stop and ask her if she wanted a ride?*

LONG: *Yeah.*

PRICE: *And then what happened?*

LONG: *She got in the car and, uh, I pulled...pulled around one of the side streets and started to do the same thing that I did to the other girls but she pulled these scissors out of her purse and tried to stab me...It wasn't bad, you know, just barely cut the skin, but, uh, it was a struggle to get her tied...*

PRICE: *Okay. Then what did you do?*

LONG: *Took her out Old Morris Bridge Road...the one that dead–ends right by the Interstate...had sex with her...strangled her...and dumped her there.*

PRICE: *What did you use to strangle her?*

LONG: *I'm not sure.*

PRICE: *The reason I ask is earlier you referred, uh, we were talking about Lisa, okay, and you prepared the blindfold.*

LONG: *You know, most of these I wasn't prepared.*

PRICE: *Okay. Where did you leave her? Vicky?*

LONG: *I left her...ah...just...Old Morris Road turns into a dirt road and runs straight into a barbed wire fence at a cow pasture. If you turn right when you hit that barbed wire fence and follow it almost to the road, exit on the Interstate...she's right there...by the fence.*

To assist officers in locating the body, Long drew a map of the site. Detective Howard Smith was one of the officers sent out to search for the remains of Vicky Elliott. Long had hidden her well. As he later reported, Smith had to follow some complicated directions to reach the secluded dump site:

"On 17 November 1984, based on information provided by Sgt. Price and Sgt. Latimer, I responded to the dead-end at Morris Bridge Road north of Fletcher Avenue on the west side of the Interstate 75 bypass. The scene had been secured the previous night by Hillsborough County Sheriff's Office deputies...The Morris Bridge Road turned north off of Fletcher, traveled a short distance, turned back east and then back north and led to a dead-end. There was a dirt path made by vehicles that led north from the pavement to the edge of wood line. The wood line ran east and west and going through the opening in the wood line I came to a barb wire fence which traveled east and west. Turning right at the fence and going...almost to the Interstate boundary line fence, there was a small circular area cleared out in some trees. The skeletal remains were found at that location."

Indeed, after seventy-one days, skeletal remains were all they found, along with a long pair of black–handled scissors.

347

The scissors had been deliberately shoved in the woman's vagina, and still rested within the bony pelvic cradle when police located the remains. One detective who was first on the scene "...noted a black handled pair of scissors, approximately eight or nine inches long, lying in what would have been the crotch or pubic area, with the sharp ends pointed towards the abdomen, an extensive rusting of the blades indicating that they might have been within the body cavity prior to decomposition."

Lt. Terry later added: "We know what he did with those scissors, probably as an act of rage and revenge for her trying to stab him. They were deliberately shoved up inside her. An act of total contempt. The only thing we don't know is if he did it while she was still alive or waited until she was dead. Bobby Joe absolutely refused to talk about those scissors, just as he refused to talk about any of the other things he did that were of a sexual nature.

"Incredibly, we also found more of those tiny red fibers in hair that remained on the skull. Mike Malone at the FBI Lab was astonished that such evidence still existed after the body had been exposed for so long."

On November 15, the day before he was arrested, Bobby Joe Long called Cindy, his former wife, to make arrangements to see his two children over the upcoming Thanksgiving holiday. During the conversation, he asked her if she had heard about all the girls getting killed in the Tampa area.

Cindy said she'd been reading about it in that paper, and Bobby Joe replied: "It's really rough out there. That's why I tell you and Holly [Cindy's roommate] to be careful."

The next day, Bobby Joe called again.

"You remember what we talked about last night?" he began. "You mean the girls?" Cindy asked. "Well, what about it?"

"Well, I did it."

"You're kidding," she exclaimed.

"Well," Bobby Joe sighed, "I wish I were, but I'm not." His last words to Cindy were instructions for his children. "Tell them," he said, "I was killed in a car wreck."

At that, Sgt. Latimer came on phone and told Cindy her

ex–husband and the father of her children was under arrest as a serial killer.

Five and a half hours after Sergeants Bob Price and Randy Latimer sat down to question Bobby Joe Long, they walked out of the interview room with a taped confession that, when transcribed, ran to forty-five pages. All three were drained, emotionally and physically, by the intense, almost intimate encounter.

Meanwhile, the major players in the Tampa Bay news media were gathering for a surprise press conference timed to go live on the 11 p.m. newscasts. Photos of Long and nine of the women he was charged with killing were prominently displayed on a bulletin board alongside the podium. Sheriff Walter Heinrich wanted maximum impact, and he got it. Blinking in the glare of the bank of television lights, Heinrich stepped to the podium and told the assembly that he and "...Pasco County Sheriff Jim Gillum, Tampa Police Chief Robert Smith, along with Danny Johnson, Special Agent in Charge, FBI, and Hillsborough County State Attorney E.J. Salcines, announce the arrest of Robert J. Long, charging him with eight counts of murder, sexual battery, and kidnaping. One additional murder charge is pending in Pasco County."

The astonishing, unexpected news hit the community like a thunderbolt. And nowhere was the impact felt more sharply than among the girls of Nebraska Avenue, and at places like the Sly Fox and the Starlite Lounge, whose topless dancers had lived in fear for months.

"It actually made me cry," one dancer told an inquiring Tribune reporter. "It's like I can't leave work and not worry about getting killed."

Since an indictment is necessary in Florida in capital cases, the Hillsborough grand jury was called into session to consider the charges against Long within forty-eight hours of his arrest. In the meantime, the Public Defender's Office had come to Long's aid, and attorney Charles O'Connor put forth a rare motion to block the indictment. O'Connor asked Judge John P. Griffin to remove the sitting grand jurors, to have them interviewed about their prejudices, or to send the case to another county, because of "inflammatory" press coverage of Long's case.

349

But Griffin ruled that the news-media coverage was to be expected in any case of such magnitude, and that he doubted if press reports were so "invidious" that they might destroy grand-jury impartiality. "Although relatively extensive and detailed, [publicity] has not been presented in a manner designed to create within a reader or listener, a vindictive and retributive feeling," Griffin added.

With the judge's go ahead, the grand jury listened to the evidence presented by the state attorney's office, deliberated for less than thirty minutes, and returned murder indictments against Long in the slayings of Ngeun Thi Long, Michelle Denise Simms, Devon Chanel Williams, Kimberly Kyle Hopps, Karen Beth Dinsfriend, Elizabeth B. Loudenback, Vicky Marie Elliott, and Kim Marie Swannn. Long was also charged with raping all the victims except Kim Swann. The ninth victim, Virginia Johnson, was killed in Pasco County, and therefore not named in the Hillsborough grand-jury indictment.

And there, as far as the police were concerned, it ended. With the case of Bobby Joe Long now resting with the judicial system, Lt. Terry and his men could take satisfaction in having done their jobs—although they regretted that so many had to die before they tracked the killer to his lair. Thanksgiving was coming, and the police who had worked almost non–stop through vacations and weekends were looking forward to some blessed time off to spend with their families.

But then, just when they thought the nightmare was over, one more horrifying specter arose to haunt them.

"Shocked," is how Lt. Terry described his reaction, when the dispatcher called that Thanksgiving Thursday with the news that the remains of an apparent homicide victim had been found. "Just totally shocked," he continued. "I almost collapsed. Bobby Joe was locked up, and my first thought was we had another copy cat killer on our hands. But then I learned that only skull and bones had been found. They'd been there eight months or longer. The same ligatures were present, so suddenly we realized that Lana Long wasn't the first, like we'd believed all along.

"This one, whoever it was, was probably the first killed, but the last found."

But who, exactly, was "this one"?

Christopher and Helma Larimer had finished Thanksgiving dinner early, and decided to take a mid–afternoon walk around their new subdivision. Their stroll carried them down along a drainage ditch running through a wooded area that bordered the Sundance property. They were looking for ferns in the woods when they came upon an area of the ditch that had recently been dredged out by a county road department dragline. Banks of sand and debris were piled up on either side of the ditch. As they approached, the Larimers noticed what appeared to be a human skull, partially buried in a mound of sand on the south side of the ditch.

Authorities were notified. Hillsborough County Detective David Luis arrived, and soon discovered other human bones near the skull. It appeared, he noted in his report, that the victim had been thrown in the ditch some time ago. When the ditch was being cleared, the remains were dragged into the pile of sand and then exposed when rainstorms washed the covering sand away.

Along with the skeletal remains, Luis found and cataloged three pieces of rope that apparently had been used as ligatures, one still tied around the tibia and fibia; a blue and white cloth belt; a blue, four–pocket professional smock; a red spaghetti– strap top with small, metal, beaded flowers around the neckline (and which appeared to have been sliced open from top to bottom in the front); a string necktie or hatband with wooden beads; a braided hairband made of shoestrings; two house keys on a metal ring; cigarettes; and a blue disposable lighter.

Dr. Lee Miller was called to the scene, and began the laborious process of identifying the extremely decomposed body and determining the cause of death.

The remains, he reported, were found 300 feet west of Ponderosa Trail and 7/10ths mile south of Lightfoot Road in southern Hillsborough County. The presence of the ligatures led

Dr. Miller to believe this was probably a homicide victim, but he couldn't be sure since the condition of the remains made it impossible to determine the exact cause of death.

To Lt. Terry, "Pops" Baker, and the other members of the Major Crimes Squad, those ligatures might as well have been a neon light spelling out the name of Bobby Joe Long. Detectives rushed to pay a visit to Long in his county jail cell, bringing with them evidence of his ligature handwork that linked him to the murder scene as surely as a fingerprint. By now, however, Long had developed some jailhouse smarts, and, with public defenders at his side, hinted that he'd talk about the recent find if prosecutors were willing to cut him some slack. "Here's the deal: First, no prosecution on this latest case if I give it up, and the evidence can't be used against me in any other prosecution. Second, you guys are still holding all my furniture and personal property. If you release the stuff to my ex–wife, I'll cop to your homicide. Third, the state attorney's office has to keep quiet about this latest confession so it won't jeopardize my defense in any of the upcoming trials."

Reluctantly, Assistant State Attorney Michael Benito, who was handling the prosecution, agreed to Long's deal, since it was the only way to solve the murder and identify the victim. Any fiber, hair, or semen evidence that might have existed was long since destroyed by the elements.

"But it really wasn't a secret deal," Terry protested. "We put the news out to the media, and I think they just totally missed it.

"Actually, we missed it too the first time around. When we confronted him with the ligatures we found at the last homicide (Wick), he did give a statement and enough information that we cleared the case, but he didn't tell us about it until after the remains were found. That's the key thing. When you look back at his confession, we were totally unaware of the Wick victim at the time. During the interview, the detectives were talking to him about each individual victim. At some point, they asked him, 'What about the victim on highway three-oh-one?' He says, 'Where on three-oh-one?' We didn't know at the time, there are two victims he'd dumped off, just the one north, by the state park. So the

352

detective told him the one across from Thonotosassa and Long said, 'Oh yeah. Her name was Sugar.' A street name—he had no idea who she was, but with that information we went to our moniker file and identified her. It wasn't until after we found Artiss Wick's body down south, off three-oh-one, that we went back to his statement and started putting one and one together. He knew about both of them, but he wanted to see how much we knew. He wasn't about to give it up voluntarily, especially when he found out that we didn't know about it.

"That's why I'm convinced today that there are other victims. I'd bet my paycheck on it. Here and possibly elsewhere. You don't start your killing with a murder like Lana Long's, without having some prior experience. The scene was too sophisticated for a first-timer. Finding the body in the Sundance development proved that Lana Long wasn't his first victim. But was it the last body found the first one killed? I doubt it."

Meanwhile, officers were digging through the files of both the Tampa police and the sheriff's office, looking for missing-persons reports that matched the time and place Long said he picked up the young woman and left her dead in the Sundance ditch. The report they hoped to find was one filed March 29, 1984 by Shannon and Terrena Nichols. A woman they identified as their "roommate," Ann Wick, had left their home the day before and never returned. The circumstances of her disappearance were, to say the least, peculiar.

At 11:00 on the morning of March 28, the Wick woman left the Nichols home, where she'd been staying for the past several weeks, to walk to the Kash 'N Karry Supermarket a half-block away for a package of Benson & Hedges cigarettes. When she left, the woman was wearing blue jeans, a red top held up by spaghetti straps, a blue striped shirt, and a straw hat. She was also barefoot, telling Shannon Nichols and her brand-new fiance, Johnny West, that she'd be right back. As Ann walked the short distance to the store, Terrena Nichols drove past, and Ann waved.

The Nichols, the parents of two toddlers, met Ann in January over in Tarpon Springs when they were visiting some of Shannon's

relatives. They immediately took a liking to the quiet, friendly young girl, who said her name was Artiss but that she preferred Ann, and who seemed so in need of a friend.

"She just acted like she was lost and didn't know where to turn next. We sort of took her in," said Shannon Nichols. "The deal was that she'd watch our girls and get her room and board for free. The kids loved her. I think it was because Ann was like a child herself.

"She had a little dog named Precious that she treated like it was her own baby. When she didn't come back from store that morning, we knew something had happened to her. She wouldn't go off and leave Precious if she could help it."

What was even stranger, thought the investigating officer, was that Ann Wick left all her belongings behind in the Nichols home—including her fiance Johnny West, the man she'd met two weeks earlier and was planning to marry on April 7. When their live–in baby sitter hadn't returned by the following day, the Nichols were alarmed enough to report her missing. One clue to her disappearance, Terrena Nichols thought, was in a conversation she'd had with Ann a couple of days earlier. Ann was having serious second thoughts about going ahead with her plans to marry Johnny West, because she thought she was pregnant with another man's baby. She didn't say who, but Terrena thought it might be a guy named Dave who worked as a roofer and had dated Ann. But there were also a couple of men over in Clearwater–St. Pete that Ann had been involved with.

As Terry's men studied the missing-persons report, they felt certain that they'd found a name to go with their unidentified skeleton. Everything seemed to match, but the final decision was left to forensic dentist Dr. Vicki Lindauer. She compared the teeth in the skull found at Sundance with dental records the missing woman's parents had sent from Indiana. There were at least six strong points of similarity. In her report dated December 11, Dr. Lindauer advised Detective Luis: "These numerous points of comparison establish positive identification of the deceased as Artiss Wick."

There were eerie similarities between Elizabeth Loudenback and Artie Wick, both so hungry for affection they were willing to go

nearly anywhere with almost anyone who showed them the least bit of attention. Both young women left Indiana when they were nineteen years old and traveled to Florida's Gulf Coast, in search of a more exciting lifestyle and maybe some romance. Like Liz Loudenback, Artie's early years also were unremarkable— small–town dullness with nothing to mark her as a potential murder victim. But in the four months preceding her death, Artie Wick, described by those who knew her best as shy and introverted, suddenly and without word to her family picked up and left her Indiana home, possibly to escape involvement in a local homicide; hitched a ride to Florida with the driver of an eighteen–wheeler; moved in with a cop; got pregnant (she thought) by a cab driver (or maybe a roofer); and agreed to marry a third man she'd known for only two weeks.

One of the photos that the Tampa police used for their missing-persons bulletin was a senior class picture that shows a smiling, pug–nosed, apple–cheeked girl with dark blond hair cut in bangs that almost cover her wide, green eyes.

Her father and stepmother, David and Bonnie Wick of LaFontaine, Indiana, had half-expected the bad news since March.

"We were shocked," David Wick admitted. "I had feared the worst for a while, but there was always the hope that she'd been kidnaped and was being held alive somewhere. The worst part was not knowing.

"Artie called home and talked to Bonnie that same day she disappeared. Talked about getting married and sounded real happy and excited about it. She wanted me to get some time off and fly down to Tampa to see her get married."

His daughter, Wick continued, had graduated from Mississinewa High School in 1981, with grades a little below average. Shortly afterwards, Artie moved out of her parents' home to room with a school friend. The two started hanging around "...with some people who were a bit rough," her father said, an association that may have put her life in danger. One of Artie's boyfriends and his brother were accused of overpowering their father in October, 1983, beating him to death, stuffing him in an old refrigerator, and

355

tossing it into the Mississinewa Reservoir. Afterwards, the brother took off for Texas. The night of the slaying, Artie Wick had dropped by to visit her boyfriend. When Artie herself suddenly left for Florida in December, 1983, Indiana police speculated she might have seen too much and was running for her life. The suspicion that someone might have tracked her down to silence her was something Indiana authorities seriously considered when she vanished in March. The two brothers eventually returned to Indiana, stood trial in June, 1984, and were acquitted.

Meanwhile, Artie made it to Tampa and linked up with her sister, Becky, who'd already made the move to Florida. For the next couple of months, Artie wandered up and down the Gulf Coast's metropolitan area—worked for a while at a waitressing job in St. Pete, then went to Clearwater for a spell, then on up to Tarpon Springs and back again, working a few days here, a couple of weeks there. Detective found where she'd worked at a Dunkin Donuts in Clearwater for two weeks, quit, then came back and worked two more days before quitting again. The manager there knew that Artie had dated a driver for one of the cab companies. The investigators also picked up a rumor that she'd moved in with a Florida Highway Patrol trooper she'd met at the donut shop.

The rumor turned out to be half true. The guy wasn't a trooper, but he was an officer with the Clearwater Police Department, who was nervous and upset at being sucked into a major murder investigation involving a notorious serial killer and his old girlfriend. In fact, the cop, Gerald Evans*, was so overwrought, he was almost incoherent during much of his interview with Detective Rick Rodriguez. Despite his agitated state, Evans still managed to convey a clear image of an unhappy young woman who might easily accept a ride from a handsome, smiling, soft-spoken, polite, well-dressed young man driving a big red car, in the hopes that this one, finally, would be the man of her dreams.

Yes, Evans conceded, he had met the woman he knew as Ann Wick when she was working at Dunkin Donuts where he often stopped on his breaks. Asked where Ann was living at the time, Evans replied that Artiss had moved several times during their

brief, "friendly-type dating" relationship. They had gone out a few times, but the relationship had never gone any farther.

Evans said he hadn't known Becky, Artiss' sister, very well, because she and Artiss were very different. Artiss, he said, was "real quiet" and "very friendly." Evans thought she might have had another boyfriend after they dated, but he wasn't clear about that. He does know that about a month after their last date Artiss called from New Port Richy, very upset about some "domestic problems" she was having with a man she was living with. Evans went down and picked her up, and Artiss stayed with him for a few days. Evans denied knowing anything about a possible pregnancy.

Evans said that after Artiss met the Nichols family and moved to Tampa, he never heard of her again until early April, when a mutual friend told him that his former girlfriend had been reported missing.

In the end, the death of Artie Wick brought the victim count to ten known bodies. But it was only by a freak chance that her remains were found at all.

"Artiss Wick," "Pops" Baker reflected, "was our 'freebie.' We swapped a murder confession for some furniture. His ex–wife wanted his furniture and belongings. We had seized everything, because a lot of the stuff we found in his apartment had been stolen from the homes where he'd raped the women. She wanted some of the things that were actually his. So the defense attorney swung a deal, and Bobby admitted to the Wick killing, if we'd release the stuff to his ex–wife and if we wouldn't charge him with the murder.

"I interviewed him briefly on that right in the courtroom. Took him into a jury room and asked him about it. Of course, at this time we were all making Lana Long number one. But Artiss Ann Wick was killed in March. He said he had picked her up on 301, up around the Fowler area [Which would have been several miles she would have had to travel, barefoot, from where she last waved to Terrena Nichols.] She was walking, Long said, which at least was consistent with the story that she'd gone out to get some cigarettes. We found her all the way down on the Manatee County line. But

even with the mess we found there, the ligatures stuck out like a sore thumb, especially the control, the leash. The two ligatures around the wrists, the distances, between them, that telltale four-teen–inch–long control rope. All this was to allow the victims enough freedom to be able to move so they could have sex.

"He gave us that one. I told him, 'Bobby, you know that by admitting to this you're telling us that Lana Long was not number one.' He wouldn't say anything about that. In fact, he wouldn't say anything more about why he did it," Baker said.

Society is currently experiencing a spasm of self–absorption in which every violent act is traced to a twisted, abused childhood, freeing the actor of responsibility for his actions. Bobby Joe Long has been riding that "poor me" wave since he was a toddler and, as an adult, has refined his "victimness" into a skillfully produced psychodrama in which he is both star and scapegoat. In one of his studies, Dr. Joel Norris ticked off the entire shopping list of reasons why Bobby Joe Long believed he should not be held responsible for his chilling, cold–blooded career of rape and murder:

"...physiological, behavioral, and experiential factors contributed to his extreme violence. The type of glandular disorder that produces gender misidentification puts Long in a possible high–risk group for confrontation with the criminal justice system. That risk was compounded exponentially by Long's head injuries, resulting in lesions to his temporal lobe and a loss of control over his violent impulses. His upbringing, in which he was dominated by his mother, who moved him from place to place and who shared a bed with him, made him more than distrustful of women and lit a flame of hostility that has continued to burn. His marriage to Cindy, based as it was on her manipulativeness, only fueled the fire and created a personality disorder in which manipulative women became Long's enemies. Finally, his near fatal motorcycle accident, which caused extensive brain damage, removed the last vestiges of neurological control over his behavior. Although he was aware of what he was doing and was consciously opposed to his actions, he was unable to stop himself from committing more than fifty rapes and nine (sic)

358

murders. Fear of punishment kept him from seeking professional help during the course of his career, although he realized that he was unable to control his almost reflex impulses. In the end he finally put a stop to his career by letting one of his victims go free and simply waiting for the police to catch him."

One of the detectives who hunted him for seven months, disagreed, "Bobby Joe Long killed because he enjoyed it. And if we hadn't caught him, he'd still be out there killing—just because he likes to kill."

From the moment the Task Force took him down, Bobby Joe Long protested that the only reason they got him was because he wanted to be got. He told police that when they cuffed him and hauled him away. He told the same story to reporters, and he repeated it when Dr. Joel Norris visited him in the Florida State Prison:

"I knew when the police task force was announced that I was running out of time," Long insisted, according to Norris. "I was sick, heaving my guts up every morning. I wanted to be stopped. I should have gotten out of the area, but I wanted to get caught. I could have gone anywhere in Florida, kept on raping and murdering, and the police would never have found me. I could have gone back to California and done the same thing. Then, right before I was caught, the police stopped me just to check on some report of a robbery in the area. But they took my license and looked over the car and then let me go. I knew they were following me then. I'm not completely stupid not to know what the police were doing. It was just a matter of days, so I made myself visible and gave them all the time they needed to arrest me. Even Cindy called me and asked me if I'd heard about all the rapes in my area. As if she wasn't giving me a clue that the police were on to me and that they'd already called her. [Not true.] But I wanted to be stopped because I couldn't stop myself."

None of the officers involved in the manhunt for the Tampa killer buy for a second Bobby Joe Long's protestations that he

couldn't help himself and that he really wanted to be caught in order to stop the killing.

"All the information Lisa provided help us zero in on him," Terry said. "It was the last link. Of course, Bobby Long would have you believe that he knew he was going to get caught, but he released her anyway.

"That's bullshit.

"He still thought he was smarter than we were. We would have gotten him eventually, but I don't know how many more victims might have gone down had it not been for Lisa McVey."

"I've worked probably five hundred homicides," "Pops" Baker added quietly. "Certainly, Bobby Joe is one I'll never forget.

I can't believe, I won't believe that he just said 'I'm going to let this one [Lisa McVey] go so they'll catch me.' Won't buy that in a million years. He made a mistake, and that's what we prayed for. Most girls, if they'd been in Lisa's place, might have gone insane and we'd have gotten nothing out of them. He just picked a girl that was sharp as a tack and smarter than he was and handled him. He didn't handle her. I don't think she deliberately made a decision to remember as many details as she could. She's just that way, and her almost total recall expedited the process immensely. We would have got him, unless he moved to another area. And, of course, after our detectives made that field stop, he was in the process of getting out. He was emptying out the water bed and going somewhere. He was making his move.

"I think that the amazing thing about this guy is that while he was killing these women, he was still violently attacking and raping women in those home invasions and not murdering them. Turn right around the next day or the next week, pick up a girl and kill her. There was no question that he absolutely hated women. Some he killed to satisfy something inside him. But I have no answer why he killed some and not the others. I doubt if anyone does. Not even Bobby. Lots of psychiatrists are making a lot of 'educated' guesses. But nobody really knows the answer."

Lt. Gary Terry has his own private thoughts about the killer who haunted his nightmares for so long.

"The best word for Bobby Joe Long or others of that type is predator," Terry said. "Smooth, cunning and very dangerous. Just lives to kill. If Bobby Joe Long was ever set free again, all you'd have to do is follow the trail of bodies to him because he'll kill and kill again. That's all he will ever do. He enjoys it.

"I heard his excuses, his explanations—abused child, broken home—we have so much of that, but I don't buy it. Maybe all that contributed to what he became, but Bobby Joe Long is just one mean predator. He preyed on these people and he'd prey on anybody else if he ever got out.

"So why should we think he'd stop at ten?

"And who's to say that's all he's done. I firmly believe he killed more than that. Will we ever find out? The only one who can answer that question is Bobby Joe Long."

REPORTER: *So going back to the thing about what you were feeling, what you were feeling throughout, not in terms of the violence, but in terms of the victims and the families of the victims...*

BOBBY: *Yeah, ummm, well I got to be honest about it, Okay? You talking about families of these girls, maybe two of them had families that gave a shit about them. Maybe. You know, I'm just guessing. I don't know. The rest of them were sluts out on the street. If somebody cared so damn much about them why were they out on the street? You understand what I mean? I mean I don't want to ... they have no right, what happened to them wasn't right. Okay?...Nobody deserves that. Nobody deserves what happened to any of those girls. Nobody does. But you asked me about the families and this is my feelings on the families. How, you know if your daughter was out working on Nebraska Avenue for twenty bucks a pop, anybody that drives along, how much do you care about her?*

REPORTER: *How about the victims themselves?*

BOBBY: *That's another story. Like I said, I don't think anybody deserves what happened to them. Anybody...But, you know, what's some street hooker going to do? Oh, oh, oh, I was raped. Who cares.*

REPORTER: *But they weren't all street hookers?*

BOBBY: *A couple of them weren't. But they were pretty close.*

361

Pretty close...You don't want to go down Nebraska Avenue if you're a decent type.

REPORTER: *Once she got it, did you feel that she deserved it?*

BOBBY: *Yeah, I guess I did. Then I did.*

REPORTER: *So that helped you do it while you were doing it, right?*

BOBBY: *Well you know, I don't really think that ... like I've tried to say, I don't believe that I had the intention of killing anybody when I picked them up. McVey is a good example of that again. You know? If I had the intention of picking somebody up and raping them and killing them, McVey would be dead. McVey would have been out in a field somewhere or with her neck broke or whatever. She wouldn't be walking around now. Does that make sense?*

REPORTER: *Yeah, it does, but what about the rest of them, the rest of them did end up...*

BOBBY: *They did and like I said, they all were that pretty certain type. (CBS News Interview)*

▲   ▲   ▲

Part FIVE

THE TRIALS

A LETTER FROM BOBBY JOE

I'm pissed, I'm helpless, this can't go on much longer. Fuck everybody, if I could I'd Nuke the whole fuckin world. Fuck em all! Follow this. I won't die in the chair. I'd much rather OD on any-thing...Anythings better than being a Crispy Critter, and just going to sleep sounds a whole lot better to me! All my thoughts are on getting out though, and pills or anything else is way down the road, only after all else fails and I still have the very good chance somethings fucked up in my brain. I've taken some hellatious clouts to the head, and I'm educated enough in anatomy & physiology and med-icine and experienced enough in dealing with head injuries to know it is a real possibility.

▲　　▲　　▲

Now began the legal contest over the person of Bobby Joe Long, confessed serial killer and sexual predator.

Although none knew it at the time, the battle line was drawn the instant that Bob Price and Randy Latimer sat down across from Bobby Joe in the small room in the Hillsborough County Sheriff's Office to begin their interrogation. At some point during that exhausting confrontation, the Florida Supreme Court decided, the detectives, intentionally or not, had crossed too far over the line, a ruling that ultimately produced two death sentence reversals, new trials, and a greatly extended life expectancy for the killer.

For the many defense lawyers who were to move in and out of the case, the guilt or innocence of Bobby Joe Long was never the issue. Their reality was much more basic than that: Life or Death.

▲   ▲   ▲

It's another Sunday morning—but without the terrible taint and stench of dead bodies left too long in the sun.

After so many harrowing, horrifying, crime–scene Sundays, the setting this time is an arena where Justice finally sits in judgement of the woman–killer—and not the other way around. Other than a swarm of news hounds, still smarting that they hadn't been notified in advance of the dramatic finale in the movie-theater parking lot, the Hillsborough County Sheriff's Office in Ybor City is all but deserted. Most of the detectives who have worked nonstop for six months tracking Bobby Joe Long, have taken some much–deserved time off to be with their families.

But some have gathered in a warm, windowless courtroom in the county jail building, which is used only on special occasions. They're here out of a strong sense of duty, or because, they can't turn the case loose or because, like everyone else in the Bay area, they're just plain curious. The semi–public appearance of Bobby Joe Long at his first presentment hearing qualifies as the special event of the year, if not the decade, for these lawmen who, for the first time in their careers, have peered into the abyss of a serial killer's mind—and come away forever changed.

For the news media, and for some of the police who jockeyed for seats in the tiny courtroom for this rare Sunday morning session, this would be their first look at the killer who had prowled the city's streets and neighborhoods for months, raping and murdering.

At 9:03 a.m., a side door leading to the court's holding cell swung open and Bobby Joe Long, wrists shackled to a body belt, ankles manacled, shuffled into the room, surrounded by stony–faced, muscular guards. He blinked briefly at the audience jammed into the narrow benches. Every eye in the room was on the man dressed in the prison–blue jumpsuit with "COUNTY JAIL" stenciled in big black letters across the back. All had vague,

preconceived notions of what a serial killer should look like. Few expected what they got—a chubby-faced guy, eyes wide with fear, who looked so...so ordinary!

Hillsborough County Judge Perry Little took his seat at the bench, determined that, despite the circumstances and the intense scrutiny from the media, this extraordinary hearing would go off with the customary dispatch of any other initial presentment hearing. As Judge Little carefully read the nine counts of kidnaping, eight counts of sexual battery, and eight counts of murder in the first degree, Bobby Joe Long stood before the bench, swaying slightly back and forth. Public defender Joseph Benito, whose prosecutor brother would later convince a jury that Bobby Joe Long deserved the death sentence, stood at his side. Task force detectives, tense and ready to pounce, hovered behind the defendant.

Long spoke only twice during the proceedings. "Yes, sir," he answered softly, when the judge asked him, "Are you Robert J. Long?" And he replied, "Right," when asked if he wanted the public defender's office to handle his case. Within five minutes, almost before the restless reporters could open their notepads, the hearing was over. Strong hands grabbed Long by each arm and hustled him out of the courtroom, back to his steel isolation cell.

The news of Long's arrest was applauded along West Kennedy Boulevard and in the joints lining Nebraska, where the air of relief was almost palpable. One of the dancers on the Nebraska Avenue flesh strip hunched over newspaper spread across the bar, her finger tracing the details of the spectacular arrest. Well, that's fine, she shrugged, but how about a more instant brand of justice, one that would fit the nature of the crimes. "They should let us women have at him," she muttered. "He didn't show us any mercy. Why should we show him any?"

Elsewhere, the stunning news that the murder spree was over and the killer in chains evoked far different reactions. At her home in Hollywood, between Miami and Ft. Lauderdale, Cindy Long Levy hung up after taking the late-night call from the Hillsborough County Jail and slumped to the floor in shock, as though someone had punched her hard in the gut. Disbelief battled painful reality.

Bobby Joe, the man she had married, the father of her children—a killer! And the way things had been going between them recently, Cindy was seriously thinking about giving in to Bobby Joe's pleas and marrying him again. As far as she could tell, he was the same old Bob Long, except older now and more mature.

The arrest also sent shock waves rumbling up through the Appalachian chain to the narrow, clapboard house in Kenova, where Joe and Louella Long struggled to cope with the news that their only child, whom they'd always suspected might be a little screwed up in the head, was, in fact, a pitiless rapist and a demented multiple murderer.

"Everywhere he turned, his life has been a dead end. It's been torture," Louella Long wept. "We were worried about him. He had such a terrible personality. He was so unlucky, sad and lost. He had so much hate for me. He hated me for leaving his father and the hate just kept building in him."

Bobby Joe had last called home on October 20—a few days after celebrating his 31st birthday by savagely raping and strangling Karen Dinsfriend and Virginia Lee Johnson. He boasted at the time that he'd been offered a plum job teaching scuba diving aboard one of the major cruise ships that sailed the Caribbean. But, he added, he hadn't decided whether to accept it or not.

The next call from their son came from the Hillsborough County Jail.

"He said he couldn't face us now," Joe Long recalled, reaching out to pat Louella's hand. "I can't accept him doing this, no sir. How can a man just destroy himself like that? How can you explain it? I wonder if he can explain it. I wonder if he understands it himself."

As expected, the capture of the serial killer, announced at a prime–time press conference which involved the heads of all the agencies comprising the Task Force, sparked a media feeding frenzy that became the focus of a scathing Memorandum of Impression filed by Long's Public Defender attorneys. The Memorandum captured the level of intense excitement and morbid curiosity that the killings aroused throughout the Bay area. Bobby Joe's defense

attorney insisited that his client could not possibley get a fair hearing because the media had already tried and convicted him. Defense counsel cited specific instances, including the unusual Sunday-morning hearing, where the media had been allowed access to Bobby Joe and been allowed to audiotape or film the proceedings for broadcast purposes. The attorney further claimed that the "nightly rehash" of the events was detrimental to his client, and claimed that Bobby Joe was the "...subject of the flimsiest, vague, unspecified, unsupported allegation of which he is in all probability not involved." The Task Force came under fire, too, for allegedly not checking their facts and allowing those same facts to be broadcast by an "irresponsible" media.

The fact that most, if not all, of those allegations were indeed true was beside the point. Still, Charles O'Connor, the lawyer from the public defender's office appointed to represent the killer, was so upset by the "unbelievably pervasive" publicity that he argued for the dismissal of the present Grand Jury, since it was so tainted by the media accounts of the crimes that it couldn't possibly hear the evidence against Long fairly and without prejudice. (First–degree murder defendants in Florida must be formally accused by a Grand Jury indictment.)

Emotions in the community were running so high due to the media hysteria that Bobby Joe Long's arrest ignited, that the murder suspect could easily become the victim of "a retaliatory feeling in the community," O'Connor argued. "I don't believe he's going to be able to find a fair and impartial Grand Jury." O'Connor urged a change of venue for the Grand Jury, far removed from the highly charged emotional atmosphere of Hillsborough County. The motion was denied.

Thus on Wednesday, November 28, the Hillsborough County Grand Jury indicted Bobby Joe Long on charges that he murdered eight women during a six–month period, beginning the previous May. He was also indicted on charges of kidnaping all eight of the victims and raping seven of them.

A month later, another Grand Jury meeting in neighboring Pasco County returned another indictment charging Bobby Joe

with the kidnaping, rape, and murder of Virginia Lee Johnson.

Almost from the moment police slapped the cuffs on Bobby Joe Long, attorneys from the public defender's office rose to protest the circumstances of the initial police interrogation of the suspect. The PDO lawyers were particularly incensed that Sgts. Price and Latimer may have continued their questioning after Long had asked for an attorney, as was his Constitutional right. Once he did so, they declared, all police questioning should have stopped. That point remained a hotly contested issue throughout the trials and, in fact, became the basis for one Florida Supreme Court conviction reversal, and played a secondary role in another reversal.

But the way Bob Price told it, the detectives had gone by the book in scrupulously reading Long his rights to an attorney and in their handling of the lengthy interrogation. Sure, maybe they booby–trapped him, talking first about Lisa McVey, letting him think that's all they had on him, and then suddenly ambushing him with the gruesome crime-scene photos of the murder victims. But that was part of the head games all good investigators played.

"We were very specific in discussing the type of evidence we had against him in the McVey case," Price said. "Once we had received all of the information that we felt was necessary in that case, it was time to confront him with the murders.

"Sgt. Latimer started by asking Bobby if he was familiar with physical evidence, like tire impressions, fibers, fingerprints, that type of thing. Bobby said yes, he understood what physical evidence was. Randy asked if he was familiar with the F.B.I. and their reputation for handling evidence and how highly qualified they were. Bobby again responded, 'Yes, I am.'

"The best procedure—in any interview or interrogation, I personally like to have some type of object, something that he's familiar with, something that will definitely convince him that I know what I'm talking about, so I excused myself from the room.

I went out and got five photographs of victims. The photographs were pictures of the young ladies when they were in fact alive, not dead. I attempted to find something else. The only other thing I

could get my hands on was the knife which had been recovered, and I was not going to take the knife back in there; it was too large.

"When I reentered the room, I handed the photographs to Sgt. Latimer who had moved his chair closer to Bobby, and he asked him if he had ever picked up any prostitutes. Bobby said, 'Yes, down around Miami.' Randy said, 'What about Tampa?'

"Bobby started getting very uneasy, shifting in the chair, body movement, crossing his arms. He says, `I don't like...I don't like the atmosphere since...—talking to me— ...since you've come back.' He said the—what were his exact words?—the complexion— `The complexion of things have changed since Price came back. I think I might need an attorney.'

"I said, 'Why would you need an attorney? Nothing's changed.' "Anyway, he definitely became uneasy when Sgt. Latimer asked him about picking up prostitutes in Tampa. I believe he said no, that he hadn't. Then Sgt. Latimer started one by one showing him photographs and asking him if he'd ever seen any of these women before. He stopped with the last photograph. He spent more time on the last photograph than the first four. He made some remarks about, 'She looks familiar, but I don't really think—like I seen her around someplace.' You know, something to that effect....

"Randy said 'Look, we're not here to ask you if you did this. We know that you did this, and we want to know why.' Randy explained to him about the Vogue tire, and that's what impressed Bobby the most. He went over the fibers. We've now got your car, we have flown experts in from Washington to examine your car. We have connected four or five of the homicides. We got you. There is no doubt. We just indicated to Bobby plain and simple, 'Look, it's not a matter of did you do this, we know you did this. We can prove you did this. This is not to make our case; our case is made or you wouldn't be here. It's that simple.'

"He looked off, looked down, just didn't seem to be upset at all, and then made the remark, 'Well, I guess you got me.' And Randy says, 'Explain that. What do you mean?' And Bobby said, 'Yeah, I killed them.' "

Naturally, Bobby Joe Long's opinion of his capture and interro-

gation was markedly different in fact, from that of his captors.

By early December, the news of Long's arrest on multiple homicide and rape charges had circulated through other law enforcement agencies throughout Florida and much of the southeastern United States. Lt. Terry was so overwhelmed with requests for information on the killer that he urged Sheriff Heinrich to call a meeting, invite all those other agencies to send representatives, and air everything out at once. Dozens of detectives, lugging stacks of unsolved case files with them, showed up for the symposium. Rape and homicide cases from as far away as New York State were examined for a match, but only two were pertinent. Palm Beach County detectives were able to clear at least one rape case with the information that was gathered at the symposium. But, unfortunately, the statute of limitation had run out so Long couldn't be charged with the crime. The same was true of most of the other cases—either the evidence against Long was too tenuous or it was too late to file charges. One exception was the kidnaping and rape of Miami hooker Evelyn Moore. The charges were later dropped, after Bobby Joe was sentenced to death on the murder charge.

▲   ▲   ▲

A LETTER FROM BOBBY

Its pretty fucking desperate as you know. Like I've said if a couple of things don't pan out, its gonna come down to something desperate or dead...
I know too, anybody can be bought.
But until the book or movie or whatever comes out, I don't have that kind of money and I know the offers will come in after the trials over.

▲   ▲   ▲

When the case of State of Florida v. Bobby Joe Long finally reached the courts, the trials and hearings often took on the aura of a made–for–television movie, hand–tailored to accommodate every

quirky taste in the book. There was, for instance, the conflicting testimony from the battery of psychiatrists who paraded to the stands to describe Bobby Joe's quirky upbringing; his questionable, incest–tinged sex life with his mother; and his ghastly head injuries, which supposedly revved up his sex drive into triple overdrive. One defense strategy turned on claims that overdoses of pornography aroused Long's insatiable desire to kill. There was even a serious challenge to the First Amendment of the Constitution, with the psychotic killer on one side and the entire CBS television network stacked up on the other side.

Once, during a recess in one of Long's many court appearances, Gary Terry was standing in the hallway when spectators emerged from the courtroom. He overheard a group of women who had been attending the hearings discussing the case.

"Just to look at him," simpered one of the spectators, a middle–aged, matronly woman speaking of Long, "you'd never think that he's a serial killer. He's so nice looking. Even kind of sexy.

"I couldn't believe what I was hearing," said Terry, years later, shaking his head over the memory. "What did they expect a serial killer to look like? Serial killers don't go around with an X carved in their foreheads. They look just like you and me. They're ordinary—and that's one of the things that makes them so dangerous. Since they don't look like a serial killer, they get away with murder. It's the perfect cover."

Dr. Helen Morrison, director of The Evaluation Center in Chicago, has spent hours interviewing serial murderers.

"On the surface, she reads from a newspaper, 'they are charming, helpful, almost nice. They're not bizarre. They don't foam at the mouth or have weird stares. They're not crazy or delusional. It's only when you regress them to a more childlike psychological state that you see how chaotic they are inside.' They know they've murdered. They just don't care that what they have destroyed is a human life. They have a total lack of empathy for a human being."

▲   ▲   ▲

A LETTER FROM BOBBY

I've put out the word that I want to start dragging the anchor, delaying tactics which will put
just trials at about 2-3 yrs. Remember I have 9 of
those babies, and even if they do get their "2"
death sentences (they'll never be happy with just
one that may be overturned) will still drag the
other trials out as long as possible—who knows, if I
don't get out of here, maybe by the time it comes to
zap me, they won't be doing that anymore! You never
know!

▲   ▲   ▲

Shortly after the first of the year (1985), when Bobby Joe had
been in jail for two months, a Tampa Bay private eye named
Richard Powell contacted Sgt. Bob Price with disturbing information that opened an alarming new avenue of the Bobby Joe Long
investigation, and had ominous personal overtones for Price,
"Pops" Baker, and Randy Latimer.   Powell, who'd been in the
PI business in the Bay area for thirteen years, said that he'd
received a call from an inmate at the Hillsborough County jail
named Jay Robert Shideler. Only twenty-six years old at the time,
Shideler was, nevertheless, a jail–wise con whose rap sheet showed
charges of delivery of cocaine; battery of a law enforcement officer
(for which he did a year in the county lockup), and, as of
November 15, 1983, first-degree murder and armed robbery.
   According to Powell, Shideler had gotten in touch with him a
couple of months earlier. The admitted dope runner and killer
wanted Powell to help him set up a deal whereby, in return for a
reduced sentence, Shideler would voluntarily lecture schoolchild-
ren about the evils of cocaine, using himself as an example of how
someone could be turned from the path of righteousness by the
demon drug. If it could happen to an all– American kid like him,
Shideler intended to moralize, it could happen to anybody.
   No one in law enforcement took Shideler's transparent deal

seriously. But now Jay Shideler was back in touch with Powell with something more solid, with which he hoped to get out of a long prison term. He had the ear and confidence of Bobby Joe Long, the worst killer to hit Hillsborough County and the current media darling. Bobby Joe was talking to him, Shideler confided to Powell, getting into the stuff he'd done and plotting a sensational escape that involved killing Bob Price and Randy Latimer, the two detectives who'd "wheedled" the confession out of him. Long was also obsessed with killing his former girlfriend, Suzette Rice and wanted Shideler to line up some of his street buddies on the outside as contract killers. But that wasn't all. Good jailhouse lawyer that he was, Shideler had convinced Bobby Joe to open up to him in a series of notes and letters. Shideler wanted nothing more than to do his duty in preventing these terrible events.

However, according to what the private investigator told the police, Shideler also had grandiose visions of writing a book about Bobby Joe Long and making a ton of money off of Bobby Joe's confessional letters. At the very least, Shideler hinted to Powell, he hoped to work a deal with the State Attorney's office for a reduced sentence or an early release.

When Richard Powell came to Sgt. Price with Shideler's information, the veteran homicide detective sat up and took notice. He had dealt with this character in the recent past—in fact, Price had helped put him in jail on a murder one charge. His dealings with Jay Shideler had left a lingering bad taste in Price's mouth. Sgt. Bob Price had little use for the likes of Jay Robert Shideler, but since they had to occupy the same bloody arena where only police and killers go, Price was prepared to deal with Shideler on his own terms.

As soon as Price learned of Jay Shideler's collection of letters, Price called in the Hillsborough County sheriff's office. Together, Price and "Pops" Baker decided to con the con man. Let Shideler go along believing that a deal might be in the offing. Nobody made any promises, but as long as Shideler was so determined to do his civic duty by duping Bobby Joe into thinking he was on his side, nobody was going to stop him.

"Jay's a very emotional young man; he also comes from a very unusual background." Price said. "He spent time in prison up north somewhere. He had taken the rap, so to speak, for a bunch of other guys, and he said he had learned a hell of a lesson because everybody else talked. He was going to play the big man and refuse to talk, and he got ten years out of it....he learned that we cannot place an agent in the Hillsborough County jail to solicit comments from inmates in regards to murders, rapes, robberies, or anything else. He learned that information gotten that way is illegal and inadmissible—but not if it comes through a third party, like if he told his brother and his brother came to us.

"I believe that that's what he did in this situation. Jay figured I got this guy, killed ten people in a cell next to me. I've got ninety-nine years to do. Let's see if I can come up with something that will help me reduce my sentence. So he got to talking to Bobby Long and they started passing their notes back and forth.

"Bobby Joe wanted Shideler to contact some people on the outside who could take a sawed-off shotgun to a certain location around Silver Springs and hide it. Then Long would contact Randy and myself and say: 'Look, guys, come on back. I'm going to take you to some more bodies, but I don't want nobody but you two.' He was going to take us to that location, utilize the shotgun to kill us both. He was going to wear Randy's clothes, because I was too fat or something. Bobby Joe was very serious about this, and he referred to it as the 'hunt.' We got page after page after page how he planned it, replanned it, planned it again, replanned it. And all the time Jay is feeding him:, 'Yeah. Well, my friends say they can come through. What kind of shotgun do you want? Would you rather use a handgun?' You know, that type of thing."

Jay Shideler was, in "Pops" Baker's opinion, just a common criminal who knew how to work the system. On the other hand, Bobby Joe Long, at that point, hadn't yet developed the mentality necessary to survive in the brutal world of big-time prison, and although his macho image of himself refused to admit it, Bobby Joe badly needed a friend inside to show him the ropes.

"Shideler," Baker described, "was a con who knew how to play

all sorts of jailhouse games, and he sort of snaked Bobby Joe into it and started pumping him for information. And he got a bunch of it, because Bobby really got to trusting him."

According to "Pops" Baker, while Shideler insisted that had no intention of helping Long escape, he did have visions of maybe writing a book about Long. If things worked out, and the state wanted to show its appreciation for his cooperation, maybe Shideler could get a little preferred treatment, or help in reducing his sentence. Therefore, Jay continued, he encouraged Bobby Joe to write his "novel" as a way of keeping the killer talking.

In one of his letters, Bobby Joe conceded that Jay was "awful close" in his speculation about why the murders occurred. The reply was in response to one of Shideler's letters, in which he had suggested several reasons why the killing began:

A. A female did you wrong, feel inferior, driven by the hatred.

B. Had bad experiences with a chick, "someone you loved fucked you." Bobby called all women "cunts."

C. You're a kinky sex pervert, had a male or female accomplice, group sex, bondage, maybe it got out of hand and you all killed someone.

The letters Powell received from Jay Shideler were passed on to Lt. Gary Terry and Assistant State Attorney Mike Benito. They decided that the plot had gone far enough— the risk that something unforeseen might happen was too great to allow it to continue. Jailers moved Long from his isolation cell in the same cell block housing the other prisoners to a special holding cell in the infirmary, where contact with other inmates was almost impossible.

That was just fine with Detective "Pops" Baker. "If Shideler and Powell had gone along with this thing," he recalled, "Bobby Joe Long might have actually gotten away with what he called his 'hunt', the plan he had to kill Bob Price and me or Randy Latimer. He would have got us out there to look for another body and if there had been people waiting for us, we would have been had. If he had said there was another body and wanted to show us, we would have believed him in a heartbeat. And he knew that. But we

shut him down and put him in an isolation cell. Decided not to play that game out, since we really didn't know who was involved.

"For all his big-shot talk, Bobby just didn't have the right connections to get the job done."

Bobby Joe Long apparently knew enough to destroy the notes and letters he received from Jay Shideler, so there's no record of what they contained. However, reading between the lines of Bobby Joe's letters to Shideler, it seems obvious that he was responding to the more seasoned con's seductive enticements and empty promises that Jay's "people" would like nothing better than to help Mad Dog Long break out of jail and join them running dope and killing police. Long's letters reveal a progression from escape as a vague abstraction to his intricately detailed plans that included maps, gun placements, disguises, and escape routes. Finally, enough reality seeped through so that even Bobby Joe himself seemed to grasp just how really preposterous the whole idea was. Taken as a whole, the series of escape letters, like an onion being peeled, progressively lays bare the corrosion of Bobby Joe Long's mind, each layer more diseased than the one before.

▲   ▲   ▲

LETTERS FROM BOBBY

Jay Buddy, you know and I know I'll "definitely" get the chair, you have a good shot at it yourself. They're gonna fry Bill Boy eventually, its just gone fuckin crazy. Ok I never claimed to be insane, I don't believe your insane...But the State wants blood. They'll get it too... You can fool yourself if you want to, but in your own mind you know I'm right. Unfortunately. You know thats why I'm gonna go the escape route.

▲   ▲   ▲

I did try to "feel out" the two Detectives I told you about for the "hunt". I wrote them a note ask-

ing them to bring me one of my 3 pc. suits, shirt tie, shoes etc...for court. Two days later here they both were, with my shit...drooling!

They all still think I did some cunt in some bar across from bush gardens, and theyre pretty sure about one in Orlando. Man all I have to do is get word to those two drooling fuckers, theyd be here in an hour ready to go! Dripping & Drooling! I think the "HUNT" is the only real chance...I know if I could think of the right place, the "HUNT" would work.

▲   ▲   ▲

The courthouse is awfully tempting. Its just me and Baker in this room waiting to go to the court-room, and I know I could take Baker out easy. Yeah theres more outside the door but I keep wondering what if I got hold of Bakers piece. I'm qualified "expert" in everything from handguns to M-60 machine guns and I know if I came out that door with a piece, none of those fuckers are gonna try anything cause they have to know I have nothing to lose. They do!

Its not like that nigger they shot not too long ago. He was outside at 6 something in the morning when there were no innocent bystanders, and the officers were free to open up on him...It really would be good to drop kick Bakers head though. He's a wormy fucker!

▲   ▲   ▲

They'll never take any chances in transit except maybe for the hunt. I know these two guys. They think that I think we're all buddies. Nothing would make me happier than to blow them both into mush!

▲   ▲   ▲

Anyone who knows me knows that if given the shot, I'll take it! The police have a pretty fucking

377

accurate (amazingly) psychological profile on me. Thats one of the reasons whenever they transport me they have 4 people, and set up a security perimeter around the bldg I'm in. Bakers the one I was gonna bounce that pad-lock off his head the other day. I had that waist chain wrapped around my hand with about a foot hanging down on the end. At the very least it would have put him "out", probably safe to say it would have killed him. I'm standing there thinking soon as that second leg shackle is off--Wham, grab his gun and go for it. I knew there was one of them outside, no problem, but I wasn't sure where the other two were, or (even more important) had they left the keys in the car? My heart was doing double time and the adrenaline was pumping. It was a hard one to pass up. Yeah, I know, I look like a harmless little fuck. Don't believe it for a second. Its like last night when I would walk around behind that sargeant and the retard. Did you see how nervous they were anytime I was near them?

▲   ▲   ▲

Your shit out a luck buddy. Detective Sgt. Bob Price and Detective Sgt. Randy Latimer are the two I've been talking about.
They're mine!
You can have this ass-hole Baker, I know how you feel about that fucker Price.
Latimer's not so bad but they all lick their mamas asshole.
Sorry!

▲   ▲   ▲

We all know what kind of heats going to be around here if I bust loose, especially if Heckle and Jeckle get wasted...We both know 9 first degree murder charges, and all the rest--twenty some charges in all--all felonies. Thats not even counting Price

& Latimer, I don't have to tell you what happens
when police get wasted...They'll have every law
enforcement agency in the state, the Coast Guard,
and anybody else they can get (you forgot the Border
Patrol) are going to be after me. If I'm not out of
the state in five or six hours at most, this place
is gonna be sealed off like nothing you ever saw!
Have no doubt.

▲   ▲   ▲

My "hunt" is now complete, from beginning to when
I get my hands on the gun. Whether I'd kill these
guys in cold blood, I don't know...What do you
think, should I just come out blasting or should I
just cuff em so they'll be a long time getting
found? I'm gonna take both their guns, I.D.'s, and
one of them, Latimer, I think his clothes will even
fit me so I'll take his clothes. I know you don't
like Price, if you want I'll do his ass just for
you, and I'll tell him who its for first. If I kill
one, I'll have to do the other. No live witnesses,
I've learned that, I won't forget it...

▲   ▲   ▲

I "guarantee" you when we pull up to that bridge
it will be me in the back seat of a 2 door car, the
two stooges will be in the front. If your boys go
for it, they could go out and check the place out
before hand. Its the perfect place for something
like this. Clear field of fire, no cover, no other
cars could be within 3 or 4 miles without being
seen. Even if they have a homing device on the car
by the time anyone got there, its too late. I know
this area really good, we'd be gone before anyone on
a homer or a radio could get close and be on a busy
road, and have 2 different ways to go from there.
It's a cinch. All I need is some help. You know
somebody who'd like to fucking Sargeants served to

them on a plater, here they are! I won't be cuffed, they'd go for it, hell they suggested it when they first got me and I was in shock and exhausted and talked. I didn't lie to them. They know that and they trust what I say. This location falls in line with the pattern of the others [murders]. IT IS PER-FECT!

▲   ▲   ▲

Once I was out, I would do a total appearance change, so even if I was ever back in U.S. territory, nobody would recognize me... I know how to be diplomatic if I have to and I've mingled with every class of people from street "bag" people to million-airs and I can do any way I need to to get by.
What about papers, I.D., passport & shit like that?
Hey, a few years, the heats off, new I.D., blonde hair, blue eyed contact glasses, no moustache! My own mamma wouldn't know me! I could visit here, or move family to me, wherever. Its a hell of a lot better than life or Old Smoky, any way you look at it.
Your boys sound like the way to go! I know how drug people are, they don't fuck around, it comes time for bleeding--its fuckin Ingrams, uzis and M-16's no fiddely fuckin around. Lets put it this way. If you can get them to put it on the line for me, I'll go to the wall for them! Go ahead and try to set it up...Once theyre ready, I'll contact these "guys" and I guarantee you within two days we'll be at that bridge alone--just the 3 of us. No doubt in my mind!

▲   ▲   ▲

As soon as you hear from your people, let me know, I'm anxious to here what they say. I'm afraid I'm too "hot" and they may be afraid to have me

380

around. You said it yourself, I escape, two Dead
Police, all the other shit that have one me FBI's #1
man--pretty fuckin hot. Has to be a consideration
for your people. I just hope it don't scare em off.
But I'll tell you for a fact, man, I get out of here
and in twenty-four hours you wouldn't recognize me
if I ran into you on the street.

▲   ▲   ▲

I've been thinking a lot about "after." I'm sure
your people will see me as an asset, not a liabili-
ty. Not only do I know weapons, and their use, they
know I will kill, I hope they can see I'm not stupid. Put me in a 3 pc suit, I blend in with anyone,
anywhere. Dumb hillbilly fucks, to millionaires, I
can do it either way, or in between. I don't run my
mouth. I'm not a real trusting soul. I had you
checked out before I started to really talk to you.
What more can I say? Except lets go, I'm ready, my
adrenaline pumps just thinking about it. He who
laughs last, laughs best, I always say.
As far as working for these guys, Love to! As
long as its not catching shrimp.
They ever want somebody "hit" I'd be more than
happy!
They want someone to make a run—no problem!

▲   ▲   ▲

I'm sending a map as detailed as I can get. We
need to get going on this. Both our court dates are
just around the corner. Who knows what will happen
then? Send your friends the map...
You never told me what you told your people in
your letter. Talk to me! I'm still trying to reach
my boys. Who knows, they may come thru before yours.
They aren't CC's but they're Bikers and they're big
and Bad and hate police like we do! If my buddies
involved, I'll feel real good just knowin he's

there. He's never let me down, he has always acted first, ask questions later. Definitely one to have on "your" side.

Maybe you should go ahead and send this map to your boys.

If a couple of items of womens clothing could be planted down by the water and all fucked up to look like theyd been there a while, that would be a good touch.

If these guys are like the drug boys I used to know, they'll jump at the chance to waste two Detective Sgts. Its such a fuckin good plan. If they decide to help and have the firepower, soon as our car is stopped (where I marked on the map is the only real place for them to park) and I'm out, I'll haul ass once I'm ten ft away, two or three guys, well armed, twelve gauge pumps 00 Buck, its all over but the cryin.

▲   ▲   ▲

You didn't answer my note yesterday, the one with the map.

What do you think? I think it sounds real good, and I haven't even told you all the little details that are gonna make those two swallow it hook, line and sinker...

I'll be honest with you, I wouldn't murder those two guys. Not unless I had to, but if it comes to that -- no fucking around -- both of them are DEAD MEAT.

I started off with 5 or 6 good places, but narrowed it down step by step to this one. Its fucking perfect.

I need to "know" some details like who these guys are how well you know them, where are they, how do I contact them, do they know about me? Theres a lot riding on this (my life) and I need to know so I can make ALL the plans I have to! Talk to me! Don't mention this to ANYONE!

I've dealt with some cold blooded mothers and I don't want to end up with one in the head, floating in the fucking Gulf, feeding the sharks!

▲　　▲　　▲

If these guys are gonna come thru, your people, I hope its soon! Keep me posted. I knew a bitch from Carta Hana Columbia--she says its beautiful, and if all the cunts look like her--okay, and I know Peru has incredible broads.

▲　　▲　　▲

Theres no problem with the "hunt."
Moneys real tight, let me know what its gonna cost just for the piece.
Like I've said, I prefer twelve gauge pump (No auto) loaded and ready to go with the pull of the trigger. If not that 41, 44, 45 revolver (No auto).
If this goes down, it could get real hairy.
I would like to "know" I'm dealing with people who will not let me down.
Yeah, I'm not a very trusting soul and I've learned about fucking "live" witnesses!
I don't forget my lessons!
You write your people, tell em about me.
I want to see them somehow.
If nothing else, they can go to the western union office straight out my window.
At a set day and time, just so I can see them. I want to see them.
Moneys tough right now. But I can come up with a little.
Just me, I don't need any help!
All I need is a "reliable" piece!
Its gonna be my ass on the line. I don't plan to fuck up again!

Go thru this for me, OK we're all set and Humpty
& Dumpty cant be put together again.

Then what?

Like I said, this is serious, dangerous shit, I
want to know some details.

If these people get me out, they have a friend
for life, to the wall if need be!

Naturally you'll be a "priority."

Why haven't you gone the route with these guys?

I have to be absolutely, positively one hundred
percent sure in my own mind about the reliability of
these guys, and I want to see them, and the piece.

All they have to do is pull up in the W. Union
parking in daytime and hold it up so I can see it,
and see what I'm dealing for.

I assume these guys are "local."

What about papers, transport to S.A.   I mean I
want to KNOW whats going.   Its gonna be my life on
the line, I have to know I'm not being set up by
anybody!

I know these police will swallow it all! They're
so fucking sure about those other two bodies. They'd
be here an hour after I call em, and we'd be on our
way.

Hey what the fuck, a few years working for these
guys, a few bucks, no heat, I.D. change (hair,
glasses, shave) and a few bucks, I could always set
something up with my people.

Its better than dead or life behind bars. Eh!

Talk to me kid!

▲   ▲   ▲

Just thought of "another" little detail to add to
the plan for the hunt.   I've been giving a lot of
thought to how to go about initiating this whole
thing, without alerting the boys.   I've come up with
what I think is the "perfect solution"...I'll send
them a note say around 7:00 the night before its to
go.

384

They'll show up here before noon the next day I'm sure. In the note I'll just say "Its important I talk to you." They'll show, drooling as usual.

When they do show and ask whats going on, after all the hi, how are you shit, I'll ask them if they think the fact that I talked before, will help me in the trial? Of course they say, sure it will--blah blah blah, the fact that you talked without asking anything in return certainly will help. Yeah theyll only kill me five times instead of six.

So anyway, these guys aren't stupid and they'll read between the lines, and know why I'm asking this and the note and all, and since they (as well as my attorney and investigator) are still sure I killed that girl from the bar on Busch Blvd. I'll say OK, I know where we can find a couple of more bodies that haven't been found yet. Got all the information I need about the one from Busch from the clipping my guys keep throwing at me, make up some bullshit about a girl I picked up in Pinellas County, and since I already have charges on me there, I don't think theyll have much trouble buying it all!

I'm thinking theyll be pretty comfortable with it and not be on guard, which is good, and even the place is good, a couple of bodies were found not to far from there, I mean if I tried to lead them over to Carrollwood, they may be a little itchy.

As it stands (and I can bullshit pretty good) I'll just shit em to death all the way out there...

This is heavy duty shit, it may go in day time or night time, this "must" be taken into account and planned for accordingly...It will go, but I want it to go "Perfect." I don't want to fuck up and get myself killed. You gotta know, if I fuck this up, they'll blow me away, attempted escape or some such shit...

Its beautiful, whether the waters up or down, its beautiful, so the stock gets wet, no problem . If that puppies as I requested, sawed off, twelve gauge pump 2-3/4" Remington Express 00 Buck, safety off

385

and one in the chamber, its all over for the boys...I'd love to have some help, its such a setup I can handle it on my own, but I'd like some help.

Say I don't get any help Jay, what do I do after I take care of things there? Remember I'm gonna be in a cop car, which aint to fuckin neat. But like where do I go, how can I get the fuck out of the country FAST!

Let me know what you think--send it back with this book—talk to me. We need to get crackin on this thing, send your people this diagram, I think they'll agree its too sweet to pass by from start to finish.

Really the finish is the only thing I worry about.

TALK TO ME!

▲   ▲   ▲

I've been thinking a lot about all we've talked about the last few days.

It sounds like a script from a "B" movie.

▲   ▲   ▲

As Bobby Joe Long plotted his moronic breakout in blissful ignorance, the state prosecutors were making solid plans to go to trial—many times if necessary, or as long as it took to guarantee that this serial killer would die in the electric chair or, at the very least, spend the rest of his life in prison. The first trial on the docket was for the murder of Virginia Lee Johnson, the only murder case over which Hillsborough authorities had no control.

The trial's setting was the courthouse in Dade City, the county seat of Pasco County, about an hour's drive north of Tampa. The people who make up the Pasco County voter rolls, from which juries are drawn, are predominantly country folks—conservative, suspicious of interlopers from the big cities, the kind whose rock–solid beliefs are rooted in the admonition that God helps

those that help themselves. Do something wrong, you stand up and take your medicine. People did good things because they were good, and bad things because they were bad. Simple as that—and all the head doctors in the world weren't going to change anything.

Bobby Joe Long came to Dade City to be judged by a jury of his peers. And Bobby Joe Long's lawyers from the public defender's office subpoenaed psychologists and psychiatrists from far-off big cities and ivory–towered universities, whose task it would be to convince all those people sitting in the jury box that Bobby Joe Long raped and terrorized scores of women and strangled ten more because he slept with his mother until he was a teenager and had his brains scrambled in a motorcycle crash.

The religious people of Dade City and Pasco County were about to have a guided tour through the cesspool soul of a sex killer, a surreal trip they didn't ask for but would never forget.

Judge Ray E. Ulmer, Jr. was on the bench when jury selection began on April 22, 1985. Only five days earlier, another jury across Pasco County, in New Port Richey, had found Bobby Joe Long guilty on six counts of home invasion rape–robbery the previous March. The judge in that case had sentenced him to ninety-nine years on each of the six counts, for a total of 693 years, so Bobby Joe and his defense team didn't come into Ulmer's court with high hopes of getting favorable treatment. In a meeting in chambers before voir dire began, Long's attorney, Robert Norgard, offered to plead his client guilty to killing Virginia Johnson if the state promised not to seek the death penalty.

No deal, said the State.

The State's case, as presented by Pasco County's Assistant State Attorney Phil Van Allen, was as straightforward as you can get: Here is the victim. Here is the suspect. Here is the physical evidence—the hairs and fibers—that the FBI experts say indisputably ties them together. Here is Bobby Joe Long, in his own words, saying, yes, I raped and strangled Virginia Lee Johnson, and here's how I did it.

Bobby Joe Long's public defenders, Robert Norgard and Randall Grantham, found themselves in an awkward position.

387

Okay, they were forced to concede, Bobby Joe Long did kill Virginia Johnson, but he couldn't help himself. He was mentally unbalanced at the time, which is why he shouldn't be executed, and here are our psychiatric experts to explain why.

Thus a pattern was set that was to be repeated in all subsequent trials and hearings over the next nine years. The only hope Long's defense team had of saving his life was to focus on the client's bizarre psychopathology which, they claimed, had been aggravated by all the neurological damage he sustained in his several injuries. This, said the half-dozen psychiatric experts who over the course of five trials were to testify for the defense, was the justification for his becoming a violent, cold–blooded serial killer. It was a long–shot and the defense drew a blank.

As it was, not a single jury ever bought the argument that Bobby Joe's scrambled brains made him do it.

▲   ▲   ▲

A LETTER FROM BOBBY

You mentioned about not draggin the anchor.   It wasn't my idea, my attorney came up with it.   He knows there gonna get me, he also knows if theyre gonna get me they're gonna have to pay out the ass for it.   We have this lady shrink coming in from Chicago, a specialist in "Serial Killer". From the time she leaves her house, to the time she gets back to her house, its $150 per hour.   Add that to all the other tests and shit, its a small fortune.   "If" they get me, its not gonna be cheap. nine trials, I couldn't even begin to guess what its gonna cost, and it would drag out the trials alone for a couple of years anyway. Then appeals and all that shit.

▲   ▲   ▲

When the trial opened, the state didn't waste time trying to prove that Bobby Joe Long was sane and responsible for his actions

when he raped and murdered. The proof of that, Assistant State Attorney Phil Van Allen stated, was in the fact that he carried out his crimes in a cold, calculating, and deliberate manner, and then took careful steps to cover his tracks and escape detection—actions that fully demonstrated he knew exactly what his was doing.

Joe and Louella Long came from Kenova to be at their son's side during the trial. So did his ex–wife, Cindy. Most of the time, family members were excluded from the courtroom, since they might be called as witnesses for the defense. The three huddled on benches in the hallway or paced nervously back and forth, refusing to talk to reporters and ignoring the curious, accusatory looks from the usual gaggle of courtroom groupies.

Security was tight. Three hefty deputies from the Pasco County Sheriff's Office stopped visitors at the courtroom door and checked them with metal detectors. Inside, the regular contingent of court bailiffs was supplemented by another trio of stern–looking sheriff's deputies.

Each day, Bobby Joe Long arrived in court wearing a navy blue, three–piece suit and light–blue tie. His dark, wavy hair was neatly trimmed. Throughout the testimony, he sat quietly, fiddling with a pencil, occasionally conferring in whispers with Norgard and Grantham.

The first order of business was choosing a jury, something the defense had argued would be impossible in light of the publicity. To ensure that there would be enough potential jurors, Judge Ulmer ordered that two separate juror pools of two hundred each be called. With that many, he figured, there would be at least twelve who hadn't heard about the case and who could sit in fair judgement.

At least two of the potential jurors admitted they couldn't be fair because they were too personally involved. Sharon Trehuba of Dade City asked to be excused because she'd known one of the other women Long was accused of killing. Trehuba, a probation counselor for the Department of Health and Rehabilitative Services in Tampa, said that Kim Swann was one of her clients "a couple of years ago."

The other prospective juror, Charles McBride of Land O' Lakes, told the lawyers during voir dire that Bobby Joe Long had twice come to the home of a woman in his church, answering an advertisement the woman had placed in the newspaper offering typing services.

"She's religious," McBride added. "She felt she had been protected because Long did not attack her."

Finally, after nearly three full days of quizzing, the prosecution and the defense settled on a jury of eight women, four men, and one alternate that accurately reflected the rural, retirement–oriented character of Pasco County

Actual testimony began on Thursday morning, April 25. Phil Van Allen spent barely a day presenting the State's case, which included a string of forensic experts, witnesses who found the woman's scattered remains, the medical examiner's testimony, and the gruesome crime-scene photos. Mike Malone, the FBI hair and fiber specialist, flew in from Quantico to testify. In a detailed and graphic presentation, Malone patiently explained to the engrossed jurors how a hair remaining on Virginia Johnson's skull was similar to one found on the floorboard of Bobby Joe Long's car. He also testified that a single red fiber found in the skeleton's hair microscopically matched the carpet fibers from his car. The odds against that being a coincidence were astronomical. At some point, the dead woman had been a passenger, willingly or unwillingly, in Bobby Joe Long's flashy Dodge Magnum.

Despite the brevity of the trial, Van Allen still managed to inject some suspense into the proceedings by building his case to a dramatic climax with the playing of Bobby Joe Long's taped confession, in which he admitted picking up, raping, and strangling Virginia Johnson.

The jury and the courtroom observers listened raptly as Long's high–pitched, nasal voice described in cold, unemotional tones how he picked up a hooker who matched Johnson's description on Nebraska Avenue. After she agreed to have sex with him for thirty or forty dollars, Long said he drove to an empty parking lot behind Cheeks Lounge on Skipper Road in North Tampa.

It was there that he overpowered the young woman, stripped her, and tied her up with shoelaces that he just happened to have with him in the car. From there, he drove with her beside him all the way out to rural Pasco County, some fifteen or twenty miles, and found an isolated side road where he raped the helpless woman, strangled her with a shoelace, and dumped her nude and still-bound body in a cow pasture just off Morris Bridge Road.

At 10:53 a.m., Phil Van Allen switched off the tape recorder, and, in the sudden silence, turned to Judge Ulmer and said quietly, "The prosecution rests, Your Honor."

For all intents and purposes, the trial was over, since Long's attorneys decided not to call any witnesses on his behalf nor offer any defense.

Following a lunch break, Van Allen stood before the jury box to deliver his closing argument. He began softly, sadly almost, by reminding them of the missing victim, evoking a sorrowful portrait of Virginia Lee Johnson. "Who is—pardon me—who was Virginia Johnson?"

"Virginia Johnson was eighteen or nineteen years of age. Virginia Johnson was five–feet three–inches to five–feet five–inches. Blond hair. Green or blue eyes. Light skin. Well built with large breasts.

"Virginia Johnson was addicted to cocaine and heroin, apparently. Virginia Johnson drank too much. Virginia Johnson was a prostitute who turned tricks on Nebraska Avenue and Florida Avenue.

"Virginia Johnson had gonorrhea, and Virginia Johnson lived with any number of people.

"She came from Connecticut.

"She went to a V.D. clinic.

"I think that's it.

"Virginia Johnson was not the nicest lady in the world; prostitute, sold sex. That, however, does not mean that she deserved to die by strangulation at the hands of Bobby Joe Long..."

Van Allen went on to explain to the jury that premeditation, the element that separates first-degree murder form second-degree murder, had to be present. There is, he added, "...substantial, uncontradicted evidence of premeditation.

"And that is the cause of death.

"Virginia Johnson wasn't shot. It wasn't a situation where a person plans and pulls his gun, and shot, and said, 'I didn't mean to do that.'

"She wasn't stabbed to death, where a person said, 'I didn't mean to kill her, I just meant to hurt her.'

"She was strangled.

"I submit to you, ladies and gentlemen, that in order to strangle somebody, whether by use of a garrote or by your hands, that your hands or the garrote goes around the neck of the victim and you hold...and you hold...and you squeeze, until that person is dead.

"At any time you want to stop, at any time you want your victim to live, all you do is let go...

"Strangulation. Strangulation requires that pressure, until there is no more breath."

Other evidence of premeditation, Van Allen continued, was the ligature, a brand-new shoestring, that was used to strangle Virginia Johnson. And after Bobby Joe Long had picked up the woman he drove her fifteen or twenty miles, bound and naked, to the place of her death.

"He took her to a desolate, isolated country rural area, bound and naked," Van Allen thundered.

"He took her clothes when he left.

"Is there evidence of premeditation?

"It screams!

"Some of you were asked what you thought of when you looked at Bobby Joe Long. And some of you said that he was a nice-looking young man.

"Perhaps he is.

"But the evidence, ladies and gentlemen, the evidence and the law has shown you that that is the last face that Virginia Johnson saw before she died.

"That while that might be a nice-looking young man, the evidence has shown you that's the face of a murderer."

The defense countered with the argument that the State hadn't proved premeditation, which was a prerequisite for a verdict of

first-degree murder. At the worst, Bobby Joe should be found guilty of second-degree murder, which didn't carry the death penalty. The defense also attempted to shift at least part of the blame for her own murder onto Virginia Lee Johnson, suggesting that the young hooker's shady lifestyle was responsible for getting her killed. Russell Grantham reminded the jury that Virginia Johnson had lived with several men in her brief life, including a "kinky man" from Lutz. He further suggested that Virginia Johnson may have consented to being tied up, as part of a bondage freak's sex game that got out of hand and resulted in her unpremeditated, unintentional death.

The jury flatly disagreed. After retiring to consider the evidence, it took the eight women and four men only forty-four minutes to reach a verdict. At 4:07 p.m., jury foreman Russell Miller stood to deliver the verdict:

"Guilty of murder in the first degree. So say all we twelve."

That ended the guilt-or-innocence phase of the trial. But with capital cases in Florida, as in most other states, finding the defendant guilty is only the beginning. Next comes the penalty phase, in which the same jury listens to all the reasons the state believes the convicted person should be put to death. The defense counters with reasons why the defendant should be allowed to live but be imprisoned for life. Usually, this involves putting sobbing family members on the stand to plead for the accused, or psychiatric experts to testify that, murder notwithstanding, there were mitigating circumstances over which the accused had no control and that forced him to kill, although it was against his better nature.

In Bobby Joe Long's case, the defense employed both tactics.

After accepting the jury's guilty verdict, Judge Ulmer ordered the panel to return the next day for an unusual Saturday session, in which they would recommend which penalty would be most appropriate for Bobby Joe Long. At this stage, it was the defense's turn to roll up its big guns, in the persons of Dr. Helen Morrison and Dr. Michael Maher, whose role was to convince the jury that Bobby Joe Long was guilty, yes, but just too crazy to execute.

Also, the defense, in an effort to sway the sympathies of the jury

and thus win clemency of its client, put Louella Long and Cynthia Long Levy on the stand, to describe how Bobby Joe had evolved over the years from a sweet–natured, quiet, and withdrawn boy into a moody, angry man, whose behavior changed dramatically following the severe head injuries he suffered in a motorcycle accident.

Louella Long, through her tear–soaked testimony, told the jury how she struggled as a single mother to provide for little Bobby Joe and how he came to resent her for going off to work in her skimpy bar maid costumes. Quizzed by Robert Norgard, Louella described episode after episode, including the two major accidents that resulted in head injuries, which demonstrated how Bobby Joe's personality changed radically. She specifically recalled the shocking spanking incident when she was visiting Bobby Joe and his family in Miami.

Cindy told how she and Bobby Joe became inseparable teenage lovers almost from the moment they met in junior high in Hialeah. She explained that despite their frequently stormy marriage, Bobby Joe was a devoted father who loved his two children. In fact, she continued, her relationship with Bobby had improved so much in recent years, that as recently as the month before he was arrested as a serial killer, they were seriously talking about reconciling.

Louella and Cindy were there strictly for the emotional dressing. But it was the rational, objective opinions of the psychiatric experts that the defense banked on to convince the jury to spare their client. They hoped to show that his mental condition was so severely diseased and his personality so grievously damaged by his life circumstances that he couldn't control his murderous impulses, was not responsible for his actions, and therefore should not be put to death.

Dr. Helen Morrison told the jury she had spent about 23 hours interviewing Bobby Joe Long. In addition, she had spoken to his family, reviewed his medical history, particularly that concerning his growth and development and had studied the results of neurological tests done on his brain.

Her conclusion: Bobby Joe Long suffered from "atypical psychosis." According to Dr. Morrison's definition, such individuals have a distorted perception of reality, or are incapable of making a

judgment or a moral decision about events in which they are involved. They are unable to process thoughts and come to rational decisions the way most "normal" people do.

Such a person, she continued, "...is not capable of taking the fragmented parts of his mind and making them cohesive, which we see with Mr. Long from the time of at least one year of age..."

Dr. Morrison testified that the most powerful memories Bobby Joe Long had of childhood were of being locked in closets by his cousins and screaming to get out. There were terrifying nightmares that did not cease until he reached the sixth or seventh grade. Also, the instability he experienced because of his frenzied family life was aggravated by the movement back and forth between Florida and West Virginia, and the constant need to change schools—four in one year, for example.

"From the evidence I've been able to gather both from Mr. Long and from his mother, the relationship is one that is extremely mixed. It's love and hate combined simultaneously. He was saying that he resents his mother, and on the other hand he says what his mother does to him is only testing him. He will say that his mother was absent and always working, but then that she was doing the best that she possibly could...It's unclear to him as to what role his mother or any other human being plays in his life..."

▲　　▲　　▲

A LETTER FROM BOBBY

I'm going fucking crazy, my sick bitch of a mother came down here and attacked every person from my ex-wife, to my best buddy, who ever meant anything to me. The guilt trip is just too fuckin much! I wont write or call either of them again, and only regret I'll have to see them in court, "If" I ever go to court, which I hope to fuck I won't.

▲　　▲　　▲

Okay, Dr. Morrison, Robert Norgard continued. What about his relationship with Cindy and the marriage, with respect to his having this atypical psychosis?

In many ways, Dr. Morrison continued, Cindy simply replaced Louella Long in the relationship "...to the point that Cindy was doing some of the same activities that mother would do in regards to Robert Long. His impression was that Cindy was also testing him, that Cindy trapped him into marrying her because of her pregnancy, that Cindy continually demanded more than he felt capable of giving to the point where he feels that he can neither trust nor leave Cindy emotionally, even though he's done so physically...He felt not ready to marry, his son was born approximately four months after the marriage, their daughter a year later.

"In the context of the marital relationship, the sexual relationship, there was a good deal of confusion and difficulty in regards to their sexually being together. There were multiple other individuals who were involved in their sexual relationship according to Mr. Long and, essentially, the same chaotic inability to maintain a job, inability to maintain a consistent lifestyle...."

Finally, Norgard reached the point that the jury had been waiting to hear: What did all this have to do with the rape and murder of Virginia Lee Johnson?

Dr. Morrison's explanation, some of the jurors later admitted, went right over their heads.

In Bobby Joe Long's thirty-one years on earth, she began, "...we see a period of gradually shortened ability to maintain control...the increased disorganization in his jobs and all aspects of his life. He began to attempt to find ways to get an external structure for himself. It hadn't worked with the job, it hadn't worked with the marriage, it had not worked with the military, it had not worked with his schooling. In a mechanical sense, the homicides provided that external structure that Mr. Long did not have..."

And because of that, she continued, Bobby Joe Long is incapable of understanding the criminality of his actions; unable to appreciate the fact that wrapping a shoelace around a woman's neck and squeezing until she was dead was the wrong thing to do.

"There was no recognition, there was no processing and there was an incapacity to make a decision about whether what he was doing was right or wrong...In my opinion, there was extreme mental disturbance and emotional disturbance at the time of the homicide...In my opinion, he was not capable of cold, calculated premeditation...It's not a person. It's an 'it' phenomenon that's happening. Something starts. It goes on. It's ended and it's over, but there's no calculation of, I will do this and this will happen and this will be the outcome, and this is what it will mean to me," Dr. Morrison concluded.

Dr. Michael Maher, a Tampa psychiatrist and professor at the University of South Florida, followed Dr. Morrison on the stand. He concurred with Dr. Morrison's opinion, but Dr. Maher cut straight to the chase when he told the jury, "In my opinion, on the day that Bobby Joe Long picked up Virginia Johnson, he was like a stick of dynamite with a short fuse, and seeing her and believing that she was a prostitute, a wicked, evil creature that was only on earth to satisfy the needs of somebody, started a sequence of events which could not be stopped by him. He didn't have the capacity to choose whether he was going to brutalize her, whether he was going to explode and destroy her in the process.

"When the impulse, when the desire, when the need for sexual release and, more importantly, aggressive, angry, hostile release, when he got to the point where he was ready to explode, his rationality, his capacity to function in a rational way was totally absent.

"After the explosion, he...was to some extent free of the emotional turmoil that caused him to lose his ability to be rational, to be sensible, to function according to any rules, so that after he had an explosion, whether someone was hurt in the process or not, there would be a period of time, possibly days or weeks, possibly longer, when he would be able to put on a pretty good show of looking normal, of reacting normal; but, inevitably, the build–up of violence would occur again....

"He was operating according to a mechanical response, to a situation which was part reality, but more fantasy...He did not and does not have the capacity to do something in a premeditated, cal-

culating way. He has the capacity only to react as one might react if you touch something that's hot and you pull your hand away. He had only the capacity to act to something that was happening within his own distorted, sick mind, and in response to what he saw of the external world, that this woman had certain characteristics, for example."

Dr. Maher echoed much of Dr. Morrison's testimony about Bobby Joe Long's chaotic childhood, and how those conditions stunted his emotional growth to the point where his emotions never matured.

Consequently, Dr. Maher told the jury, Bobby Joe Long suffers from a mental defect that renders his thinking, his feelings, his emotions, and his ability to control his behavior inadequate. And this mental defect was behind the "...impulsive, unpredictable, and explosive violence which resulted in Virginia Johnson's death."

"There are three factors which are a part of this mental defect," Dr. Maher elaborated. "They are the inherited constitution that Mr. Long had at the time he was born.

"The second is the physical factors which developed as a result of those inherited tendencies and as a result of experiences in life, the things that happened to him. For example, the head injuries that occurred during his lifetime.

"The third factor is the environmental...or the specific experiences that he had throughout his life with different people at different times.

Dr. Maher also emphasized how the head injuries Long suffered as a child, and particularly in the motorcycle crash as an adult, affected his personality and behavior. Damage occurred to that part of the brain that seems to govern self– control.

"The head injury exaggerated...the inability to deal with frustration, the inability to control sexual urges, the inability to control violent impulses...He did not work consistently for quite a long period of time partly related to his physical disability and severe leg injury, which occurred at the same time, and partly related to his inability to remain focused and consistently involved in anything in

his life—his social isolation, his desperate need to be close to someone...got progressively worse...

"There was a period he moved away from his wife and children...and worked as an X–ray technician. That was actually rather brief. He was constantly on the move. The already established pattern of chaos in his life became even worse. He withdrew into an emotional fantasy world that contained only him. His contact with the world as a place where there are other human beings was utterly and completely lost. People at that point in his life were no more human than a thing, than a cup that you might put milk in to drink...If you were annoyed with it or you didn't like its color, you might just toss it aside. That's what people were to him at that point, and his frustration and anger and rage, his hurt, continued to grow and explode."

In the end, the psychiatrists might as well have stayed home.

After listening patiently, the jury went to put all this together and decide what penalty to recommend. It took them less time to sentence Bobby Joe Long to death—thirty-five minutes—than it took to convict him. The condemned man himself barely blinked when the unanimous death penalty vote was announced. Afterward, as Judge Ulmer polled the jury, asking each in turn if this was, in fact, his or her individual decision, Long stared intently as each juror answered "Yes" in a firm voice.

On May 3, 1985, Bobby Joe Long was back in the Pasco County courtroom of Judge Ray Ulmer to learn his fate. There wasn't much suspense as the judge settled into his chair, glanced down at the well–groomed killer standing before him, and waved to the attorneys to proceed.

Up to this point, the defense team had religiously avoided any mention of Bobby Joe Long's other rapes and murders, for fear such information might prejudice the jury. But now, paradoxically, they embraced those other killings as proof that Bobby Joe was too insane to be put to death. Robert Norgard, in a last attempt to head off the death sentence, spoke fervently about sparing Long's life, on the grounds that Bobby Joe suffered from a unique and newly

399

recognized disease called "serial killing." For that reason, he should be preserved and studied like a laboratory specimen to learn what causes the disease and to discover possible cures.

"This particular area of what has been characterized as `serial murder' is a rather new area of psychological study," Norgard told the Court. "There are very, very few people in the country that understand it, there are very few people that have studied it and there is very little material on it...

"What we have here, Your Honor, is a unique psychological condition in which studies are just beginning to evolve...I have reviewed cases of many other people who have been labeled 'serial murderers.' And when you start reading those books, it's frightening when you see the similarities. In Mr. Long's case, when you look at it...it is frightening how he compares to these other people.... "I would submit to the Court that a further study of this disease would be necessary...

"And by executing these individuals that suffer from this disease, in no way can we let society know or benefit from their mistakes...The magnitude of it is frightening. The fact that a mental illness results in a person going out and committing nine homicides is so frightening that it's hard to imagine.

"Incarcerated, Mr. Long could flourish. He's an intelligent man. He can read books, he can write well. In custody, under close supervision and scrutiny, he would properly develop and his emotional problems would be confined. But to execute this individual would be cruel and inhuman. I would like to think that society has gone much further than executing people with mental problems."

In his turn, Phil Van Allen, who would have loved to describe in detail for the jury how Bobby Joe Long kidnaped and murdered at least nine other young women and savagely raped countless others, now found himself urging Judge Ulmer to rule solely on the brutality of Virginia Johnson's death.

Murder alone might not be enough to earn Bobby Joe Long a reserved seat in the electric chair. It was the way Virginia Johnson died that was particularly cruel and heinous. The young hooker was "slowly and agonizingly" strangled to death with a shoelace. It took

her a long time to die, a long time to know she was dying—and to realize there was nothing at all she could do about it.

Moreover, Van Allen continued, Bobby Joe Long and his lawyers never offered any justification, however remote, for the murders.

"I had somewhat expected," Van Allen said, "that we would hear that Mr. Long was trying to clean up Tampa singlehandedly by getting the prostitutes off the street, a job which he cannot do legally...But at least there would have been some justification on his part.

"But the evidence is clear that he was killing Virginia Johnson simply to kill her, for no reason at all."

As for the psychiatrists who came at the behest of the defense to explain away Bobby Joe's crimes as the actions of a mentally ill person, Van Allen told the Court: "They have been confronted by an individual who committed murder and were working backward to find out why he committed murder. They are trying to create a niche in the law that has not previously existed...They are operating under the preconceived idea that anybody who would commit this murder has to be crazy. That simply is not the law."

Finally, when there was nothing more to be said, it was Judge Ulmer's turn. In a voice that trembled under the strain of what the law required him to do, Ulmer said he'd carefully read Long's pre–sentencing report and seriously considered Norgard's arguments that it would be better to have a live serial killer to study than a dead one. Nevertheless, he could find no legal reason to go against the jury's recommendation that Long be executed.

"Mr. Long," said the judge, "in keeping with my responsibility, I do accept the recommendation of the jury. The aggravating circumstances do outweigh any mitigating circumstances. And I would suspect that any further comments I would make to you, Mr. Long, would fall on deaf ears."

He then ordered Bobby Joe Long to be "electrocuted until you are dead," concluding with the admonition: "Mr. Long, may God have mercy on your soul, sir."

The moment when a death sentence is passed on a defendant in any courtroom is a somber one. The gravity of death weighs

heavily on everyone from the Judge to the bailiffs to the prosecutors who have fought for just such a conclusion. No matter how justified, sending a man to his death can be a dreadfully intense moment.

Long, who had shown virtually no emotion throughout the trial, exhibited even less during the hour–long hearing to determine whether he would live or die. He appeared only mildly interested in what the attorneys were saying about him, and even looked a bit bored when asked to stand while Judge Ulmer sentenced him to death. And when it was all over, Long, dressed in the same dark-blue, three–piece suit he'd worn throughout the trial, was fingerprinted and handcuffed. He wiped the ink from his cuffed hands and, as he was led from the courtroom, Bobby Joe Long began whistling a jaunty tune.

▲   ▲   ▲

A LETTER FROM BOBBY

When I go, if its anything but natural causes, I want to take as many with me as I can! Really, I don't think I'm cut out for this shit, the minute I stop reading, I start getting strange visions of my charred and smoking body as they unstrap it and put it in a fucking body bag to take it away. Yuk yuk--no joke.

▲   ▲   ▲

Even as the Pasco County trial was being heard, the Hillsborough County state attorney's office was busy gearing up for eight separate murder trials that conceivably could stretch on for years. Assistant State Attorney Mike Bonito would be the prosecutor in charge. After plowing through Long's voluminous file, Bonito decided to prosecute the Michelle Simms murder first, for several reasons: One, because the body was discovered so soon after the slaying, the case had the strongest physical evidence—mainly fibers

and tire impressions—that tied Bobby Joe Long to the killing in a kind of unbreakable Gordian knot. Second, there was the stomach–turning nature of the murder. The young prostitute had been beaten, strangled, and had her throat slashed. The brutality of the murder was certain to grab a jury's attention and, although prosecutors would piously deny any deliberate attempt to inflame the jury's sentiments, the grisly photos of Michelle Simms' slashed and mutilated body would be enough to provoke most jurors to return a guilty verdict and a death sentence.

The second Hillsborough trial would be for the slaying of Karen Dinsfriend. As with Simms, Benito decided to go with this case on the strength of the abundant forensic evidence.

And so on down the line, until all eight murder cases had been tried.

Before that happened, however, Long's attorneys from the public defender's office sat down with the prosecutors, and hammered out a plea bargain designed to save the state the time and expense of eight separate first-degree murder trials that would most likely have identical outcomes, given the overwhelming evidence and Bobby Joe's own confession.

On the positive side for the defense, the plea bargain greatly reduced—but did not eliminate—the risk that Bobby Joe Long would be executed for his crimes.

On September 24, 1985, the two sides met in Circuit Judge John P. Griffin's court to formalize the details of the negotiated plea bargain. Bobby Joe Long agreed to plead guilty to eight murders in Hillsborough County—those of Ngeun Thi "Lana" Long, Michelle Denise Simms, Elizabeth Loudenback, Vicky Marie Elliott, Chanel Devon Williams, Karen Beth Dinsfriend, Kim Marie Swann, and Kimberly Hopps. He also pled guilty to multiple kidnaping and sexual-assault charges.

Judge Griffin then sentenced Bobby Joe Long to a total of twenty-six life sentences. Twenty–four of the sentences were to be concurrent, while seven of those (all for murder) provided that he could not be considered for parole until he had served twenty-five years on each of the seven sentences. In addition, two of the twen-

ty-six life sentences, Judge Griffin ruled, would run consecutively to the first twenty-four, leaving little doubt that, even if he was never executed, the odds "...that he'll ever walk out of prison a free man are slim and none, and Slim just left town," remarked a detective sitting in the back of the courtroom.

But the State was holding a card in reserve just in case. An important provision of the plea bargain allowed the state attorney's office to seek the death penalty against Long for at least one of the killings, that of Michelle Simms.

Speaking on behalf of his taciturn client, Public Defender Charles J. O'Connor said Bobby Joe Long and the defense team agreed to the terms of the state–proffered plea bargain "...to minimize the opportunities the State will have to argue for the death penalty. It's obvious that he never will be released from the penitentiary," O'Connor said.

So it was that on July 14, 1986, both sides gathered in Judge Griffin's Hillsborough County courtroom to empanel a jury to hear the evidence against Bobby Joe Long. Because Long had already confessed to the murder and agreed to the terms of the plea bargain, the question of his guilt or innocence was not an issue. The jury was in the box for one purpose only, to decide if Bobby Joe Long should be electrocuted for killing Michelle Simms, or allowed to spend the rest of his life in prison—along with the twenty-six life sentences for the Hillsborough cases, the six life sentences for the home-invasion rape and robbery in Palm Harbor, the 696 years for the Port Richey rape conviction, and the death sentence just delivered in Pasco County for the strangulation murder of Virginia Johnson.

And if the case of Bobby Joe Long, serial killer, wasn't sensational enough by itself to attract vast media attention, along came Miami attorney Ellis Rubin.

While Ellis Rubin has been a fixture on the Florida legal scene for decades, his skill at involving himself in melodramatic, high–profile criminal cases has frequently thrust him into the national spotlight. Ordinarily, his name is appended with such descriptive terms as colorful, unorthodox, flamboyant, eccentric,

controversial, and unconventional. To many, Ellis Rubin was either a champion of the little guy, or a relentless self–promoter and quixotic gadfly, going for any case that guaranteed him a headline. Rubin first attracted national attention in 1977, with his unconventional "television intoxication" defense of a fourteen year old Miami boy. The teenage killer, Ronny Zamora, had wandered next door with a buddy, robbed and murdered his elderly neighbor, Elinor Haggart, and used the proceeds to finance a weekend spending spree at Disney World. Like most youngsters of his generation, Ronny Zamora had watched thousands of hours of television which, Rubin contended, left him incapable of distinguishing the make-believe violence he saw from real-life violence, in which dead people don't get up and walk away when the show's over.

"I never expected a jury to excuse Ronny Zamora for what he did because he watched too much television," Ellis Rubin later wrote. "I wanted to get a disturbed young man the medical help he needed...The defense I was left was... 'not guilty by reason of insanity.' 'Television intoxication' was what brought on Ronny's bizarre form of insanity." In the end, the jury disagreed. Ronny was found guilty, and sentenced to life in prison without parole for twenty-five years.

The Bobby Joe Long–Michelle Simms hearing began on Monday, July 14, 1986. On Friday, July 11, Rubin was tossed into jail in Miami to begin serving a contempt-of-court sentence. After nine hours, he was ordered freed by the Florida Supreme Court, pending his appeal of the contempt charge. Rubin and his son, Mark, rushed to Tampa to take on the State of Florida v. Bobby Joe Long. The following Monday, while Rubin was quizzing potential jurors in Tampa, state prosecutors were back before the high court, urging the justices to send Rubin back to jail to finish serving his 30 days. The Supreme Court refused to act, and Rubin remained free to continue his defense of Bobby Joe Long. The Rubins took the case as court–appointed attorneys, accepting the State's customary maximum fee of $3,500, although their actual costs would exceed that amount by many thousands of dollars.

"We took the case because it's a challenge," Rubin explained,

405

adding that, whatever the outcome, the case seemed destined to provide valuable insights on sex crimes and serial murder.

The defense Rubin formulated for Long's penalty phase hearing in the Michelle Simms murder was in character with his penchant for taking national issues and twisting them into justifications for his clients' behavior—in the case of Bobby Joe Long, pornography produces serial killers.

On July 10, the day before Rubin did his nine–hour stint in jail, the front pages of newspapers across the country announced the latest report from Washington—the release of the U.S. Attorney General's Commission on Pornography, a highly disputed and roundly criticized report ordered by Attorney General Edwin Meese. Among its main conclusions: Pornography was linked to crimes of sexual violence.

The report was thoroughly discredited even before it was published, and condemned in many quarters as a blatant political maneuver by the Reagan administration to exert censorship control.

Most Americans got a hoot out of the report, which became known, euphemistically, as "Uncle Sam's Dirty Book." Within days of its release, the expensive boondoggle began collecting dust in some dark government warehouse.

However, Ellis Rubin instantly seized on the report as the basis for a great defense strategy—an idea that made just about as much sense as the report itself, and had just about as much impact. Before the trial began, Rubin announced that he expected to use the government report to demonstrate that pornography was a "contributing factor" in Bobby Joe Long's mental deterioration, which culminated in rape and murder.

This, Rubin promised, will be "...the first documented case to prove the attorney general's report."

A Tampa Tribune reporter, wondering if the porno defense could be the new thing in other major murder cases, called Harvard Law School professor Alan Dershowitz—he of the Claus von Bulow and O.J. Simpson defense-team fame—seeking his views on the matter.

"If this is Ellis Rubin's notion of truth, he has a very, very strange notion," Dershowitz snorted. "I think it's a ridiculous defense...an insult to the jury. People [not pornography or television violence] are responsible for their own actions."

Rubin only smiled when told of the Dershowitz criticism. "If Professor Dershowitz is telling you that no link exists [between porno and violence] then he should have his own brain examined. Not by the Meese commission but by a lunacy commission."

During jury selection, the Rubins pursued the porno defense by closely questioning potential jurors about their feelings toward pornography and their own exposure to televised violence.

But that, as it turned out, was only peripheral to Rubin's primary intent, which was to drive home the point that Bobby Joe Long was a serial murderer of ten women. Evidence that their client had committed other crimes—in this case, multiple rapes and murders—is something that most defense attorneys would rather suppress. Yet at times, Ellis Rubin sounded more like a fiery prosecutor hell–bent on hanging the bastard than a defense attorney pleading for his client's life. But, as Rubin indicated, his purpose was not to set Bobby Joe Long free to walk the streets again, only to spare him from death in the electric chair.

Indeed, it was Rubin himself who brought up publicly for the first time that there were, in fact, ten known murder victims, not nine, as had been reported since Long's arrest. Prosecutors and lawmen were forced to admit that the previous December they had struck a deal with Bobby Joe Long. In order to clear the case, they promised not to prosecute him and to keep his confession quiet if he would admit to slaying Artiss Ann Wick.

Rubin told jurors about the tenth victim because he wanted them "...to know everything there is to know about our client's record. Anybody that would commit ten murders is sick." And that was the whole point—convincing the jury that Bobby Joe Long was too sick to be executed. That stratagem was outlined when Mark Rubin rose to deliver the defense's opening statement to jury.

"It's important for us to make clear from the beginning that under no circumstance are we attempting to walk Bobby Joe Long

out that door into freedom. It's become very clear that that is not what should happen. He is a convicted murderer of nine women. And, in fact, this morning you heard that he even killed a tenth woman. And the reason that was brought out is because we are going to attempt to bring you every possible piece of information that you can use in your deliberations whether Bobby Joe Long lives or dies...Bobby Joe's exposure from an early–on age to pornography, drugs, various head injuries...his perverted adult sexual life and his whole family system...

"...Bobby Joe was pulled out of his bed in the middle of the night, sometimes, so the mother could sleep with strange men in his bed while he would sleep in the same room on a couch.

"You will hear about perverted holes that were knocked in the wall where he would look through while his mother was performing strange sexual acts with men.

"You will hear about his father when they were separated, grabbing his mother off the street in the middle of the day and dragging her out in the woods, the same way many of these [murder] victims were dragged out in the woods and raped. His father raping his mother...

"You will hear about the times when as a little child his parents had porno films in their house, and he used to sneak in because his parents didn't think he knew how to use the projector. He used to watch those porno films, the early–on impressions he got about what sex life, morality, was like and should be like...

"You will hear how Bobby Joe thought his mother was a prostitute. How Bobby Joe's aunts, who lived with Bobby Joe and his mother, would always tell Bobby Joe that his mother was a prostitute and a whore and a hooker and a bad woman. And these things were tearing on him because he had to sleep with her at night until he was thirteen years old...and how this reaction was manifested on the women that he killed....

While the Rubins urged the jury to consider why Bobby Joe Long did what he did, Mike Benito heatedly countered that, no, not why but what he did, and the way he did it should be foremost in the jurors' minds when they considered the appropriate penalty.

Under Florida law, the state had to prove that "aggravating" circumstances existed in the murders to justify the death penalty. All of those conditions were present in the murder of Michelle Denise Simms, which Benito described as especially heinous, atrocious, cruel, cold, calculated, and premeditated; committed in the course of another felony—kidnaping; and committed by a killer with prior felony convictions. Another aggravating factor, Benito added, was the murder of Virginia Johnson and Long's recent conviction for that crime.

Again, as in the Virginia Johnson trial, the prosecution's case rested primarily on the physical evidence and Long's own statements to Sgts. Price and Latimer, while the defense again called half-a-dozen psychiatrists, psychologists, and criminologists to explain to the jury how Bobby Joe Long's psyche became so twisted, and why that caused him to become a serial rapist and serial killer.

Dr. Robert Berland, for example, described Bobby Joe as a psychotic who placed women in two categories— "sluts," who took advantage of men; and "madonnas," or pure women. Michelle Simms, he continued, was sort of the embodiment of all the sluts in Bobby Joe Long's world, "That is, immoral, sleazy and manipulative, who subjugate and dominate men through sex."

As the trial concluded, Benito told the jury in his closing argument, "I am not going to stand here and argue with you or Mr. Rubin that Bobby Joe Long is a normal individual. Ten murders? Forty rapes?...You don't have to go to medical school to say that a man who has committed ten murders and forty rapes is not normal. But is he responsible? Of course he is. Was he in control of his actions? Of course he was.

"Doctor Walter Afield, the defense's own witness, tells you clearly that this man knew the difference between right and wrong. He knew what he was doing...

"Doctor Kathleen Heidi, the defense's own witness [who said that Bobby Joe raped and murdered out of "rage" toward the world] testified this man made conscious decisions to rape, to rob, to kidnap, to kill....

"He left a trail of women that would no longer make him feel inadequate."

At one point, Benito placed an enlarged color photo of Michelle Simms' slashed and bloodied throat on an easel, only feet from the jurors' eyes. He then grabbed the hunting knife that Long had admitted using to cut her throat, and waved it dramatically in the air.

"Don't lose sight of Michelle Denise Simms," Benito said, his voice rising to a shout. "She's gone! She is gone! And he killed her. She is dead because, within this man right there, there burns a violent flame...a violent flame which must now be extinguished. You should have no reservations about your decision.

"Bobby Joe Long is a cunning, intelligent, cold–blooded killer. That is what Bobby Joe Long is. He is not some poor soul with a bad background that committed these killings because he is reading Hustler magazine in a Seven-Eleven Store, and he falls down and hits his head. That is not what Bobby Joe Long is. He is a cold– blooded, cunning, intelligent killer."

Benito attacked the defense's position, which was, as in the Virginia Johnson trial, that since so little was known about what produced serial killers, they should be preserved and studied to try and prevent such horrors in the future.

"To think, if one man kills one woman, he might be executed," the prosecutor said, shaking his head in disgust. "But if one man kills ten women, he is something special. He should be kept alive. He should be studied. That is ludicrous. That flies in the face of logic.

"There is no guarantee we will learn anything from studying them. There is no guarantee that we will be able to stop them by studying them. A hundred years ago, Jack the Ripper, no pornography, Victorian Age...A few years ago, the Boston Strangler. Now, Bobby Joe Long. And a hundred years from now, we could have another Bobby Joe Long.

"You can't hold his mother responsible. You can't hold his father responsible or Playboy or drugs or his well–fed dog. That man is responsible.

"That man killed Michelle Denise Simms, and that crime cries out for the death penalty."

When it came his turn to speak, about the only prosecution point Ellis Rubin disputed was that Bobby Joe Long should be put to death for killing Michelle Simms. Oh, he killed her, Rubin agreed. But he also killed nine other women—which is why he should be spared. Bobby Joe Long is a serial killer and that, Rubin argued passionately, should be enough reason to keep him alive.

"Bobby Joe Long deserves to die," Rubin began. "So does every person who takes another person's life.

"Bobby Joe Long is vicious. Bobby Joe Long contains a flame of violence. And Mr. Benito wants to extinguish it. So do I. So do you. And so does every other rational, thinking human being...

"Anyone who would terrorize another human being the way that Bobby Joe Long did ten times and forty more in these sexual assaults is not normal...And what were you doing when this terrible spree of terror was going on? It doesn't take much imagination to figure out that anybody who was reading and listening and watching television while this unknown killer stalked this community, there was stark raving terror in women and men who were fathers and husbands and brothers. And everybody wanted to catch this man, this maniac, and execute him in twenty-four minutes, let alone twenty-four hours or twenty-four days or twenty-four months...

"This man, from the moment of conception, was programmed for murder. The doctors have said it...If you ignore them, it's at your risk. And it's at the risk of young women who are going to be in this community and others for generations to come, who will be the prey of Bobby Joe Long and others who are programmed to kill.

"Now, we've got to alter that program. This isn't a gimmick to try and keep Bobby Joe Long alive...I took this case because the United States has thirty to thirty-five of these maniacs walking around at any one time, killing innocent people. You don't stop it by burning them alive. You put out that flame by understanding what made it spark in the first place...

411

"Yes, he is responsible for his acts because he is a human being. And that human being has been created to commit murders. He is smooth. He is cunning. He is articulate. But that doesn't explain why he murdered ten girls...

"I am here asking for his life, so that these girls won't be the forerunner of other serial killers because we just didn't know where they come from, how they develop, and what symptoms we can spot at an early age...

"Don't go back to Jack the Ripper. Don't go back to the days when they sliced a man up on the public square because he did something wrong.

"Let this verdict ring out from Tampa that serial killers must be stopped. And this man, as intelligent as he is, can help. He can contribute...

"Mr. Benito speaks for death. I speak for life. Life that can contribute to other lives...You are voting on whether or not to help the future, regardless of this maniac. He isn't going anywhere. The rest of his life will be in prison or it'll be snuffed out with the electric chair...

"In this case, I hope that you will join with those who say, 'When a jury kills, it is the same thing that Bobby Joe Long did.'

"When a jury says, 'There is a better way for this man to pay for these crimes,' I hope that'll be your verdict," Rubin concluded quietly.

▲   ▲   ▲

REPORTER: *Did you want to get caught?*

BOBBY: *I don't know. I don't think consciously I really sat down and said, Gee, I want to get caught and I want to go to prison for the rest of my life or sit in the electric chair and let them fry me. You know? To tell you the truth I never even considered the electric chair. I never considered it. I figured it was so obvious that there was something wrong with me that when they did catch me that they would fix me. But I learned real quick that nobody gives a damn, nobody cared what causes this. (CBS News Interview)*

412

The Simms jury took just over an hour before returning with an eleven-to-one recommendation that Bobby Joe Long receive the death penalty. ("You can print that I wasn't surprised," Long sarcastically told a reporter on the way back to his jail cell.) A week later, Bobby Joe stood before the bench while Judge Griffin affirmed the jury's recommendation of death, and pronounced sentence.

In a last-ditch effort, Ellis Rubin told the judge: "Putting him to death isn't going to serve any purpose. We ask that you spare him in the name of society and humanity and preservation."

However, Judge Griffin stated that he was acting in the name of society in carrying out the will of the jury. "There is no question in this court's mind that the defendant, Robert Joe Long, had serious mental and/or emotional problems," the Judge said. "But the outrageously wicked nature of the murder, its cold and premeditated manner, and the fact that it occurred during a kidnaping outweigh any reasons for mercy."

The sentence was death. Again.

Soon after the penalty hearing ended, while Ellis Rubin was still Long's attorney of record, he gave his permission for a crew from "The CBS Evening News" to visit Bobby Joe at the Florida State Prison in Stark, as part of a report the network was preparing on serial killers. Reporter Victoria Corderi and the camera crew spent about an hour and a half interviewing Bobby Joe Long. Dan Rather used a brief segment in his newscast on December 26, 1986.

In that segment, Bobby Joe is seen telling the reporter: "All in all, I guess I've probably destroyed about a hundred people...It was like ABCD. I'll pull over. They get in. I'd drive away. Stop. Pull out a knife, a gun, whatever. Tie 'em up. Take 'em out. And that would be it. And the worst thing is, I don't understand why."

The decision to allow the interview was one that Long and Rubin would both come to regret, although it did figure in yet another reversal by the Supreme Court and a third trial for the murder of Virginia Johnson.

In the meantime, Ellis Rubin's boast that he has never lost a client to the electric chair still holds. It's been eight years since

Bobby Joe was sentenced to die for the sadistic rape slaying of Michelle Simms, and so far he continues to cheat the executioner.

After that sentencing in the Simms' slaying, not much was heard of Bobby Joe Long for the next year and half. Then, in November, 1987, the Florida Supreme Court tossed a legal bombshell in the laps of the Hillsborough and Pasco prosecutors and investigators, who had come to believe that the horror of Bobby Joe Long was behind them for good.

The unanimous ruling handed down from the high court in Tallahassee ordered a new trial in the Virginia Lee Johnson murder, on the grounds that Long had asked for an attorney following his arrest, but that Detectives Bob Price and Randy Latimer had ignored his request and continued questioning him. In doing so, the court ruled, the detectives had violated Long's rights, established in the U.S. Supreme Court's landmark 1966 Miranda case. The four justices also cited a second, 1981 decision by the nation's highest court, which allows police to clarify a suspect's request for an attorney if it is ambiguous.

"This [second] safeguard was designed to assure that the individual's right to choose between silence and speech remains unfettered throughout the interrogation process," the Florida court noted.

Long had obviously requested an attorney during the interrogation and the questioning should have stopped at that point, the court said. Instead, the interrogation continued, and Long soon confessed to nine murders. To continue the questioning was a clear violation of the suspect's rights, and for that Bobby Joe Long deserved a new trial.

The State Attorney's office disagreed and appealed the ruling, which put the case on hold for several more months.

May and June, 1988, were bad months for the prosecutors in both Pasco and Hillsborough Counties, who remained convinced they had Bobby Joe Long—what with all the indisputable forensic evidence, his confession, and plea bargain.

The first bit of bad news arrived on May 16, all the way from the U.S. Supreme Court in Washington. The Justices refused to

reinstate Bobby Joe Long's murder conviction and death sentence in the Johnson slaying. Florida's Attorney General, Bob Butterworth, had urged the nine Justices to "...decide the correct standard for determining the effect of an accused's ambiguous or equivocal reference to counsel during a custodial interrogation."

Without comment, the federal court let stand the Florida ruling that Long was entitled to a new trial because he wasn't allowed to talk to an attorney during the questioning. The high court's decision, in effect, ruled that Long's confession was invalid because of the apparent rights violation, and therefore couldn't be used against him in any subsequent retrials.

Then, on June 30, it was the State Supreme Court's turn to destroy the prosecution's fervent hope for an early execution with another reversal. This time, the four Florida justices, in essence, told Hillsborough County: You screwed up on the Michelle Simms penalty phase.

The justices overturned the death sentence Long received at the end of the penalty phase of the Simms hearing, on the grounds that prosecutors had used the conviction and death sentence from the Pasco County case as aggravating factors that justified the death penalty in the Hillsborough case. In other words, since the conviction in the Virginia Johnson murder had been ruled invalid, that made the death sentence for Michelle Simms' murder invalid as well.

When he heard the news, Mike Benito threw up his hands in frustration. "It's beyond me how the Supreme Court's ruling affects the jury's recommendation for death," he said. "When you look at the defense put up by his attorney, Ellis Rubin made it clear to the jury that his client not only was guilty of killing the Pasco woman, but he also had killed eight other women...and that his client should be studied and not destroyed.

"Well, at least the convictions and the judge's ruling were upheld. That's on the up side, so if the Court says 'do it again,' we'll do it again. And again and again if necessary. If we can't seat a jury in Hillsborough County, I'm prepared to follow Mr. Long to Timbuktu."

By the fall of that year, Pasco County was ready to try again to convict Bobby Joe Long of strangling Virginia Lee Johnson to death. However, it quickly became evident that, after all the publicity generated by the first trial in Dade City, the chances of seating a second, unbiased jury drawn from the same jury pool were not good. Pasco County judge Wayne Cobb granted a defense motion for a change of venue, and the whole operation packed up and moved down the coast to Fort Myers, in Lee County.

When Bobby Joe Long was brought in from a holding cell at the Lee County Justice Center for the first time, courthouse observers noted the striking change in his appearance. Gone were the bushy, mustache and the thick, wavy, brown hair. Faint streaks of gray touched his short–cropped hair. Long appeared puffy from the jailhouse diet, and pale from the sunless prison life. But he still came to court nattily attired in a light-brown sports jacket and dark-brown tie, the same meticulous, well–groomed appearance he carefully cultivated before going out to "shop" the classified ads.

A jury of eight men and four women was selected fairly quickly, and on Wednesday, November second, the prosecution prepared to call its first witness. Earlier, Assistant State Attorneys Phil Van Allen and Alan Allweiss had announced that they intended to employ the Williams Rule in this second trial—a ruling that allows evidence of a pattern of similar crimes to be admitted. Ordinarily, evidence of prior crimes or convictions is inadmissible. To support the evidence of prior crimes, the state planned to show the jury the portion of the videotaped interview that had been broadcast on CBS, in which Long talked about the killings.

But before the State could begin, Bobby Joe Long's new attorneys from the public defender's office, William Eble and Robert McClure, lobbed their first grenade by challenging the edited version of the interview, arguing that the network had distorted Bobby Joe Long's comments by taking them completely out of context. Unless the jury was allowed to view the entire 90 minutes that had been taped at Florida State Prison, then the jury would get only an abbreviated and prejudicial view of their client. Eble wanted to view the entire tape, in the event it contained material that was

favorable to Long but that had been edited out to make the network's telecast more shocking and dramatic.

Judge Wayne Cobb sided with the defense, and gave the network until 5 p.m. the next day to turn over the tape, adding a threat to subpoena the reporter if the tape was not turned over. That got the high–octane lawyers from CBS's New York headquarters in an uproar.

CBS attorney Tom Julin rushed to Fort Myers to protest the order that "...would undermine the integrity of the editorial process. News reporters would become professional witnesses in every case." CBS, as well as other news organizations, he said, generally oppose demands for unpublished notes or "outtakes," (as the unused portions of videos are called), because to do so would make them an arm of the courts and destroy their impartiality.

Julin immediately filed an appeal of Judge Cobb's ruling with the 2nd District Court of Appeals in Lakeland. While the appeal was pending, Cobb agreed to postpone the defense's other motion to subpoena reporter Victoria Corderi.

So with the threat of a massive challenge to the First Amendment of the Constitution looming, the trial moved into its third day of testimony, with prosecutors calling Lisa McVey to the stand as part of their strategy to use the Williams Rule to portray Bobby Joe's pattern of similar criminal behavior.

Once more, the spunky young woman, took the witness stand and defiantly told the spell–bound jury how she had been snatched off her bicycle in the middle of the night, forced at gunpoint into the kidnaper's car, blindfolded, driven to his apartment, marched upstairs and "...raped numerous times." She described being held prisoner until late the following day, when the man she now identified as Bobby Joe Long dressed her, drove her back to the neighborhood where he had grabbed her, and set her free.

Tampa detectives followed Lisa to the stand to tell how her coolness during the ordeal and her careful observation of details led them to the man who turned out to be the sadistic serial killer who had been terrorizing Tampa nightlife for months.

They also testified about the rape–murders of four other

women in Hillsborough County, whose slayings bore striking similar earmarks to that of Virginia Johnson.

That same day, word came down that the appellate court had temporarily blocked Judge Cobb's order that CBS must provide the outtakes to the defense. Judge Edward F. Threadgill, Jr., granted the network's emergency motion for a stay until the entire appellate court had had time to review the potential thorny constitutional issue.

Meanwhile, the trial progressed and, over the vehement objections of Bill Eble and his team, Judge Cobb allowed the prosecutors to play about fifteen seconds of the CBS interview. The jury heard Long tell the reporter how his victims were killed, but that he didn't understand why he stalked, raped, and strangled the ten women.

However, Cobb also blocked the showing of portions of the tape in which Bobby Joe speculated that he might, indeed, be mentally ill. And he refused to let the jury view a segment of the same CBS News report that featured medical experts expounding theories that serial killers may be the products of brain damage or of an abused childhood.

Late Friday, just as testimony was concluding for the day, Judge Cobb was notified that the appellate court had rescinded its stay, which placed Cobb's order to CBS to surrender the outtakes back in effect. CBS attorneys immediately dashed to the state supreme court in Tallahassee, requesting an emergency hearing. The outtakes, they continued to insist, were protected by the First Amendment, and to force the network to turn them over would be a serious violation of the Constitution.

But Chief Justice Raymond Erhlich didn't think so. In an unusual Saturday action, Erhlich sided with both the appellate court and Judge Cobb. With that, CBS caved in. Although there was still talk about a direct appeal to the United States Supreme Court, the network decided instead to turn over the outtakes for viewing when the trial reconvened on Monday.

And after fighting for the right to view the entire interview, Long's attorneys took one look at the tape and decided they didn't

want the jury to see the outtakes after all. They had hoped to find statements that would aid Bobby Joe's defense, but now feared that the interview would focus even more attention on the broadcast portion the jury had already seen.

Prosecutor Phil Van Allen gleefully seized on the opportunity to put the shortened version of Bobby Joe Long's television confession on the record for all the world to see. So devastating was the image of Bobby Joe, coldly and apparently without remorse, discussing rape and murder that Van Allen made sure the jury watched the tape again during the penalty phase of the trial.

After that, events moved swiftly. The defense quickly presented its lineup of psychiatric experts, and rested its case.

In his closing argument to the jurors, Phil Van Allen reminded them: "We have shown you that every time a hooker gets together with Bobby Joe Long, she dies by strangulation."

Assistant Public Defender Robert McClure countered that prosecutors had failed on two counts: They hadn't shown that the murder was premeditated, nor had they been able to prove that Virginia Johnson was killed in Pasco County.

"You have to put aside your hatred in this case and apply the law," McClure urged.

By late afternoon, the jury retired to consider the verdict. It was back in sixty-two minutes after deciding, for the second time, that Bobby Joe Long was guilty of killing Virginia Lee Johnson. Long wasn't surprised. He turned to a bailiff and sneered, "It took them longer than I thought it would,"

The penalty phase of the trial began the following day.

Once more, the question of Bobby Joe Long's state of mind before, during, and after the rapes and murders consumed much of the testimony. Most of it was repetitive, instant replays of opinions and counter–opinions presented in the previous trial. But at one point, Dr. Arturo Gonzalez, a prosecution witness, was questioned in some detail about why Bobby Joe killed some women but allowed others, such as Lisa McVey or those in the home invasion rapes, to live.

"I think the key to why some ended up murdered and some

didn't lies in the unconscious of Bobby Joe Long," Dr. Gonzalez testified.

"Somewhere in the unconscious, every time he killed one of these girls, he was trying to kill his mother by extension. I venture to say that once the connection was made that this woman is a whore, that triggered the unconscious image of the mother, which he wants dead. He wants to kill the mother. He even said that in my interview with him, that he would like to kill her."

Defense attorney Bill Eble asked Dr. Gonzalez if he had read Lisa McVey's testimony of what had happened. When Gonzalez replied that he had not, Eble paraphrased the girl's account of her ordeal at the hands of Bobby Joe Long, and asked the witness, "Can you draw any conclusions from that scenario?"

"Sure," Dr. Gonzalez replied. "We are talking about the same thing. She did not meet the criteria for being killed. And there were the scenes of love, of caring that Mother never gave him, the love that he would like Mother to give him. The McVey girl— somehow he interpreted she was giving it to him, and that's the taking the blouse off and laying on her breast or chest...That's a very maternal–evoking image that you have there. Madonna/whore type of thing."

Another expert, called by the defense to offer mitigating circumstances as to why Bobby Joe should not be executed, was psychologist Robert Berland. Since his arrest four years earlier, Bobby Joe had never satisfactorily explained to anyone why he brutalized and killed the ten victims.

Berland offered the Fort Myers jury the best reason anyone had come up with yet: He liked it.

"He derives pleasure from the pain that he might inflict or that he might observe in other people," Berland testified, adding that sadistic tendencies were a major part of the psychosis that drove Long to kill, and that his mental and sexual disorders diminished his capacity to obey the law and to realize the nature of his crimes.

Assistant State Attorney Allweiss jumped all over that explanation in cross-examination, making sure the full impact of Berland's conclusion reached the jury.

"He loved to destroy people, is that what he told you?" asked Allweiss.

"Yes," Berland said.

Dr. John Money, an internationally renowned psychologist and specialist on sexual disorders from Johns Hopkins University, also took the stand on Bobby Joe's behalf. Originally, the noted expert became involved in the case only after Long wrote to him pleading for help. However, the court refused the defense's request to appoint Money as an expert witness, so Joe and Louella Long scraped together enough to pay for the psychologist's round-trip ticket to Tampa, plus a $1,000 contribution to his research fund.

Bobby Joe's problems, Money testified, actually started in the womb. It was likely that Long carried an extra female chromosome in his genetic makeup, which was probably why he started developing large breasts at puberty. The motorcycle crash in 1974 exacerbated what was already a dangerous pathological condition, and was likely the trigger that ignited his murderous rage. The accident damaged Bobby Joe's hypothalamus, a pea–sized part of the brain that regulates nervous impulses for appetite, sexual drive, and anger, Money said.

Dr. Money further testified that the brain damage, along with all the other genetic and environmental factors that impacted on Long's fragile psyche, combined to produce "...a very specific sexual insanity, which I often refer to as a `Jekyll and Hyde syndrome.'

Whenever Bobby Joe Long encountered a woman he perceived as "sleazy," an automatic set of reactions kicked in that escalated into extreme violence, Money continued. Of the ten women Long murdered, six had been charged with soliciting for prostitution, two had worked as exotic dancers, and two others worked or lived in an area along Nebraska Avenue where street prostitution was rampant.

All the psychological testimony on the part of the defense experts was designed to establish "mitigating circumstances" to counter the state's "aggravating" factors. To that end, Eble told the jury: "The evidence is uncontroverted that there is something wrong with that man's head. I ask you if we can sentence the mentally ill to death?"

But the state had brought out its own mental-health experts to testify that Bobby Joe Long was perfectly sane, in the legal sense, and therefore eligible for the death sentence. They conceded that Bobby Joe obviously exhibited an "anti–social personality," but pooh–poohed the idea that the motorcycle accident had jumbled his brain and triggered the uncontrollable rages and sexual impulses.

Tampa psychologists Sidney Merin told about examining Bobby Joe Long. "It was clear," he testified, "that I wasn't dealing with a psychotic. He was not seeing little green men from Mars, he didn't think he was Napoleon. I guess I would compare Long to a Mafia killer who murders because it's a job.

"What we were dealing with here was a vile, despicable, depraved individual," he concluded.

Phil Van Allen also surprised the court when he read several letters that Bobby Joe had written to Jay Shideler while both were in the Hillsborough County Jail. Those letters contained Long's vile boasting about how he raped and terrorized countless women, plus his elaborate escape plot that included plans to murder two detectives. The letters, Van Allen said, provided clear evidence of aggravating circumstances and supported his argument that Bobby Joe Long should be put to death.

Finally, to drive home his point, Van Allen had the jury watch the brief CBS interview with Long. "I want you to watch a cold–blooded killer as he outlines the deaths of those women and tries to con you as you sit there...he plotted, he schemed, he planned, he killed, and as a result, Bobby Joe Long has forfeited his right to live," he concluded.

At that Long leaned over the defense table and muttered to Robert McClure, "This makes me sick!"

When it was his turn, Bill Eble implored the jury not to be swayed by the gory details of the crime, reminding them that Bobby Joe Long was serving several other life sentences.

"If the life sentence is appropriate in the other cases, I ask you, before walking out of here today, to figure out what about the Virginia Johnson case is different," Eble said.

"With medication and chains and cinder blocks and bars we can

protect society from him without executing him. He'll never hurt your children, and he'll never hurt my children."

The jury made sure of that. It took only thirty minutes to come back with a nine to three recommendation of death by electrocution.

Bobby Joe Long, his hands stuffed in his pockets, rolled his head from side to side as he listened to the verdict. In the brief silence that followed the pronouncement of death, Bobby Joe Long smiled his thin, mirthless smile and shrugged. "I'm not surprised."

Surrounded by heavily armed deputies, Bobby Joe Long was again bound in chains and hustled back to Death Row to await the next round. He still had a long way to go before facing the executioner.

That next round—the rehearing of the penalty phase only for the murder of Michelle Simms—was scheduled for the following year. Hillsborough County Circuit Judge Richard Lazzara wasted no time in granting a defense motion to move the hearing out of Tampa due to the extensive publicity that the name of Bobby Joe Long still generated, nearly five years after his murderous reign of terror ended.

The resentencing hearing began on Monday, June 26, 1989, in a Daytona Beach courtroom, where Lazzara hoped potential jurors would not be influenced by the name and reputation of Tampa Bay's infamous serial killer. To ensure that the jurors wouldn't be contaminated by the publicity, Lazzara also granted a second defense motion to sequester the jury after it was selected.

By now, both sides had the routine down pat: Present the physical evidence. Present the police and forensic experts. Present the gruesome crime-scene photos. Rest the case. Defense's turn. Describe Bobby Joe's bizarre childhood. Describe the accidents that left him brain damaged. Bring on the shrinks. Rest the case.

By Thursday, it was all over. The jury, as most expected, returned with yet another death recommendation.

Judge Lazzara, although he was not bound to follow the jury's recommendation, did his part. Back in Tampa on July 21, the judge told Bobby Joe Long that he recognized his history of mental problems and his inability to control his rage toward women. But none of that justified the violent rape and murder. In his sentence,

Lazzara added two more life terms, one for kidnaping and one for raping Michelle Simms. He then ordered Bobby Joe to die for her murder.

The sentencing pleased Mike Benito, but the system was beginning to irritate him. As he left the courtroom, Benito told assembled reporters that the constant delays in carrying out the death sentence were "...a joke. This is no deterrent. You can't scare anybody with the death penalty if it's carried out in this fashion.

"Bobby Joe Long confessed almost five years ago to murdering ten women and now, the way it stands, it could be another eight years or more before the appeals for all his convictions and two death sentences run out. There is a very serious flaw in the criminal justice system that allows a man to remain alive thirteen or fourteen years after he admits to murdering ten women."

Benito's frustration was far from over. Three more years passed. Then, on Friday, October 16, 1992, the Associated Press bureau in Tallahassee reported:

"Confessed serial killer Bobby Joe Long got a thumbs up and a thumbs down on Thursday when the state Supreme Court vacated one of his death sentences but affirmed the second.

"In Thursday's unsigned opinion, the high court unanimously upheld his sentence for the May 1984 slaying of Michelle Denise Simms in Hillsborough County. The Court rejected all 13 issues raised by Long in his appeal...

"Long had both his second conviction and sentence overturned on Thursday in the case of Virginia Johnson, whose badly decomposed body was found off a dirt road in Pasco County in November, 1984. The first conviction and sentence were vacated in 1987 because his right to an attorney was violated.

"This time, the justices found that the trial judge was wrong to let Long's second murder trial continue with only a two-minute edited version of a 90-minute television interview with Long...."

In addition to the CBS interview, the Supreme Court also said

that the jury in Fort Myers shouldn't have been permitted to hear evidence about other murders in Hillsborough County, nor the testimony of Lisa McVey. Therefore, Long's second conviction for killing Virginia Johnson should be overturned and a new trial ordered.

The Supreme Court's order noted that during the second trial, prosecutors spent three days presenting evidence on four of the Hillsborough slayings, but presented only four hours of testimony about the murder of Virginia Johnson. Those killings became the "central feature," when the focus should have been on the Pasco County killing.

"Under the unique circumstances of the case," read the Court's opinion, "including the [Hillsborough] plea agreement, we find that the four other murders could not be presented at this trial.

"Little doubt exists that one of the major benefits intended to be received by Long in entering into the plea agreement was that his guilty plea could not be used against him in subsequent proceedings."

The Court added that in any retrial some,but not all, of Lisa McVey's testimony could be used, specifically that which led to the identification of Bobby Joe Long and his car.

The courts had given Bobby Joe Long his third shot at beating one of his death sentences, and Assistant Public Defender Bill Eble exulted in the news. "It would be an absolute waste of Pasco County taxpayers' money to retry him. They've taken two shots at him and come up with nothing."

Despite the third setback, Phil Van Allen sighed, took a deep breath, and went back to what had become almost a full-time job for him—closing off all the legal loopholes, one by one, until Bobby Joe Long was finally strapped into the electric chair.

Another year passed. Now it was the fall of 1993, and all members of the cast reassembled in Pasco Circuit Court Judge Wayne Cobb's Dade City courtroom.

The only thing that made this round different was the presence of that litigious CBS interview tape. Should it or should it not be shown? And if so, how much?

During a pre–trial motion, Judge Cobb was asked to rule on the relevancy of the taped interview. The prosecution wanted to show the whole thing to the jury; the defense wanted it excluded for the negative image it projected of Bobby Joe. This jury wasn't likely to be any more understanding than the other when they watched and heard Bobby Joe Long's chilling gloat: "All in all, I guess I've probably destroyed about a hundred people...It was like ABCD..."

As part of that motion, Long and his former defense attorney, Ellis Rubin, who had approved the CBS meeting in the first place, told Judge Cobb that the interview was granted with the understanding that Rubin could review and edit the tape before broadcast. He said that promise was not kept.

After studying the matter, Judge Cobb came back with an atypical, blistering denunciation of Rubin's tactics:

"Based on the totality of the evidence and the credibility of the witnesses, this Court finds that these statements were made voluntarily to Miss Corderi by Mr. Long," Judge Cobb noted.

"It's clear from the testimony of—I find that there was a limited agreement or a promise by or statement by Miss Corderi that she would not get into any specific cases, but was going to limit her questions to background. And I find that she did that. She honored that agreement. Although Mr. Long talked about some specific cases, she didn't ask him about any of them. He just brought those up.

"But there was no agreement, I find, that Mr. Rubin would have any kind of control over the product. That's—Mr. Rubin did nothing to enforce it. He didn't show up; he didn't have any written contract; he didn't do anything to enforce it after it was published. I think it's patently absurd for me to believe at this time that there was any agreement that he would have any kind of editorial control over that tape.

"The testimony by Mr. Rubin...also convinces this Court beyond any reasonable doubt that this was all strategy, approved by Mr. Long and discussed with Mr. Rubin, that they were going to present some psychobabble defense. Mr. Rubin is famous for his psychobabble defenses. And that's all Mr. Long wanted to talk about in this interview, was these murders and these rapes were caused by his second

toe being longer than his first one or something almost as ridiculous...

"The statement [by Long] was voluntary, and I agree with Mr. Van Allen that it's now in the public domain, and...that the Fourth Amendment does give the State the right to use it.

"I'm not finding relevance or materiality, but I'm finding that this was a voluntary statement."

On November 12, Judge Cobb summoned the first group of Pasco County citizens, from which a jury would be selected to try Bobby Joe Long for the third time. Five days later, the judge threw up his hands in futility. Neither side had been able to find twelve jurors who didn't have strong opinions about Bobby Joe Long or the application of the death penalty in his case.

"The longer this goes on in this atmosphere, especially with the press writing and broadcasting about efforts to get a jury, it's going to be much harder," Judge Cobb decided, in finally granting Bill Eble's oft-repeated motion for a change of venue.

This time the trial was moved to Ocala, the Marion County seat in the center of the state. The last day of January, 1994, a jury was seated. By the end of the week, the jury was back with what by now had become an almost rote recitation: Guilty of First Degree Murder. Recommendation: Death. As the clerk of the court read the now-familiar sentence, a bored Bobby Joe Long nonchalantly poured himself a cup of water and sipped it while the jurors were polled on the guilty verdict.

Judge Charles Cope accepted the verdict, and set sentencing for March 19. That morning, when Long was brought into court, Judge Cope nodded to the scowling defendant.

"Good morning," he said.

"Nothing good about it," Long growled. For the next several minutes, while Judge Cope slowly read the solemn legal document that directed state prison officials to take control of the person of Bobby Joe Long and legally put him to death for the "unnecessarily torturous" murder of Virginia Lee Johnson, the condemned man stood with his arms folded and head tilted, rocking back and forth.

When the sentencing concluded, Bobby Joe Long turned

abruptly, pushed aside one of his defense attorneys, and rushed out the side door into the waiting chains of the court bailiffs.

It was as if Bobby Joe Long couldn't wait to get back to his five–by–nine, windowless home on Death Row.

▲   ▲   ▲

A LETTER FROM BOBBY

    Personally I think FL will go the lethal injec-
tion route before too long--Politics--the people
don't get as upset about putting someone to sleep
permanently as they do about frying em...I'd much
rather have the injection, but I don't plan to have
either. A lot of guys talk shit about death, "I'm
not afraid to die," all that shit. I'll buy it to
an extent. I'm not afraid to die, but I want to be
around every second I can, at least while I'm young
enough to enjoy things...I figure I have another
"good" 25 years left. Maybe more! First I need to
get the fuck out of here!

▲   ▲   ▲

In the ten years that Bobby Joe Long has resided on Death Row awaiting execution, the serial killer has developed a prison reputation as a world–class whiner, among a Death Row population noted as top-notch complainers. Ever since he arrived on the exclusive East Unit that houses the death watch at Florida State Prison, Long has produced a blizzard of complaint letters that now overflow the files at the Department of Corrections in Tallahassee. His demands range from the fantastic to the frivolous, continuing his lifelong habit of bitching by mail.

"I'd be willing to bet," said one police official who worked hard to put the killer where he is today, "that when they strap him in the chair and just before they throw the switch, Bobby Joe Long will bitch that the seat's too hard!"

But, given the bizarre twists and turns the case has taken over

428

the years, no one is counting on the switch being thrown.

"Pops" Baker, who came to know the killer as intimately as any-one, believes the day will come when Bobby Joe Long finally pays the ultimate price for the senseless, unmerciful murders.

"I don't have any thoughts for him personally," Baker said. "He's just some type of animal that got turned loose in society and I'm sure there's thirty or forty more like him out there.

"What makes me fearful, after being involved in three different serial murder cases, is how vulnerable and how exposed we are to this kind of thing. Especially women. They're fair game. And it scares me that we have no way of picking serial killers out of a crowd. No way of finding them before they start. And we have to find out a way to do that.

"I've heard people trying to excuse what he did by saying, well, he just slipped through the cracks. He did, but that happens every day. You go look at any hundred rape cases coming through the courts today, and nearly every one of them will be watered down, plea-bargained away. So that person you could say slipped through the cracks.

"But in my opinion, those people—and Bobby Joe Long—did-n't slip through the cracks. We let them fall through the floor! We did it. Not him. We did it as a society, because we don't take time to make that extra effort to ensure that such an animal doesn't get out.

"How many times does a person have to rape before he becomes such a threat to society that we decide we don't ever want him turned loose again?. Sometimes they go on for ten-fifteen rapes before we get around to locking them up for good. And the death penalty as a deterrent to that? I don't know if it is or not. I just know that Bobby Joe Long deserves it."

One aspect of the Bobby Joe Long case that continues to haunt Gary Terry is that, somewhere out there, more photographs may exist of Bobby Joe in the act of rape, possibly even murder.

"I feel there are other photographs in possession of someone that may show some of our victims, but I don't know if we'll ever locate them," Terry said. "We know how much he paid to have the

429

company in New York process pictures and how many we recovered. There's a discrepancy in the numbers. Maybe Bobby Joe got rid of them. Maybe someone else has them. We had a seal on his post office box for a period of time, but had to take it off because we couldn't establish for the courts that we had cause to search it. The key to that box went to the defense. So we have no idea what could or could not have been there. But based on the fact that photos were taken of at least one victim, it's logical to assume there might be others.

"If he did it with one victim, he more than likely would have done it with others. Could be rape victims only. Or it could be rape victims who then became murder victims. Or could be both. He progressed. He started with rape and then began murdering rape victims. So there's reason to believe that if he raped and photographed, he may also have murdered and photographed. It's still a possibility, because photographs were part of his trophy-taking.

"I agree that there's something missing here, but it's such a sensitive area that, from our position, we have to be very careful with speculation."

Of far greater importance than the possible existence of photographs, however, is Terry's concern for the survivors of Bobby Joe's destructive rampage and for the families of the murdered women.

"There are still families of the murdered girls and the rape victims who survived and who continue to go through this emotional roller coaster—again and again and again. There is no finality for them. One time, I made a promise to Bobby personally, to myself, and to those families, that I would be there the day they pull the switch. I may be old and retired and living in a wheelchair, but I'll be there. Someone has to be there to speak for the victims and their families.

"His response to me was to get out of my face. Bobby Long doesn't like me. Or anybody else, for that matter," Terry said.

And while he awaits a visit from Florida's executioner, Bobby Joe Long continues to blame just about everybody and everything else for his killing spree, while dodging any responsibility of his

own. When he talked to Dr. Joel Norris, the killer complained:

"What kills me the most is that the girls that I raped were all dope addicts and whores. Not that anybody really deserves to get killed, but they weren't saints. I'm sick. I know there's something wrong with my brain. I knew it from the first times in the hospital when I felt what I felt. I told doctor after doctor what I felt, but it made no difference. I'm no killer, not like the other guys here on the row. But it made no difference to the court or to the governor. Bloody Bob Graham [the former Florida governor, now a United States Senator] needs me to die because he has to get reelected, just like he needed Ted Bundy to die to get reelected. He kept on signing death warrants for Bundy and putting him on death watch even though he knew that the court was going to step in. Everybody knew it. But it made no difference because we're here just to die so that people can get elected back into office. As far as I'm concerned, they're the real killers because they're not sick and are using the state to kill so that they can get ahead in their careers. I'm sick and I'm going to be fried alive. After I'm dead, they're going to open up my head and find that just like we've been saying a part of my brain is black and dry and dead. But they're not going to give a fuck."

In 1984, after Bobby Joe Long was finally captured and confessed to killing Vicky Elliott and defiling her with the scissors she carried to protect herself from the likes of such night crawlers. Joyce Culbertson, the manager of the coffee shop where Vicky worked, made a vow: "We're going to write letters or do whatever it takes to make sure he doesn't sit on death row for the next twenty years. He had no right to kill anybody. Vicky didn't deserve that."

Nevertheless, Bobby Joe Long continues to take up space on Florida's overcrowded Death Row. He's now on the downhill slide of that twenty years. With a little bit of luck and a generous hand from the courts, he could make it to 2004—Joyce Culbertson's vow to the contrary.

In the meantime, Vicky Elliott and the other nine victims are more than a decade in the ground.

A LETTER FROM BOBBY

Believe it or not, I know a lot of cunts that care for me and know I'm not a fucking Fiend. If I could just get out of here...